T0386673

For Alan and Barbara

First published 2025 by Picador
an imprint of Pan Macmillan
The Smithson, 6 Briset Street, London EC1M 5NR
EU representative: Macmillan Publishers Ireland Limited, 1st Floor,
The Liffey Trust Centre, 117–126 Sheriff Street Upper,
Dublin 1, D01 YC43
Associated companies throughout the world
www.panmacmillan.com

ISBN 978-1-5290-3416-5

Pan Macmillan does not have any control over, or any responsibility for,
any author or third-party websites referred to in or on this book.

1 3 5 7 9 8 6 4 2

A CIP catalogue record for this book is available from the British Library.

Typeset in Garamond Premier Pro by Palimpsest Book Production Limited, Falkirk, Stirlingshire
Printed and bound by CPI Group (UK) Ltd, Croydon, CR0 4YY

Visit **www.picador.com** to read more about all our books
and to buy them. You will also find features, author interviews and
news of any author events, and you can sign up for e-newsletters
so that you're always first to hear about our new releases.

TIFFANY JENKINS

STRANGERS
AND
INTIMATES

The Rise and Fall of Private Life

PICADOR

STRANGERS AND INTIMATES

'There is no private life which has not been determined by a wider public life.'

George Eliot, *Felix Holt* (1866)

'A life spent entirely in public, in the presence of others, becomes, as we would say, shallow.'

Hannah Arendt, *The Human Condition* (1958)

'Private and public are two essentially different worlds and that respect for that difference is the indispensable condition, the sine qua non, for a man to live free.'

Milan Kundera, *Testaments Betrayed* (1995)

'He has a sense of total privacy between them. He could tell her anything about himself, even weird things, and she would never repeat them, he knows that. Being alone with her is like opening a door away from normal life and then closing it behind him.'

Sally Rooney, *Normal People* (2018)

Contents

List of Illustrations

Introduction:

AN UNNATURAL STATE

Harry and Meghan, the Duke and Duchess of Sussex, are not the most sympathetic of privacy advocates. 'I am not going to take lectures on privacy invasion from Prince Harry,' stormed the journalist Piers Morgan in 2023, amid allegations of his involvement in hacking the Prince's phone during his tenure as editor of the *Daily Mirror*. Pointing to the revelations in Harry's bestselling memoir, *Spare*, Morgan called him 'the biggest invader of privacy in royal history'.[1]

Harry's 400-odd-page tome, published worldwide with great fanfare, is a tapestry of intimate detail. It covers everything from the loss of the Prince's virginity when he was seventeen (in a field behind a pub, to an 'older woman' who treated him like a 'young stallion') to the discomfort of his 'frostnipped penis' during his brother William's wedding to Kate Middleton. Harry also discloses personal text messages from his late mother, the Princess of Wales, as well as private conversations with his brother and his father during a fraught time for the family at his grandfather's funeral.

Morgan could also have mentioned *Oprah with Meghan and Harry*, in which the celebrity couple bared their souls to the queen of confessional TV in March 2021; or the time Meghan wrote about her miscarriage in the Opinion section of *The New York Times*. She painted a vivid portrait of heartbreaking loss, recalling how she had clasped her husband's 'clammy' hand in the hospital bed and kissed his knuckles, 'wet from both our tears'. The 'path to healing', she counselled readers, begins with asking three simple words: 'Are you OK?'. Speak your truth, she implored, to encourage those 'silently suffering' to do the same.[2]

Such was their openness about their own private lives – while also calling for privacy – that the couple became a target of the satirical animated TV show *South Park*. 'We just want to be normal people. All this attention is so hard,' complains the cartoon duchess in an episode, swishing her long brown hair during a talk-show appearance. Her red-haired husband hangs banners above their house that read 'We want privacy' and 'Stop looking at us', while they host parties on their lawn illuminated with fireworks. They then board a private jet to embark on a 'Worldwide Privacy Tour'.[3]

Rupert Bell, TalkTV's royal correspondent, spoke for many journalists when he advised, 'If Prince Harry really wants his privacy, then he must shut up!'[4] Commentator and former tabloid journalist Dan Wootton called Harry 'the prince of hypocrisy', highlighting the apparent discrepancy between his words and actions.[5]

But these critiques of Harry and Meghan risk missing the broader context, oversimplifying the complexities at play. Their contradictory statements and actions reflect the bewildering reality of how a great many people, from celebrities to everyday citizens, perceive privacy today. When Oprah Winfrey defended Harry and Meghan's desire for privacy, she clarified that it didn't mean the couple must remain silent. 'I, too, value privacy, but I talk constantly,' she said on the *Today* show. 'It's about living a life without being hounded by photographers or people invading your space.'[6] Indeed, many non-journalists and especially younger observers have exhibited sympathy for the couple, whose conflicting demands hold up a mirror to our society's deep confusion over the issue.

We live in an era characterized by calls for transparency and demands for authentic revelation, in which boundaries – between public and private, personal and professional, personal and political, work and home, online and offline – are ever more indistinct. Expressing one's inner feelings and troubles is culturally validated; keeping something private can elicit mistrust. In the spring of 2024, Kate, the Princess of Wales, tried to step away from royal duties for three months after abdominal surgery. Her short absence from public life was met with wild online conspiracy theories: that her marriage was in trouble, that she had been replaced by a body double, even that she was dead. The idea that a senior royal might choose to withhold access to her private life for a matter of weeks after a major operation was apparently incomprehensible, and for some it served as proof she no longer existed. Out-of-control speculation eventually forced Kate to record a video statement revealing her cancer diagnosis and explaining that she had wanted some time away from the public gaze to focus on her family.

Opponents of privacy often characterize it as inherently suspicious or fraught with danger. Eric Schmidt, the former CEO of Google, encapsulated the former sentiment with a revealing comment. When asked whether search engine users should be sharing information with Google as if it were a 'trusted friend', he responded without hesitation: 'If you have something that you don't want anyone to know, maybe you shouldn't be doing it in the first place.'[7] Schmidt's words highlight society's discomfort with the idea that private and public lives differ and that it may be beneficial to shield certain parts of our lives from others.

This same unease finds voice in figures like the veteran tabloid reporter Paul McMullan, who has asserted, 'Privacy is the space bad people need to do bad things in. Privacy is for paedos; fundamentally nobody else needs it.'[8] Or the radical feminist and legal scholar Catharine MacKinnon, who argued in the late 1980s that a border between the public and private spheres 'works to protect systematic inequality' and serves 'male supremacy'. MacKinnon called for the dissolution of this division to address these pressing threats.[9]

*

It's neither 'natural' nor universal to have a private life. Neither fixed in definition nor eternal in form, the idea, condition and evaluation of a private domain – a fortress against authority and a shield from collective scrutiny – varies significantly over time and place.

Consider the thriving city-state of ancient Athens in the fifth century BCE, which comprised two distinct realms: the *polis*, a domain of action, politics and freedom, and the *oikos*, the household and family unit. A strict divide between public and private life was integral to Athenian life.

Public life, limited to free adult male citizens, unfolded in the *polis*, in grand and open spaces like the agora where great speeches were delivered and heroic acts recounted. The animalistic aspects of life were relegated to the *oikos*. Everything essential to life's maintenance and reproduction – work, economics, sex, eating, cooking, birth, death – was hidden from public view.

The *oikos* served the public realm of the citizens, who had status and property. Their freedom was predicated on the unfreedom of others: the women and enslaved people who attended to the needs of the heads of each household, enabling them to spend their days in the public world of the forum and the army. Women were excluded from public life. They had virtually no political rights. They couldn't vote, nor could they stand for election. They had no lasting public voice and were silenced on the issues of the day. They were confined to the *oikos* and were veiled and chaperoned when out in public. A male relative or guardian represented them in all dealings with public authorities. Their most important duties were to bear children, preferably male, and to run the household, in which the patriarch had absolute authority. The public and private realms were not just separate but imbued with different values and purposes. The private sphere was necessary and meaningful, but it was the public arena that was celebrated. Pericles, the renowned general, emphasized this in a powerful address during the state funeral for the war dead of Athens following the Peloponnesian War. He praised Athenian democratic culture and characterized the public realm as a place of action and significance. He argued that men who did not participate in public duties were 'useless'.[10] Indeed, the word 'privacy' derives from the Latin word *privatus*, meaning 'deprived' – specifically, of public office.

Athenian citizens denigrated the private realm because, as far as they were concerned, one was only fully human as a *zoon politikon*: a social or political animal. Only in the *polis* was man understood to realize his true nature. As Aristotle put it, man was 'by nature a political animal'.[11] This disregard of the private sphere was a direct corollary of the elevation of the public sphere, with its conception of man as a political actor. The boundary between the public and private realms emerged from this exalted vision of politics.

In contrast, there was no such sharp border dividing the public from the private domain in medieval Europe. Public power was fragmented and intensely personal, and there was no longer a clearly identifiable private realm. The two spheres had blurred into one: everything was public. Large and wealthy households were places of power, transferred down through families. Households of all sizes were the site of professional as well as domestic work. Almost every room was used for every purpose and many activities spilled outdoors.

This is not to say there was no distinction between what people did in front of others and how they behaved alone. All societies draw a line somewhere to distinguish between what is open to view and what takes place in private, and all have ideas about taboo and shame. In most cultures, people shield themselves when toileting (although in ancient Rome, the emperor's palace had elaborately decorated three-seat commodes where guests could sit and converse). There's also little evidence that people have ever had much sex in public.

But in Europe between the fall of the classical world and the eighteenth century, societies were not organized in ways that delineated sharply between a public and private sphere. For centuries previous, a semblance of private life – somewhere away from the intrusions of authority or from the watchful eye of the community – either had to be wrested from the encroachment of powerful authorities, or achieved through subterfuge. Attempts to do this were widely seen as dangerous, or as evidence of moral disorder. As a seventeenth-century English preacher warned his congregation: 'The murderer and the adulterer are alike desirous of privacy'.[12] Privacy was sinister, even frightening: a shelter for sin and immorality.

It was only in the eighteenth century, first in Europe and then beyond, that a private sphere came to be understood as a space bound by different rules and conventions, *and* positively and rigorously championed. This was a transformation that would have astonished the Athenians.

By the Victorian age, the delineation between public and private realms was starkly defined. This division, coupled with the high esteem now placed on the private world, transformed the protean concept of privacy into something to be celebrated and fiercely protected. By the nineteenth century, what was once considered to be a state of deprivation and something to be feared came, in the West, to be conceptualized as an essential resource for the self.

'Every house has its skeleton in it somewhere,' William

Makepeace Thackeray wrote in *The History of Pendennis* (1848), a novel about a young gentleman born in the countryside who travels to London to seek his place in society. With a wife who had suffered a nervous collapse and was in confinement, and a half-Indian sister born to his father's mistress in Bengal, Thackeray understood well the realities he wrote about. Only his intimates were aware of his father's Eurasian family; until the mid-twentieth century, his biographers mostly refrained from mentioning it.

By contrast, in the twenty-first century, the biographer of a public figure typically dives deeply into such private details, picking over the subject's personal life, which is considered more authentic and revealing than their public persona. Public figures are no longer assessed solely on their feats and accomplishments; their personal lives are key to their reputations. Private words and deeds can have career-ending consequences for public figures and citizens alike.

From the halls of Westminster to the corridors of the White House, figures like Boris Johnson, Donald Trump, Gordon Brown and King Charles III, along with politicians of all persuasions, police officers, students and everyday citizens, have experienced the sting of seeing their private conversations exposed for public consumption. The sanctity of private discourse has given way to a culture of leaks and exposés that envelops everyone.

The fact is, we are all different in private. We may not be our best selves when we shut the door. We misspeak, we think the unthinkable, we let off steam, we rant and we rave, and we say and do stupid things. Privacy conceals harmful behaviour and impedes accountability, and yet we all require that space away from public view. As the sociologist Erving Goffman astutely observed, individuals, like actors in a theatre, need backstage areas where they can remove their public masks, collect themselves and relieve the pressures and tensions of social life.[13] Members of the royal family, celebrities, politicians, normal, everyday people – all of us need time away from the watchful eye of others, where we can develop ourselves and our personal relationships.

The private realm is where we cultivate our inner lives, explore our consciences and enjoy intimacy in all its forms. Only here can we find respite from the incessant demands of public life and afford to stumble, to err, to question and refine our beliefs, feelings and actions. It is within this secluded environment that we can be vulnerable with those we love and build the foundations of trust. We can prepare ourselves to step back into the public eye, renewed and ready to engage with the world once more. In this respect, private life is essential to public life. But today all that is at risk. The historic achievement of establishing those two distinct realms, private and public, each governed by its own set of norms and values, is in mortal danger.

To understand the contemporary world, where personal lives are exposed for public consumption and the act of maintaining privacy is viewed with suspicion, it's necessary to delve into the societal shifts that have muddied the boundary between public and private life. Many of the trends that shaped our current situation began long before Mark Zuckerberg or any of today's other tech giants were born.

Digital technology has of course brought about profound changes to the way we live our lives, but the current discussion about privacy is shallow and narrow, primarily focused on recent decades rather than placing developments in a historical context. This perspective tends to view new technology as the primary driver of change, overlooking the context in which it was introduced and how that context, in turn, influenced the technology.

Only by exploring the deep historical roots of our concept of private life, and of the challenges it now faces, can we build a clear picture of what is new and what is not. Only by understanding how and why private life is at risk can we take steps to protect it.

*

Beginnings can be hard to pinpoint, especially when it comes to elusive concepts like 'private', 'public' and 'privacy' that have been in use for centuries but with widely varying definitions. Scholars examining privacy often start with the household: the idea of property, the laws that keep others out, and the design of physical spaces – doors, locks, windows, corridors and curtains. Linguistically, while the word *private* in the fourteenth and fifteenth centuries already covered 'a concealed affair', 'something concealed or hidden' or 'an ordinary person', it's not until 1502 that the *Oxford English Dictionary* (*OED*) records the first reference to 'private' property, and in 1542 to a 'private house'.[14]

But *Strangers and Intimates* is not a history of the minutiae of people's private lives, a peek behind closed doors to see how our ancestors lived. Instead – concentrating on Britain, and informed by parallel developments in Europe and the USA – it examines the underlying forces and crystallizing moments that shaped the private realm as an entity with clear boundaries, rules and conventions, and considers how it came to be publicly celebrated and protected. It also shows how and why the border separating public life from private life has dissolved, and why that matters. How societies distinguish between what is public and what is private affects all aspects of human life. It defines what concerns others, shapes the nature of private life and influences the cultural significance we assign to privacy.

The focus of this book is not on whether people over the centuries have spent time on their own, sought not be observed, or had thoughts they did not share with others – all of which, arguably, are universal to the human condition – but on how our attitudes to those behaviours have evolved. Key moments and specific influences have shaped society's ideas about what belongs in the private sphere and how it should be distinguished from the public sphere (if at all). Those social factors, in turn, have helped to determine how far authority – be it that of a king, the state, religious, or corporate power – extends into our lives and the degree to which individuals can be free of it, or even imagine that possibility.

Strangers and Intimates begins at a critical juncture during the turbulent aftermath of the Reformation, a period riven with religious strife that tore Europe apart for 130 years. Amid the chaos, individuals from all across society – elites, common folk, Protestants, Catholics, followers of lesser-known sects – began quietly, and then publicly, separating themselves from prevailing authorities in order to follow their faiths. Out of the convoluted twists of history and the English Civil Wars, England's people eventually forged a path towards the idea that political communities could survive in the midst of religious diversity if they limited their activities to a 'private' sphere, thus endorsing its possibility.

The emergence of a private domain in the Western world wasn't the deliberate result of solitude-seekers. Rather, it was an accidental journey. Historical change is complex; particularly in this context, where development is inconsistent and uneven, with progress for some rarely equating to progress for all. It was only by defining the borders of the political realm that the private realm could take shape. The trajectory of private life has been influenced by the concurrent rise of public life. Without a public sphere there can be no private sphere, and vice versa. Through their differentiation, they attain their contours and distinction.

To grasp what is at stake – to fully understand the extent of the threat – we need to begin with a look back at the first people to stumble upon it, rediscovering their needs, desires and efforts to stake out a private domain.

PART I:

Borders Drawn

Chapter 1:

THE SPARK OF CONSCIENCE

In January 1521, an ancient city along the Rhine River in modern-day Germany became the backdrop for a pivotal assembly of the Holy Roman Empire's most influential power brokers – the Diet of Worms. On the fringes of the gathering stood Martin Luther, a troublesome professor of theology from the remote University of Wittenberg. Discussions centred on foreign affairs: the threat of Ottoman expansion, the conflict in France. It was also a trade event, and merchants milled about.

Luther awaited his summons. He had brazenly defied the Roman Catholic Church, branded Pope Leo X the Antichrist, and described the Church as a brothel. The Pope had responded with a papal bull giving Luther sixty days to recant or face excommunication. Now Luther was called to face the secular authority of Charles V, the Holy Roman Emperor, and explain himself. Would he dare challenge the Emperor's might as well?

Luther had hinted at his resolve despite the risk to his own life. He wrote to Charles: 'As long as conscience is capital to the Holy Scriptures, which have furnished evidence for all my books, I cannot recant if I am not proven wrong.'[1] For Luther, following one's conscience was a matter of an individual's beliefs based on the authority of scripture as revealed in the books of the Bible, not the dictates of the pope.

*

What had started as a minor academic dispute had escalated into a fierce argument, involving the religious and secular authorities of medieval Europe, over how a soul might be saved. In writings and sermons, including his famous *Ninety-five Theses* (1517), Luther had challenged Church doctrine on salvation. He condemned the practice of selling 'indulgences' – wringing money from parishioners with a promise to absolve them of their sins, and using the profits to pay for elaborate cathedrals and the lifestyles of wealthy clerics.

At the core of Luther's message lay a profound belief: salvation could not be bought, and only through God's grace could one attain redemption on Judgement Day. That meant he repudiated a central tenet of the Church, the belief that good works – financial donations, good deeds and fasting – would be taken into account by God. Luther proposed a direct and intimate connection between the believer and the divine, bypassing traditional hierarchical structures and established rituals. This audacious proposition struck at the very core of the religious establishment and had implications for every believer.

Religion was the framework of meaning and order within society, intricately woven into its fabric, binding people together day and night. Church authorities organized the lives of individuals and their communities twenty-four hours a day. Church bells rang with hourly instructions, demanding unwavering devotion in the service of God. This encompassed both public obligations – attending church, participating in collective worship in the community – and private acts of piety, which extended to the management of household affairs. Its reach began before birth and extended until after death.

Medieval Catholicism was collective and communal. God was everywhere and in everything, and the Church too was universal. People gathered in various groups – whether in parishes, guilds, or monastic settings – to pray for themselves and for others, for both the deceased and the living. The medieval church acted as an intermediary, teaching that prayers, whether offered personally or paid for, could help ease a loved one's passage through purgatory into heaven, or grant forgiveness for one's own sins.

Pope Leo X, who had been born into the illustrious Medici political and banking dynasty, was head of the Church as well as ruler of the Papal States. He requested Luther's silence. But Luther kept preaching and churning out papers. The printing press circulated his writings alongside illustrations of satirical woodcuts, significantly broadening the appeal of his teachings. His works were translated from Latin into German, enabling laypeople to read them without relying on a priest's interpretation. Luther's sermons, delivered in German, spoke directly to the people in their own language, and he conveyed his ideas through powerful hymns and songs. He was a brilliant polemicist and he rapidly gained supporters.

No one – least of all Luther himself – had anticipated that his message would so captivate many of the faithful. But he emerged at a time when anti-papal sentiment was rising in all quarters of German society. German princes smarted at the flow of money from the German church to the Italian princes of the papacy; laypeople resented paying for ornate basilicas in distant cities. And ultimately, beneath the surface of this dispute pulsed a fundamental question, one that occupied the thoughts of both men and women daily: how should one serve the divine and secure the salvation of the soul?

By the time Luther set out for Worms to account for his words and deeds to the highest authorities in the land, he was a celebrity. Men and women hailed him as he passed through city gates and flocked to churches to hear him preach. When, in April, he arrived, thousands surged onto the streets, greeting him as a hero. A priest brushed the hem of his robe.

*

On 17 April 1521, Luther was finally called into the hall. Clad in a plain cassock, he stood amid a sea of opulent regalia, facing some seventy princes and senior prelates. Johann Eck – a theologian whose writings Luther had provocatively set fire to at the gates of Wittenberg, along with canon law and the papal bull that had condemned him – interrogated him. Eck pointed to a tower of books on a table, challenged Luther to confirm that the writings were his, and demanded that he recant their content. Luther admitted that they were but asked for time to consider the second question, which he was granted.

The overnight delay built anticipation but only strengthened Luther's resolve. Pope Leo wanted him reined in, obedient; Charles sought unity and peace in his empire. But as far as Luther was concerned, what was at stake was nothing less than the truth about how Christians ought to pursue holiness.

The Diet reconvened the following evening, this time in a larger gallery to accommodate the influx of spectators. Illuminated by flickering torchlight, attendees were on edge to see what the foul-mouthed monk would do next. Having composed himself during the night, Luther spoke clearly and loudly but with care. He apologized for the tone of his writings. He then ventured that he would retract his words, but only if the authorities could show that he had spoken against scripture. 'I believe neither in Pope nor councils alone,' he stated.[2] 'My conscience is captive to the Word of God. I cannot and I will not retract anything, since it is neither safe nor right to go against conscience.'[3]

For Luther, the word of God, as revealed in the books of the Bible, surpassed that of either the Church or the pope, and he could not act or speak against the Lord. Aware that he might be executed as a heretic in front of all the great men of Europe, he did not retract. The first editor of his collected works, Georg Rörer, summed up his testimony in the memorable phrase now attributed to Luther himself: 'Here I stand; I can do no other.'[4]

In his emphasis on an essential biblical command – obey God, not man – Luther challenged the two great powers of medieval Europe in front of its highest political authorities. His sermons were a rebuke to the papacy, which ruled all Christians. His message defied all kings and princes who ruled in God's name. He deferred to scripture over their claims to authority.

Charles withdrew to make his decision on Luther's fate. Two days later, he ruled that Luther was a heretic and banned his writings but granted him safe conduct to the outskirts of Worms. Luther was given three weeks to leave the city before he would be vulnerable to 'liquidation'.[5]

As Luther left the city, his protector Friedrich the Wise, Elector of Saxony, secretly staged his kidnapping and confined him safely in the Wartburg, a castle in the Thuringian forest. There, under constant threat of discovery and complaining of constipation, Luther spent the next year translating the New Testament into German.

*

The Diet of Worms was a seismic event, creating fault lines that shaped the course of history. The Reformation laid the groundwork for centuries of conflict, fracturing societies and creating repercussions that reverberated from the thrones of kings and the courtiers that surrounded them to the daily lives of laypeople. As Luther's ideas swept across much of Europe, they shattered the notion of a universal church, leading to a split into two branches: Catholic and Protestant. Over time, Protestantism itself would fragment into various denominations. Once Luther made the argument that God could be worshipped by following scripture rather than the authority of the pope, the way was open to others to promote their own interpretations of God's will. Ulrich Zwingli, who led the Reformation in much of Switzerland, and the French theologian John Calvin, who triggered a second

Reformation across northern Europe and Geneva, established
their own churches.

Luther was horrified by the iconoclastic forces he had unleashed.
He might have challenged the Pope and condemned the corruption of the Catholic Church, but he was by no means opposed to
authority. During the German Peasant Rebellion of 1524–5, a
massive uprising influenced by the radical reformism of the
German preacher Thomas Müntzer, Luther was initially sympathetic to the peasants but eventually sided with the nobility. He
urged them to 'slay' the rebels like 'mad dogs', and some 100,000
peasants were slaughtered in the repression that followed.[6]

Luther believed in obedience. He had not meant for the
people to rebel, only for a select elite to question how things
were done. But his revolutionary ideas took on a life of their
own, evolving away from him in unexpected ways. Within the
gap he had created between Church authority and the believer's personal relationship with God, the seeds of the individual's
separation from traditional authority were able to germinate.
Luther's desire to follow God rather than man opened up the
possibility of individuals making their own decisions about
how best to follow the Lord. The revolutionary idea that man
might instead choose to follow his individual conscience –
which was not Luther's message at all – was loosed upon the
world.

This is not to say that the notion of a private life originated
directly from Protestantism. Its evolution was far more intricate,
and it had additional and equally accidental originators. Protestants did not advocate for an expansion of the private sphere.

As Luther warned a friend: 'By all means flee solitude, for the
devil watches and lies in wait for you most of all when you are
alone.'[7] Protestants made all sorts of allegations about hermits
and what they considered to be their filthy habits. Being under
constant observation provided a sense of security that reduced

the likelihood of danger. Being alone was threatening to the social order and the individual alike.

Yet by underscoring the duty of believers to consult scripture directly and live in accordance with its teachings, both in action and in thought, Protestantism did encourage interiority. Protestant theology developed ideas about creating a direct relationship with God by getting rid of intermediaries. The translation of religious texts into vernacular languages such as German and English also highlighted each believer's responsibility to engage personally with God's word, sparking a greater emphasis on individual understanding. Salvation was to be a matter between God and the Christian.

What Luther did was set in motion a series of conflicts over authority – papal, monarchical, and the believer's own interpretation of authority – which, after many twists and turns, gradually fostered a nascent sense of the individual conscience. This would become the cornerstone of private life.

But all of that was still to come. Like Pandora with her jar, Luther had released a powerful force into the world. As a consequence, unsuspecting players across Europe would be drawn into a whirlwind of change, with England emerging as a major battleground. Here, Luther's adversaries unwittingly dealt decisive blows of their own to an edifice that had once seamlessly melded public and private realms, in a struggle that would reverberate through the corridors of power and the hearts of laypeople alike.

*

A decade after Luther's defiant stand at Worms, Henry VIII initiated the English Reformation in a fit of pique. In the 1530s, he used Parliament to break the centuries-old relationship between England and Rome and declared himself supreme head, under Christ, of the Church of England.

Henry, however, was no religious reformer. He had ordered the burning of Luther's books and written the *Defence of the Seven Sacraments* of 1521, a theological treatise in which he denounced Luther as an *'inferorum lupus'* (wolf of Hell), and the *'diaboli membrum'* (devil's member). The Pope had rewarded his loyalty with the title 'Defender of the Faith'. Luther, never one to shy away from a fight, fired back, calling Henry a 'dunghill', a 'stupid and sacrilegious king' and a 'mad fool with a frothy mouth and whorish face'.[8] But when the King's marriage to Catherine of Aragon failed to produce a male heir, he asked the Pope to annul the union so that he could marry Anne Boleyn. The drawn-out refusal set Henry on course to break with Rome. His chief minister, Thomas Cromwell, assisted him with finesse.

Henry assured his subjects that things would remain largely the same and that he had no intention of altering the articles of the Catholic faith. At first, people continued to worship in the same churches and go about their business, religious and secular. But the break with Rome was a constitutional revolution that precipitated a moral crisis. The English Reformation saw fewer deaths than its counterparts in Europe, but it set in train tectonic changes.

By insisting that all ecclesiastical law required royal assent and that canons or constitutions could only be revised or repealed with his approval, Henry destroyed the independence of the English Church. The monarch became the final legal authority in matters both secular and religious. This was a major development that tied politics and religion tightly together, effectively relegating the pope to the status of a foreign bishop. Henry wielded his sceptre not only over matters of state but also over the souls of his subjects.

The King demanded obedience to this disturbing reordering of authority, and formal consent. He required that his subjects (in practice, mostly men over the age of fourteen, thanks to their privileged legal and social standing) take two oaths. With the

Oath of Succession, Henry declared his first marriage to Catherine of Aragon null and void. The kingdom was sworn to accept only the children of his new queen, Anne Boleyn, as heirs – starting with the infant Princess Elizabeth. In the Oath of Supremacy, Henry demanded an even more radical shift. No longer would England look to the pope in Rome for spiritual leadership. Instead, the king himself – Henry VIII – would be the Supreme Head of the Church of England. With this, the old religious order crumbled.

Henry also formalized the charge of treason for not taking the oaths. The Treason Act of 1534 specifically made it treasonous to deny the validity of Henry's marriage to Anne Boleyn, to reject the legitimacy of their offspring, or to refuse to recognize Henry as the Supreme Head of the Church of England.

In a massive royal bureaucratic effort, the country was divided into regions and commissioners were sent out to administer the oaths. Every man had to sign or make his mark, whether or not he could write.[9] Those who resisted faced a range of severe consequences, which included imprisonment, and the confiscation of property and titles.

Oaths invoking God and with saints as witnesses were commonly taken in late medieval England. Bishops swore obedience to both the Crown and the pope. Oaths were pledged in courts of law, on the taking of office, and upon admission to an esteemed trade or guild. They were exchanged amid the solemnity of marriage ceremonies. But never had the nation been instructed to swear loyalty to such a significant change in policy.

Swearing an oath was a serious matter. It was thought that individuals who made false oaths – said what they believed to be an untruth – would face divine retribution, in both the present and the afterlife. Their soul was at risk of eternal damnation.

Almost everyone swallowed their reservations and swore Henry's Oath of Succession. John Forest, a Franciscan friar with the strict Greenwich Observants, did so, but later confided that he 'denied the bishop of Rome by an oath given by his outward man, but not in the inward man'.[10]

This was a dangerous position, *verboten* by the King and faith. The prevailing sentiment in the temporal and secular corridors of thought followed the decree of Augustine, the eminent theologian: 'He lies, moreover, who holds one opinion in his mind and who gives expression to another through words of any other outward manifestation.'[11] There was to be no distinction made between one's words and one's thoughts.[12] Henry's men were on high alert to look for those who did not swear with conviction. Ever suspicious, he ordered all his sheriffs to watch their bishops closely to make sure they preached his supremacy 'truly, sincerely, and without all manner, cloak, colour, or dissimulation'.[13]

Most saw no choice but to do just that. Among them was the last abbot of Reading, Hugh Cook, a man torn between loyalty to his king and fidelity to his faith. When swearing to the King's supremacy, he later admitted that he added silently, 'of the temporal Church, but not the spiritual'.[14] Outward conformity did not always signify acceptance of the King's terms. The whispers accompanying affirmations and quiet hesitations of the obedient were more difficult to control.

Henry's oaths were the start of a series of oaths of conformity enforced by English governments over the next 150 years. Though intended to assert authority and ensure compliance, as well as to identify dissenters and dispel them, they also created friction: resistance, mostly silent, yet occasionally vocal.

These oaths got to the heart of the changes wrought upon England and forced people to consider their beliefs. Not everyone could bring themselves to go along with them. Braving considerable risk to their own lives, there were those who refused to submit.

*

Sir Thomas More, a deeply spiritual man who had faithfully served Henry VIII as Lord High Chancellor of England, could not countenance the break with Rome. On 16 May 1532 he met with the King and resigned, seeking to withdraw from the turbulent world of politics. A humanist scholar who supported reform within the Church, he had been horrified by Martin Luther's impact and likely assisted Henry in writing the *Defence of the Seven Sacraments*.

More was the first English writer to use the Greek term *anarchos* – anarchy – applying it to Luther and his followers.[15] He understood that Luther's attack on aspects of the Catholic Church risked tearing down the entire institution and would spread disorder. He was convinced that if Henry used the Lutherans for his own purposes, the chaotic and blood-soaked fate of Germany could be visited on England.

On 12 April 1534, he received a summons to take the Oath of Succession. The next day, after a long night of prayer, he travelled by boat from his Chelsea home to the Archbishop of Canterbury's palace in Lambeth. There in front of Thomas Cromwell, Thomas Cranmer, Thomas Audley and William Benson, More was asked if he was ready to swear. Relying on his considerable rhetorical prowess as a seasoned lawyer, More employed every stratagem to avoid doing so. He prefaced his refusal with a diplomatic disclaimer – 'My purpose is not to cast aspersions on the Act or its authors, nor to impugn the oath or its takers' – before declining to take the oath.[16] He did not criticize the Act of Succession, the King, nor any subject taking the oath, but he refused to swear it himself. He feared God more than he feared his king.

After repeatedly refusing, on 17 April he was imprisoned in the Tower of London. He was not entirely alone; he had a servant with him, tasked with reporting any treasonous comments he might make. A month later, he was allowed to receive a visit from his beloved daughter, Margaret.

*

Fearful for his life, More's family pressured him to take the oath. 'Why should you refuse to swear, Father, for I have sworn myself?' pleaded Margaret.[17] More wrote to her using the charcoal he was permitted, explaining that his conscience would not permit him to comply. He described how the formation of conscience was the result of a long process in which he uncovered the truth – the correct understanding of God's law. It was not the right to be wrong. True conscience, More said, was not merely the word of an individual like himself. It required knowledge derived from reason, universal to all human beings, and extensive learning in the word of God.

This wasn't conscience in the modern sense, where individuals assert the right to follow their personal beliefs. More was following the period's accepted ideas that conscience was not subjective, but an objective truth to be uncovered by experts. But those ideas were in flux.

In the corridors of academic theology, complex debates surrounding conscience had been a steadfast focal point since the eleventh century. By the thirteenth century, drawing on Paul's Epistles, Aquinas distinguished between two aspects of conscience: *synderesis*, the 'spark' that kindles within, the innate disposition of conscience; and *conscientia*, the reasoning process applied to this spark. Aquinas argued that *synderesis* was inherently truthful, but grave errors could arise when reflecting upon it. Heretics, according to Aquinas, were individuals who had reasoned incorrectly about their initial moral intuitions.[18] Despite their sincerity, their incorrect beliefs would not save them from punishment. They could faithfully follow their consciences and still be wrong – and for this they would be sent to the pyre. The flames were a prelude to the eternal torment awaiting them in hell.

But within the framework of English law, questions were being raised about whether conscience could be invoked as a mitigating factor in legal matters. These debates were heavily influenced by the writings of Christopher St Germain, a prominent jurist of the early sixteenth century. William Tyndale, the theologian and translator known for his English Bible, also argued that the law should show restraint towards a person's conscience and should not 'break into the consciences of men'. He asserted that the law has no place in a person's soul and that no judge should compel a man to swear against his will.[19]

As Lord Chancellor, More had shown no patience for such whimsy. He had vigorously enforced order and demanded obedience, supporting the burning of heretics, who, he believed, were an infection in the community that had to be purged. Heretics, he asserted, should be 'kept but for the fire first here and after in hell', unless 'they repent and call for grace'.[20] Though he denied allegations that he had tortured evangelicals in the backyard of his Chelsea house, he admitted to keeping them in his home under the watch of clergymen.

More had written several works attacking Tyndale, accusing him of numerous theological errors and outright heresies, portraying him as a deceitful, malicious figure who sought to pervert the true faith. More condemned Tyndale's rejection of key Catholic doctrines such as the authority of the pope, the sacraments, and the importance of tradition in interpreting the Bible.

Tyndale, who had been forced to live in exile to continue his work safely, defended his translation and his theological positions in his own writings. He argued that his translation of the Bible was based on the original Greek and Hebrew texts and was more accurate than the Latin Vulgate used by the Catholic Church. In his view, the Church had corrupted the scriptures over centuries, and his work aimed to restore the purity of the Christian message.

The conflict between More and Tyndale had been not

merely a personal feud but a microcosm of the larger battle between Catholicism and the Protestant Reformation. More represented the ecclesiastical authority striving to maintain its control and doctrinal uniformity: the Church was the authority, full stop. Tyndale embodied the reformist impulse to return to what he saw as the original, unadulterated Christianity of the Bible.

Now, however, More found himself on the receiving end of Henry's wrath. It was his turn to be persecuted for his beliefs.

*

In 1535, a year after first refusing to swear the Oath of Succession, Sir Thomas More faced trial for treason. The Treason Act, conveniently just passed, had rendered it a capital offence to maliciously deny, either verbally or in writing, members of the royal family their dignity or title. The trial thus focused More's silence.

In the vast hall of the Palace of Westminster, which for centuries had accommodated royal courts and been used for state trials and impeachments, the King's attorney argued: 'Sir Thomas, though we have not one word or deed of yours to object against you, yet we have your silence, which is an evident sign of the malice of your heart: because no dutiful subject, being lawfully asked this question, will refuse to answer it.'[21]

More, pale and slender with an unkempt beard, appeared in a long woollen gown over his hairshirt. He calmly denied the charge. His silence, he assured the court, was no sign of any malice in his heart, as evidenced by his loyal service to the King. He argued that his stance was not one of defiance, suggesting instead that 'he that holdeth his peace, seemeth to consent'.[22] More then addressed the heart of the matter. He maintained that his silence was neither 'corrupt' nor 'perverse'. He suggested that human law could not judge what St German described as 'inward things'. He asserted that this issue was fundamentally a matter of conscience. As More explained, in matters 'touching conscience', every 'true and good subject is more bounde to have respect for his conscience and soul than for anything else in the world'.[23]

When Lord Chancellor Audley presented him as the lone voice of defiance against the general view of the bishops, the universities and the learned men of England, More replied that it was the English view that was in the isolated minority – he was with the law, established Church and the authority of Rome, not on his own. Rather than proclaim the autonomy of his conscience as an independent source of authority, he provided it as 'proufe' of his conformity with the larger part of Christendom.

*

Having spent over a year in the Tower of London, More had used the time to engage in a long dialogue about conscience. In the twilight of his existence, confined within prison walls as he grappled with his impending fate, he sought solace and justification for his decisions, both to himself and his beloved family. In his letters, the word *conscience* appears with striking frequency – forty-three times in a single letter, and seven times within the first hundred lines alone – revealing his intense struggle with its various meanings.[24] Although More had told his family that conscience was not a question of following one's own beliefs but those prescribed by the Church, while in prison he wrote a memorandum on perjury arguing that: 'No one has the power to tender an oath to anyone else binding him to reveal such a secret as can and should be kept secret.'[25]

As trial proceedings continued, the King's attorney pressed harder. He alleged that not only had More refused to take the oath, he had denied the Act of Supremacy in private conversation in his prison cell with officials who were working for Thomas Cromwell. But even if this were true, More protested, it should not count against him, because it was spoken in 'familiar' and 'secreate talk'.[26]

Henry was determined to extend the border of his new state ever further into the minds of his subjects: More would have to submit both in public, by saying an oath, and in private, by not speaking against the King. More's refusal to make the oath, combined with the testimony about his alleged private conversation, sealed his end. He was sentenced to death. In his final letter to his friend Dr Nicholas Wilson, who had also been imprisoned for having refused to take the oath, More bade him farewell, saying: 'Leaving every other man to their own conscience my self will with good grace follow mine.'[27]

The one concession the King made was to commute More's sentence from hanging and disembowelment at Tyburn to beheading on Tower Hill. Henry also granted More's family the liberty of being present at his burial, but not at his execution. More may have wanted it that way. His wife and children had not fully reconciled with what he had done. His corpse was taken to the church and was interred. His head was boiled and impaled upon a pole on London Bridge. The head was eventually taken down and buried by his daughter, Margaret Roper, who had it wrapped in a red cloth and interred in the Roper family tomb in the Church of St Dunstan-in-the-West in London.

The meaning of More's actions and his ideas about conscience were much discussed after his death. Martin Luther had followed his conscience, based on the higher authority of scripture, knowing that he might die for it. Thomas More justified his silence by his Christian duty to obey God, making his conscience paramount, based on the higher authority of the Catholic Church, and was executed for it. Despite their radically different views on the authority of Rome, neither More nor Luther could betray what their conscience told them was true. They followed different masters, but fundamentally, and without intending to, they both authorized the individual to follow their private convictions of faith over the authority of the day.

*

The execution of the Carthusian monks, a hermit-like order, began on 4 May 1535, when three Carthusian priors – John Houghton, Robert Lawrence and Augustine Webster – were hanged, drawn and quartered at Tyburn for refusing to acknowledge King Henry VIII as the Supreme Head of the Church of England. This took place two months before Thomas More was executed on 6 July 1535. Their martyrdom marked the beginning of a series of executions of Carthusians and other Catholics who resisted Henry's establishment of the Church of England.

In 1537, the remaining Carthusian monks of the London Charterhouse, who had long resisted taking the Oath of Supremacy, finally yielded and began with prayers to the divine: 'Nor is it hidden from thee, O God, Thou searcher of hearts, how contrary to the law of our mind is the consent which we are constrained to give . . . We beseech thee therefore of thy inexhaustible goodness and gentleness mercifully to pardon thy servants for the sin which, though heart and conscience resist, we are about to commit with our lips.'[28] They erected a division between their outward actions and their inner beliefs.

Executions demonstrated the consequences of public dissent, but taking the oaths didn't guarantee internal agreement. In secret, many began to follow their own consciences, carving out a mental space away from the mandated belief system and practices. From these quiet beginnings, those faithful to Rome formed covert networks of belief and resistance. More may have feared anarchy and sought to prevent it, but his actions and death inspired an underground movement of Roman Catholics who began to rationalize how they might legitimately follow and practise their faith.

In unleashing the English Reformation and demanding obedience from the nation, Henry sought to command not only people's bodies but also their souls. His actions transformed religious dissent and certain forms of intellectual exploration into political crimes. By attempting to impose a singular way of thinking, he ignited resistance that revealed alternative perspectives and ways of understanding. This prompted people to question who truly held power and where Henry's control should rightfully end.

Before the Reformation, religion required devoted living in the service of God, in a manner that encompassed public duty and private piety in ways that were highly interconnected. That practice mostly continued across the sixteenth century. However, as prominent elite figures and laypeople alike felt forced by the actions of the state to live a public religious life that differed from their private beliefs, this unity of public and private began to crack.

And the disruptive, violent switchback between different faiths was only just beginning.

*

After Henry's death in January 1547, his nine-year-old son, Edward VI, ascended to the throne. Edward became the first English monarch to have been raised as a Protestant. His advisers, Lord Protector Edward Seymour and Archbishop of Canterbury Thomas Cranmer, were committed to establishing a fully Protestant England. Catholic priests were imprisoned in the Tower of London. The Latin Mass, which had been the order of English churches and people's lives for centuries, was abandoned. Services were now conducted in English, and the new English-language Book of Common Prayer was introduced.

Royal injunctions unleashed iconoclastic destruction on England's churches. Men with axes dismantled altars, beheaded alabaster statues and shattered stained-glass windows. They removed rood screens and demolished side chapels. Protestant missionaries travelled across the country, preaching to large crowds, and English Bibles were forcefully placed in the hands of the laity. Resistance emerged in Devon, where priests and peasants rebelled but were defeated.

After Edward died of tuberculosis aged sixteen, Lady Jane Grey, a devout Protestant who had been named his successor, was deposed after just nine days on the throne by supporters of Mary Tudor. Mary I, the daughter of Henry and Catherine of Aragon, was crowned queen in 1553 – just twenty years after her father had ushered in the English Reformation. In a dramatic reversal, Mary, a Catholic, repealed all of Edward's religious reforms and restored England's allegiance to the pope. The Latin Mass was reinstated and the Protestant simplicity in church furnishings gave way to the rich ornamentation of Catholic practice. The English prayer book was discarded and Catholic preachers were dispatched to confront Protestant beliefs and root out heresy. Public recantations, clergy disciplining, and the exposure of Protestant conspiracies became common sights.

Between February 1555 and November 1558, 283 individuals were burnt at the stake for refusing to renounce Protestantism and accept papal authority. Thomas Cranmer joined their ranks. Despite having renounced Protestantism, he was sentenced to death regardless. In his final moments, he defiantly renounced his recantation, reclaiming his faith with conviction. Leading Catholic preachers sermonized from pulpits set up next to the crackling pyres, while the faces of the condemned were deformed by the flames. Foxe's *Book of Martyrs* (first printed in 1563) described gruesome scenes of 'fat, water, and blood' flowing down the bodies of the dying, their lips moving in prayer until they were 'shrunk to the gums', instilling fear in Protestant communities.

The Burning of Latimer and Ridley at Oxford, *1555. From John Foxe's
'Book of Martyrs' or 'Actes and Monuments', 1570.*

Notable among the martyrs was Nicholas Ridley, Protestant
Bishop of London, who had supported Lady Jane Grey's claim to
the throne. Arrested for treason and condemned for heresy, Ridley's writings first linked 'conscience' to liberty.[29] By the late 1550s
and early 1560s, 'liberty of conscience' had become a rallying cry
among Catholic recusants, who refused to attend Anglican services. This notion was now more than a mere spark. It was a flame
that spread through both Catholic and Protestant communities.

Chapter 2:

SECRETS OF THE HEART

Elizabeth I claimed the throne of England on 17 November 1558, following the death of her half-sister, Queen Mary I. While their father, Henry VIII, had pursued religious conformity with an iron will, Elizabeth adopted a more pragmatic approach. She sought to reconcile the schisms within her kingdom, even if it meant turning a blind eye to the dissonance between public piety and private belief.

Her aim was clear: to re-establish England as a Protestant nation. But Elizabeth understood that such a transformation would require patience and care. She initially rejected the persecution of Catholics, recognizing that previous efforts had only fuelled resistance. The flip-flopping between various demands on public behaviour had made it impossible for pretty much any individual to retain a consistency between private thought and public behaviour. The pendulum swings over the country's official religion, and the pursuit of those who did not submit to the doctrine of the day at any one time, risked turning people against authority itself.

She tacitly acknowledged her subjects' right to a private realm for their deepest convictions. As a letter to a French official, put it, 'Her Majesty is not inclined to peer into men's hearts and secret thoughts' – a sentiment that would later be immortalized into the famous line: 'I have no desire to make windows into men's souls.'[1]

Elizabeth's primary concern was not the inner beliefs of her subjects, but rather outward conformity to the established order. In the
words of a 1559 proclamation, she sought, 'the soul health of her
loving subjects, and the quieting of their consciences in the chief
and principal points of Christian religion'.[2]

Yet, serious threats both domestic and foreign tested Elizabeth's commitment to religious tolerance. In time, consciences,
including those of Catholics and Puritans, *were* molested.[3] And
rather than the quieting of consciences, such measures only aggravated them. When, in 1603, King James I succeeded Elizabeth to
the throne, he inherited a realm grappling with the scars of religious persecution and burgeoning resistance to monarchical
authority – not only from individual believers, but from other
sources of authority rising to challenge the Crown.

*

In December 1614, Edmund Peacham, a sixty-one-year-old rector
from the Somerset village of Hinton St George, stood before the
Court of High Commission. This special ecclesiastical tribunal
had been established during the reign of Elizabeth I to uphold the
authority of the Church of England and ensure adherence to its
doctrines. Determined to eradicate any trace of dissent or heresy,
the Court adopted inquisitorial methods.

Peacham, a steadfast Puritan convinced that the Church of
England had not sufficiently purified itself of Catholic influences,
was renowned for his fiery sermons denouncing the policies of the
King and bishops. The court found him guilty of libel and
stripped him of his holy orders, but worse was to come. When
officers of the Crown searched his lodgings for unlicensed books,
they found notes for an undelivered sermon in which he planned
to complain about the monarch, his son, and his advisers and
counsellors. It was also said that Peacham imagined the death of
the King.

It was never wise to insinuate a threat against a monarch, even in the jottings for an unspoken sermon, and doubly unwise in the case of this king. After the Gunpowder Plot of 1605, the failed conspiracy by English Catholics to assassinate King James I and blow up the House of Lords during the State Opening of Parliament, James remained vigilant against any conceivable danger. His caution reached such heights that he fortified the walls of his chamber with feather beds to shield himself from lurking assassins.[4]

James was suspicious of the Somerset gentry, including Peacham's associates. Some of them had refused to pay the benevolences, a form of direct taxation that he had imposed. There was an increasingly obvious contrast between louche behaviour at his court – drunkenness, bawdy jokes and gossip about his relationships with his favourite male courtiers – and the restrained lives of the Puritan classes. He had reason to suspect that their lips pursed and their fingers wagged in his direction.

The King's men subjected Peacham to the excruciating torment of the rack, mercilessly stretching his limbs to the brink of snapping. Yet, the elderly rector remained resolute. He did not confess to any plot. Nonetheless, James and his attorney-general, Francis Bacon, an ambitious political operator and brilliant natural philosopher, were convinced that Peacham's undelivered but written sermon was sufficient to charge him with high treason.[5]

In preparation for Peacham's trial, Bacon set out to test and effectively steer the opinion of the judges. It was common practice for them to be assembled for a consultation with the Attorney-General, but as a group. In this case, Bacon approached each judge individually – and in secret. If his intention had been to ensure they arrived at the desired opinion, it had the opposite effect on the Chief Justice, Sir Edward Coke, Bacon's enduring adversary.

Coke was tall and robust, sporting a moustache and a short, pointed beard. His booming voice conveyed unwavering self-assurance to all within earshot. Renowned for his brutal prosecution of high-profile defendants including at the trials of the Earl of Essex, Sir Walter Raleigh and the Gunpowder Plotters, he was a determined figure not easily swayed. Elizabeth Hatton, his second wife, reputedly said of him, 'If he enters through one door, I shall exit through the other.'[6]

At the time of Peacham's case, Coke had already triumphed in love, captivating Hatton in 1598 – whom Bacon had once desired – while also becoming Bacon's political nemesis. The two men clashed repeatedly over the decades, their enmity shaping the course of their careers and the governance of their era. The conflict came down to their interpretation of tradition, precedent and common law: the source and scope of power.

Bacon, a pragmatist with a talent for aphorisms such as 'Knowledge is power', had a knack for aligning himself with the reigning monarch and harboured suspicions regarding judicial overreach. Coke started as a government man, rising through the ranks of the judicial hierarchy and evolving into a principled disputer. His convictions clashed with those of monarchs and their men.

The power of the monarch, buttressed by religious faith in the divine authority of the Crown, was immense. But doubts had spread. The religious turmoil of the sixteenth and early seventeenth centuries illustrated the political and social challenges of having the English monarch as the leader of the national church. Catholic, Anglican and Puritan alike had begun to follow their own conscience in secret over the best path to salvation. While the Gunpowder Plot had failed, it hinted at deeper discontent simmering beneath the surface.

Meanwhile, Parliament was increasingly populated by lawyers who believed in their mandate to shape the country's direction. It had become a battleground for conflicting views on the nature of sovereignty and the role of the law.

Into this state of turmoil stepped Edward Coke, boldly asserting the supremacy of the law – seen as a fixed and public entity – over the monarch's prerogatives. His numerous legal judgments, coupled with his groundbreaking writings, transitioned medieval common law into the Elizabethan and Stuart era. Coke consistently challenged royal claims to be the ultimate source of English law, firmly stating that the monarch was subject to common law, not above it. By establishing fundamental common law principles, he left an indelible mark on political and legal systems worldwide. In practical terms, this involved bolstering the authority of the judiciary while challenging that of the monarch, both as an individual and in their role. Coke's efforts to curb royal authority and elevate the law played a pivotal role in defining the boundary between power and the private realm.

*

By the time of Peacham's case, Coke had established a reputation for resisting royal authority and pushing for a space free from its reach. One such ruling during Coke's tenure as attorney-general (1594–1606) had been Semayne's Case, decided in 1604. The case arose from a dispute over property rights involving Richard Gresham and George Berisford, who shared a residence in Blackfriars, London. When Berisford died, leaving debts to Peter Semayne, Semayne sought to seize Berisford's possessions, but Gresham refused him entry. The case hinged on whether the sheriff had the legal right to enter the property. The Court of King's Bench ruled that while individuals have the right to defend their property, this right is not absolute and can be overridden in certain situations, such as executing a lawful warrant.

Though a relatively minor ruling, it established a key principle: the state and its agents could only intrude upon private property

under specific conditions, such as with a valid warrant or legal
authorization. In delivering this judgment, Coke argued that
ordinary homes should enjoy the same right to be left undisturbed as a baron's castle. In so doing, he drew on and reinvigorated
Magna Carta, the legal document signed in 1215 that protected
the lives, liberties and estates of 'free men' from arbitrary royal
decrees.[7] Coke invoked a popular proverb, writing: 'The house of
every one is his castle, and if thieves come to a man's house to
rob or murder, and the owner or his servants kill any of the thieves
in defence of himself and his house, it is no felony and he shall
lose nothing.'[8] This idea quickly seized the public's imagination.
Over the course of centuries, it was transformed into one of the
most familiar phrases in the history of private life: 'An Englishman's home is his castle.'

Edward Coke opposed the arbitrary use of power by the
Crown and perceived institutions like the Court of High Commission as perilous to the rights of English subjects. He argued
that such ecclesiastical courts undermined the authority of
common-law courts and infringed upon the legal rights of individuals. Coke criticized the High Commission for its lack of
procedural fairness, its use of coercion and intimidation, and its
tendency to act beyond the limits of its authority.

When, in 1607, the High Commission under James I pursued
Puritans as well as Catholics, Parliament asked Coke, now Chief
Justice, for an opinion on the propriety of this approach. His reply
was forthright: 'No man ecclesiastical or temporal shall be examined upon secret thoughts of his heart or of his secret opinion. And
the defendant must have, as in [the] Star Chamber and Chancery,
the bill [of particular charge] delivered unto him, or otherwise he
need not answer to it.'[9] Otherwise, he continued, laymen might too
easily be trapped into false confessions of heresy.

In delivering this opinion, Coke articulated a ringing defence
of private thought. By challenging the monarch's influence and

championing common law and individual liberties, he played a crucial role in defining and expressing what would come to be understood as private life – encompassing both physical property and, crucially, a mental space.

*

It would have surprised no one that when Bacon sought to confer with Coke about his verdict on Peacham's case, the King's philosopher came up against firm resistance. Coke reasoned that while the preacher's verbal attacks had been unwise and intemperate, he was not guilty of treason. But Coke also had another problem with Bacon's and the King's approach. To take such opinion in secret, Coke reprimanded, was not the custom of the realm; it would give the Crown excessive influence over the judiciary. As far as Coke was concerned, common law was the supreme law and the King in his own person could not adjudge any case; the law was sovereign and judges must have their own liberty of judgement. Bacon in turn argued that judges were there to advise the monarch and no more.

Peacham died in Taunton jail in March 1616, having been sentenced to death for high treason by Coke's peers. That same year, James dismissed Coke from his position. He would soon return to prominence.

*

Borders were beginning to form, though faint and easily erased. The lines between property and power, as well as the distinction between the inner world of thought and belief – the mind – and authority, were taking shape. But the concept of a distinct private sphere, separate from the public realm, had not fully developed. Privacy in itself was not yet a goal.

The word *privat* proliferates in its use in the late sixteenth and early seventeenth centuries in telling ways. The *OED* records 1549 as the first reference to the word *private* in terms of a 'private or personal matter', or as in 'a person's private affairs'. Other new expressions resonated with significance: *private interpretation* (1526), *private judgement* (1565), *private opinion* (1586).[10] They highlighted a shift in thinking, underscoring the growing importance of personal belief and interpretation as matters solely for the individual during this transformative era.

The term *private* is also found extensively in the diaries of religious men and women who write about praying in 'private', often in a 'prayer closet'. A notable example is the diary of Lady Margaret Hoby, a Puritan who lived on her estate in Hackness, a small village surrounded by the moors of North Yorkshire, in the early seventeenth century. Her diary is the oldest known such book in English written by a woman.

On many a page she writes: 'After I was readie I praied priuatly,' and this is how most of her mornings began.[11] In the hours that followed, she often attended 'publect prayer' within the household, conducted by her chaplain, Mr Rhodes; visited the parish church with the rest of the community; and then retired again for 'priuat prayer'. (The spelling of 'private' and 'public' varies.) Hoby records no feelings or emotions in the diary, though she reminds herself of God's mercies and chastises herself for her failings. Her illnesses and other unfortunate events, including the plague, are taken as demonstration of divine retribution. The day often ends with: 'I went to priuate praier and so to bed.'[12]

Even when praying privately, one might not be alone. Margaret Hoby also records praying 'in private' with her husband, and with the chaplain. The London-based woodturner Nehemiah Wallington, a Puritan artisan, also recorded his commitment to private worship in all kinds of busy places, especially when travelling. When at home, he noted that he woke at three and four in the morning for private prayer in bed while his wife and children snuggled beside him.

Frontispiece to Edward Wetenhall's Enter into Thy Closet; Or, a Method and Order for Private Devotions, *printed for John Martyn, 1670.*

Rather than physical isolation, what mattered was mental seclusion. 'Shut the door twice over . . . the door to the closet and your own lips when praying,' urged the Puritan preacher Thomas Brooks in *The Privie Key of Heaven, A Discourse of Closet Prayer, or, Twenty Arguments for Closet-Prayer* (1665), one of a number of instruction manuals in circulation.[13] After all, even when Hoby and Wallington were by themselves, kneeling in worship and deep in thought, they were not strictly by themselves – they were present before God, who saw everything, knew everything and forgot nothing. And their efforts would have been evident to those around them. The Suffolk clergyman John Carter prayed privately every day, 'in his Closet, very loud and mostly very long'. According to his biographer, this was to 'give a good example of secret prayer to children, and his servants'.[14]

Privacy would not, in all likelihood, have been sought by Hoby or Wallington. For while private prayer showed the believer's true commitment, and an expression of an intimate relationship with God, being alone placed them in a precarious position. 'Wee must, when we are solitary and alone, keepe a narrow watch over ourselves,' is how one is how one Puritan put it.[15]

As Richard Brathwait, an early seventeenth-century writer of social conduct books, warned: 'Task yourselves then privately, lest privacy become your enemy.' Brathwait also cautioned: 'Be you in your chambers or private closets, be you retired from the eyes of men, think how the eyes of God are on you. Do not say, the walls encompass me, darkness o'ershadows me, the curtain of night secures me . . . do nothing privately which you would not do publicly.'[16] Everyone knew that the devil made work for idle hands and wandering minds. People could not be trusted to be alone; they were used to being watched. If anything, it was reassuring. It meant they were safe and less likely to do something wrong.

From birth to death, every aspect of life was intertwined with the community. Women gave birth at home with local midwives present, accompanied by ministers, their wives, and 'gossips' – a term used for companions during childbirth who shared news of the event with others.

Family life and its breakdown was other people's business. Neighbours intervened, restraining abusive husbands and counselling couples, facilitating a separation if this seemed necessary to protect a wife from injury.[17] The violent could not invoke a right to privacy to defend their actions or to limit oversight (as would come to be the case in the Victorian age). It was a broadly protective environment if, by modern standards, a rather oppressive one.

People died in their beds rather than in hospitals. As death approached, the local parish church bells tolled to invite neighbours to visit or pray for the dying. In 1614, Thomas Adams described the 'sinner's passing bell' as a 'speedy messenger' that travelled from house to house, urging everyone to assist with their prayers.[18] Deathbed 'watchers' provided comfort, paid their respects and ensured the dying person was in a suitable state of grace. They recorded last wishes: parental blessings or apologies.

These areas of life that we, in the twenty-first century, think of as private or personal, as separable from others, were not so in the seventeenth century. The household was embedded in the community. Each person had a particular role within it and all followed the same rhythm of life. Everything that went on inside the household, at some point, concerned others. It was impossible to avoid scrutiny. People had interior lives. They could and did retreat for reflection. But against the structures of power, the demands of society and the community, there was no strictly separate private sphere, no aspect of life where others could not legitimately intrude. The outside world could pry into anyone's business and was expected to do so. Curiosity and nosiness were mandated. Especially in intimate relations.

*

On 14 September 1610, Humphrey Philpott, a clothier, was deposed before the Gloucester consistory court, a type of ecclesiastical tribunal so closely associated with the policing of vice that they became known as the 'Bawdy Courts' or the 'Bum Courts'.[19] Though the Church had long regulated sex, policing people's sex lives was central to the Protestant Reformation's reshaping of the world. Whereas Catholics had considered lust reprehensible but inevitable, Protestants viewed the Catholic Church as lax, tending to believe that sexual immorality would lead to social disorder, and they sought to banish unchastity.

From 1604, the Church courts had upheld canon law, one

aspect of which was to police the laity's morals. All sex outside marriage was illegal. Transgressions therefore included adultery and 'fornication' (premarital sex). The courts also tackled 'any other uncleanness and wickedness of life'. That could include gambling, drinking in the alehouse during church services, and playing sport or dancing on the Sabbath.

The courts relied upon members of the community to police each other. When a good Christian observed immorality, it was to be reported to the churchwardens. Trials, which were inquisitorial and with witnesses, but without a jury, took place in church – the heart and soul of the community. Offences that would once have been confided in private to a Catholic confessor in a dark closet were aired among officials in this more public setting. In some ways, the old religion had been more respectful of privacy than the new. Now, the depositions of witnesses were circulated widely.

Philpott was one of five witnesses called against Jone Anslett and Michael Payne, who were on trial for adultery. Philpott lived in the same building as Jone and her husband, Richard Anslett, and had on several occasions seen Payne come into the house to solicit Jone's 'private company'. He made his disapproval clear. He would have needed to. Had he not condemned the adulterous couple or made his case against them, he could have been charged with 'bawdry' – pimping, procuring and other forms of aiding and abetting sexual offenders. It was 'very vnfitt' that a young man should keep 'privat company' with another man's wife when her husband was away, Mr Philpott began, before describing everything he had seen.[20]

At six o'clock in the morning on the Friday after Whitsunday, he saw Mr Payne visit Mrs Anslett. They were alone together, in her bedchamber, for as long as a quarter of an hour. Philpott said that he had rushed to tell a neighbour, Jane Hall, a brewer's wife, so that she could confirm if what they were doing 'in privat' was 'suspicious or scandalous' and in need of 'redress'. Hall's testimony corroborated Philpott's. She told the Gloucester consistory court that she had seen, through 'a hole in the wall' in her room, which directly adjoined Jone Anslett's bedchamber, Michael Payne 'lieing in naked bed hauing onely his shirte on', 'embracinge kissinge her in most notorious and scandalous manner'. Jane Hall had then sought further corroboration, calling on Elisabeth Morrice, a shoemaker's wife, whose testimony supported that of her neighbours. Mr Payne, Morrice confirmed, did 'carnally know the body' of Mrs Anslett. Two other witnesses confirmed that they too had observed the same scene.

Who knows exactly what went on between Jone Anslett and Michael Payne in those fifteen minutes, or what exactly each of the five onlookers actually saw. What is significant is that they were obliged to report wrongdoing, that neighbours spied and reported on each other enthusiastically, and that conventions for doing so included evidence secured via holes in the wall. The very attempt to secure privacy might provoke a neighbour's suspicion.

There is no record of Anslett and Payne's punishment. But the Church courts had few sanctions: they could enforce penance, fines and excommunication on the guilty, but had no right of arrest, imprisonment or corporal punishment. Instead, they relied on public shaming. Culprits had to make an open confession and show remorse by weeping, going barefoot or wearing a white sheet in public. Penance might be performed in the even more public marketplace as well as, or instead of, the church. And – although in 1617 the Norfolk minister William Yonger complained that 'so renowned and famous a church as this of England, should have no sharper censure for adultery than a white sheet' – public humiliation was effective.[21]

Rather than make an open display of repentance, records show one man from Banbury paid £3 for the crime of fornication. He explained that this was because the public humiliation would have severe consequences: it 'would be a great disparagement unto him in respect for preferment in marriage and, in all likelihood, an occasion of his loss of his present service and also of his friends' goodwill and inclination towards his future preferment'.[22] In a tightly interconnected world with strict moral codes of behaviour, the exposure of sinful activity could ruin lives.

A petition in 1606, made by the residents of Castle Combe in Wiltshire, called on local magistrates to act against an unmarried woman who was pregnant.[23] As the parish was responsible for destitute infants, private sin had both collective consequences and public repercussions. Women were closely monitored. If they went walking alone after dark, they would be stopped on suspicion of immorality. An unmarried woman who put on weight might find herself being strip-searched by a respectable matron. The mother of a child of unknown paternity would be interrogated for hours until she revealed the name of the father. There were frequent searches for evidence of infanticide.[24]

Intimate life was under constant corrective review, which is why many headed outdoors for romantic purposes. But nowhere was safe from prying eyes, not even the long grass. Church court records tell of Joan Thorne, a married woman from Ely, who was sent to court 'for behaving herself most uncomely in the fen . . . by stripping off herself into her smock'. The court ruled it was 'a thing very unseemly before men, & very much offensible unto women that did see the same'.[25]

The Church courts and community policing impacted on many aspects of community life and individual sexual behaviour.[26] When Church courts cracked down on prenuptial sex, the number of prosecutions increased.[27] Between 1590 and the 1620s, the number of women recorded as pregnant when they got married declined from around 20 per cent of all brides until fewer than 5 per cent of babies were conceived out of wedlock.[28]

And yet, during this era of piety and devotion, of spying, peeping, prying, and fearing solitude, the boundaries of a private realm took shape.

*

Edward Coke lived long enough to cause trouble for James's successor, Charles I. Charles was a firm believer in the divine right of kings, considering himself God's representative on Earth. However, the nation's acceptance of that conviction was about to be shaken.

In 1628, at the grand old age of seventy-six and on the eve of his retirement, Coke took a central role in framing and drafting the Petition of Right. This was a major constitutional document setting out specific English freedoms that should be respected by the monarch in all cases (except where the subject was a Catholic). They included: no taxation without parliamentary approval; no imprisonment without cause; no billeting of soldiers in a subject's home – a small victory for private life; and no martial law in peacetime.

Charles's response was defiant. It was his 'sovereign power' to rule the country, he argued, entirely confident of his position as the supreme ruler of his kingdoms. Despite intimidation from the Crown, Coke rose to his feet before a joint session of both houses of Parliament to defend the petition and remind parliamentarians of the importance of Magna Carta: 'Take we heed what we yield unto,' Coke boomed. 'Magna Carta is such a fellow that he will have no sovereign.'[29]

Charles was pressured into confirming the Petition of Right – a historic achievement in restraining the power of the Crown, and an event which confirmed that cracks were appearing in the authority of a monarch who ruled by appointment from God. Coke had made it clear that judges possessed their own liberty of judgement and that there *were* limits on the power of kings.

Common law was a bulwark against royal authority and its imposition on the subject. By seeking to limit the authority vested in the monarch, he contributed to the formation of private life, aiding in its early demarcation.

Edward Coke died on 3 September 1634 at the age of eighty-two. Legend has it that at his funeral his wife Elizabeth said, 'We shall never see his like again, praise be to God.'[30]

Chapter 3:

THOUGHT IS FREE

It was Monday, 22 March 1641, and Thomas Wentworth, 1st Earl of Strafford, was fighting for his life. The first week of his trial for treason had begun. He was standing in Westminster Hall, where Thomas More had stood before him. Once again, the hall was hosting a show trial, and thousands wanted to witness the spectacle.

At the centre of the west wall stood the sovereign's throne, a high-backed, Gothic-style armchair. Before it, an oval of courtiers and judges in red robes trimmed with white ermine sat on wool-stuffed cushions, flanked by two long lines of court officials in black robes. At a side table sat the clerks of Parliament and the prosecution. Rising into the hammer-beam roof were rows of terraced seating for the members of the House of Commons, members of the nobility, and the public.

The hall had started to fill as early as five o'clock in the morning. Many of the ladies attending had long feather plumes in their hair in accordance with the fashion of the day, obscuring the view of those sitting behind them. There was chatter and hissing and coughing as well as the continuous eating of sweets, bread and meat. Wine and beer were drunk from the bottle. Many brought their own chamber pots.

At nine o'clock, King Charles, Queen Henrietta Maria and the ten-year-old Prince of Wales arrived. The boy took a seat on the steps of the throne but the King did not proceed to the dais. Protocol dictated that his subjects should remain silent in his presence, so it was left empty. Instead, he walked with the Queen into a wooden cabinet erected at the side of the hall, where a lattice window shielded their faces. Those watching the trial would see his fingers grip the slats until, one day, they broke through. It was the King's man whose neck was on the line.

Strafford, a Yorkshireman in his early forties, had curly brown hair. The time spent in the Tower had begun to erode his once-handsome appearance. His brooding demeanour and authoritarian tendencies had long ago earned him the moniker 'Black Tom Tyrant'. As a younger man, as mere Thomas Wentworth, he had opposed the

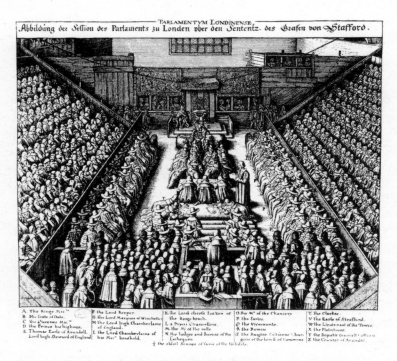

The Trial of the Earl of Strafford in Westminster Hall, *1641*.
Engraving by Wenceslaus Hollar.

autocratic use of royal prerogatives and supported the rights of
the House of Commons to limit the power of the monarch. But
then – in a move that would prove to be his undoing – he had
changed sides.

*

Between 1629 and 1640, Charles had governed without conven-
ing Parliament, a period known as his 'Personal Rule'. This
unilateral exercise of power frustrated members of Parliament,
who perceived it as a descent into tyranny under unchecked royal
authority. Charles's insistence on extending 'ship money' to
inland counties – a tax traditionally reserved for coastal regions
during wartime to fund the Royal Navy – aggravated parliamentarians who were convinced of their right to participate in
taxation decisions.

Wentworth, appointed Lord President of the Council of the
North in 1626, efficiently gathered funds for his royal master.
Recognizing his loyalty, Charles elevated him to the position of
Lord Lieutenant in Ireland, the third realm within the King's
domain. In this role, he skilfully manipulated the dynamics
between the native Gaelic Irish and the Scottish and English set-
tler communities to further his objectives.

The divided religious loyalties of the country festered. Puritans
were concerned that Charles had encouraged William Laud, the
Archbishop of Canterbury, to be sceptical of the Calvinist belief
in predestination. This doctrine holds that God had predeter-
mined who should go to heaven or hell before they were born,
hence there was no possibility of earning one's salvation through
works, including sacramental ceremonies. Laud also advocated
religious services that seemed to resemble Catholic practice. Both
Charles and Laud were relaxed about the playing of games on the
Sabbath and other holy days, which many strict Protestants saw
as wholly sacred. While Charles was not a Catholic, his French

wife, Henrietta Maria, was openly so. Puritans suspected a hidden agenda to restore Catholicism to England and challenge the true word of God.

Social changes added to the sense of tension and tumult. England's population had doubled from just over two million people in 1500 to over four million in 1600.[1] People were also more geographically mobile, and there was a huge migration into London. In Henry VIII's time, the city's population had been around 80,000 inhabitants. By 1640 that number had increased to around 400,000.[2] The city teemed with tradespeople come to make their fortunes, and the streets bristled with new ideas: radical books and pamphlets were published, and plays and entertaining sermons were performed before rowdy crowds. In 1623 the Puritan preacher William Gouge was shocked when, as he instructed congregations on 'female submission & inferiority' in domestic life, the women in the audience 'squirmed' and 'murmured'. Such behaviour was considered the height of female rebelliousness and reflected the relative freedom the city afforded to women.[3]

Charles's government cracked down on the reading public, determined to wipe out dissent and disorder. In 1632, the Court of Star Chamber banned 'news books', the precursors to today's newspapers. Five years later, William Laud passed a decree restricting the number of licensed printers in London to twenty. But that didn't stop the flow of seditious literature. Covert publications filtered out, reaching secret networks of unorthodox believers.[4] Books and pamphlets printed in Amsterdam, known for its relative religious tolerance, were smuggled into the country. With literacy rates for men in London approaching 80 per cent, reading illicit works freed ordinary people to think for themselves.

In 1637, John Lilburne, a cloth merchant's apprentice, was arrested for printing and distributing unlicensed Puritan books and pamphlets. When he was required by the Court of Star

Chamber to swear an oath that he would answer truthfully the questions put to him (though he had not been informed of any charges to which these questions might be related), he refused and remained silent. Officers whipped him through the streets, set him up in the pillory and then sent him to Fleet Prison, where his convictions only strengthened. He fired off a series of pamphlets describing his persecution and calling for separation from the Church of England.

It was not only Parliament and the people of England that the King had troubled. Scotland was effectively a separate country, despite the 1603 Union of the Crowns, with its own parliament and its own state church: the Kirk. The Reformation had taken a more Presbyterian turn north of the border, but in 1636 Charles imposed upon his Scottish subjects a new Anglican Prayer Book, with a set liturgy that restricted more extemporaneous preaching. When, a year later, the dean of Edinburgh, James Hannay, read from the new prayer book at Edinburgh's St Giles' Cathedral, his words were met with a barrage of church stools thrown by the congregation in disgust. Among the throng, according to legend, one figure emerged as the harbinger of defiance: Jenny Geddes, a spirited market trader whose voice rose in fury: 'daur ye say Mass in my lug?'[5] Her ears were offended. It was a phrase that speaks to the physical sense of invasion felt by the congregation at the imposition of the new liturgy. A riot broke out, and spread.

A year later, Scotland was in open rebellion. The rebels signed in blood a National Covenant in front of the pulpit of Greyfriars Kirk in Edinburgh, pledging the rights of ordinary Scots to exercise their 'God-given consciences' in matters of faith and agreeing to resist Catholic innovations. The signatories spread across the Lowlands of Scotland and into the Highlands. A war between the Scottish Covenanters and the King's Army broke out in 1639.

After a short truce, Charles intended to wage war again – but he required money to do so, and for that he had to reconvene Parliament. By now, however, the parliamentarians had had enough. They refused his demands, proposing instead that they debate his Personal Rule. Charles, in defiance, returned to battle the Scots, bolstered in part by a promise by Strafford of 8,000 Irish Catholic troops. But he found himself defeated in the Second Bishops' War of 1640. Once he surrendered, only lightly chastened, Charles agreed that he would not interfere again with Scotland's religion and that he would pay the Scots' war expenses.

Throughout all this, Strafford had been Charles's right-hand man, his enforcer in the north of England. He was closely associated with a king who was making enemies and losing allies, and was widely held responsible for the King's misrule. Finally, a group of MPs took it upon themselves to arrest Strafford.

Strafford's trial focused long-standing tensions. Within Westminster Hall, the two sides in England's impending civil war were forming: the champions of the rights of the English Parliament, who would be called Roundheads by their opponents in reference to the short hair of the Puritans. The supporters of monarchy and of the divine right of kings were known as Cavaliers, which to their enemies implied dissolute, violent gentlemen.

John Pym, a stout West Country lawyer with inexhaustible determination, led the prosecution. He was convinced that the King's religious policies undermined English Protestantism, and that taking down Strafford would rein in the monarch.

Strafford, meanwhile, was fighting not only to maintain the King's powers, but for his own life.

*

Strafford left his cell in Traitor's Gate at the Tower of London every morning accompanied by his guards and travelled along the river Thames in a flotilla of six barges rowed by fifty pairs of oars. He then inched his way through King Street and Palace Yard, which was lined with soldiers to protect him from the jeering, jostling crowds. Upon entering Westminster Hall, he gave a low bow, followed by a second and then a third. He knelt, before standing to salute the House. A few Lords lifted their hats in response. Only then did Strafford take his seat.

On the first morning it took three clerks three hours to read out the twenty-eight charges against him, which, it was said, amounted to cumulative treason.[6] Though the proceedings were meant to take only a few days, Strafford refuted each charge, and his trial dragged on. He disputed most of the charges on points of fact, but his central defence was that none of them, even if proven, amounted to treason.

Many of those present were surprised by the robustness of his defence, until the prosecution delivered what it believed would be the decisive blow. Members of the King's Privy Council, the formal body of advisers to the sovereign, would testify about treasonous remarks they had heard Strafford make at Council meetings the previous year. By convention, the proceedings of these meetings were ordinarily considered private, with participants' observations treated confidentially. But on this occasion the prosecution was determined to make use of them.

The Hall stilled in expectation. With each passing day his appearance had waned, broken by gout, dysentery and mortal fear. He was dressed almost entirely in black. According to Robert Baillie, a Scottish Presbyterian minister who attended the trial, he looked like a man in mourning shrouds.[7]

Pym informed the crowd that the notes he had obtained from the meeting showed that Strafford had advised using an Irish army against the King's enemies, to bring the English kingdom to obedience – advice he presented as treasonous.[8] It was a sly move. Pym would have understood that Strafford had meant using the Irish army against Scotland; not, as he implied, England.

It was Strafford's turn. He stood and allowed himself a pause before mocking his own and anyone else's ability to remember exactly what a person had said in company as long as twelve months ago. He then turned to why evidence of this kind could not be used to convict him, contending that no recollection of private conversations should be admitted. 'If, my lords,' he argued,

> 'words spoken to friends in familiar discourse, spoken at one's table, spoken in one's chamber, spoken in one's sick bed, spoken, perhaps, to gain better reason, to gain one's self more clear light and judgment by reasoning, – if these things shall be brought against a man as treason, this (under favour) takes away the comfort of all human society.
>   'By this means we shall be debarred from speaking – the principal joy and comfort of life – with wise and good men, to become wiser and better ourselves. If these things be strained to take away life, and honour, and all that is desirable, this will be a silent world! A city will become a hermitage, and sheep will be found among a crowd and press of people! No man will dare to impart his solitary thoughts or opinions to his friend and neighbour!'[9]

'It was a passionate defence of private conversation. Strafford, who had been on the stand for nine hours, was taken back to his cell, exhausted.

While his vigorous defence may have improved his reputation, it didn't save his life. With the prosecution's case floundering, they changed tack and presented a bill of attainder: a legal mechanism that allowed Parliament to vote on the accused's guilt without recourse to evidence. Who had said what no longer mattered.

By this point, 20,000 men of 'good rank and quality' – mostly apprentices and tradesmen – had signed a petition calling for

Strafford's execution, and a crowd of some 10,000 surged outside Westminster Hall in further support.[10] With momentum building on the streets, a majority in both houses of Parliament moved against Strafford. The vote on the bill of attainder decided he was guilty, and thus he was condemned. Charles's signature on the death warrant was all that was needed to seal his fate.

The King was conflicted. He didn't want to give up his man, but the situation was spiralling out of control. Eventually, on 10 May 1641, Charles signed the warrant for Strafford's execution. Two days later, armed guards marched Strafford from his cell to Tower Hill for the last time. A chaplain blessed him; he knelt before the block; and Thomas Wentworth, 1st Earl of Strafford, was beheaded in front of 100,000 jubilant spectators.[11] Bonfires were lit across London that night in celebration. The windows of those who didn't participate in the rejoicing were smashed.

Civil war broke out the following year.

What followed was one of the most tumultuous, violent and confusing periods in British history. The English Civil Wars, a series of interconnected conflicts between 1642 and 1651, saw England, Ireland and Scotland torn apart, with counties, towns and families set against each other. More than one in ten men took up arms in a conflict where Parliamentarians fought for the ancestral rights of the English people, while the King fought for his own. Each camp believed that God was on their side. Some 84,000 people were killed, while a further 100,000 died from typhus, dysentery and other war-related diseases.[12]

With ancient certainties such as the divine right of kings called into question, the war forced ordinary people to consider their beliefs and give thought to how they might follow them. Powerful thinking about conscience coursed through Britain, intersecting with other new ideas about the natural rights and liberties of the common man. By the century's end, a distinct boundary had been established between authority and the populace, as well as between public power and private life. However, the path to this separation was anything but clear.

*

On 28 October 1647, soldiers of the New Model Army – a body of professional soldiers raised by Parliament and committed to the parliamentary cause – gathered in the pews of St Mary's Church, Putney. Sitting in their pale-yellow buff leather coats, they were ready to have their say. King Charles had been defeated in what would later come to be seen as the first stage of the Civil Wars, and had been imprisoned in the royal apartments at Hampton Court Palace as a settlement was discussed.

Oliver Cromwell, the parliamentary Lieutenant General who was negotiating with the Royalists, chaired the meeting. The son of East Anglian landed gentry and a devout Puritan, Cromwell had proved a brilliant leader on the battlefield. Despite having no military training, he led forces loyal to Parliament to victory over the King. Every step of the way, Cromwell had felt the guiding hand of predestination. 'God made them as stubble to our swords,' he said, after the decisive battle of Marston Moor in 1644.[13]

Fighting a national war generated a sense of common purpose that united men from disparate religious sects. In a transformative act, Parliament had accepted anyone into the New Model Army who would fight against the King, regardless of their religion – even Anabaptists, who rejected infant baptism in favour of a consciously chosen adult baptism and were considered unorthodox by all sides. And the New Model Army was partly run on democratic principles: every regiment elected a representative onto the army council. Now, with victory apparently assured, it was time to debate their situation.

Cromwell opened the meeting stating that it was for public business and encouraged anyone with something to say to take the floor. He and his fellow generals had assumed that discussion would concentrate on military grievances, including arrears of pay. But over the meeting's several days, many men raised questions on a more fundamental topic: England's future political constitution.[14]

'We have engaged in this kingdom and ventured our lives,' said a soldier named Edward Sexby, who spoke passionately about how the men had spilled blood in the struggle against the monarch. He believed that they should now contribute to the future direction of England, referring to 'our birthrights and privileges as Englishmen'.[15] Another, Colonel Thomas Rainsborough, powerfully stated the case for suffrage: 'For really I think that the poorest he that is in England has a life to live, as the greatest he; and therefore truly, sir, I think it's clear, that every man that is to live under a government ought first by his own consent to put himself under that government; and I do think that the poorest man in England is not at all bound in a strict sense to that government that he had not had a voice to put himself under.'[16] Rainsborough, the son of a naval officer, also argued that the power of the House of Commons and the Church to intervene in the lives of ordinary men should be limited.

The men were not advocating universal suffrage; they did not ask that the vote be extended to women, servants and paupers. But their arguments for democracy were, in the context of the time, strikingly radical – too radical for their generals. Cromwell argued that giving the franchise to unpropertied men who had 'no interest but the interest of breathing' could lead to anarchy. His son-in-law, Henry Ireton, Commissary General of the New Model Army, held that without property – without a 'fixed permanent interest in the kingdom' – a man should not be permitted to have a say in its future. 'Liberty cannot be provided for in a general sense if property is to be preserved,' he asserted.[17]

This was a significant discussion about political order, and one that relied upon a common idea of the natural and political rights of man. Previously, such conversations would have taken place behind closed doors, in the household; but increasingly ideas were being tested out in front of others and even aired in print.

The collapse of royal authority in the heat of war had ended formal censorship, and there was a deluge of pamphlets on matters of conscience and political ideas. Many of the men at the Putney debates had read these, passed them around and debated them with one another. Titles such as *Conscience Puzzel'd*, *Conscience Caution'd* and *Nineteen Cases of Conscience* reverberated with discussions on faith, morality, the tangled web of political and religious allegiance and the implications of conscience in everyday life.[18] Some tracts, authored mainly by Puritans, dared to argue for freedom of worship. The writers believed in the supremacy of their faith, but they had had to confront when dissent was legitimate. They had also started to believe that their spiritual goals could not be attained if they themselves were denied the freedom to practise their religion. And they began to consider the concept of the rights of man, regardless of who was king, and of rights assertable against all civil authorities.[19]

In this way, what today would be described as civil liberties appear to emerge from within Puritanism in this period. This is a curious paradox. Puritans regarded God's arbitrary grace as the only source of redemption and denied any possibility of achieving it through a life of good works. And yet some were beginning to argue for civil rights, on the basis that all men had natural rights. As doctrinal differences faded or became less strongly felt, what was left was a belief in natural rights of man, laying the groundwork for later democratic movements in Britain.[20]

The eventual widespread acceptance of these ideas should not imply that they emerged fully formed or unchallenged in the minds of their originators. On the contrary, they were initially tentative, subject to rigorous testing, frequent challenge, and abandonment. However, once articulated and fixed in print they gained an enduring foothold in the collective consciousness, never to be forgotten.

*

On 20 January 1649, King Charles himself stood before the High Court of Justice in Westminster Hall. Eight years after his man Thomas Wentworth had faced John Pym, the King was on trial for treason. A second Civil War had broken out, the Royalists had again been defeated, and the army had quickly recaptured the King after his attempt to escape. But Parliament now faced a great challenge: what to do with a monarch, a man purportedly appointed by God, who continued to threaten the peace.

Their plan had been to reform the monarchy, not remove, let alone execute, a king. But Charles, resolute in his belief that God had appointed him, refused to recognize the authority of the court and showed no remorse for the carnage of the war. He even appeared to have every intention of provoking another conflict. The usurpers began to think that there could be no peace while Charles lived.

Oliver Cromwell added his signature as the third among fifty-nine on the death warrant. He justified the execution on grounds of divine providence, arguing that Charles was not the rightful guardian of the faith and therefore God's will mandated his death. Nonetheless, the King's beheading outside Banqueting House in Whitehall on the bitterly cold day of 30 January 1649 – by an executioner whose face was hidden by a mask, false wig and beard for his own safety – was a monumentally shocking act. According to one contemporary account, women miscarried and men 'fell into melancholy'; 'some with consternations expired'.[21] Four months later, the monarchy was abolished.

Oliver Cromwell now assumed a preeminence that no English commoner could previously have imagined. In 1653, after four years of revolutionary republican experiments, he accepted the title of Lord Protector to the Protectorate, a quasi-monarchical system, though he was obliged to summon Parliament at least once every three years. Cromwell was master of Britain and Ireland, and he was determined to transform the country into a model godly commonwealth.[22]

Under Cromwell, strides were made towards formalizing freedom of conscience, and Parliament passed the Toleration Act of 1650. This meant that some dissenting Protestant groups were allowed to practise their faith without fear of persecution, but other groups, particularly Roman Catholics, were still subject to discrimination and persecution.

The trial of the Quaker James Nayler for heresy in 1656 shows the extent of the progress. By riding into Bristol on a donkey, Nayler, a charismatic and unconventional figure, had reenacted Christ's Palm Sunday entry into Jerusalem with a group of followers. The House of Commons placed Nayler on trial for blasphemy, with some Presbyterian parliamentarians advocating for his execution. Cromwell intervened and saved his life. They did not burn Nayler at the stake, but he was whipped and pilloried, and his tongue was bored with a red-hot iron. His forehead was branded with the letter B, for Blasphemer, to publicly shame him for his offence against religious doctrine. Parliament could not accept that someone like Nayler, an extreme Protestant with non-Trinitarian views, could have acted out of conscience. But he was spared the pyre.

*

Thomas Hobbes, who had fled England for France before the outbreak of the military conflict between Charles and Parliament, found himself amid a community of displaced English Royalists at the French court. There, at the age of sixty-three, he penned his magnum opus, *Leviathan* (1651), in which he describes life outside civil society as 'solitary, poor, nasty, brutish, and short'. At its core, *Leviathan* is an investigation into how social order might be maintained.

Speaking to fellow Royalists, Cromwell and the new regime, Hobbes argued that the ultimate authority in society – the Leviathan of his book's title – depended on sovereignty and was essential to political stability. For Hobbes, there could be no society without the state. He accepted that sovereign authority derives from a covenant based upon the individual consent of each man. (He recommended monarchy as the best outcome of such a covenant.) But he argued that if the sovereign failed to fulfil its end of the social contract by not protecting the lives and property of its citizens, or if the sovereign threatened the very existence of the society, then subjects might have a right to rebel. Such rebellion should only be a last resort, undertaken only when the very survival of society is at stake and when there is a reasonable expectation that uprising would lead to a better situation.

Hobbes argued that the individual subject must follow the sovereign's law, regardless of the beliefs of their heart. He rejected the notion that every individual could be a judge of good and evil, entitled to follow their own conscience. He argued that would lead to anarchy and 'the war of every man against every man'. In Hobbes' ideal society, there was no space for individual sincerity of view. He called, in effect, for acquiescence, and for silence from people who wanted to follow a different faith, to deny individuals the right to express their external disagreements outwardly. He advocated hypocrisy – the gap between public utterance and private belief and conduct – in the name of social cohesion, in ways that Henry VIII would not have permitted with any of his subjects, especially Thomas More.

Hobbes recognized and sought to limit the private sphere to the internal realm of the mind. As he stated, 'A private man has always the liberty, (because thought is free,) to beleeve, or not to beleeve, in his heart . . . But when it comes to confession of that faith, the Private Reason must submit to the Publique'.[23] He challenged those who wished to expand the private sphere to encompass the home and private religious gatherings, while affirming the freedom of belief within one's own thoughts.

For Hobbes, uniformity of religion was central to a well-functioning civil society. Amid all the disorder, he believed that the need for security, order and control trumped freedom of religion. The end of political life – order – was both his starting and his end point. In his way of thinking, lying or publicly concealing one's true nature or motives was an acceptable and necessary aspect of political life, whether for sovereign or subject. Indeed, he regarded politics as inevitably a hypocritical business.

Centuries later, Thomas Hobbes is considered a conservative thinker, but his argument was radical for its time. Many Royalists were shocked by his writings and unprepared to accept the logic of *Leviathan*, which implied that they should not only accept the Puritans as the rightful rulers of the realm, but keep quiet about it.

*

Toleration under Cromwell concerned matters of religious faith. However, in other respects there were zealous attempts to intrude into people's lives. Moral crusaders now came from the state itself as well as from the Church. The vision of a new society, guided by God's chosen people, loomed large, and its leaders sought to mould the populace into a nation deserving of Christ's imminent return. The Protectorate took the common puritanical view of immorality and had grand ambitions to reform private behaviour: government considered its subjects' private lives very much its business. And in a period that saw inflation, rising population numbers and prices, and widespread poverty, MPs and government shared the Puritan conviction that strict social and moral discipline was necessary to maintain social order.

The Protectorate cracked down on drinking, dancing and the playing of 'lascivious' music. They had inns and theatres shut down and there were calls for an end to horse-racing and cock-fighting, as well as attempts to ban make-up and to encourage modest dress in women. Legislation was passed to ensure that every Sunday was stringently observed as a holy day.

In 1650, Parliament enacted the Commonwealth (Adultery) Act, aimed at quashing the 'detestable' sins of incest, adultery and fornication.[24] The Adultery Act stipulated the death penalty for the sins of incest and adultery by a married woman and her partner. (Married men and single women were spared capital punishment.) These changes brought English law into line with that of the Old Testament and were endorsed by radical churchmen: 'God would have put the adulterer to death,' preached Thomas Warson, a fierce Presbyterian.[25]

People who had sex outside marriage were to be jailed for three months and possibly worse, though the wording is unclear. Brothel-keepers were to be whipped, branded with a capital B and imprisoned for three years. Prostitutes, who, prior to the Adultery Act, would have suffered dunking or banishment from the city where they worked, now risked being deported to the colonies.[26] Every parish in England was sent a copy of the Act.

In Devonshire in 1654, Susan Bounty, who was married to Richard Bounty but was pregnant with another man's child, became one of the new act's victims. Shortly after giving birth, she held her baby boy and said goodbye to him. She had been found guilty of adultery by the Exeter assizes court and sentenced to death by hanging.[27] Richard Bounty took in the illegitimate child. Yet Susan's execution appears to be one of the few sentences that were carried out. Although there were at least thirty-six prosecutions for adultery at the Old Bailey, criminal records suggest that judges did not want to enforce the death penalty.[28] The Act lapsed in 1660 and was not renewed. It would have been no consolation for poor Susan Bounty, but she was probably the last person in England to be executed for the crime of adultery.[29]

*

Oliver Cromwell's death from natural causes in 1658 unleashed political chaos once again, and by 1660 the republican experiment was over. In that year Charles II, who as a young prince had attended Thomas Wentworth's trial and who, since his father's execution, had been living in exile in France (where he was briefly tutored by Thomas Hobbes), claimed his father's crown. Britain had a king again. Order had been restored, with a new balance of power that respected the central role of Parliament.

But once the Anglican Royalists were back in power, they passed laws declaring religious dissent to be a matter of civil disorder. Nonconformists and dissenters were subject to imprisonment and persecution, even execution. There was more violence. By 1679, the nation was yet again on the brink of civil war.

Among those bearing witness to the turmoil was the philosopher John Locke. Raised in a Puritan household in Pensford, a small village near Bristol, he had been ten years old when the first Civil War erupted in 1642. Reflecting on those early years, he recalled, 'I no sooner found myself in the world than I found myself in a storm.'[30] Locke wondered if there might be ways to structure society such that people of differing religious beliefs could live together without violence. Politically, he threw in his lot with the Earl of Shaftesbury, a leader of the Radical Dissenters – Protestants who had left the Church of England entirely – and in 1683 he fled to the Dutch port of Rotterdam. Within Holland's tolerant atmosphere, Locke embarked on one of the most renowned treatises in the annals of political philosophy.

Locke's *Letter on Toleration*, finally published in 1689,

solidified numerous debates on conscience from preceding centuries and propelled them further forward. According to Locke, the key to preventing violent disputes over religion did not lie in state coercion to enforce conformity, as advocated by earlier monarchs and argued by Hobbes, and, indeed, by Locke himself as a young man. Instead, in his *Letter on Toleration*, Locke championed a benevolent tolerance that permitted sincere conscience to freely express itself not only privately, but publicly in community with others. He also argued that one's religious affiliation should not affect a person's civil rights. However, he excluded atheists and Catholics from this tolerance.

He argued that the 'magistrate' had no legitimate authority to impose religious doctrine or belief on individuals; he wrote, it 'hath nothing to do with the good of men's souls'.[31] Civil interference in matters of religion was tyrannical and should be resisted. Individuals could only truly be saved if their consciences were sincere, and they could not be coerced into genuine belief. Attempting to do so would only breed hypocrisy and, potentially, violence.

In advocating toleration Locke drew on his understanding of God, who demanded sincerity of conscience, as well as on his belief in the inherent rationality of the human mind and his conception of the self. Unlike Hobbes – who depicted humans as driven by destructive passions, perpetually at risk of conflict, and in need of state authority to protect and maintain order – he posited that individuals could employ their rational faculties and adhere to natural laws for the betterment of society. He envisioned humanity's natural condition as one of freedom and equality.

Locke further argued that if people were to be truly moral beings, it was unacceptable that they should not be able to follow their consciences. Only reason and judgement could change people's minds, and the state therefore needed to treat citizens as

rational subjects. Locke defined the self as that 'conscious thinking thing', fully aware of pleasure and pain and largely concerned
for itself.[32] This was a transformative notion that helped shape a
new understanding of politics and human nature. A view of
humans as rational beings points to their capacity to lead what we
now regard as complete private lives, in which they can autono-
mously determine how to worship and conduct themselves.

From a modern perspective, Locke's case for toleration is limited and restrictive. He excluded atheists, reasoning that without
faith, they required no freedom to practise it. He also said they
could not be trusted to be good citizens. His intolerance towards
Catholics was primarily political rather than religious; he was not
alone in regarding allegiance to the pope as a threat to the civil
state.

Amid lingering anxieties over the threat of Catholicism, all
eyes turned apprehensively towards James, the younger brother of
Charles II. When he publicly declared his Roman Catholic faith
in 1673, Locke and others viewed the announcement as a threat
to the stability of the kingdom. Following Charles's death in 1685,
Locke found himself embroiled in what amounted to a coup: Angli-
cans and radical Whigs united to compel James to flee the country,
meanwhile extending an invitation to James's Protestant son-in-law,
William, Prince of Orange, and his wife, Mary, to sail from Holland
and jointly ascend the throne. Locke returned to England with the
same fleet as William on a mission to uphold Protestantism. William was crowned King under terms agreed upon by a 'convention
parliament', which maintained checks on royal authority. These
events became known as the Glorious Revolution.

An early landmark of William and Mary's reign was the
enactment of the Toleration Act of 1689. This law exempted
Trinitarian Protestants from penalties previously imposed for
non-attendance at Anglican services. Other Protestants did not
benefit from the suspension of punishments. Catholics and

non-Trinitarian Protestants were denied such protections and continued to face legal discrimination and persecution in England for years thereafter.

Even so, the Toleration Act was an advance towards religious tolerance and pluralism in England, paving the way for future developments in religious freedom. Moreover, the Act was accompanied by a bill of rights affirming 'the rights and liberties of the subject' and was followed by provisions guaranteeing annual parliamentary sessions, safeguarding judicial independence and ensuring qualified freedom of the press.

Toleration had become a principle of mutual restraint, demonstrating that political communities could endure even amid religious diversity, as long as believers confined their practices to a private sphere. It was not liberalism as we have subsequently known it. There were, for example, no guarantees of freedom of speech. (Though John Milton defended intellectual freedom, even he called for unorthodox opinions about sexual licence and 'popery' to be censored.) But the new political order nevertheless established that there were places the state could not go. From this the private realm was built.

This dawn of private life had three components: freedom of conscience and religion; what would become known as civil liberties; and the understanding of sexual and domestic mores and behaviour as 'private' matters. None of these concepts started out fully formed, nor did one inevitably lead to another. They did not emerge at the same time, or develop consistently, or at the same rate. But once it had been accepted that religion and conscience might be matters of private freedom and that subjects had liberties, the possibility that the same approach could be applied to other, more intimate areas of life hung in the air.

PART II:
The Age of Separations

Chapter 4:

PUBLIC FACES, PRIVATE SPACES

When the essayist Joseph Addison arrived at the Royal Exchange in the City of London on a May morning in 1711, he encountered a noisy hum, as if he had been engulfed by a swarm of bees. Fashionably adorned in a brocade waistcoat over a crisp ruffled shirt, with his wig impeccably coifed and powdered, he made his way towards the arcade. This was the place to find sellers who traded from all over the world. The areas dedicated to Norway, Jamaica and Virginia all buzzed with energy.

Mr Addison squeezed past a Japanese man in dispute with an English alderman and was jostled by a group of Armenians. He overheard French and Spanish before finding himself surrounded by a sea of Dutchmen.

All around him were luxury goods brought by ships laden with the harvest of many countries: citrus fruits from Portugal, sweet, spongy white Indian sugar cane, cloves from the Spice Islands. Brocade petticoats from Peru were piled so high that they threatened to topple over folds of Persian silk. The sparkle of a diamond necklace from India captured his attention. Up on the first floor were around 200 shops where women stood behind the counters busily folding ribbons, trying to sell patches and pins, hoping to catch the eye of each passer-by.

Addison, the eldest son of a clergyman, found himself irresistibly drawn to the world of commerce and the changes it heralded.

In an essay for *The Spectator* – the bestselling and most influential periodical of the age, which he co-edited with the exuberant retired army officer Captain Richard Steele – he detailed his observations with palpable delight. The format featured daily essays penned by a fictional 'Mr Spectator' who roamed the vibrant streets of London. The ostensible anonymity of the writer allowed them freedom to chronicle the social scene.

At the Exchange, 'Mr Spectator' described how tears streamed down his face and his heart swelled with pride. He was overcome by the sight of private men – men who once would have been mere vassals to barons – negotiating like princes for sums of money that dwarfed the former royal treasury. It was a scene that encapsulated the transformative power of commerce, highlighting the propulsive shift from feudal subjugation to economic empowerment.[1]

At the dawn of the eighteenth century, known as the 'long century' for its sweeping transformations, an era of economic, political, intellectual and cultural awakening was under way. Britain was a thriving commercial trading nation to rival the Dutch. In 1700, some 2.5 million tonnes of coal was produced here, roughly five times more than in the rest of the world combined.[2] And while continental Europe was Britain's most important export market, Britain's economic dynamism came from its imperial possessions in North America and the West Indies, and its trading outposts in India.

During the first half of the eighteenth century, imports from North America increased almost four times in value. West Indian imports more than doubled.[3] The amount of tea shipped into Britain by the East India Company – the first commodity to reach a mass market – expanded from 67,000 pounds in weight in 1701 to close to three million pounds fifty years later.[4] The addition of sugar, harvested in the Caribbean by enslaved people and imported in mountainous quantities, transformed an exotic luxury into the national drink. Village grocers sold crates of tea leaves at every end of the country, and sweet tea in porcelain bowls arranged on lacquer tables provided the centrepiece during flurries of fashionable visiting.

The ports of Liverpool, Bristol and Whitehaven in Cumbria thrived. London grew into the centre of world trade, including in consumer goods, and, with the establishment in 1694 of the Bank of England, of the banking, brokerage and insurance industries. Mercantile capitalism transformed the state from an institution organized around the king and the nobility to one organized around the treasury. Economics was taken over by laymen; the clergy moved to the periphery of power. The government's bureaucracy, the Church and the army became public institutions. The middling and professional classes – bankers, insurance brokers, clerks and tradesmen – assumed a more central role in the life of the country and were able, increasingly, to hold the state to account.[5]

In 1720, the German-born composer Georg Friedrich Händel made London his home, bringing with him the sounds that would define an era. By 1759, the British Museum opened its doors to visitors with clean shoes and a written request. People formed private clubs and associations. Theatres offered rowdy entertainment. Public pleasure gardens bloomed, illuminated by thousands of oil lamps that burst into life as dusk fell. The English novelist and dramatist Henry Fielding described these places as 'great scenes of rendezvous . . . where the nobleman and his tailor, the lady of quality and her tirewoman [maid] meet together and form one common', and all soon 'dissolved in pleasure'.[6] There were operas, concerts, debating clubs, societies, libraries and balls.

The Master of Ceremonies at Bath's Assembly Rooms, Richard Nash, explicitly endorsed social mixing. In his smart white hat, the Welshman helped transform the city into the most visited and decorous place in the country. He instructed men to leave their dirty boots and swords at the door before they twirled with women in satin dresses, and encouraged them not to dance only with other nobles. Nash urged the aristocracy to mix on the dance floor with rising gentry, the wealthy landowners who had entered society.

Merchants from distant corners gathered, and a burgeoning middle class embraced the vibrant social life, leading to the development of new norms for conducting oneself among strangers whose rank and position were no longer fixed by birth. The once unchallenged supremacy of monarchy and court began to wane, giving way to the intellectual tides of the Enlightenment that fostered novel modes of thought. Ideas about conscience spread into all areas of life. It was a time of dazzling acquisitiveness, social interaction and the clash of intellectual discourse. Above all, it heralded the arrival of public and private realms.

The rise and fall of private life is not a story of the progressive growth and decline of a private space free from the reach of authority. One of the most critical influences on the private sphere, on its expansion and definition, was the rise of public life. There is no private sphere without a public sphere, and the reverse is equally true; they exist in a state of complex interdependency. The condition of one influences the other in a dance of sorts.

Over the course of the eighteenth century, powerful economic, political and cultural influences – the dynamism of the economy and the receding domination of life by religious and Crown authority – etched sharper contours upon the landscapes of public and private life. They were aligned with the secular currents and a new, energizing confidence in reason. This was an age of separations, when the divide between public and private life, which in varying forms exists in all societies, went from being implicit to explicit. It was a time when these two spheres began to be seen not as overlapping shadows but as two distinctive realms.

*

When the Royal Exchange closed each night, business didn't stop. Men spilled out of its doors and into the coffee-houses that clustered on the surrounding streets. Soon, row upon row of gentlemen were seated at long communal wooden tables, flickering candles in glass lanterns illuminating their faces. In rooms that reeked of tobacco, with straw underneath their buckled shoes, they talked and drank and gossiped, inhaling snuff and exchanging information.

Pasqua Rosée, the former servant of a Levantine merchant, had opened London's first coffee-house in a shed near the Exchange in the middle of the seventeenth century, and queues formed immediately. Before long, coffee-houses had popped up all over the city – and the country. They spread beyond Britain's borders, but not as extensively. Amsterdam only had thirty-two coffee-houses by 1700. Those in St Mark's Square in Venice would not seat more than five customers.[7]

London Coffee-House in the Reign of Queen Anne (engraving).

The rapid growth of international trade increased the need for any information that could provide competitive advantage. 'What news have you, sir?' might be the first question asked of an arriving customer. The coffee-house was where a trader would hear about events affecting his commercial interests, like a storm destroying an East India Company ship, or the outbreak of war. The Jamaican Coffee-House in Cornhill, one of the ancient streets that radiate out from the Royal Exchange, drew merchants who traded from the West Indies; the Baltic served those dealing with Russia and the Baltic. New Lloyd's Coffee-House specialized in marine insurance. In the Marine Coffee-House, Sir Isaac Newton, the greatest mathematician and astronomer of the age, who would lead both the Royal Mint and the Royal Society, delivered lectures by candlelight on his theories to tradesmen and seamen who needed to establish longitude at sea.[8]

Members of the Royal Society of London for Improving Natural Knowledge met weekly to debate, experiment and record investigations, predicated on the idea that by observing the natural world and conducting experiments, a person could accumulate knowledge – and thus learn more about God's design. They discarded the book-based approach to learning that dominated the old universities, and which revered tradition and the wisdom of the ancient thinkers. A new scientific approach, then in embryo, revealed parts of life hitherto unseen. Thinkers such as Voltaire, Kant and Rousseau advocated for reason and scientific enquiry over dogma and superstition. They wrote treatises questioning the divine right of kings, proposed new forms of government and promoted the idea that all men are created equal. These revolutionary notions ignited a firestorm of public discourse, seeping into the very fabric of society.

Intellectually, society moved from a fundamentalist belief in the validity and certainty of the Bible to one in which people were able to trust their private judgements. The spark of conscience, ignited so long ago now and accidentally spread by Martin Luther and Thomas More, found new Enlightenment underpinnings. Seventeenth-century pamphlets that provided religious guidance on matters of conscience fell out of favour. The economist Adam Smith brushed them off as 'generally as useless as they are commonly tiresome'.[9] Smith proposed that rather than consulting religious authorities, 'nice and delicate situations' should be left to 'the man within the breast'.[10]

Men flocked to the coffee-houses in search of all kinds of knowledge; unlike every other social institution, rank and birth had less import here. The new middle classes, most of whom had not attended university, were hungry to educate themselves. Books circulated widely and could be rented 'by the candle', granting the reader time to read until the end burnt out. The social fluidity was relative, often mocked and overstated, but theoretically anyone with sufficient wealth to afford the penny entrance fee could enter – so long as they were male. Apart from the women who ran them and the prostitutes who frequented them, coffee-houses were dominated by men. The discourse conducted over the tea tables of the domestic household was more the domain of women. Not unlike the Athenian agora, the new public realm was a male place.

Samuel Johnson, the prolific scholar and reader whose *Lives of the Poets* was commissioned in a coffee shop, praised the 'ready man' of conversational society over the scholar 'buried among his manuscripts', who considered his ideas to be 'incontestable truths'. Johnson argued that knowledge only becomes truly understood when it is tested through interaction with people, rather than remaining confined to dusty books.[11] Rigorous criticism and social interaction would illuminate truth and separate insight from error: this was, in effect, the mission statement for the public sphere.

At Waghorn's coffee-house in Westminster, politicians were taken apart for their tedious speeches. Bedford's in Covent

Garden displayed a giant thermometer, its temperatures rising to 'excellent' or plummeting to 'execrable' as customers passed searing judgement on new plays. Or they went to Buttons coffee-house, a stone's throw from Covent Garden, where the stars of literary London – including Alexander Pope and Jonathan Swift –assembled each evening, delivering their devastating verdicts after attending a performance or reading a poem, novel or manuscript, making and breaking literary reputations in an evening.

Debates were rowdy and riotous and, because their verdicts mattered, coffee-houses became a locus of public opinion. By the 1730s, the phrase *publick opinion*, a term hardly previously used in England, peppered the discourse.[12] The very possibility of criticism was premised on an ideal of the public. '[T]he public is everything to me, my school my sovereign, my trusted friend. I shall submit to this and to no other tribunal,' wrote the German poet Friedrich Schiller.[13] London's *Theatrical Guardian* declared the public's sovereignty over the stage when it proposed: 'the public is the only jury before the merits of an actor or an actress are to be tried, and when the endeavours of a performer are stampt by them with the seal of sanction and applause, from that there should be no appeal'.[14] The 'public' was increasingly the arbiter of taste and judgement.

German philosopher Jürgen Habermas characterized the development of this new social realm, distinct from the state, as the emergence of a bourgeois public sphere. It was composed of financially secure private individuals whose social relationships and connectedness transcended the boundaries of their personal lives, coming together as a public that was increasingly aware of itself as a social force.[15]

The heated conversation in the coffee-houses, the news media, the explosion of private clubs and associations, the fluttering fans cooling dancers in assembly rooms, the hissing from the theatre stalls, the raucous politicking and the animated public discourse – ranging from the calmly rational to the savagely satirical – all contributed to a vibrant social scene. Conversations about religion and politics that would once have taken place in the shadows of the household had migrated out into a new public realm of strangers, largely men who shared an interest in the modalities of culture, manners and morals. In the interest of fostering trade (and the revenues and prestige that came with it), governments promoted these developments, but their social and economic integration established an expanding area of social and public life that was broadly independent from the state and the court. It was widely understood as the realm of the increasingly influential bourgeoisie. It was in 'society' that individuals could gather as a public, a place that in aggregate could articulate the public interest.

From a modern perspective, the eighteenth-century public sphere was exclusive in terms of class and gender. Even at the time, this prompted Jonathan Swift's caustic comment: 'It is a folly of too many to mistake the echo of a London coffee-house for the echo of the kingdom,' observing that the average coffee-house was filled with 'censure, coffee, pride, and port'.[16] Public spaces such as assembly rooms and other centres of culture were dominated by the middle and upper classes. But compared to what had gone before, the public realm did represent something novel and expansive. By extending the political centre of gravity from the landed aristocracy to the merchant bourgeoisie, the newly formed public sphere brought more people together to discuss public matters. Although the men, and occasionally women, in the public sphere did not and could not speak for everyone, they began to represent an ideal of the public with its own prestige and legitimacy.

*

As economic and intellectual developments forged a public sphere, the fabric of household life was being transformed too. In the preceding agrarian era, households had served as the epicentre of economic activity. Each family tended to its land, producing essentials for sustenance and engaging in local trade. It was a crowded hub of production, commerce and consumption, with every member contributing to both household needs and the local marketplace.[17]

With early modern capitalism, paid work was sought outside the home. Nearly half of English families by the mid-eighteenth century were reliant on external employment. Whether toiling as farmhands, factory workers or professionals in industries like law or finance, many relinquished the reins of household production for the promise of a wage.[18]

Where once a rural English household had prided itself on self-sufficiency, by the eighteenth century such aspirations dwindled. Textile production, for instance, transitioned from a domestic affair to a commercial exchange. Rather than cultivating and spinning flax in-house, families increasingly turned to linen drapers for their fabric needs. Homemade soap and starch gave way to shop-bought alternatives. Gradually, but unmistakably, the household shed its economic obligations, transitioning from its role as a linchpin of local commerce to become a retreat from its demands – a change that gained momentum as the century unfolded.

Households were secured and parts within defined. By 1700, the principle that 'the house of everyone is his castle', given rhetorical legs in Edward Coke's 1604 ruling, had become embedded in English common law. This notion was cemented in 1765 by William Blackstone, a prominent jurist and Tory politician, in his *Commentaries on the Laws of England*. The ethos rang out in Parliament in 1763 when Prime Minister William Pitt proclaimed: 'The poorest man may in his cottage bid defiance to all the forces of the crown. It may be frail – its roof may shake – the wind may blow through it – the storm may enter – the rain may enter – but the King of England cannot enter.'[19]

Burglary and housebreaking were capital offences, even if the burglar failed to steal any goods. It was legal to own firearms and use them on intruders. Laws strengthened long-standing regulations limiting the 'overlooking' of neighbours' property. A ruling passed in 1709 noted that windows could not be altered 'if before . . . they could not look out of them into the yard . . . for privacy is valuable'.[20] These were not new rights, but they reiterated and extended rights that now gave explicit recognition to privacy.

Within, a revolution in building design hammered out private spaces. Rooms became smaller and more specialized, acquiring distinct functions. Curtains were drawn, cushions were plumped and the home began to embody a sense of separation and intimacy. Servants, once a constant presence at the foot of their masters' beds or in common rooms, were relegated to annexes or attic spaces. New wire bell-pulls connected to their quarters allowed instant summons. The introduction of back stairs, which rerouted staff through parts of the house without bringing them into contact with members of the household, was equally transformative. The architectural historian Mark Girouard indelicately describes the scene: 'The gentry walking up the stairs no longer met their last night's faeces coming down to them.'[21]

In 1716, the Duchess of Marlborough took issue with Sir John Vanbrugh's design for her new property, Blenheim Palace, finding the room arrangement peculiar. Vanbrugh explained that the concept of the 'corridor' was 'foreign', but signified 'no more than a passage'.[22] To Abraham Swan, the architect of homes for the average gentleman, it represented a revolutionary innovation that offered desired seclusion. Swan advocated for its widespread adoption in new designs: 'All the Rooms in this House are *private*, that is there is a Way into each of them without passing through any other Room; which is a Circumstance that should always be attended to in laying out and disposing the Rooms of a House.'[23]

In time, the corridor found its way into homes far less grand than Blenheim Palace. It took a century for this architectural feature to become commonplace, but once it did, the Victorians embraced it wholeheartedly.

A desire to create personal boundaries permeated all levels of society. Drawing upon the records of the London criminal court, the Old Bailey, historian Amanda Vickery finds that testimonies frequently referenced 'private house', 'private gardens', 'private door of my house and small 'private boxes'.[24] For a servant, a lockable wooden box held significance. Adorned with paper flowers, it was not just a repository for valuables: a locked box allowed a modicum of autonomy.

These changes to the household didn't mean that it was cut off from society. Far from it. Within these abodes, specific quarters teemed with sociable activity, and not solely with the comings and goings of servants for those affluent enough to afford them, or the chatter and footfall of lodgers for the less well off. The first floor of a prosperous residence was a whirl of social interaction akin to a miniature semi-public square. Satin curtains adorned the expansive windows, drawn aside to offer passers-by a tantalizing glimpse of the festivities within. The arrival and departure of carriages at the entrance proclaimed the inhabitants' presence, further enlivening the atmosphere and establishing the home as a locus of social engagement and spectacle.

The lavish dinner parties of the era, brimming with guests and boisterous merriment, elicited a mix of admiration and exasperation from participants. Renowned writer and socialite Hester Lynch Thrale wrote in her diary of the relentless procession of guests, bemoaning: 'here we have dined 30, 40 people every day for three weeks together'.[25] A beleaguered correspondent, writing to the *Dublin Mercury*, expressed dismay at the incessant influx of visitors through his front door, ruefully remarking that his house was 'as public as any tavern in town' due to his wife's stream of guests.[26] The weight of social obligations proved taxing for Mary Delany, celebrated for her intricate botanical drawings: visitors caused her such strain that she fled to the local assembly rooms, well known for public entertainment and social mixing, for 'privacy'.[27]

*

By the early eighteenth century, four events had shaken the political landscape. The first two were the Glorious Revolution of 1688, which saw the deposition of the Catholic James II and the ascension of his Protestant daughter, Mary II, and her husband, William III, to the throne; and the Toleration Act of 1689, aimed at quelling a century of religious conflict. The third was the formation of the Whig and Tory parties. The Whigs, champions of parliamentary authority and opponents of absolute monarchy, saw themselves as guardians of liberty. The Tories, with their leanings towards High Church Anglicanism, represented a more conservative strand of British society. The fourth was the inadvertent expiration of the Licensing of the Press Act in 1695. Up until then, two secretaries of state, plus the Lord Chancellor, the Earl Marshal, the archbishop of Canterbury and the bishop of London, as well as the chancellors of Oxford and Cambridge, had decided what could and (more likely) what could not be published.

Like an unblocked dam, the news press, books, and periodicals flowed freely. The year 1702 saw the launch of London's first daily newspaper, the *Daily Courant*, followed by the first newspapers in Bristol and Norwich.[28] By 1712, there were twenty newspapers in London and fifteen others in major towns.[29] By 1735, around twenty-five provincial newspapers were published, a figure that had doubled by the 1780s.[30] Whereas in 1670 around two dozen printing houses in London, Cambridge, Oxford and York had been authorized to print, by 1724, there were seventy-five publishing firms in London and twenty-eight outside the capital.[31] And by 1800 there were hundreds of printers and publishers dotted around, with at least one in every town in England.[32] Unlike in Catholic France, where hundreds of pre-publication censors were at work, Britain was engulfed by a tidal wave of print.

The press emerged as a vital authority, expanding the sphere of debate and placing the government under scrutiny. *The Craftsman*, a popular journal, subjected the Walpole ministry and the Whig party to intense examination, filled with the language of exposure. (The title itself was inspired by the 'craftiness' of politics.) It proudly declared that it would 'unravel the dark secrets of *Political Craft*,' and that it 'trac'd *Corruption* though all its dark lurking Holes, and set its Deformity in a true Light'.[33]

Britain became a world leader in rapidly rising literacy rates. Most people were self-taught, responding to demands in commercial society. Merchants and traders, the backbone of Britain's economic engine, required a workforce proficient in reading, writing and arithmetic – skills essential for navigating the complex world of commerce and finance. The ability to tally profits and losses, to account for every penny, became indispensable. Ordinary citizens also wanted to keep abreast of the news, especially events like wars, which directly affected their material interests. Access to information became a necessity, not a luxury.

Though many of the coffee-houses and forums for debate were largely urban and physical in form, their impact spread deep into society, streaming outwards into minds and homes via the press and periodicals. Newspapers and journals were found in every aspirational middle-class and educated house, including in the USA. Benjamin Franklin observed that *The Spectator* taught him how to write, talk and argue.[34] While the first series of the periodical, running from 1711 to 1712, officially sold more than 3,000 copies per issue, it reached many thousands more as it was passed around in the nation's coffee-houses, where it was read out loud, discussed by provincial societies and perused at home.[35]

The periodical intended to create what Addison termed a 'Fraternity of Spectators', addressing the world as if it were a grand theatre.[36] It placed itself outside of politics and made sure to attract female readers. Addison and Steele wrote as private gentlemen rather than noblemen, navigating and commenting on an expanding social landscape. They were figures in a broader cultural movement that championed a new way of being in public as a way of navigating the new times: how one might present a public face and interact with one's peers. Country folks wanted to learn what to spend their money on and how to behave when they visited the smart cities of London, Bath or Liverpool. Previously, elite conduct had taken its cues from the royal court, and the principles governing this behaviour were little changed since Baldassare Castiglione's *Book of the Courtier* (1528), an interminable treatise on how to be the ideal courtier or court lady. But this new commercial society was far less bound by aristocratic ties or royal patronage: it was a society of strangers, invigorated by nascent capitalism, who needed to know how to conduct themselves when they met others without always knowing their exact rank and status. They turned to *The Spectator*. The periodical advised people who were socially mobile – and socially ambitious – how to behave in society. It was one of an array of widely read handbooks and manuals about how to act in public that were eagerly devoured by the literate public, offering detailed guidance on the nuances of engaging discourse, elevating everyday interactions to an art form.

Politeness was then a popular modern concept reflecting secular ideals surrounding social interaction and self-presentation. The word came from the Latin, by way of French – *polir*, to polish – and reflected a positive sense of social interaction. As Anthony Ashley Cooper, 3rd Earl of Shaftesbury, who had been educated by John

Locke, enthused: 'We polish one another, and rub off our Corners and rough Sides by a sort of amicable Collision.'[37] Politeness, he believed, was fundamental to society; codes of behaviour meant that people who were different could get along.[38]

The handshake, originally a marketplace custom for sealing deals, began to signal egalitarianism. Although there was initial resistance due to concerns about hygiene, erosion of social distinctions, and some discomfort with women adopting the practice, by the 1790s it had replaced bowing and curtsying among the middle classes.[39]

While some, like the Quakers, decried such codes of behaviour and polite speech as hypocritical, most Britons accepted that civilized life required a degree of artifice and dissimulation.[40] The Scottish philosopher David Hume asked rhetorically, 'Am I a liar because I order my servant to say I am not at home?' In Hume's view, compliments were lies that did no real harm – it was far better to be tactful.[41]

The new norms of politeness promoted self-improvement and socially agreeable behaviour, avoiding excessive formality or ostentation. They were seen to moderate religious and political conflict, aligning with the ideals of tolerance. The improving nature of social engagement applied to upwardly mobile men who had begun to frequent the gentlemen's clubs, and also to women. As Addison observed, the endeavours of men to captivate the hearts of women served as a catalyst for their own transformation, instilling a sense of refinement. Without the influence of women, he noted, a man would remain as 'a rude and unfinished Creature', lacking the finesse and completeness that only the presence of the opposite sex could inspire.[42]

*

In his groundbreaking exploration of eighteenth-century discourse, the historian John Brewer dissects the evolving semantics of *public* and *private*. Delving deep into the literary landscape of the era, Brewer scrutinizes books published in English between 1700 and 1800. He evidences that commentators spoke of the 'public' and 'private' spheres in new and modern ways, and people became conscious of the categories.[43]

Brewer shows that of the two, *public* has more entries (7,607) and is more stable in its meaning. As an adjective, *public* referred to 'belonging to a state or nation', 'open, notorious, generally known', 'general, done by many', 'regarding the good of the community' and 'open for general entertainment'. As a noun, it meant 'the general body of mankind, or a state or nation; the people' and 'open view; general notice'.

The world *private* appeared in 1,594 records and was, as ever, more complicated. It retained the residual, negative definition of 'that which is not public'. But it too had expanded and specified its meaning. Economic activity was described as 'private' in the sense that it was not the activity of the state, but of individuals, and because it had particular rather than general ends. For example, there were references to 'private wealth', 'private traders' and 'private credit'. And then there were private institutions, like the private clubs and private libraries, which were not open to everyone.

Brewer finds that use of the term *private* also applies to the territories of mind and body: 'Private judgement' was contrasted to church 'authority' and described, sometimes pejoratively, as 'free thinking' or, more positively, as 'individual conscience' or 'private devotion'. Bodily, medical or sexual matters were also repeatedly described as private. It was not yet usual to equate the private with the domestic. Brewer finds the terms *domestic, domestick* and *domesticial* used more often to refer to national matters as contrasted to international foreign affairs, rather than in the context of the home. That is, until the 1780s, when the number of titles that associate the domestic with the household increases.

With the emergence of a modern state and economy, public

and private began to take on their modern forms. In time, *public* was understood to relate to public authority, civil society and the state, while *private* described economic activity and the family. The private realm, though connected to public life, was gradually differentiated from it, shedding its old functions, dropping its economic significance and acquiring the trappings of romance and intimacy. This marked a seismic change in human behaviour. For the first time in history, sex became a private matter – a change that would reverberate through the ages and redefine the very fabric of relationships.

Chapter 5:

IN THE HAPPY MINUTE

After enduring four and a half days in the cramped discomfort of a post chaise, James Boswell arrived in London from Edinburgh on the morning of 19 November 1762. He was twenty-two and – thanks to an allowance from his father, the Calvinist judge Lord Auchinleck – in pursuit of a commission in the Foot Guards. He was also in pursuit of carnal pleasures, a quest in which he achieved remarkable success.

Boswell's voluminous diaries offer a window into his life as a man about town, indulging his insatiable appetites. One episode, dated 10 May 1763, encapsulates his hedonistic exploits with bold candour: 'At the bottom of the Hay-market I picked up a strong jolly young damsel, and taking her under the Arm I conducted her to Westminster-Bridge, and then in armour complete did I engage her upon this noble Edifice.'[1]

In contrast to the Puritans, who filled their diaries with records of their prayers, Boswell unabashedly boasts of his virility on nearly every page. His chronicles detail sexual encounters with three married women, a liaison with the mistress of the philosopher Jean-Jacques Rousseau, and trysts with four actresses. He recounts keeping three mistresses simultaneously and indulging in the company of at least sixty prostitutes.[2] No wonder that, despite his use of 'armour' – condoms made out of animal gut – he suffered frequently from venereal disease.

But Boswell was also given to melancholy and often found himself wracked with guilt about his lifestyle. That same 1763 diary entry captures this inner conflict. 'The whim of doing it there with the Thames rolling below us amused me much,' he writes; but 'after the brutish appetite was sated', he 'could not but despise myself for being so closely united with such a low wretch'.[3]

Boswell's reflections deepened after he encountered Samuel Johnson, a staunch opponent of licentiousness. He confessed that he had begun to consider more seriously the duties of morality and religion, and the dignity of human nature. He condemned 'promiscuous concubinage' as inherently wrong, believing it to be a source of social disorder and misery. He imagined that unchecked carnal desires could lead to the collapse of society. Like every soul battling a vice, he resolved to do better: 'I am now resolved to guard against it,' he wrote, capturing the timeless struggle between moral aspiration and human frailty.[4] Yet even as he chastised himself for his appetites, he continually succumbed to them.

From the mid-eighteenth century to the dawn of the nineteenth, Britain underwent a revolution in sexual behaviour. While extreme libertines like Boswell may have been exceptional in their promiscuity, changing attitudes were evident across all social strata. In 1650, the birth of a child out of wedlock was a rare scandal, with fewer than 1 per cent of all children born illegitimate. All sex outside of marriage was a sin. Secular and religious authorities dominated life within the household, pressing, as we have seen, watchful neighbours to peek into its crevices and corners to monitor its members' sexual relationships. By 1800, the growing number of children born out of wedlock was a testament to the rising frequency of premarital sex, which was increasingly tolerated. Nearly a quarter of all first-born children in England were now born outside of marriage. Forty per cent of brides approached the altar already pregnant. This shift signalled a broader relaxation in social attitudes towards sexual morality.[5]

Religion and sexual morality had long been intertwined, with the prevailing belief that sexual behaviour was a matter of public concern necessitating strict regulation. The Church, alongside ordinary citizens, played a role in policing these morals. Yet by 1800, such extreme measures had become relics of a bygone era.

The growth of the city provided opportunities. London was a metropolis with more than a million inhabitants: the second-largest city in the world after Peking (now Beijing). It was easier to pursue a brief sexual encounter without one's neighbours spying through the holes in the wall. Additionally, secular courts had taken over many issues that were once handled by ecclesiastical courts, and most forms of consensual sex outside of marriage were no longer illegal. People across the country were also talking and writing about sex in new ways. 'For, tho I am a Reformer,' opined Richard Steele in *The Tatler*, 'I scorn to be an Inquisitor' – and he elaborated on the pointlessness of policing sex.[6] 'Love is free: to promise for ever to love the same woman, is no less absurd than to promise to believe the same creed', declared Percy Bysshe Shelley in *Queen Mab* (1813), a tenet he followed in his own intimate relationships.

Previously, sex had been considered a public matter, subject to scrutiny by the law and by society. But now, there was an overall perception of intimate life as a private rather than public concern. Like many of the transformations that comprise the history of private life, this one was set in motion unintentionally.

Advocates of toleration in the late seventeenth century had been adamant that while freedom of conscience applied to religious belief and observance, it did not imply liberty of thought in other areas. When John Locke argued for religious toleration he had proposed that spiritual beliefs, if they posed no threat to others or to society, should remain outside the purview of civil government. In contrast, Locke maintained that actions detrimental to society warranted intervention. He insisted that there should be no 'toleration of corrupt matters, and the debaucheries of life' and singled out 'adultery, fornication, uncleanness' and 'lasciviousness'. These were 'properly the magistrate's business', who should punish, 'restrain and suppress them'.[7]

But once the arguments for freedom of conscience were loose in the world, they proved uncontainable. The acceptance of toleration and private conscience over the most important question of all – how to achieve eternal salvation – led to the acceptance of other kinds of belief and behaviour. In essence, notions of religious freedom had a liberating effect on other ideas of freedom. The realm of conscience was extended.

When Hobbes warned in *Leviathan* that the idea of 'every private man [being] his own judge of good and evil actions' was a seditious doctrine that would have consequences for the commonwealth, he was correct on the latter point. But, while Hobbes viewed the notion that individuals could be the best judges of their own behaviour as toxic, others would take a different view.

*

In Susanna Centlivre's comedy *Love's Contrivance*, which premiered at London's Drury Lane Theatre in 1703, Octavio addresses Belliza with the phrase, 'Liberty of conscience, you know, Madam.' Belliza, understanding the implications, replies with a knowing nod: 'Ay, and men's consciences are very large.' As well as highlighting the characters' views on sexual liberty, their exchange reflects the societal conversation taking place at the time about moral freedom.[8] This notion was central to the work of Peter Annet, a freethinker known for his controversial views on religion and his critical stance against the established Church.

Annet became a notable figure advocating for reason and scepticism over traditional religious dogma.

Annet's beliefs were shaped by his strong commitment to deism, a philosophical position positing the existence of a rational God who created the universe but does not intervene in human affairs through miracles or revelation. Deists like Annet emphasized the use of rationality and empirical evidence as a basis for understanding the world, rejecting the supernatural aspects of religion and the authority of religious institutions. He became a schoolmaster and a popular debater, known for applying concepts of conscience and natural law to sexual morality. In his 1749 pamphlet *Social Bliss Considered: In Marriage and Divorce; Cohabiting Unmarried and Public Whoring*, he argued that men and women should be free to have sex with whomever they choose, cohabit, and divorce at will. He maintained that this freedom was in line with both God's intentions and human nature, writing, 'God has given these natural affections and lusts to be gratified with reason, to make life sweet and agreeable . . . the gratification of carnal lust to the injury of none, is no evil; nor is the lust or desire itself.'[9]

Annet's outspoken views brought him into conflict with the authorities, one incident occurring in 1763, when he was convicted of blasphemous libel for his pamphlets criticizing Christian religion and the Bible. He was sentenced to a year of hard labour and fined. But despite the challenges he faced, Peter Annet's contributions to religious and philosophical thought had a lasting impact.

Initially, those advocating for sexual freedom were outliers, although rakes like Lord Bryon and Casanova quickly seized upon the ideas. However, serious and influential thinkers gradually began to explore similar arguments. Among them was David Hume, one of the most significant voices of the Enlightenment. As a religious sceptic, he sought to disentangle the study of human behaviour from the theological assumptions that had traditionally constrained it.

Central to Hume's musings was his contemplation of the waning influence of divine providence. 'The providence of the deity,' he wrote, 'appears not immediately in any operation, but governs everything by those general and immutable laws.'[10] In other words, God did not intercede in the minutiae of life, but instead set the parameters for it. Hume also considered the essence of human nature. He posited that human behaviour was governed by a dynamic interplay of reason and passion. Venturing into the realm of ethics, he argued for an inherent moral sensibility in people, a fountainhead of natural virtues – virtues which did not encompass chastity. 'The confinement of the appetite is not natural,' he asserted.[11] To Hume, lust was not a vice but a conduit to all 'agreeable emotions', positioning sex and desire as natural impulses and chastity as artificial.

Against a backdrop of European exploration, Hume's observations of diverse sexual norms across different societies further reinforced his thesis. These varied customs suggested that moral distinctions were less the result of divine ordinance and more the products of human reason and social custom. Hume still held to the moral standards of his day. He disparaged polygamy and divorce. But he shared the fashionable view that libertine love and adultery were less odious than drunkenness.

Individuals who challenged the rigid conventions of their time invoked the ideals of liberty and conscience to justify their actions. When James Boswell sought a brief period of good behaviour and tried to end his relationship with the married woman Jean Home, she was unwilling to let go of their 'delicious pleasures'. She told him that she loved her husband as a husband and Boswell as a lover, that each had a place and that no one suffered: 'My conscience does not reproach me, and I am sure that God cannot be offended by them,' she said.[12] When her husband later divorced her after an affair with an army officer, she reflected that she hoped God would not punish her for the passions that he had given her in her nature.

Women indulged in and wrote about their own desires. As when in 1751, Frances, Lady Vane anonymously published a 50,000-word narrative of her adulterous love life, thinly veiled under the title *Memoirs of a Lady of Quality*. Her appetite for sexual relations shocked society just as much as it thrilled them to gossip about it.

Yorkshire gentlewoman Anne Lister was a diarist of lesbian desire and of romantic love. As she wrote in her journals, she believed and hoped that her relations with other women would be understood and forgiven, not damned by God: 'Lord have mercy on me and not justice.' Her emotions and desires were not unnatural, 'my conduct & feelings being surely natural to me inasmuch as they were not taught, not fictious but instinctive'.[13] Lister wasn't just after sex, she longed for marriage. She bought a ring to pledge herself to the women she fell for.

The era of licentiousness was not without its critics or punishments, and Anne Lister made the point that sexual norms were more unfairly oppressive of women. But campaigns launched against brothels proved largely ineffective. Publications like *The Spectator* discussed prostitutes not as sinners but as victims of circumstance.[14] William Hogarth's *A Harlot's Progress* exposed the stark realities faced by young women lured to the city. The prostitute at the centre of the story is pitied as much as condemned.

The landscape had changed from the days when women selling sex were whipped, branded and deported under the Commonwealth (Adultery) Act of 1650. Even that old stick-in-the-mud Samuel Johnson observed: 'That every man should regulate his actions by his own conscience, without any regard to opinions of the rest of the world, is one of the first precepts of moral prudence.'[15]

In his 1732 series A Harlot's Progress, *William Hogarth tells the tragic story of 'Hackabout Moll', a country girl who is lured into prostitution upon arriving in London. In the first plate, Moll is charmed by the notorious brothel-keeper Mother Needham, while a lecherous gentleman watches, signalling the start of her descent into ruin and eventual death.*

Homosexual men faced the severe threat of capital punishment under the Buggery Act of 1533. Despite such draconian laws, the early eighteenth century saw an increasing visibility of same-sex male relationships, particularly in the larger cities of London and Edinburgh. These urban centres exhibited a degree of leniency and acceptance. Certain public parks and gardens were known as places where men could meet. Within the clandestine confines of 'molly houses', men found spaces where they could dance together and form connections. These establishments occasionally attracted the ire of the Society for the Reformation of

Manners, one of several groups formed in response to perceived moral decay. Nevertheless, a moderate tolerance prevailed.[16]

Terminology developed to describe same-sex relationships between men. *Mollies* were more effeminate, while *back-gammon players* was a term noted in a 1785 *Dictionary of the Vulgar Tongue*.[17] When men were reprimanded or prosecuted for their sexual conduct, the discourse surrounding their actions had been influenced by the ideals of the time. Such as when, in 1726, William Brown, a married man, was apprehended in an area along the London City Wall locally known as 'Sodomites' Walk', where he had been looking for sex with a man. Prosecuted at the Old Bailey, Brown justified his behaviour in terms that twenty-first-century readers would recognize: 'I did it because I thought I knew him, and I think there is no crime in making what use I please of my own Body.'[18] Brown was found guilty of an attempt to commit sodomy and sentenced to stand in the pillory in Moorfields, pay a small fine and go to prison for two months. But he had lived by and articulated a modern conception of consensual sex.

Not everyone was as fortunate as William Brown. While precise numbers are elusive, documented cases and scholarly estimates indicate that this period could be a perilous time for men accused of homosexual acts in Britain. The last two individuals to face execution were John Smith, a forty-year-old labourer, and James Pratt, a thirty-year-old groom. Both were hanged in front of Newgate Prison in November 1835.[19]

Although adultery remained a crime, prosecutions were far less frequent – the last is likely to have been in 1746 – and when they did occur, they were widely publicized. This was not for the purpose of shaming the participants, as would have been the case just over a hundred years earlier, with men and women forced to parade in the market square. Now it was for titillation: the press and publishing world had discovered that the scandal and troubles of private life could be monetized. Depictions of sex were becoming more mainstream, less secretive and a major part of print culture.

In the 1720s, the Scottish traveller John Macky observed that as night fell in London, thousands of prostitutes would 'arrange themselves in a line along the footpaths of the main streets', often grouped in companies of five or six. Macky noted that they were 'more numerous than those in Paris' and exhibited 'more liberty and effrontery than in Rome itself'. What struck him most was the open acceptance of this trade; it had become so normalized that the names of prominent prostitutes were 'publicly cried in the streets', and their residences were widely known.[20]

Although sex was now considered a private matter, subject to individual conscience, it was not confined to the shadows. Public figures openly maintained mistresses, and European pornography was widely accessible. The mass media of the era delighted in the exploits of celebrity courtesans and enthusiastically reported on sexual scandals, with the women involved often leveraging them to their advantage. One such was the actress Mary Robinson.

In 1779, at the tender age of twenty-one and having been tutored by the esteemed David Garrick, Mary graced the stage as Perdita in Shakespeare's *The Winter's Tale*. Audiences were charmed by her charisma and the youthful George, Prince of Wales, a mere seventeen years old, also fell under her spell. Taking the pseudonym 'Florizel', the Prince initiated a rapid exchange of letters with 'Perdita'. His confidant George Capel, Viscount Malden, assumed the role of intermediary, imploring Mary to entertain the Prince's entreaties. Mary, who was married, reciprocated with her own missives, counselling the Prince to exercise restraint and extending sisterly guidance. Before long, however, their communication transcended mere written correspondence.

Mary's affair with the Prince became fodder for the pens of pamphleteers, the strokes of caricaturists and voracious appetite of the public, who hungrily consumed every detail of the liaison. From the pages of newspapers to the idle chatter of society, curiosity soared about 'Perdita'. Celebrity-spotters were obsessed with her trend-setting clothing: a puffed and ruffled muslin dress, inspired by one worn by Marie Antoinette, an elaborate fur muff, and the donning of the peasant girl look complete with a straw hat.

The Prince provided Mary with a residence on Cork Street, where she played hostess to him and his companions, and he was seen with her in public: at the theatre, concerts, and events like military reviews in Hyde Park and the King's hunt at Windsor. Her audacity in occupying a side box at the Opera House, assuming the airs of nobility, ignited indignation.

Satirical illustrations mocking the Prince and his paramour perturbed his father, the monarch. Meanwhile, George grappled with doubts regarding Mary's loyalty. Such suspicions were not necessarily unfounded, as she may have been entangled in an affair with Capel. As 1780 drew to a close, Mary's allure waned, eclipsed by the attractions of other women. In a decisive turn of events, the Prince ended the affair.

Mary resolved not to retreat without a fight. Her lavish lifestyle had left her drowning in debt, and the Prince's abandonment only compounded her woes. Armed with a trove of his impassioned letters, she wielded them as a bargaining chip, leveraging their potential publication to secure compensation for the irreparable damage he had inflicted upon her reputation and prospects. After protracted negotiations, Mary relinquished the letters in exchange for £5,000 and the assurance of a steady annuity.

It was the first kiss and (almost) tell. For years afterwards, the press continued relentlessly intertwining their names, but in time Mary would reinvent herself as a woman of intellect and letters.

*

The ideas of the late seventeenth century, which stressed the importance of private conscience, had by the mid-eighteenth century, seeped into the way people thought and wrote about relationships and sex. With the decline of church authority and the rise of scientific thought, coitus was transformed from a matter of public concern, into a private one. Indeed, given that religion and sexual discipline had been so bound together in the seventeenth century, it was likely inevitable that changes in religious tolerance would impact the way people thought about personal morality and sex.

At first, this libertinism primarily benefited property owners and heterosexual men (who were often one and the same). It also had uneven consequences. Over the course of the eighteenth century, increased toleration of 'natural' sexual behaviour led to a sharper definition of, and resistance to, 'unnatural' conduct. Persecution of homosexuals became more intense.[21] The belief in natural differences between men and women restricted women's freedoms. The sex lives of the working classes also continued to be policed by their supposed betters. Even so, compared to earlier periods, sexual matters became less regulated and more private. By the century's end, the idea that public authorities had minimal business interfering in matters of faith or conscience had been not only established but extended further, to moral choices.

Chapter 6:

THE LANGUAGE OF THE PASSIONS

When Samuel Richardson set out to create an instruction manual for letter-writers, he could hardly have foreseen the sensational impact his work would have. Published in 1740, *Pamela; or, Virtue Rewarded* evolved from a simple guide into a work of fiction that became a literary phenomenon. It altered the course of Richardson's life and immortalized the values of the private self in print.

In 1739 a consortium of booksellers had approached Richardson, a fifty-one-year-old Fleet Street printer, with a modest proposal: to compile a book of model letters for those struggling to pen their own correspondence. Literacy rates were continuing to rise and the market was flooded with guides advising people on how to write with the cultivated informality that had become fashionable. 'Yours Sincerely' first appeared here as a recommended sign-off. To express one's feelings naturally and conversationally was not merely a skill, it was a coveted art form.

As Richardson worked on the project, he realized the potential of using letters as a medium for storytelling – an insight that led him to develop the epistolary novel. He created the character of Pamela, a virtuous fifteen-year-old maidservant, who writes to her parents about how she resists the advances of her wealthy master, Mr B, a country landowner, who does not expect to be refused. The law cannot help her because Mr B is also the local justice of the peace.

The narrative climax arrives with the interception of Pamela's private letters by Mr B – a moment of reckoning that transforms his perception of her. Confronted with the purity of Pamela's convictions and her private self, Mr B undergoes a metamorphosis. His initial pursuit of her virtue evolves into admiration and, ultimately, love. Seeing that he is a changed man, she comes to love him in return. Eventually Pamela, a young woman of lower birth, agrees to marry the more socially elevated Mr B.

Richardson reported that the first edition, published in November 1740, had a 'large Impression'. This batch sold out swiftly, necessitating the printing of a second edition by February 1741. As demand soared, a third edition followed in March, a fourth in May and a fifth by September of the same year. The European reception of *Pamela* was a whirlwind of translations and reviews that surpassed all expectations. Within five years of its publication in England, there were editions in Dutch, Danish, German and Italian. French translations sold well in Sweden and Switzerland. Benjamin Franklin printed *Pamela* in Philadelphia.[1]

Richardson's mailbox overflowed with letters from readers touched by Pamela's tale. 'Pamelists' celebrated its moral lessons. Lady Mary Wortley Montagu, an intellectual and writer, lauded the novel's portrayal of virtue and its gripping emotional resonance. The clergy too embraced *Pamela*, heralding its lessons as invaluable for young women and advocating its use as a guide for nurturing virtue and propriety. Literary salons and societies buzzed with discussion lauding the novel's rich exploration of social and moral quandaries.

A consumer paradise of associated merchandise, from decorative fans and playing cards to murals and waxworks depicting its characters, celebrated the work. The novel was not without its critics; Eliza Haywood's *Anti-Pamela* and Henry Fielding's *Shamela* (both 1741) lampooned the heroine, casting her as a manipulative social climber. Regardless, the bulk of public feeling was with the critics. Readers hadn't encountered anything like it before.

The French philosopher Denis Diderot praised Richardson's work, saying that as he read it, he felt that he was hearing 'the genuine language of the passions' and that Richardson 'brings the torch into the depths of the cave'.[2] One letter to Richardson from the 'Publick' praised the novel's 'Spirit of Truth', its stimulation of 'Concern and Emotion' and its '*Instruction* and *Morality*'.[3] Samuel Johnson, whom Adam Smith described as knowing more books than people, was an ardent admirer. He esteemed *Pamela* over another celebrated novel by Fielding, declaring: 'There is more knowledge of the heart in one letter of Richardson's than in all *Tom Jones*.' Richardson, Johnson summarized, had revealed the 'inner mechanism rather than the broader clock face'.[4]

Up until this point, the main form of public entertainment in English culture had been the theatre. The novel offered a uniquely interior cultural form that allowed readers to spend time inside other people's heads – and, unlike the stage, a book could be enjoyed in the privacy of one's home. While people still read out loud to one another, especially in coffee-houses, the spread of literacy meant it was possible to read alone and in silence.

In *Robinson Crusoe* (1719), one of the first modern novels published in English, Daniel Defoe focused on Crusoe's pleasure in the quotidian: sleeping in his tent, shaving, and cooking with a kettle and a pot. The word *home* appears a dozen times in the first chapter, and over sixty times in the book as a whole.[5] Another literary sensation was *Tristram Shandy* (1759), by Laurence Sterne, a rambling, bawdy attempt to capture on the page the inner life and opinions of its eponymous (and frequently absurd) hero. The emergence of the novel in England was the beginning of such portrayals of an individual's inner world.

A growing body of non-fiction writing expressed as never before the everyday and inner lives of ordinary individuals. The success of Boswell's *Life of Samuel Johnson* (1791), widely regarded as the first modern biography, showed that one man's life story could become an object of widespread interest and a commercial success. As the century progressed, more and more private individuals began to document their own lives – not just their religious observance and private prayer, as Margaret Hoby and Nehemiah Wallington did, nor their conquests as Boswell had done, but their everyday, secular habits and practices.

Roger North, a Tory lawyer, advocated keeping such a journal for his own benefit and that of his family. As he explained upon turning fifty, in the preface to his *History of My Private Life* (1796): 'The history of private lives adapted to the perusal of common men, is more beneficial (generally) than the most solemn register of ages, and nations, or the acts and monuments of famed governors, statesmen, prelates, or generals of armies. The gross reason is, because the latter contain little if any thing, comparate or applicable to instruct a private economy, or tending to make a man either wiser or more cautelous [*sic*], in his own proper concerns.'⁶

The classical view of the private realm as less important than the public gave way to something new. No longer was the private world seen solely as a realm of deprivation, or a place in which to hide the less salubrious aspects of life, as with ancient Athens; nor was it merely a place of economic production, as in medieval times; nor a threat or a place of danger, as in the seventeenth century. Instead it became understood as a refuge, free from the rules governing social and political life; valued on its own terms. So much so that, for some, the private side of life started to matter more than the public one.

*

Jean-Jacques Rousseau's *Julie* (1761) – an epistolary novel about a nobleman's daughter who falls in love with her impoverished tutor, Saint-Preux – moved readers across Europe to tears. Like all great love stories, this one is doomed. Obeying her father's wishes, Julie marries Wolmar, a Russian nobleman, but continues her correspondence with Saint-Preux. Tragedy strikes when Julie dies while attempting to save her drowning child. Her last wish is that she and Saint-Preux will be reunited in heaven.

Rousseau's more sophisticated readers, like the aristocratic thinker Voltaire, found the novel overblown. 'No more about Jean-Jacques' romance, if you please,' he grumbled. 'I have read it, to my sorrow, and it would be to his if I had time to say what I think of this silly book.'[7] But Voltaire was in a minority. Readers rushed to get a copy. They rented the book by the day and even by the hour. With at least seventy editions in print before 1800, it was a bestseller of the era.[8]

Rousseau, the man behind the literary sensation, was transformed into a figure as coveted as his own writings. Closeted away in a cottage in the small French town of Montmorency, where he delighted in the nightingales that sang through the treetops, he received postbags stuffed with letters raving about how *Julie* had affected its readers. One claimed to have sobbed so violently that he cured himself of a severe cold.[9] Another only made it as far as Julie's deathbed scene before she broke down, her heart crushed, and could barely continue.[10] So powerful were the sensations effected in one reader, she doubted the book was a work of fiction at all.[11]

Rousseau welcomed the feelings the book evoked, as well as the celebrity status its success conferred upon him. His fame and his intellectual prowess were so compelling that he boldly claimed there wasn't a single female reader who wouldn't have surrendered herself to his charms, had he but asked. But he also triumphed in the popularity of the message. The moral of *Julie*, which is 800 pages long and contains lengthy philosophical digressions, is that in suppressing her love for Saint-Preux, the book's heroine betrays her own heart. It describes the difficulty of being true to oneself when society, so in thrall to the god of Mammon, to property and the artificiality of appearance, rewards fakery.

*

Rousseau wrote *Julie* during a great crisis in his life, when he had broken ranks with the thinkers known as *philosophes*, an intellectual movement championing reason, including Denis Diderot, co-editor of the *Encyclopédie*, an epochal attempt to map all the branches of human knowledge. France at that time was still under the Ancien Régime: the monarchic–aristocratic political system that would be overthrown in 1789. The *philosophes* spent their time conversing in the elaborately decorated rooms of the salons, new social spaces run by prominent literary hostesses. They were joined by idle aristocrats wearing long silk coats buttoned from neck to hem, silk stockings, and beauty spots placed at the corners of the eyes (to suggest passion) or beside the lower lip (to denote candour and frankness). They draped themselves over elegant chairs, pontificating about the ideas of the day. Madame Geoffrin, who subsidized the encyclopedists' project, hosted her salon over one o'clock lunch. Madame de Bouffler, in whose mirrored rooms the young Mozart had performed, introduced Rousseau to David Hume.

Rousseau may have been one of the most influential writers of all time, but he was prickly. For him, these salons were suffocating arenas of forced conviviality. He railed against the squandering of countless hours on trivial chatter in stuffy parlours. Beneath his frustration was a deeper disdain for pervasive deceit cloaked in high-minded airs. Above all, he was disgusted by the pretence. As *Julie* suggests: '[T]he men to whom you are speaking are not the ones with whom you converse; their sentiments do not emanate from the heart, their perceptions are not in their minds, their words do not represent their thoughts, all you see of them is their shape.'[12] But then, Rousseau, as a self-educated lover of solitude, had never been the kind of person who easily gets along in society. Germaine de Staël, a formidable woman of letters who held her salons in the Swedish embassy, observed that 'everything struck him too deeply'.[13]

In *Emile, or On Education* and *The Social Contract* (both published in 1762), he had developed a searing critique of society with a line that would echo down the centuries: 'The more [men] come together, the more they are corrupted.' These treatises dismantled established social constructs, advocating instead for a radical reimagining of governance and education. Central to Rousseau's vision was an impassioned plea for a natural education, unshackled from the fetters of convention, through which children could reach their innate potential and be liberated from the stifling grip of social norms. These ideas were scandalous, leading to condemnation by the authorities, book-burning and Rousseau's eventual exile from France. Hume helped him find a home in London, but they quickly fell out when Rousseau, feeling paranoid, began to suspect Hume had brought him to England in order to dishonour him.

After returning to France and publishing *Julie*, he turned his back on Parisian society and aspirations of wealth and advancement, vowing to devote himself to a life of independence and poverty. Leaving the city behind, he sought refuge in the serene countryside. He discarded the flashy garments that once defined him. He stripped away his decorative gold trimmings and abandoned his pristine white stockings. The long, elaborate wig he had worn for years was replaced by a short, simple one. His sword, once a symbol of his status, was laid aside, and he sold his watch, marking his break from the regimented hours of urban life. Embracing a simple life, he dressed in rough wool.

The response of his friends was ridicule. Diderot quipped that he was retreating into 'brute stupidity under a bearskin mantle'.

He sent Rousseau a copy of his latest play, *The Natural Son*, which included a biting line: 'Only the wicked man lives alone.'[14] This thinly veiled jab was the final straw, severing the fragile threads of their friendship.

There were those in the mid-eighteenth century who experienced the transition from traditional to modern society as a devastating disruption. They viewed the breaking down of external authority, from the Church to feudal custom, as undermining meaning and the grounding of the moral life and sense of self.

In his *Confessions* (1782), often regarded as the first modern autobiography, Rousseau recalls a momentous day when he sat down by the roadside and wept as he came face to face with the insight that progress – contrary to what the *philosophes* claimed about its civilizing, liberating effects – was leading to new forms of enslavement. He perceived the so-called civilized society of adornment and manners as conformist, enforcing adherence to fluctuating currents of taste, behaviour and opinion, with individuals pressurized to play the appropriate roles. When in public among others, people had to wear the mask of artificiality and be untrue to themselves. The social man existed only in the opinions of others. He contrasted this with the self-reliant 'savage' who lived fully within himself.

Rousseau's writings laid bare the enslavement of man's inner world. He argued that individuals were bound not only by property relations and economic dependency – working relentlessly until death, just to survive – but also by an emotional and psychological servitude to others. They sought approval, flattered those who held power over them, and looked down upon those exploited for their own gain. Holding these beliefs, when the flood of letters praising *Julie* began to arrive, Rousseau found himself grappling with the duality of celebrity. It irked him deeply that his true essence was often obscured by the roles society projected onto him: a Protestant, a one-time Catholic, someone who had served in the military, a pacifist, a famous writer. It was this sense of being misunderstood that drove him to pen his auto-biography, a corrective narrative aimed at setting the record straight. In *Confessions*, he championed the notion of aligning one's actions with the laws of the heart, with one's innate nature. He elevated personal experience gained to a level of importance that had never been seen before.

Whereas, a century earlier, solitude had widely been seen as something to fear, Rousseau instead thought of it as the epicentre of a singular private self, a self whose authenticity and moral free-dom are rooted in the secret world of subjectivity. Society started to be viewed as an alien force or pressure that distorts people's true natures by insisting they conform: to fashion, etiquette and all that is false.

Unlike Thomas Hobbes, who had argued that humanity in its natural state turns violent, that life would be 'nasty, brutish, and short', and that mankind therefore needed the security and safety brought by law and an all-seeing state, Rousseau claimed that man on his own, in the original state of nature, and conditional on a certain level of social development, could be free and happy. He thought that to cultivate an independent, self-sufficient individ-ual, able to reason and exercise free will, the inner nature must be cultivated. Man should grow and develop 'according to nature's law, not man's'.

Rousseau never used the word *authentic*, but he embodied its spirit. He dramatized the tension between private feelings and the oppressive demands of a conformist society. In his writing we can see the beginnings of the Romantic movement, which would come to value living sincerely and authentically according to one's true nature, prioritizing the private self over the public persona.

Chapter 7:

FEMALE VIRTUES

'It was very full and I had several good political fights,' wrote Georgiana Cavendish, the Duchess of Devonshire, describing a night at the opera in a letter to her brother, George, in March 1784. Her pleasure was due entirely to the spirited debates among members of the audience rather than the melodious strains of dramatic arias.[1] From opulent velvet boxes, aristocratic ladies with towering grey wigs, their faces powdered white with lead and cheeks ablaze with rouge, vociferously exclaimed, 'Damn Fox!' while others retorted, 'Damn Pitt!'

The cause of this uproar was the impending Westminster parliamentary election. 'Damn Fox' referred to Charles James Fox, leader of a revived Whig faction. His party advocated for curbing the king's powers, bolstering parliamentary authority, American independence, and the abolition of slavery. 'Damn Pitt' was Fox's arch-rival, the Tory prime minister William Pitt the Younger.

All members of Parliament were landowners, or nominees of landowners; all were Protestants; and all were men. Property restrictions on who could vote meant that only about 300,000 men, from a population of roughly ten million people, had the right.[2] Legal anomalies and customs enabled peers and wealthy gentlemen to own a seat outright, and they had considerable influence on such constituencies. There was no secret ballot, which meant that choices were public and voters open to influence. The House of Commons, and indeed the country itself, was effectively controlled by what radicals derisively termed the 'two hundred families': an oligarchy of aristocratic landowners and their allies.

Although the electorate was a mere sliver of society, the appetite for political debate was large. From the smoky confines of coffee-houses to the ink-stained battlegrounds of the press, and even out in the streets with parades and rallies, citizens eagerly threw themselves into the fray. And, as the scene at the opera suggests, women, especially those from aristocratic families, engaged – none more so than the Duchess of Devonshire.

As the eldest daughter of Earl John Spencer of Devonshire and Lady Georgiana Spencer, Georgiana had been born into privilege. Her family was one tier down from royalty. Her marriage on 7 June 1774, her seventeenth birthday, to William Cavendish, the 5th Duke of Devonshire, was regarded as a perfect match but soon became an infamous disaster. By the terms of his father's will, the Duke could only inherit the estate once he had a male heir, which meant the couple's future relied upon the birth of a son – an event that, alas, was not forthcoming. Georgiana found it difficult to get pregnant at all. She then had miscarriages and daughters but, until 1790, no boys.

As time ticked on, William's indulgences became flagrant. He brazenly conducted affairs, even going so far as to invite his lover – Lady Elizabeth Foster, who was also Georgiana's friend – into their home. This domestic arrangement was scandalous, yet not entirely one-sided. Georgiana, too, sought solace outside her marriage, finding companionship with the future prime minister Charles Grey, with whom she had a daughter.

Boredom and restlessness drove her to the gaming tables, where she racked up astronomical gambling debts. Yet her mind craved more than mere diversion. She devoured books and immersed herself in the world of ideas, letters and politics, finding a way to exert her influence.

As a hostess, Georgiana's soirees were legendary: lavish dinner parties and all-night balls beneath ceilings adorned with fresh roses. She thrived in this environment, engaging her guests in spirited debate. She was a celebrated supporter of the Whig Party and found public ways to champion its leader, Fox; when out on the town clothed in the colours of her chosen party, she turned heads with her sartorial choices. Ostrich feathers, worn aloft in her hair like a crown, danced in the breeze, their hues of blue and buff yellow a proclamation of her political allegiance.

Georgiana was not alone in her activism. Indeed, she belonged to a lineage of aristocratic women who had long wielded their influence. In a society where property ownership determined one's voice and worth in the political arena, women of her class possessed a currency of power unmatched by their male counterparts without estates or titles. They had considerably more sway than women from the lower classes who had no well-connected, well-heeled men to pressure.

But Georgiana would eventually step too far out from the backstage of political machinations. In doing so she breached her era's firm boundary between the private realm, deemed appropriate for women, and the public domain, which was reserved for men.

*

In the spring of 1784, just after the shouting match at the opera, the Duchess of Devonshire and a cadre of notable ladies went out campaigning for Charles Fox in his bid to become MP for Westminster. Dressed in Whig colours, with foxes' tails in their hats, the women canvassed for votes, distributed propaganda, and appeared prominently in processions of Fox supporters. The crowds they drew to their cause were loud and boisterous.

At one point, as Georgiana left her carriage to meet and talk with people, gangs of sailors began to follow her around. It was a step too far. The next day brought an avalanche of vicious pamphlets, newspaper reports and obscene cartoons. The report in the *Morning Post* of 8 April 1784 sniped: 'The Duchess of Devonshire's attendance at Covent Garden, perhaps, will not secure Mr Fox's election; but it will at least establish her pre-eminence above all other beauties of that place, and make her a standing toast in all the ale-houses and gin-shops of Westminster ... Ladies who interest themselves so much in the case of elections, are perhaps too ignorant to know that they meddle with what does not concern them, but they ought at least to know, that it is usual, even in these days of degeneracy, to expect common decency in a married woman.'[3]

One satirical print, 'Political Affection' by Thomas Rowlandson, depicted the Duchess tenderly pressing a large fox to her breast while a human baby by her feet clamoured for milk. The cartoon implied that she was neglecting her responsibilities as a woman in the private realm of the nursery to interfere in the public sphere. In another vicious print, 'The Devonshire Amusement', published shortly after the election, the male and female roles were reversed. The Duke of Devonshire was shown in one panel sitting in a nursery, changing a baby's nappy. In an adjacent panel the Duchess, her robes and hair loose, was out campaigning.

All this commentary captured the highly gendered nature of the public and private spheres. The reaction to the activism of the Duchess of Devonshire, from a press that usually praised her, revealed the limitations on a woman's ability to contribute to political affairs. Influence in private was fine, up to a point. But too much independent political activism in public could be seen as deeply suspect. That a woman of Georgiana's standing consorted with ordinary folk was also seen as improper. For a woman to

*'The Devonshire Amusement', 24 June 1784. The Duchess of Devonshire
(left): on the ground at her feet is a paper inscribed 'Secret Influence'.
The Duke (right) sits on a chair, an infant face down on his knee; he
appears to be changing the baby's nappy; clean towels hang over a line
beside him; at his feet is the cradle. The Duke is saying, 'This Work does
not suit my Fancy. Ah William every one must be cursed that like thee
takes a Politic Mad Wife'.*

emerge from the household to participate in public life was unbe-
coming, unwomanly, unnatural – almost (as Rowlandson's political
cartoon so savagely suggests) a form of marital infidelity.

The age of separations, as well as creating the public and private spheres, had forged a division within the private realm. Male
and female roles came to be more explicitly distinguished and
associated with each domain. The achievement of private life, a
positive development, also entailed the subjection of women,
which was not.

*

In his *Commentaries on the Laws of England* (1765–70), jurist William Blackstone outlined the principle that a husband and wife were in law a single person – represented by the husband. Through the English common-law doctrine known as coverture, when a woman married she effectively became her husband's property. No matter how wealthy or important she might be, she was 'covered' by her husband – he acted for her.

A married woman could not own property; it would pass to her husband when they married. Without her husband's consent, she could not enter into a contract or write a will. She could not sue or be sued in her own name. She had no legal rights over her children. A text explaining the laws concerning women was to the point: 'By marriage the very being of or legal existence of a woman is suspended.'[4] Within Edward Coke and William Blackstone's 'castle', women were subjugated: erased as citizens and legal subjects. There were exceptions, but essentially a married woman could only act through a man in any legal context. An unmarried woman could, in theory, take legal action on her own behalf, but there was immense social pressure on her to get married. Although these were medieval legal principles, they still carried weight, reinforced by the social arrangement that had evolved with the emergence of the public and private spheres.

As the development of capitalism freed the private realm of the home from the demands of economic production, the family was detached from wider networks of work and community. Men left the home to participate in public life, perhaps working as merchants, bankers or lawyers and spending hours in coffee-houses – meanwhile, it became a woman's duty to stay at home and care for her husband, manage the household and nurture a family. Though women might sometimes participate in cottage industries or small-scale entrepreneurial activities, the Church, universities, military, medical schools and the bar were all closed to them. For Samuel Johnson, the idea of a woman preacher was 'like a dog walking on his hind legs'.⁵

Women took part in social life, attended the theatre, assembly rooms, pleasure gardens, dinners, balls and parties, but remained excluded from many engagements in the civic sphere or any activity that might develop their intellect and harm their marriage prospects.

Rousseau's *Emile* (1762), which was so popular that it appeared in five different English editions before 1770, encapsulated the widespread feeling about the different natures of the sexes. 'Even if [a woman] possesses genuine talents,' Rousseau argued, 'any pretension on her part would degrade them. Her dignity depends on remaining unknown; her glory lies in her husband's esteem, her greatest pleasure in the happiness of her family.'⁶ A woman's anatomy determined her place in society. The social arrangement was presented as the natural order of things. As Joseph Addison wrote, directing his comments at women involving themselves in policies: 'Female Virtues are of a Domestick turn. The Family is the proper Province for Private Women to Shine in.'⁷

In the lives of the powerful and expanding propertied and monied minority, boys were educated for independence and public life while girls were taught how to be more attractive, virtuous, pious and possessed of self-restraint. While men were reasonably free to have sex before marriage, women were expected to be virgins. A husband had a right to demand sexual servicing. There was no crime of marital rape.

As ever, there were some women, especially in cities, who worked, or who remained single, or whose family wealth helped to secure their independence.⁸ But they butted against powerful social expectations, and there were limits to what they could achieve. Although married women might exert influence over their spouses – and sometimes, like Georgiana, over their male acquaintances – they were viewed overwhelmingly as the private

property of their husbands, and as mothers to the next generation. The barriers to women's involvement in public life were real.

Women were understood as upholding morality and social
stability through enforcing cultural norms within the household
and producing and raising children. But their domain did not
extend beyond the private world: they were expected to embody
these virtues as wives and mothers while supporting their husbands in their public roles. Rather than being recognized as the
product of a specific social and political context, women's relega-
tion to the private domain as the nurturing sex was seen as an
inevitable consequence of their nature. The distinction between
public and private spheres appeared self-evident, eternal even,
requiring no further justification. And almost immediately, some
women seized their pens and voiced their objections.

*

Mary Astell was born in 1666, the daughter of a downwardly
mobile Newcastle coal merchant and his Catholic wife. From
these modest beginnings, Astell carved out a life that defied the
expectations of her era. As a single woman, she ventured into the
realms of philosophy and politics – nearly unthinkable pursuits
for a woman of her time and social standing. Equally unusual,
Astell was a High Tory Anglican who believed in the divine right
of kings, and who also held radical ideas about a woman's position
and role in society.

Astell challenged the view that the social division between
men and women was natural and inevitable. She argued instead
that woman's subjection was the result of an imbalance of
power. It was custom, rather than nature, that dictated why
things were the way they were. Women were not naturally
stupid, nor were they inferior, Astell asserted. Her debut publication, *A Serious Proposal to the Ladies*, catapulted her into the
limelight. Published in 1694 and signed 'A lover of her sex', this

groundbreaking work championed women's right to intellectual fulfilment. It boldly proposed that women, particularly those of the bourgeois class, should unite their resources to create secular monasteries. These would be dedicated to study, contemplation and charitable endeavours, offering women the unprecedented opportunity to cultivate their minds and spirits.

Astell surveyed the intellectual currents of her time and logically, meticulously picked holes in them. In 1704, the philosopher of the age, John Locke, had just died, and Astell took aim. In his *Second Treatise on Government* (1690) he had made a distinction between the public realm, where men were naturally free and authority had to be earned, and the private realm, in which patriarchal authority was legitimate. Locke argued that within marriage, women were unequal and should obey men. This meant that although Locke's work was important in arguing for the rights of mankind – which created the theoretical possibility of full political membership for women – he chose not to explore this further.

Mary Astell had little time for philosophers who argued for public liberty but were tyrants in their own castles. Locke and the Whigs with whom he associated had famously complained about being enslaved to a king. Addressing his work directly, Astell asked why, then, he would condemn wives to the same situation. As she sharply wrote, 'If all men are born free, why are all women born slaves?'[9] If, she went on, 'absolute sovereignty be not necessary in a State, how comes it to be so in a Family?'[10]

Astell disputed the conventional idea that women were inferior because they were ruled by their passions and slaves to their bodies. Drawing on the ideas of Locke and René Descartes, she argued that women too could be rational, coming to knowledge through their own observations and on the evidence of their own reason. Locke had described the self as 'that conscious thinking thing'. Astell extended rationality and reason to women, arguing that a woman's mind was no different to that of a man and that there was no good reason why a woman should not be educated. As far as she was concerned, if women were educated like men, they would be free to evaluate their own lives and even their marriage proposals. She developed these ideas further, arguing that marriage should be a woman's choice, not her vocation.

Mary Astell's books went through numerous printings, but hers was a marginal voice. Richard Steele lampooned her in *The Spectator* and in *The Tatler* he opined: '[The] Soul of a Man and that of a Woman are made very unlike, according to the employments for which they are designed. The Ladies will please to observe, I say, our Minds have different, not superior Qualities to theirs . . . To manage well a great Family, is as worthy an Instance of Capacity, as to execute a great employment.'[11]

*

Where Astell was a High Tory Anglican, Mary Wollstonecraft was a political radical who in 1792 travelled to France to observe the French Revolution, to which she was initially sympathetic. Unlike Astell's structured and devout life, Wollstonecraft's personal life was marked by unconventional relationships and a series of passionate affairs. Yet, despite their differences, Wollstonecraft shared Astell's critical eye for the gendered inequities embedded in mainstream Enlightenment thought.

In *Emile*, Rousseau had outlined a vision of education that consigned women to lives of domesticity and subservience. In *A Vindication of the Rights of Woman*, Wollstonecraft dismantled his arguments, which she found invigorating but vexing. She saw them as a deliberate curtailment of women's potential, a systematic effort to keep them in a state of perpetual childhood. Woman's so-called stupidity and their 'natural' characteristics', she argued, were artificial. They were a consequence of women's lack of education, rather than stemming from inherent ignorance and idleness. Women were socially engineered to be lovely creatures, and also stupid ones.

Wollstonecraft envisioned a world where women were active participants in the intellectual and moral spheres of society and she called for an overhaul of the education system, for women to be taught to think critically, so that they could develop their reason. Wollstonecraft also argued for political change, with reform in the electoral systems. She said that women ought to have representatives, instead of being arbitrarily governed without having any direct share allowed them in the deliberations of government; that they were not a possession of men but should have their own civil existence.

She advocated for women to be free to carve out careers; advocated free love to end the sexual double standard; and denounced marriage as legalized prostitution. Though she did, late in life, marry the political philosopher William Godwin, this was in no small part because she didn't want her daughter, Mary Wollstonecraft Godwin (the future Mary Shelley and author of *Frankenstein*) to be illegitimate.

Wollstonecraft wasn't opposed to family life. Her two autobiographical novels celebrated aspects of female domestic fulfilment. She envisaged a world in which women could be both independent and nurturing, uniting the qualities traditionally parcelled out between Adam and Eve – rationality and feeling; participation in the public realm, motherhood in the private domain. Indeed, she argued that the immense importance of women's contributions in the private realm meant they should also be free, autonomous participants in the public realm: 'But in order to render their private virtue a public benefit, they must have a civil existence in the state, married or single; else we shall continually see some worthy woman, whose sensibility has been rendered painfully acute by undeserved contempt, droop like the "lily broken down by a plow-share".'[12]

Wollstonecraft argued that a society which kept women ignorant was itself crippled. True progress would only be achieved when women were freed from the shackles of custom and allowed to realize their full potential. She believed passionately that an enlightened society required the full participation of all its members, regardless of sex. This debate over women's natural abilities, duties and rights intensified as the eighteenth century gave way to the nineteenth. Mary Astell's and Mary Wollstonecraft's challenges to the idea of the 'natural' position of women in the private realm would reverberate for centuries.

PART III:
A Sacred Domain of Privacy

Chapter 8:

SEALED LETTERS IN AN ENGLISH POST OFFICE

After arriving in London in 1837 as a political exile, Giuseppe Mazzini – once the heart and soul of Italy's unification movement – saw his political influence not diminish, but expand. Unable to live on the modest sums sent to him by his long-suffering mother, the only option open to him was to write. Industrial processes were drastically changing the speed of the manufacture of newspapers and the spread of their distribution. But the many dailies were too full of sensationalist reporting for his liking: stories of broken families and drunken, violent louts were splashed across the pages. Instead, Mazzini took up his pen for the influential cerebral periodicals that were also proliferating.

For the *Westminster Review*, founded by the utilitarian philosopher Jeremy Bentham, he enthused about Italian literature. In *Le Monde*, he praised Britain's Representation of the People Act (1832). Quickly becoming known as the Great Reform Act, it transformed the electoral system by reducing the power of the landed aristocracy and extending the franchise to small landowners, tenant farmers and shopkeepers. The Act accepted the principle of representation and conceived of a public with a say and a stake in democracy. Though its provisions only extended to male property owners, it was more expansive than anything that had gone before, and once the principle of representation had been accepted, there were energetic attempts to extend it.

Mazzini formed links with the leaders of the Chartists, a mass movement demanding that *all* men might have the right to vote, irrespective of property. He supported the cause of Irish independence, opposed slavery in America and supported the Union cause, and advocated for women's rights. Horrified by London's poverty and deeply affected by the Italian street boys – children of the city's many illiterate Italian migrants who sought out a living as hawkers and grinders – in 1842, he established the Free Italian School in the heart of London's Hatton Garden. Charles Dickens admired him immensely and assisted him in his endeavours.

Most Fridays, Mazzini found himself at the dinner table of the Scottish historian Thomas Carlyle and his wife, Jane. Their political ideologies clashed. Carlyle, a brooding reactionary, saw civilization teetering on the edge of chaos. Yet he was captivated by the dashing Italian, with his big brown eyes and black velvet suit – worn in mourning for his country. Carlyle worried about his meagre diet and admired his ceaseless energy.

Mazzini continued to correspond with nationalists across Europe about revolution. Their shared vision was that the nation state, rather than empire, was the best vehicle for a people to express their collective will; and that democratically elected republican government offered the public a form of agency and a means to pursue shared goals. His indefatigability meant that he was soon, once again, a person of influence. Some believed he was the most subversive presence in all of Europe.

As Mazzini's ideas spread across the continent, Italy's rulers steeled themselves to face down all revolt. The 'spectre of revolution', as Karl Marx would later describe it, sent spasms of alarm through the ruling classes. Towards the end of 1843, the Austrian ambassador, Baron Philipp von Neumann, asked the Secretary of State for the Home Office, Sir James Graham, a stalwart baronet in Sir Robert Peel's Conservative government, to intercept Mazzini's mail and that of other nationalists in his London circle, to anticipate any plot. Sir James duly issued a warrant mandating the opening of all the men's correspondence. The Permanent Secretary of the Post Office arranged for the letters to be taken to the Black Chamber, a secret location in the Central Post Office. Here, five clerks opened and copied the contents before resealing and sending the letters on. There was no expectation that this covert operation would ever come to light.

But one day early in 1844, in his dank bedsit, Mazzini noticed something peculiar as he turned to his letters. One envelope bore two distinct stamps; it was as if one had been deliberately placed to obscure the other, masking the exact time of delivery. His suspicions raised, he sought certainty. He asked friends to send him letters containing small, barely noticeable items: strands of hair, poppy seeds, grains of sand. When the envelopes arrived, he opened them only to find the items missing. This was the evidence he needed. Clandestine forces were at work. The time had come to act.

On 14 June 1844, Thomas Duncombe, the Radical MP for Finsbury in north London, stood in the House of Commons and presented a petition from Mazzini and three of his associates. It alleged that their letters, sent through Her Majesty's Post Office, had been intercepted and their seals broken, despite containing no political propaganda, libellous matter or treasonous comments. Duncombe's petition condemned this intrusion, accusing the government of importing 'the spy system of foreign states', a practice 'repugnant to every principle of the British constitution' and 'subversive of the public confidence essential to a commercial country'. Duncombe challenged his fellow members: would they tolerate 'their private letters being opened, their family secrets copied, and sent to the Secretary of State?' With this, he demanded an immediate explanation.[1]

Rising to his feet with an air of comfortable authority, Sir James Graham attempted to address the issue. 'The House must be aware,' he began with leaden solemnity, 'that since the reign of Queen Anne, the Principal Secretary of State has possessed the power to detain and open letters passing through the Post Office.' Reminding the assembly of the legality and historical precedence of mail tampering, Sir James sought to downplay the specific allegations, asserting that they were 'largely untrue'. Endeavouring to close the chapter on the matter, he reminded the Commons that Parliament had placed its confidence in the individual exercising the power (namely him) and that it did not serve the public good to pry into particular cases. Concluding his remarks, he declared his intention to refrain from further discussion on the subject.[2]

Confident that his subtle non-denial would quash Duncombe's cause, Sir James settled back into his seat. But he would soon realize that he had misread the mood of the nation. A revolution in the value and esteem of privacy had taken place. Nowhere was this more obvious than in disputes over opening and spying on a man's private letters. Sir James would soon find that he was out of step with his times.

Ripples of disquiet first appeared in *The Times*, already an influential newspaper, popularly nicknamed 'the Thunderer'. Responding via the letters page to its news summary of the events in the Commons, Thomas Carlyle gave a rousing defence of his friend and clarified the issues at stake in the 'disgraceful affair': 'Whether the extraneous Austrian Emperor and the miserable old chimera of a Pope shall maintain themselves in Italy, or be obliged to decamp from Italy, is not a question in the least vital to Englishmen. But it is a question vital to us that sealed letters in an English post office be, as we all fancied they were, respected as things sacred; that opening of men's letters, a practice near of kin to picking men's pockets, and to other still viler and far fataler forms of scoundrelism, be not resorted to in England, except in

cases of the very last extremity.'³ Within the week, a *Times* editorial had denounced the letter-tampering, catapulting discontent
from the margins to the heart of the newspaper's coverage.

Though typically aligned with Tory principles and pro-
Austrian, *The Times* raged that who Mazzini was or what he
believed were no matter: the paper opposed the detainment and
opening of his private letters. Such action was the most 'odious'
of liberties granted to a British minister. The editorial argued
that these measures should be employed 'very seldom', with
'extreme caution' and 'tender moderation'. Moreover, it demanded
that any use of this power must be fully justified and transparently
explained by the government, leaving no room for evasion or
denial.⁴

*

Three factors had converged to ignite the controversy, each
rooted in the shifting landscape of British society. First, as the
Mazzini scandal erupted and spread, Jeremy Bentham's essay *Of
Publicity* (1843) had just been posthumously published, and was
recognized as a founding text of open government. Bentham
argued that a nascent democracy required 'publicity' – a kind of
transparency – that replaced mystery and concealment. 'Publicity,' he wrote, 'is the fittest law for securing the public
confidence ... secresy [*sic*] is an instrument of conspiracy; it
ought not, therefore, to be the system of a regular government.'⁵

Indeed, back in 1791, in the throes of a quest for transparency,
Bentham had conceived an architectural innovation that would
come to symbolize the ultimate invasion of privacy: the Panopticon. Its name, derived from the Greek word *panoptes*, meaning
'all-seeing', was apt. The design for a prison ensured inmates
would never be able to discern when they were under watchful
eyes, exploiting the psychological weight of perpetual surveillance
to compel better behaviour. Bentham imagined extending the

Panopticon's principles to the design of factories, hospitals and schools, creating environments where efficiency and discipline could thrive under the omnipresent gaze of authority. Yet Bentham's proposal encountered political resistance. Funding was repeatedly denied and, despite his efforts, the Panopticon remained an unbuilt dream, a powerful idea that never materialized in brick and mortar.

Reforming Victorians were working out what should be the purview of government and publicly known, and what should be private. The destruction of the mystery surrounding government was a shared endeavour as it became increasingly accepted that the modern state required openness in its workings. Government needed to be free from the imposition of private interest.

The idea – and hope – was that open government, and social programmes like education, could also instruct the public in the workings of government and improve the nature of debate. In the 1830s, the Whig administration had committed itself to educating a population through the grant subsidy of elementary education. Over the course of the century, governments made newspapers cheaper, put a shorthand gallery for journalists into the House of Commons and made its proceedings public in Hansard, the official report of all parliamentary debates.

The shining ideal of 'publicity' was one reason for the widespread hostility towards proposals for a secret ballot, which would not be introduced until the Ballot Act of 1872, and then only after heated disagreement. Robert Peel, serving as Home Secretary in 1838, argued passionately in the House of Commons, 'It is a system totally at variance with all the institutions, usages, and feelings of the people of this country, with all the maxims which have taught them to believe that free discussion, that publicity, that the light of day, that public opinion, are the great checks upon abuse.'[6]

The new appreciation of openness influenced the Mazzini

letter-opening scandal. *The Times* underscored the paramountcy of open government. The newspaper suggested that in an age of mass society and the expanding frontier of democracy, the pursuit of public objectives through clandestine means was an affront to democratic values. Secret interception of letters amounted to treason against the public trust, undermining the very essence of democratic governance.[7]

In the long, heated Commons debates that followed the opening of Mazzini's letters, no MP demanded an end to *all* forms of surveillance. The Tory statesman Benjamin Disraeli said it was fine for letters to be opened so long as the recipient was informed. He also quipped that the Home Office 'may open all my letters, provided they answer them'.[8]

The second factor was the new Post Office system. Under the guidance of Sir Rowland Hill in 1840, the Whig government had introduced a communications revolution by slashing the cost of postage to a penny irrespective of distance and introducing pre-payment to expedite delivery: a penny stamp bearing the image of the young Queen Victoria. The intention was to democratize communication and reinforce intimate bonds between those whose lives had been fragmented by urbanization as the Industrial Revolution swept through Britain. The penny post, as it was called, followed the establishment of the Manchester–Liverpool railway line in 1830.

The reformed Post Office became so efficient that letter-writers could correspond several times within a single day, and they did so with alacrity. In 1839, around seventy-six million letters were mailed within Britain. By 1850, that number had soared to almost 350 million, including the first Christmas card.[9] Valentine's Day grew in renown and favour. In the mid-1820s, Londoners sent some 200,000 tender missives. With the advent of the penny post, the volume of romantic messages swelled to twice its number; by the 1860s, it redoubled again.[10]

The Post Office encouraged householders to add letter boxes to the entrances of their homes, changing front doors forever. A few found the idea intolerable: the Marquis of Londonderry fired off a letter to Sir Rowland Hill demanding to know whether 'the Postmaster-General actually expects that I should cut a slit in my mahogany door?'[11] The invention of the post box meant that the sender no longer had to visit a post office and show their letters to the clerk. It became accepted that addressees would open and read letters inside their own homes. The ritual of letter-writing, the special kinds of paper it required, and its regularity, acquired meaning and significance.

Secure, regular private communication between citizens was an important right in a democracy and in a country that led the world in technology and commerce. In an age before telephones or email, letters were the lifeblood of an expanding society, connecting friends and loved ones across long distances and creating virtual private networks. It was this connective tissue that Sir Graham was seen to have assaulted. The Post Office's role as a public institution was to guarantee a private realm, which was idealized as never before: this was the critical third factor of the scandal that unfolded as revelations about letter-tampering continued to surface.

For the liberals in the chamber, the affair was an outrage. They believed individual freedom and property were paramount and no one, no authority, should interfere with them. A letter was a letter, raged the Whig politician Thomas Babington Macauley, whether it was on someone's desk or in transit: 'they are both alike my property; and the exposure of my secrets is the same, and attended with the same consequences, whether from the reading of a letter which is to be delivered or from the reading of a letter which has been delivered.'[12]

In 1814, at a time when Europe was emerging from the turbulence of Napoleonic Wars and the revolutionary fires of the previous decades, Benjamin Constant, one of the most eloquent defenders of liberalism, wrote a stirring manifesto for personal freedom and the private domain. In his essay, *De l'esprit de conquête et de l'usurpation* (*On the Spirit of Conquest and Usurpation*), Constant argued that the protection of the private sphere was not only necessary, but the very essence of modern liberty. He saw the intimate spaces of life – the spaces of family, friendship, work and leisure, belief, and personal pursuits – not as an escape from the public realm, but as the true core of human existence.

For Constant, freedom in the modern world was not about wielding power in the public sphere, as it had been for the ancients. It was about securing the right to retreat into the private sphere, where individuals could live according to their own desires. It was where the true richness of life unfolded – the nurturing of close relationships, the exercise of one's beliefs, the pursuit of work that gave purpose, and the experience of pleasure. Without protection of this private realm, Constant warned, people risked losing what made life meaningful.

The private sphere, in Constant's view, was not a place of isolation or disengagement, but the very foundation of a healthy, democratic society. Constant envisioned a citizen – the liberal subject – who was the embodiment of this new era and the cornerstone of democracy: a person who, through rationality and autonomy, could navigate both the public and private spheres with a sense of balance and integrity. Constant was clear: the government had its role, but it must be limited. It was there to protect the rights of citizens, to maintain peace and order, but it must never overstep its boundaries and invade the intimate aspects of individual lives.

*

Debates on the Mazzini affair in the House of Commons came to fill 550 pages in Hansard. The furore penetrated all layers of society, in what Sir James's biographer bitterly complained was a 'paroxysm

THE POST-OFFICE PEEP-SHOW.—" A Penny a Peep—Only a Penny ! "

'The Post-Office Peep-Show'. 'A penny a peep – only a penny!'

of public anger'.[13] The controversy provoked the newly founded *Punch* magazine to fire salvo after salvo of satirical comment and cartoons. One mocked: 'my letters – and the thousands I receive! – had all of them been defiled by the eyes of a spy; that all my most domestic secrets had been rumpled and tousled, and pinched here and pinched there – searched by an English Minister as shuddering modesty is searched by a French custom-house!'[14]

The periodical sold 'anti-Graham' envelopes, decorated on the reverse with a picture of an overweight, prying busybody in a top hat and a cherub's wings. Each was stamped with the sarcastic request: 'If this letter be OPENED at the General Post Office, the writer will be glad to have it forwarded the same day.'[15] Members of the public scribbled comments of their own onto ordinary envelopes. Charles Dickens, whose novels *Bleak House* (1852–3) and *Little Dorrit* (1855–7) pivot on purloined letters that threaten to expose family connections and economic fortunes, wrote on his envelopes: 'It is particularly requested that if Sir James Graham should open this, he will not trouble himself to seal it again.'[16]

The scandal resonated beyond Britain's borders. In the United States, the *New-York Daily Tribune* reprinted Thomas Carlyle's letter, which argued that 'sealed letters' be 'respected as sacred', in full. The paper itself condemned the secret opening of Mazzini's letters as a 'disgraceful . . . barbarian breach of honor and decency'.[17]

The impact of the controversy was long-lasting. The Black Chamber of the Post Office was abolished. The decipherer of foreign correspondence, Francis Willes, whose family had held the position since 1703, was pensioned off. The scandal was also addressed by a typical piece of Victorian inventiveness: the gummed envelope. The accompanying advert, which ran in *The Times*, promised that it was impossible to read the contents without destroying the envelope.[18]

And thus Britain's interception of foreign communications came to an end, at least until the First World War. For what was probably the first time in history, the British state largely stopped opening the letters of its citizens, although budding revolutionaries remained scrupulously careful. Marx and Engels considered their letters vulnerable to surveillance, and Mazzini used code in his letters until his death in Pisa in 1871. He did get to see the unification of Italy before he died, but it was as a monarchy, not the republic he had so desired.

Sir James Graham's failure to appreciate the heightened sensitivities surrounding private letters was to haunt him. His reputation never recovered: for the rest of his life, he would be known only for having invaded the privacy of Englishmen. But as he had rightly observed, back in the 1790s, the espionage of the Post Office had been widely known. People may have desired privacy in communications – and, with coded messages and intricate wax seals on their envelopes, taken elaborate lengths to achieve it – but they did not assume it. By the middle of the nineteenth century, however, expectations were rather different.

The national outcry at government mail tampering illustrated the fireball of outrage that had spread from political revolutionaries through the historians and radical politicians of the time, burning through English society and crossing the Atlantic to the USA.

*

In his *Dictionary of the English Language* (1755), Samuel Johnson defined *secrecy* and *privacy* as interchangeable. Privacy, Johnson described as the 'state of being secret; secrecy'. Secrecy was 'privacy; state of being hidden'.[19] But by the nineteenth century, these terms had come apart and their meanings had evolved. In 1814, the dictionary definition of privacy was recognizably modern: 'the state or condition of being alone, undisturbed, or free from public attention, as a matter of choice or right'. By contrast, secrecy, according to Bentham's *Of Publicity* (1843), is 'an instrument of conspiracy; it ought not, therefore, to be the system of a regular government'.[20] While secrecy had taken on negative connotations, privacy was aligned with positive ones. Privacy, as the German sociologist Georg Simmel observed, had become akin to 'spiritual private property'.[21]

In the seventeenth century, privacy had been seen as dangerous; two centuries later, it was no longer threatening but under threat, as the Mazzini letter-opening scandal served to highlight. Factors such as a strong capitalist economy, the rise of liberal democracy, mass society, new information networks, and the idealization of the private sphere fuelled the belief that privacy was an unquestionable good. The public sphere expanded while the private domain deepened, and as these realms became more distinct, public life grew more visible and private life more secluded. This separation only heightened the drama when boundaries were breached.

Chapter 9:

THE FAMILY MUST HAVE PRIVACY

Queen Victoria and Prince Albert spent their leisure time etching – capturing each other's likenesses, their children, faithful hounds, and the landscapes around Windsor and Claremont House. Although created for personal enjoyment, in late 1848, they decided to produce a limited number of bound volumes as gifts for dear friends and kin. As the year drew to its close, they entrusted a selection of plates to Mr John Brown of Castle Street, Windsor, for printing.

Brown took precautions to ensure that none but those approved by the royals might catch a glimpse. The plates were locked away, and the amount of paper in the workshop was regulated. Alas, despite such efforts, an apprentice by the name of Middleton purloined over sixty plates and sold them to one Jasper Tomsett Judge, a specialist in royal reportage. Judge planned to hold a public exhibition of the illicitly obtained etchings in London. He searched out a venue of good repute and approached William Strange, a publisher based at 21 Paternoster Row, to commission a descriptive catalogue.

When he wasn't in the bankruptcy court or embroiled in a web of legal disputes, Strange busied himself with publishing political satire, cheap periodicals and penny-part serials. He eagerly embraced the opportunity presented. The result, 'A Descriptive Catalogue of the Royal Victoria and Albert Gallery of Etchings', soon rolled off the presses, priced at a modest sixpence.

Judge forwarded a copy of the catalogue to the royal household along with a detailed account of his plans, apparently seeking their permission, somewhat optimistically after the fact. Advertisements for the exhibition ran in *The Times*, promising the inclusion of portraits of the young Princess Royal, executed with maternal devotion by none other than Her Majesty the Queen herself.

Victoria, Princess Royal, 1840–1901. Daughter of Queen Victoria and future German Empress and Queen of Prussia by marriage to German Emperor Frederick III. After an etching by her mother, Queen Victoria, dated 1841.

Victoria and Albert were horrified. They immediately sought the counsel of their legal advisers and promptly issued a writ for an injunction to ban the exhibition and ensure the return of the etchings. Because the Queen cannot sue in her own courts, the claim was brought in her husband's name.

At the end of January 1849, in a packed Court of Chancery, Sir James Knight-Bruce issued an instruction restraining Strange, his agents, servants and workmen from exhibiting the etchings, making copies or publishing any description of them.[1] The ruling also demanded that Judge surrender the plates. After Strange appealed, believing he had done nothing wrong and certainly nothing illegal, the Lord Chancellor, Charles Christopher Pepys, 1st Earl of Cottenham, confirmed the ruling.

Prince Albert v. *Strange* relied on two legal doctrines – first, the authors' right and property in the etchings. Her Majesty's Attorney-General argued that the concept of private property was expansive enough to include the act of mental creation, and therefore the etchings could not be reproduced or summarized in the descriptive catalogue. The second doctrine was breach of confidence. Strange, on appeal, argued that he had been unaware the impressions were improperly obtained and thus believed he retained the right to publish the catalogue. However, his appeal was decisively rejected. The court held that the prints could only have entered the publisher's possession through surreptitious means.

The *Lady's Newspaper & Pictorial Times*, a publication cherished by the middle and upper classes, expressed palpable relief. The courts, it declared, had rightfully defended the royals' unassailable prerogative to shield their private lives from prying eyes. This judicial stance, the periodical asserted, affirmed that every individual in society should possess the means to 'stop the evil . . . of impudent or injurious inquisitiveness'.[2]

Knight-Bruce had determined that the printmaker's actions were more than an intrusion – they breached conventional rules and offended a deep sense of propriety. He condemned the act as: 'sordid spying into the privacy of domestic life – into the home (a word hitherto sacred among us).'[3] The historian Thomas Carlyle had characterized Giuseppe Mazzini's letters – and, by extension, the letters of all English men – as sacred and inviolable; now Bruce was describing domestic life and the home in the same reverent tone.

The Victorians elevated the private sphere to a near-religious sanctity. In *The Home Life in Light of Its Divine Idea* (1866), Congregational minister James Baldwin Brown wrote: 'God made the first man after a divine original, and after a divine original too, he made the first home' – underscoring the celestial blueprint of the household.[4] Similarly, the critic John Ruskin described the domestic sphere as 'a sacred place, a vestal temple, a temple of the heart'.[5] It was a haven from a forbidding outside world and the wellspring of civic virtue.

*

As the British Empire expanded, the fireside and hearth became symbols of refuge from the destructive forces of capitalism. Victorians viewed the eighteenth century as soulless – too rational, cynical and materialistic – and believed people needed a sanctuary from commercial society.

Nineteenth-century Britain was a society of strangers. The population had doubled between 1801 and 1851 and doubled again by 1911 – faster growth than in any other European nation. In London alone, it had soared from one million to reach six million over the century.[6] Millions of unknown faces, seeking a better life away from the back-breaking toil of rural hardship, congregated in cities, detached from their village communities. The administrative state faced the colossal challenge of managing and addressing the welfare of a huge, expanding, mobile and anonymous population.

A revised social contract between private citizens and the state was required to define obligations and responsibilities and delineate boundaries. The population was tracked and provided for. New data, such as the medical statistics gathered by the General Register Office, were used to chart disease and death and to devise public health measures. New forms of bureaucracy were instigated. The Income Tax, first raised to the fund the Napoleonic Wars during 1799–1815, was reinstated permanently in 1842. The idea that society could not be improved without the production of orderly facts and numbers became commonplace.

But right from the start, the state was sensitive to questions of privacy. Authorities understood that they could not intrude upon and extricate personal information as they chose. Simply gathering some of this information had been a fraught exercise. The first census, in 1801, was only rolled out after an acrimonious five-decade argument over whether an official population count should be made at all. A national census would 'molest and perplex every single family in the kingdom', thundered William Thornton, MP for York.[7]

The Statistical Society of London, founded in 1834, was explicit about its intention to 'carefully exclude all Opinions' and to restrict 'its attention rigorously to facts', that 'as far as possible' could 'be stated numerically and arranged in tables'.[8] The aim was to understand 'the average man', not the private business of the individual. The legitimacy of an increasingly powerful state rested on openness about government business and respect for private individuals and their families. The responsibility for raising the next generation fell primarily on the family, especially the mother.

While the eighteenth century was marked by the proliferation of manuals on public conduct, the nineteenth century shifted its focus to matters of domestic life. At the forefront of this stood Sarah Stickney Ellis, a devout Congregationalist from Yorkshire, who wrote a series of bestselling tomes that illuminated the path of domestic virtue and societal duty. Her titles alone speak volumes about her subject matter: *The Women of England: Their Social Duties and Domestic Habits* (1839), *The Daughters of England: Their Position in Society, Character and Responsibilities* (1842), *The Wives of England: Their Relative Duties, Domestic Influence and Social Obligations* (1843) and *The Mothers of Great Men* (1859).

Under the guidance of a husband and, most importantly of all, a wife, the Christian nuclear family would generate the values and behaviours necessary for the stability of society. It was one of the most important institutions for ensuring a well-behaved populace. As Ellis wrote, 'There is an honest pride which every true heart has a right to feel, and England's pride should be in the inviolable sanctity of her household hearths. When these are deserted, the sentence of her degradation will be sealed.'[9]

As the private domestic realm grew in status it became isolated from the rest of society, a seclusion that intensified over time. The middle classes began their migration to the suburbs, giving rise to the phenomenon of commuting. The separation between home and work grew ever more pronounced. In 1871, the introduction of statutory bank holidays and designated days off underscored the importance of family life.

There was a preoccupation with sealed letters, locked doors and the edges of gardens. 'Fences not only define boundaries and ensure security,' advised Mr Beeton, husband to Isabella, the renowned author of *Mrs Beeton's Book of Household Management*, 'they also convey ideas of possession and seclusion.' He issued a warning: if not properly tended to, fences could also project 'a reputable or disreputable character to a property'.[10]

Despite this growing emphasis on seclusion, most households remained bustling, noisy environments. In the mid-nineteenth century, only one-third of households were limited to the nuclear family; nearly half extended to include relatives, lodgers or the help. The wealthier the household, the more likely it was to employ servants.[11]

In *The Gentleman's House* (1864), architect Robert Kerr emphasized that the ideal house was a monument to privacy. 'It is a first principle with the better classes of English people that the Family Rooms shall be essential private, and as much as possible the Family Thoroughfares.'[12] The servants' quarters were to be separate, or designated routes were to be established to prevent unexpected encounters between the family and the staff. This arrangement, he emphasized, also applied to gentlemen of more modest means: 'However small and compact the house may be, the family must have privacy.'[13]

But in a sharp essay in the *Cornhill Magazine*, an influential literary periodical, the judge James Fitzjames Stephen (uncle to Virginia Woolf) described the triumph of domesticity over public life as a cultural catastrophe: 'it is in the highest degree dangerous ... to allow any one side of life to become the object of idolatry; and there are many reasons for thinking that domestic happiness is rapidly assuming that position in the minds of the more comfortable classes of Englishmen.'[14] What alarmed Stephen was the possibility that his countrymen might choose the pleasures of home life over the strenuous demands of distinguished achievement.

*

The significance of the private sphere also made it a tantalizing target for those who sought to penetrate its veiled mysteries. With the family held in such high regard and a boundary between public and private so strictly delineated, breaking through the protective carapace of private life was titillating – and good business. There was an appetite for the spectacle of domestic failure. Newspapers profited by covering the very indiscretions they decried. Editors invited victims to pay to keep their bad behaviour out of their pages.

Publicity and blackmail loomed as threats over households. Shame could strike without warning: an illegitimate birth, a son with a penchant for 'unnatural crimes', adultery, bankruptcy – each held the potential to plunge the ideal family into public disgrace. 'There are private histories belonging to every family, which, though they operate powerfully upon individual happiness, ought never to be named beyond the home-circle,' warned Sarah Stickney Ellis.[15]

'I only wish I could write something that would contribute to heighten men's reverence before the secrets of each other's souls,' wrote Mary Evans in 1859. Evans is now better known as George Eliot, and at this point her authorship under a *nom de plume* had recently become public knowledge.[16] She lived with her long-term lover, George Henry Lewes, who was married and had a family, and they had long fought to keep 'George Eliot's' identity secret so as not to alienate the respectable reading public. Failure to live up to high social expectations was a risk for every household, and the theme found its way into Eliot's literature. In her novella *The Lifted Veil*, she abandoned her realist style for a supernatural storyline that draws attention to the danger of invading the privacy of the mind. The central character, Latimer, is a sensitive and introspective man cursed with the mysterious gift of clairvoyance. This ability to foresee future events and read the thoughts of others reveals more than just the outer actions of people – it lays bare their inner lives, their unchecked, meanest and most unpleasant thoughts.

Latimer's gift is a double-edged sword. It grants him insight into what his friends and family really think, but at great personal cost. His marriage to Bertha is stripped of any comforting illusions as he sees her disdain and deceit. He is painfully aware of his father's disappointment; and his ability to hear the unspoken thoughts and judgements of acquaintances reveals their superficiality and insincerity. Casual, otherwise harmless social engagements are transformed by the brutal clarity of his perceptions, isolating him from meaningful human connection. His awareness of the inner world of others deprives him of the comforting illusions that typically sustain social bonds and relationships.

*

In the 1850s, Henry Mayhew, editor of *Punch*, conducted a detailed study of London's working class in *London Labour and the London Poor* (1861–2). His four-volume study chronicles life in the city, revealing poverty, illness and the devastating effects of the 1849 cholera outbreak. The pages vibrate with the voices of the unheard: an eight-year-old watercress seller near Farringdon market, a soot-covered chimney sweep labouring through darkness, a sewer-hunter navigating the murky underworld in search of discarded treasures, and the dog-dung collectors, trawling through the streets to scrape a living from waste. Mayhew recoiled at the 'heaps of indescribable filth' and the graveyard stench that permeated the air.

Britain's cities had rapidly expanded, but they were ill-prepared to accommodate the influx of people seeking better lives. Family homes were divided into cramped lodgings. New buildings were crammed in behind old ones, creating the infamous 'courts' in which hundreds of families lived cheek by jowl, their homes leaning together and blocking the air. Reports from the *Quarterly Review* depicted London's notorious slums, arranged like grey honeycomb, housing the poorest classes, thieves and prostitutes. The pubs were rowdy and lodging houses were overcrowded with men, women and children packed into fetid rooms. The police deemed these areas too dangerous to enter.

Social reformers, concerned about the highly uneven impact of industrialization and urbanization, sought to mitigate its harmful effects, leading to a raft of major social reforms. The Factory Acts of 1833 and 1867 first regulated working hours for children and then outlawed their employment. The Poor Law Amendment Act (1834) overhauled the system of welfare and poverty relief in England and Wales. The New Liberal philosopher, T. H. Green, an early proponent of the welfare state, called on the state to 'remove all obstacles' to individual development, which meant addressing education, public health and housing. The social contract around welfare entitlement would be an attempt to square the liberal circle: empowering individuals to make the best of themselves, *and* improving the lot of society.

Such concern became almost routine by mid-century, leading to the passage of two acts sponsored by Lord Ashley. The first was direct legislation aimed at improving the housing conditions of the working class in Britain. The Labouring Classes Lodging Houses Act of 1851 (also known as the Lodging Houses Act) allowed local authorities to build and regulate affordable lodging houses for workers. The second, the Common Lodging Houses Act of 1851, introduced regulations for existing lodging houses, requiring them to be registered and regularly inspected to ensure minimum standards of hygiene and safety for their often overcrowded residents.

In the parliamentary debates, Lord Ashley beseeched the honourable gentlemen in the room to listen to tales of horror about the lodging houses, arguing that 'nothing produced so evil an effect upon the sanitary conditions of the population as overcrowding within limited spaces; and if people were in a low sanitary condition, it was absolutely impossible to raise them to a just moral elevation'.[17] As the architect George Godwin tersely commented: 'it cannot too often be repeated, that the health and morals of the people are regulated by their dwellings'.[18] Godwin further remarked, 'If there were no courts and blind alleys, there would be less immorality and physical suffering.

The means of escaping from public view which they afford, generate evil habits.' Overcrowding and unsanitary conditions were tied to moral dissolution. It was widely thought that improvements in dreadful living conditions would also address the moral pestilence.[19]

These social reforms improved people's lives dramatically and may seem unquestionable today; public health reforms increased life expectancy exponentially and saved many lives. But they were also often loaded with moral baggage about how people should live and restrictions that were highly invasive and prescriptive. Those who built new housing or improved the old demanded the monitoring of lifestyles in return: the Commissioner of Police had to register each lodging house and ensure the separation of the sexes. Residents were questioned about how much they drank and where, or if, they worked.

There was always a tension within liberalism between freeing the individual and seeking their improvement, between liberty and social reform. Helping people also meant changing them, a project that might not always be welcomed by those on the receiving end. Social reformers who concerned themselves with how people lived, or who walked through the slums, often met resistance.

Henry Mayhew himself noted that there was a strong sense of community generated by the collective experience of hardship and resistance to outside interference. He records the case of a boy who had kicked at a policeman in a scuffle, noting: 'The whole of the court where the lad resided sympathized with the boy.' A young street seller informs him that 'all as lives in a court is neighbours'. Mayhew describes the daily social ceremonies of the shared space between the clustered rooms: the gathering of men and women at the mouth of the alley, where they meet for a chat and a smoke.[20] Alongside poverty and desperation, illegality and immorality, there was also a sense of community, rather than the more isolated experience of the middle classes.

While government provided the legal framework for institutions to deal with extreme problems of crime and punishment, it relied not only on the family but on the educational, cultural and social institutions of civil society to persuade certain sections of the population – usually the destitute and working poor – to behave. Churches and new civic institutions such as friendly societies were charged with enforcing appropriate moral conduct without the need for direct state intervention. Attempts to improve the conditions of the poor were accompanied by worthy campaigns that many found objectionable, and they were met with defiance.

In *Bleak House*, Dickens describes a visit to the home of a brick-maker's family by a well-heeled female philanthropist. She is duly rounded on for being a 'poll-pry', then a well-known description for someone who invaded people's privacy:

'I wants it done, and over. I wants a end of these liberties took with my place. I wants an end of being drawed like a badger. Now you're a-going to poll-pry and question according to custom – I know what you're a-going to be up to. Well! You haven't got no occasion to be up to it. I'll save you the trouble. Is my daughter a-washin? Yes, she IS a-washin. Look at the water. Smell it! That's wot we drinks. How do you like it, and what do you think of gin instead! An't my place dirty? Yes, it is dirty – it's nat'rally dirty, and it's nat'rally onwholesome; and we've had five dirty and onwholesome children, as is all dead infants, and so much the better for them, and for us besides. Have I read the little book wot you left? No, I an't read the little book wot you left. There an't nobody here as knows how to read it; and if there wos, it wouldn't be suitable to me. It's a book fit for a babby, and I'm not a babby. If you was to leave me a doll, I shouldn't nuss it. How have I been conducting of myself? Why, I've been drunk for three days; and I'da been drunk four if I'da had the money. Don't I never mean for to go to church? No, I don't never mean for to go to church. I shouldn't be expected there, if I did; the beadle's too genteel for me. And how did my wife get that black eye? Why, I give it her; and if she says I didn't, she's a lie!'

Social reformers often failed to understand that even people living in slum conditions might jealously guard their own private space. Social improvement involved a kind of surveillance that imposed its own burdens.

The Contagious Diseases Act (1864) enforced highly invasive medical inspections of all prostitutes, which were vigorously opposed – not least by the feminist Josephine Butler and her Ladies National Association, who argued that the laws were an insult to the liberty and dignity of women. Their campaign drew the support of thousands of people opposed to this invasion of privacy, even though the majority of them did not approve of prostitution.

Investing the home with political and moral significance, as the Tories did, made it ripe for intervention. Investing the private realm as the locus of human meaning, as the Whigs did, similarly granted it immense standing and opened the door to reformers and social improvers. The idealization of the private realm, and the social role attributed to it, led both Tory and Liberal reformers to seek to penetrate its fortress, to improve the welfare of those within. It also increased interest from scandalmongers and social moralists seeking to do good.

The question of the age was where to draw the line between the public realm, open to scrutiny and state intervention, and the private domain of the individual. These were not abstract debates, and they engaged much of society. It was a demarcation that applied not only to government and law but to the constraining influences of norms and customs. And it was an issue that preoccupied, among many others, John Stuart Mill – the greatest liberal philosopher of his time – and the love of his life, Harriet Taylor.

Chapter 10:

EXPERIMENTS IN LIVING

John Stuart Mill was not a charismatic speaker. But at the London Debating Society on the evening of Friday, 30 January 1829, arguing that William Wordsworth's poetry was superior to Lord Byron's, he was a determined one. Poetry, after all, had changed Mill's life.

The utilitarian John Arthur Roebuck opened the debate, proposing that Byron's work was the poetry of human life; Wordsworth, he mocked, was just flowers and butterflies.[1] It was a playful speech, and Roebuck, at twenty-seven, with brown hair and long, bushy sideburns, was an energetic opponent.

When it was his turn, twenty-two-year-old Mill stood tall and thin, radiating earnestness. He argued that a great poet must possess three gifts: a mastery of description, an ability to evoke the deepest of emotions, and the power to elevate the reader's character. Byron, he claimed, fell short of this ideal: he could paint pictures with words and stir the soul, but he lacked the ability to positively shape character. Wordsworth, Mill asserted with unwavering conviction, was the embodiment of poetic greatness. He excelled in descriptive brilliance and emotional depth, and he guided his readers towards moral and spiritual betterment.[2]

Both Roebuck and Mill were members of the Philosophical Radicals, an influential group advocating for radical political, economic and social reforms based on utilitarian principles. Their beliefs were heavily influenced by the ideas of Jeremy Bentham. Bentham was now eighty years old and his prolific output spanned everything from proposals for state governance to innovative designs for refrigerators, not to mention the Panopticon. Yet poetry held no place in his rigorous world of logic and reform. Bentham was adamant that 'All poetry was misrepresentation' – a departure from precise logical truth.[3] Above all, he deplored its tendency to heighten feelings, whether for effect or to persuade.

At the heart of the debate over poetry was a conflict between rationalism and sensitivity. Though Mill conceded that Roebuck was not devoid of feeling, he accused him of being closed to great emotion. He suggested that Roebuck, and by default Bentham, could not see the value of painting, music and poetry.[4] Mill, on the other hand, had opened himself up to the power of art, for which he owed Wordsworth a debt of gratitude. While he would never completely break with the Benthamites and the Philosophical Radicals, the case he made in favour of Wordsworth over Byron that night was his first declaration in public of his departure from pure Benthamite utilitarianism.

This was a turning point on Mill's path to becoming one of the nineteenth century's most influential philosophers. It established his intellectual trajectory and his position as a key advocate for the sanctity of the private sphere.

*

Mill was born on 20 May 1806, the son of James Mill, a Scottish-born historian who worked for the East India Company and had high ambitions for his son. In the hope of forging an accomplished and virtuous young man, and influenced by his good friend Jeremy Bentham, James Mill oversaw an intensive programme of home schooling for young John.

Mill's early life was a test case for John Locke's theory that every individual is born a *tabula rasa* on which learning can energetically be written. By the age of three, he was learning Greek; by seven, he was reading Plato. Aged eight, he was learning Latin. He helped his father write a *History of British India* (1817) when he was only twelve, even though he didn't yet know how to tie his shoelaces. By the age of thirteen he had completed a course in political economy, and by fifteen he was thoroughly versed in Bentham's philosophy.

His childhood was governed by an austere regime – no toys, no holidays, no amusements and no friends, other than books. While he was permitted to read poetry and write in verse, it was with the caveat that he must not enjoy it too much. Nothing was allowed to divert him from his studies, though he was occasionally permitted the indulgence of dancing.

By seventeen, young Mill had joined his father as a clerk at the East India Company, working in the office of the Examiner's Department, where he would remain for thirty-five years. It was not a strenuous job. He walked to his office in Leadenhall Street, arriving at ten o'clock, and took a breakfast of tea and a boiled egg with bread and butter. By one o'clock, his work was done. For the rest of the afternoon, he conversed with acquaintances about the reforming issues of the day. In the early days of his career, Mill was still committed to Benthamism, but he was restless. He had yet to make his mark and find himself intellectually. That would take a nervous breakdown.

As he turned twenty in the spring of 1826, Mill suffered a mental crisis. His life, meticulously structured according to rational and utilitarian principles, began to feel desolate and insufficient. He would recount this period of despair in his autobiography, describing how he felt trapped by the deterministic worldview he had inherited. He wrote of feeling like a slave to circumstance, his character shaped by forces beyond his control.

A breakthrough came when he encountered a passage in the memoirs of the French historian Jean-François Marmontel. As

Marmontel described the death of his father, Mill was suddenly overcome with emotion and wept. In that moment, his burden grew lighter and the dead feelings within him vanished. 'I was no longer hopeless,' he wrote. 'I was not a stock or a stone.'[5] This emotional release marked the beginning of his recovery. He found solace in the poetry of the early Romantics, particularly William Wordsworth and Samuel Taylor Coleridge, whose works provided him with the 'culture of feelings' essential for his mental and spiritual renewal.

Mill became convinced that the focus of the Philosophical Radicals was too narrow, that their proposals for technocratic reform of political arrangements and social education were not enough. He didn't give up on utilitarianism entirely, but aimed instead to find a place for feelings in an intellectual and political school of thought dominated by narrow rationalism. It was a journey away from Benthamite utilitarianism and towards the full realization of the individual – and the foundation of Mill's case for a private life. He came to believe that developing the 'internal culture of the individual' and the 'cultivation of feelings' was as important as changing the external structures of society.[6] It was a dramatic change in direction, reinforced in Mill by a second epiphany.

*

In the summer of 1830, Mill attended a dinner party in north London at the Finsbury Park home of John Taylor, a pharmacist, and his wife, Harriet. Mill had just turned twenty-four; Harriet, a slight woman of twenty-three with a luminous, pearlescent complexion, was not only striking in appearance but also a sharp intellect immersed in the pressing social and political debates of the day. Her husband, whom she had married at eighteen and with whom she had two sons, was indifferent to the causes that animated her spirit. However, her convictions about female equality and universal suffrage were, to Mill, both coherent and stimulating.

'Mrs Taylor, tho' encumbered with a husband and children, has ogled John Mill so successfully that he was desperately in love,' wrote Jane Carlyle, mildly scandalized.[7] Mill and Harriet began writing together and were soon a romantic couple. The Taylors tried separation. She travelled to Paris, where Mill spent six weeks with her. Theirs was to be one of the most discussed affairs of nineteenth-century Britain.

In the 1830s, divorce could only be granted by an Act of Parliament, which was expensive and available only to the rich. Women who did go through with it had to give up their children, who remained the property of their husbands. Both Taylor and Mill argued for liberal divorce laws that would allow couples to separate without giving reasons and without great expense, subject to a minimum two-year pause between suing for divorce and contracting another marriage. Yet even if such laws had been available, Harriet would not have abandoned her husband and children: 'I should spoil four lives & injure others,' she explained in a letter to Mill.[8] She remained married to Taylor and continued to live with him, but the three of them came to an arrangement that also allowed her to be with Mill. The precise personal details of the set-up are not known, though biographers have long speculated about them. Records do show that Mill paid for the wine for the Taylors' cellar.[9]

In the spring of 1851, twenty-one years after they met and two years after her husband died, Harriet Taylor married John Stuart Mill. After seven years of marriage, Harriet died of tuberculosis. Mill remained devoted to her memory, and she would influence his philosophy and political activity for years to come.

At the core of John and Harriet's intellectual partnership lay a question: what are the optimal conditions for human flourishing? Their answer, illuminated through vigorous discourse, resided in the concept of embracing a protected private sphere. They vehemently advocated for government restraint and the establishment of an arena free from the oppressive grip of social custom.

Mill's *On Liberty* (1859), one of the most celebrated works of political theory in history, is dedicated to Harriet's memory and influenced by her. In an earlier work, he had argued that the paramount principle of social organization is freedom. This, Mill argues, requires clearly defined borders. 'There is a circle around every human being,' he wrote, 'which no government, be it that of one, or a few, or of the many, ought to be permitted to overstep.'[10]

In *On Liberty*, Mill contended that any limits placed on individual freedom should be infrequent and strictly justified. 'His own good, either physical or moral, is not a sufficient warrant' to interfere with an individual's liberty, he argued, emphasizing that no one can rightfully be compelled to act in a certain way simply because others believe it to be better for him. Interventions are justified only when an individual's actions cause 'harm to others', which he defined narrowly.[11]

Rather than encroaching on the individual, Mill argued that laws and values should respect and support 'the moral and social relations of private life'. He characterized these relations as a powerful interest, even a 'right', imbued with a sense of 'moral necessity'. This respect was essential for the collective good as well as for the individual's well-being. A state which 'dwarfs' its men is not going to help the individuals composing it, he wrote.[12]

Mill did not oppose the state in principle. His focus – the oppressive force that he and Harriet had decried – was the assortment of social norms and opinions. In defending private life they were concerned with the deleterious influence of custom, as an excerpt from an unpublished essay by Harriet indicates: '[T]he root of all intolerance ... what is called the opinion of society, is a phantom power, yet as is often the case with phantoms, of more force over the minds of the unthinking than all the flesh and blood arguments which can be brought to bear against it. It is a combination of the many weak, against the few strong.'[13]

Neither Mill nor Harriet believed that 'anything goes'. They treasured, for example, the institution of marriage, even though they themselves had lived 'in sin'. But Mill and Harriet thought that individuals should be the authors of their own lives. They advocated for free spaces where people could experiment with different ideas and ways of living, even those with which they personally disagreed. As Mill put it in *On Liberty*: 'As it is useful that while mankind are imperfect there should be different opinions ... so it is that there should be different experiments in living; that free scope should be given to the varieties of character ... and the worth of different modes of life should be proved practically, when any one thinks fit to try them.'[14]

On Liberty is as much a book about self-improvement as it is about the absence of state interference and the pressure of social custom. Mill believed freedom fostered self-development, enabling individuals to emerge as moral agents. He argued that to live a good life involves continuously working upon oneself as an individual in a project of growth. Self-development and self-reliance encourage people to behave better and more consciously.

That said, Mill also believed that a person's pursuit of their own way of living should not exist in isolation from other people, because each individual's actions have direct and inevitable consequences for other members of society. But Mill and Taylor were inclined to be tolerant of those who made decisions about their own lives, even if they personally disapproved of those decisions. As Mill desired a poet such as Wordsworth to cultivate feelings and the self, so too did he value private life for the same reason.

*

In 1865, Mill was elected as the MP for Westminster on a platform that included votes for women. No MP before him had attempted to put down legislation for women's suffrage. His advocacy was influenced by Emily Davies and Elizabeth Garrett, both members of the Kensington Society – a group for educated middle-class women who were barred from higher education – and by his stepdaughter, Helen Taylor.

'Miss Mill joins the Ladies' (Edward John Eyre; Robert Wellesley Grosvenor, 2nd Baron Ebury; William Henry Smith; John Stuart Mill), wood-engraving by John Proctor, published in Judy, or The London Serio-Comic Journal, *25 November 1868.*

Mill agreed to present a petition to Parliament in favour of women's suffrage, providing they could get 100 signatures. They achieved 1,521. Mill spoke to the petition in Parliament on 17 July 1866. A year later, the House of Commons held the first debate on votes for women. The cause lost by 196 votes to 73, but Mill nevertheless welcomed the level of support, which came from both sides of the House. The press wielded its pen as a weapon, turning Mill into a figure of ridicule for his support of the 'fanciful' rights of women. Cartoonists often portrayed him in a dress and referred to him as the 'women's member'. In 1868, Mill would lose his seat. He continued, with Helen Taylor, to campaign for women's rights.

Mill went on to publish *On the Subjection of Women* (1869), which argued for full legal parity between men and women, including voting rights and equality in divorce law. Like his advocacy for a private life, Mill viewed personal autonomy as central to the issue of women's rights. This perspective led him to argue for changes in both the political and private spheres. He believed legal equality for women was a necessary condition for the well-being of the individual, and also for social progress: 'The legal subordination of one sex to another,' he argued, 'is wrong in itself, and now one of the chief hindrances to human improvement.'[15] As for the private sphere, he raged against the legally sanctioned power of husbands, which gave them power over their wives. In the House of Commons he had called attention to the physical abuse that saw women beaten, kicked and even trampled to death – violence that was effectively sanctioned by law.[16] The legal regulation of relations between husbands and wives, he argued, was a justifiable exception to the liberal principles of individual freedom. Reform was necessary to turn the family from a 'school of despotism' to a 'school of sympathy in equality' and a 'real school of the virtues of freedom'.[17]

The century saw a law in 1858 preventing aggravated assault of women and children, and another of 1878 that enabled women to obtain separation orders if they could demonstrate that their husbands were cruel to them. The Married Woman's Property Act (1870) finally gave women the right to hold private property in their own name after matrimony. But this was not enough for Mill. In *The Subjection of Women* he criticized the heavy hand of custom, as he had in *On Liberty*, eviscerating the dominant idea that it was 'natural' for women to be subjected. In this he followed on from the work of Mary Astell and Mary Wollstonecraft. He and Harriet had always contended that it wasn't possible to know what women were naturally good at if they weren't free to explore their talents.

Mill was confident that after his proposed reforms, women would still desire marriage and a family and be at home in the private realm – something for which modern feminists have since criticized him. But he advocated for women's suffrage for the same reasons he supported it for men: he believed that voting was essential for self-development, the protection of individual interests, and that political participation would 'enlarge the capacities' of each individual, and create subjects who are better equipped to contribute to the collective good. When women finally won equal rights in February 1928, Millicent Fawcett of the National Union of Women's Suffrage Societies led a delegation to lay a wreath beside Mill's statue.

*

Britain in the nineteenth century saw tumultuous change, with every aspect of life transformed. Private life became the focus of intense controversy between the individual's right to be left alone and the state's obligation to intervene to promote the greater good, a liberal ambivalence over privacy and the private realm that has persisted ever since.

Mill's contribution to the debates over where the borders of private life should begin and end was to show that the private domain is necessary for the individual to be able to explore different ways of thinking and living, away from interference and the stultifying force of social custom. By arguing that for women to realize their full potential, they needed legal protection in the private sphere and equal rights in the public sphere – without which, true autonomy or independence would be impossible – Mill demonstrated the mutual interdependence of the public and private spheres.

This interconnection resonated with many women, who would soon begin to advocate more forcefully for their liberation from the constraints of the private realm.

Chapter 11:

THE RIGHT TO BE LET ALONE

Marion Manola – star of the Broadway comic opera *Castles in the Air*, which opened in 1890 – was known for her vocal artistry, temperamental manner and incredible legs. On stage, Manola wowed audiences in her daring costume of fringed bodice and grey silk tights, but she was determined to control how she was photographed. She sought to shield her young daughter, Adelaide, and prevent the ordinary man on the street from seeing her in such revealing clothing.

Unfortunately for Manola, the march of technological progress threatened to dismantle her carefully constructed boundaries. The recent invention of the Kodak camera meant photography was no longer confined to professional studios but was available to anyone, anywhere. Advertisements for the portable device promised the 'thrill of capturing the likeness of a person without their knowledge'.[1] *The New York Times* ran articles warning of the 'Camera Epidemic'.[2] To be branded a 'Kodaker' became a stinging insult, while 'Kodak fiends' were decried as being in league with an 'evil spirit'.[3]

Photographs of members of the public snapped on the street or sunning themselves in the park – particularly women – were plastered over newspapers. They were shamelessly used by advertisers to sell products ranging from ashtrays to flour and soap, all without the subjects' consent. The affronted women, along with

*A party of camera 'fiends' in Yosemite Valley, California,
USA, c. 1902.*

their indignant husbands, occasionally sought redress. In 1888,
Republican congressman John Robert Thomas introduced 'A Bill
to Protect Ladies' into the House of Representatives. It held that
women who were related or married to American citizens (they
did not have the vote, and would not until 1920, so were not
strictly citizens themselves) were 'entitled to protection from the
vulgar and unauthorized use, for advertising purposes, of their
likeness'. But his bill did not pass.[4]

On the night of 14 June 1890, one Kodak fiend surreptitiously snapped a photograph of Manola on stage from an upper
box in the theatre. Using a camera with a magnesium flash, he

immediately caused a disruption. Manola stormed off into the wings, leaving the audience booing and jeering at the intruder. To the journalists who rushed to her side for her account of the incident, she made her position unequivocally clear. She told *The Baltimore Sun*, an influential daily newspaper, that she did not want her image 'to become common property, circulated from hand to hand, and treasured by every fellow who could afford it'.[5]

Ben Stevens, her theatre manager and the mastermind behind the stunt, dismissed Manola's complaint with a wave of his hand. Actresses had to understand that this sort of promotion was part of the game. To Stevens, the photograph and the storm of controversy it generated were valuable assets of publicity. Manola, however, was not to be so easily dismissed. She marched to court and sought an interim injunction preventing Stevens or the photographer from developing and using the photograph. And she won, but only because they failed to appear in court to lodge their defence.

The Baltimore Sun stood by Manola, grandly describing her claim as a defence of the 'sacredness of the person'.[6] But many other commentators were unconvinced, given that she was, after all, performing in public in those tights. Stevens was likely satisfied: the copious press coverage of the whole incident meant both his star and his production had achieved the attention he sought. Manola was victorious. She wanted to control her public image and would later pose for publicity photos wearing the same outfit that she had on when Stevens took the photograph.

As Victorian society struggled to reconcile advancements in technology and the demands of publicity with a desire to safeguard personal dignity, two studious lawyers entered the fray, claiming they had found the solution to this conflict.

*

*Dancer Marion Manola, photographed with her
permission in tights, 1890.*

Samuel D. Warren and Louis D. Brandeis hoped that their twenty-eight-page article 'The Right to Privacy', published in the *Harvard Law Review* in 1890, would stimulate a little more interest than their previous publication on the public's right to access ponds. To say their hopes were rewarded would be an understatement. The two Boston lawyers had written what would become the most famous article in the history of privacy. In it, they advanced an influential argument for privacy law and articulated a modern conception of privacy.

They had met at Harvard Law School. Warren, distinguished by a neatly trimmed moustache, was the scion of a wealthy paper

magnate; Brandeis had more modest beginnings. Born in Louis-
ville, Kentucky, in 1856, he was the son of Jewish immigrants
from Bohemia (now the Czech Republic) who had fled to the
United States following their involvement in the failed Austro-
Hungarian uprising of 1848 – a historical event foreshadowed by
Baron Philipp von Neumann, as revealed in the Mazzini letter-
opening scandal.

America was entering the dizzying rush of the Gilded Age,
marked by the rise of colossal corporate empires led by titans such
as John J. Astor, one of the wealthiest men in the world. Newspaper presses surged forward to cater to a growing population of
urban workers. Between 1850 and 1890, newspaper circulation
skyrocketed by 1,000 per cent, fuelled by advancements in the
telegraph and high-speed printing. By 1880, the nation boasted
11,000 newspapers, some with circulation figures exceeding a
million. Daily papers became the focus of a rapidly growing urban
society, feeding the endless hunger for information and shaping
the public discourse.

Stories of political corruption helped to fill column inches, as
did the behaviour of wealthy and high-status individuals, which
became the lifeblood of the society pages. The novelist Henry
James observed that 'the spirit of the age' was represented by 'the
invasion, the impudence and shamelessness of the newspaper and
the interviewer, the devouring publicity of life, the extinction of
all sense between public and private.'[7]

What was described as 'yellow' or 'keyhole' journalism was
characterized by sensationalized, exaggerated reporting aimed at
boosting sales and attracting readers. Such as when the actress,
chorus girl, and model Evelyn Nesbit Thaw found herself at the
heart of one of the most sensational scandals. In 1906, her husband, Harry K. Thaw, fatally shot renowned architect Stanford
White – Nesbit's former lover – at the rooftop theatre of Madison
Square Garden in New York. The shocking murder set the stage

Evelyn Thaw dodging a camera, White Plains, 1909.

for what would become known as the 'Trial of the Century'. The trial, which began the following year, captivated the press, with journalists and photographers relentlessly hounding Mrs Thaw. In the image below, she is seen attempting to shield herself from the camera's gaze.

In 'The Right to Privacy', Warren and Brandeis deplored the state of affairs created by instantaneous photographs and newspapers, which, as they put it, 'invaded the sacred precincts of private and domestic life' so that 'what is whispered in the closet shall be proclaimed from the housetops'. The press, they argued, was 'overstepping in every direction the obvious bounds of propriety and decency', intruding upon 'the domestic circle' and thereby 'lowering social standards and morality'.[8] Gossip columns featured members of Samuel Warren's own family and social circle, much to their dismay. Their close friend Mrs Grover Cleveland, wife of the 22nd and 24th US president, was also routinely pursued by Kodakers.

Scouring the law books for a remedy, they discovered that there was no specific mention of privacy in the Constitution. The Fourth Amendment of the Bill of Rights did guarantee the inalienability of the domestic sphere based on property. Ratified in December 1791 and inspired by the ideas of Edward Coke, the amendment prohibited 'unreasonable searches and seizures' in people's homes. But its authors had not, of course, foreseen the concept of privacy invasion in the age of portable cameras and newspapers, where personal lives could be exposed without physical intrusion. Nor was there any redress for offences against the person when truthful but embarrassing gossip harmed an individual's dignity and honour. The First Amendment, in fact, guaranteed free speech and protections for newspapers.

Warren and Brandeis pored over recent international court decisions with earnest determination, seeing within them the embryonic principles of privacy rights. With scholarly gravity, they acknowledged the courageous stand of Marion Manola. They nodded knowingly at the outcome of *Prince Albert* v. *Strange*, in which the Prince defended his and Queen Victoria's ownership of their private etchings. Legislation passed in France in 1868 also caught their interest with its pioneering framework that limited what the press could reveal about an individual's personal life. It was time, they argued, for America to pull together all these legal nods to privacy and formalize its own law: the modern person had 'a right to be let alone'.[9] Their borrowing of this expression from Judge Thomas Cooley's dry text *The Law of Tort* was a masterstroke. It struck a chord and entered the vernacular.

'The intensity of modern life, attendant upon advancing civilization,' they wrote, 'has rendered necessary some retreat from the world.' They observed that 'under the refining influence of culture', the individual had become more sensitive to publicity, making solitude and ever more privacy essential. The threat of invasions was now so dire that the resulting mental pain and distress were 'far greater than could be inflicted by mere bodily injury'.[10] Their idea of privacy wasn't about limiting the state's reach into private thoughts or stopping it at the door. Instead, Warren and Brandeis described it in terms of protecting 'the inviolate personality', or, as *The Baltimore Sun* had put it, the 'sacredness of the person'.[11] The modern self needed privacy.

In Edith Wharton's novella *The Touchstone* (1900), a renowned female novelist's confidences are posthumously broken when a collection of her love letters – filled with 'tragic outpourings of love, humility and pardon' – are published. The letters, sold by Stephen Glennard, the man she loved but who never returned her feelings, were used to fund his own romance and marriage. Glennard is consumed by guilt as the letters become the talk of the town. The 'book is in the air', thrills one member of society, 'one breathes it in like the influenza'. Another, Mrs Touchett, condemns the publication: 'It's the woman's soul, absolutely torn up by the roots – her whole self laid bare . . . I don't mean to read another line; it's too much like listening at a keyhole.' Despite her objections, she is irresistibly drawn to the letters, intrigued by their promise to reveal a well-known woman's private truth.

Warren and Brandeis proposed a radical solution. While the law should not restrict the publication of matters of 'public or general interest' or information about 'public figures', it should protect the privacy of individuals who did not hold public roles. Judges and the courts would decide what the public had a right to know, ensuring that 'public matters' like Congressional deliberations remained accessible while press coverage of 'the private life, habits, acts, and relations of an individual' would be limited. For private individuals, they argued that the right to privacy should prevent not only inaccurate portrayals but any depiction of private life. In their view, the truth was secondary to safeguarding individuals from the invasive public gaze. Warren and Brandeis argued that ordinary people should have the right to control how their thoughts, sentiments and emotions were published. They believed that letters, diary entries and photographs should receive the same protection as valuable poems or essays.

The article was an immediate sensation. Certain more cerebral publications embraced their proposal. *The Atlantic Monthly* enthused, 'Surely it is impossible that the law, which we are accustomed to regard as an agency for protecting our lives and our pockets, with a perfect disregard of feelings, should stoop to concern itself with the privacy of the individual, and yet nothing less than this appears to be the conclusion of a learned and interesting article.'[12]

However, the reception in the broader public sphere was notably cooler. The *Texas Galestone Daily News*, in a characteristically acerbic appraisal, dismissed the men as 'thin skinned'.[13]

While the courts did not accept their analysis, Warren and Brandeis's arguments did influence civil law. In the decades that followed, arguments over 'The Right to Privacy' dominated discussions in courtrooms across America. According to Roscoe Pound, dean of Harvard Law School from 1916 to 1936, it did nothing less than add a chapter to the law books.[14]

The publication of 'The Right to Privacy' was a seminal moment. Privacy had been forged as a particular concept and positively valued in Britain, but it was the United States that first saw systematic attempts to protect it in law. Warren and Brandeis endeavoured to broaden and extend the concept from safeguarding property to protecting the modern self.

*

Almost as soon as 'The Right to Privacy' was published, Brandeis revisited the work with a critical eye. He admitted to his fiancée, Alice Goldmark, that he no longer found it as compelling as he once had. After considering the potential consequences of restricting press freedom – particularly the loss of essential public oversight – he revised his conclusions, believing that democracy could not endure limitations on the circulation of knowledge. He told Goldmark about his intention to write a companion piece, 'The Duty of Publicity', in which he would argue that exposing actions to the 'broad light of day' would purify them 'as the sun disinfects'.[15]

Brandeis never wrote that piece, but he spent much of his later career addressing the tension between privacy and free speech. He argued that preventing journalists from saying unflattering things about public figures would severely harm public discourse, allowing falsehoods and wrongdoing to go unchecked and undermining accountability.

Brandeis understood that meaningful civic engagement required the public to have unrestricted access to information. But while he maintained that free speech should prevail in conflicts with privacy, he did not abandon the concept of privacy entirely. He recognized the challenges posed by emerging technologies and a powerful government and continued to address these issues throughout his career, leaving a legacy on the twentieth century.

*

In the waning months of 1924, at the height of Prohibition, Roy Olmstead, a notorious figure in the clandestine alcohol trade of the Pacific Northwest, found his empire under siege. Olmstead was famed for the quality of his liquor, which was never tainted by dilution, and had built an impressive operation that defied bans on the sale and importation of alcohol. But that operation came crashing down when federal agents planted wiretaps in the basement of the building housing his office and along the streets near his home. The conversations they recorded provided evidence of Olmstead's illegal activities. In *Olmstead* v. *United States* (1928), he and his co-defendants were convicted.

Olmstead, a former police officer, was confident in his knowledge of the law. He was convinced that the tap had violated his Fourth and Fifth Amendment rights: the rights against unreasonable searches and seizures and against self-incrimination, respectively. On those grounds, he appealed the conviction. In the 'whispering wires' case, as it became known, he also pointed to the fact that wiretapping was illegal in Washington state, as it was in twenty-seven other states. The surveillance of his telephone calls, he said, had been executed without a warrant. The Ninth Circuit Court of Appeals rejected his appeal. It ruled that the federal agents' wiretapping of Olmstead's telephone had not trespassed on his property, and thus did not violate the Fourth Amendment.

Olmstead fought on. He took his case to the Supreme Court, which, in a narrow five to four decision, upheld his conviction. Speaking for the majority, William Howard Taft argued that the United States did not consider telephone conversations to be protected as much as mailed and sealed letters. Referring to the Fourth Amendment, he noted that there had been no searching and no seizure. There was no entry of the house or offices.[16]

By this time, Louis Brandeis was a Supreme Court justice. In his dissenting opinion he argued that listening to a private phone call was akin to reading a sealed letter, and that wiretapping should be covered by the Fourth Amendment. Brandeis also contended that the government should not violate state laws to gather evidence, as the federal government had done in Washington, where wiretapping was illegal.[17]

He later warned that without constitutional protections, emerging technologies beyond wiretapping could be exploited by the government to threaten individual privacy: 'Through television, radium and photography, ways may soon be developed by which the Government can, without removing papers from secret drawers, reproduce them in court and by which it can lay before the jury the most intimate occurrences of the home.'[18]

Although he would be proven wrong about television and radio, Brandeis was right in this respect: technological change would facilitate governments and other entities unprecedented access to sensitive personal information without breaking down the doors of private homes.

Chapter 12:

A ROOM OF ONE'S OWN

On a rainy summer's day in 1896, Charlotte Perkins Gilman stepped onto the speaker's platform in a corner of London's Hyde Park where speech was unrestricted. Standing alongside such luminaries as the Irish socialist and playwright George Bernard Shaw, she surveyed a crowd of eager faces shielded by umbrellas. With her chin held high, Gilman began to address the audience on the topic of 'the woman question', encompassing female suffrage, economic independence and the sobering reality of privacy for women.

Born on 3 July, 1860, in Hartford, Connecticut, Gilman had always defied the social norms imposed on her gender. As a young woman, she rejected the boned corset and ingeniously crafted one of the earliest modern bras for herself. She attended classes at the Rhode Island School of Design and began a career as a designer of trade cards. She also confided to her diary that she would never marry, because doing so would limit her ability to improve the world.

Gilman was deliciously happy when she fell in love with Martha Luther, and planned to set up house with her. But when Luther became engaged to a man, those dreams turned to dust. A few years later, in 1884, Gilman broke her own vow not to marry and accepted a proposal from the painter Charles Walter Stetson. Gilman gave birth to a daughter, Katharine, a year later, and succumbed to a tidal wave of debilitating postnatal depression. She spent years feeling wretched and continually in tears.

After she could bear it no more, in the spring of 1887, she travelled to Philadelphia to consult Dr Silas Weir Mitchell, a venerated nerve specialist (and, incidentally, the only medical doctor to have a rattlesnake named after him: *Crotalus mitchellii*). Weir Mitchell diagnosed her with hysteria and prescribed that she live a life as domestic as possible. She was to eat a diet rich in dairy produce and have much bed rest. Intellectual stimulation was to be completely avoided – she was not to touch a pen, pencil or brush. She was to isolate from her extended family and friends but always have her child with her. Weir Mitchell believed that if modern women stopped wanting things that were not good for them – education, work, the vote – they would find happiness. He called it the 'rest cure'.

Gilman followed his instructions for two months, by which point she was crawling into closets and hiding under beds to escape her grinding distress. As she came perilously close to losing her mind, she had an epiphany. Her problem wasn't too *little* rest. It was too *much*. Ripping up Weir Mitchell's prescription, she pursued her own course of treatment. She named it the 'west cure'.[1]

After persuading Stetson to agree to a divorce, she moved to Pasadena, California. Soon she was writing up a storm in the cause of becoming a 'world-server', and she never stopped. In her first year of 'freedom' she wrote thirty-three short articles, twenty-three poems and ten short verses.

The Yellow Wallpaper (1892) is Gilman's most renowned work. The novella features an unnamed narrator, her physician husband John, and their new baby, who retreat to a long-deserted country house for the summer in hopes of providing her with much-needed rest. The narrator, battling what her husband describes as a 'temporary nervous depression – a slight hysterical tendency', is forbidden from working and designated a room with iron-barred windows and repellent wallpaper the colour of sulphur. Her days blur together as she starts to obsess over the wallpaper, leading her to discern intricate patterns and perceive a woman imprisoned within its confines. Gradually, she comes to identify herself as this trapped figure. For Gilman, this fictional descent into claustrophobic insanity mirrored the grim reality of 'privacy' – a reality she herself had fled in search of a different life.

In her book on women and economics (1898), Gilman confronted the reality of 'privacy' as it applied to women: 'From parlour to kitchen, from cellar to garret, she is at the mercy of children, servants, tradesmen, and callers. So chased and trodden is she that the very idea of privacy is lost to her mind; she never had any, she doesn't know what it is.'[2] As she put it, 'Such privacy as we do not have in our homes is family privacy, an aggregate privacy; and this does not insure – indeed, it prevents – individual privacy.'[3] She reflected on how the home came with clearly assigned gender roles that limited women's choices, while men were free to pursue their interests and work in whatever industry they chose.

Gilman argued that the reality of marriage and the nature of family life had to be improved and that women needed economic independence. She argued that three measures were required to change women's lives: first, the private realm, her place of 'aggregate privacy', needed reforming; second, it had to be possible to leave it; and third, public life had to be open to women. Gilman sought thus to transform the private *and* the public spheres. Her work was translated into seven languages, catapulting her into the role of an intellectual leading light in the women's movement.

Warren and Brandeis had acknowledged that all individuals, regardless of social standing, were vulnerable to privacy breaches, but many of the examples and potential legal remedies they cited were focused on safeguarding women. Terms like 'propriety', 'decency' and 'modesty' were frequently linked with privacy. Ideas surrounding privacy and private life tended to reinforce specific expectations of female conduct, and could serve as justification for men to exert power over women and children within their households. In fact, opponents of women's suffrage referred to *their* right to a private life as a reason not to give women the vote. As one American senator put it in 1881, the enfranchisement of women was the equivalent of breaking in 'through a man's household, through his fireside . . . to open to the intrusion of politics and politicians that sacred circle of the family'.[4]

Generally, the law protected the privacy of the man in the home, a space where he could control the lives of his wife and children. Such respect for privacy could be a respectable cover for abuse.

*

In January 1868, Elizabeth Rhodes sat in a wood-panelled courtroom and braced herself for the verdict. The case was the first time the Supreme Court of North Carolina had considered whether wife-beating was a criminal offence.

The previous year, Elizabeth had taken her husband, A. B. Rhodes, to the Wilkes County Courthouse in the north-west of the state to have him charged with assault and battery. She alleged that he had whipped her with a switch as thick as his thumb. No one disputed her testimony. The jury heard from the defendant himself, who conceded that he had struck his wife with three licks, 'without any provocation' except for 'a few slight words' that he could 'not exactly recollect'.[5] Nevertheless, the verdict was unfavourable to Elizabeth. Despite the court recognizing that her husband had committed the assault, the jury did not rule in her favour.

Elizabeth filed an appeal, but the Supreme Court of North

Carolina upheld the lower court's decision. The judge's explanation makes for interesting reading. 'The violence would without question have constituted a battery,' Justice Edwin G. Reade acknowledged in his written opinion – but only if the subject had not been the defendant's wife. Justice Reade clarified that the law of the state 'did not recognize the right of the husband to whip his wife', but that the courts were 'loath to take cognizance of trial complaints arising out of the domestic relations'. 'Not because those relationships are not subject to the law,' he went on, but because 'the evils of publicity would be greater than the evil involved in the trifles complained of' and 'because they ought to be left to family government'.[6]

The costs of invading a married couple's privacy were, in the justice's view, greater than the damage wreaked by beating a spouse: 'For, however great are the ills of evil temper and even personal conflicts inflicting only temporary pain, they are not comparable with the evils which would result from raising the curtain, and exposing to public curiosity and criticism, the nursery, the bedchamber.'[7] Justice Reade warned that attempts such as Elizabeth Rhodes' to rely on the courts to settle domestic disputes would transform 'private trifles' and turn them into 'public traumas'. He argued that drawing a 'crowd around the seclusion' of the family would do harm. Intervention into the private realm, he concluded, would only make disagreements worse; and things 'which ought to be forgotten in a day, will be remembered for life'.

The ruling was a landmark because it formally subordinated women's protection under the law to the protection of family honour. It would later enrage campaigners for women's rights, many of whom in the next century came to see the very existence of the private realm as the precondition for violent oppression.

*

Charlotte Perkins Gilman distinguished between 'aggregate privacy' for the family, which she saw as detrimental to women, and 'individual privacy', which she considered essential for female emancipation. The need for women to have their own private space within the home was a concern for many early twentieth-century women writers, including Virginia Woolf.

Woolf also experienced the 'rest cure' pioneered by Dr Silas Weir Mitchell. Like Gilman, she rejected it, and she discreetly ridiculed Weir Mitchell in *Mrs Dalloway* through the character of Dr Bradshaw, a greedy physician who dominates his patients and prescribes them weight gain and bed rest. Woolf, too, had something to say about private life and privacy. As a rejoinder to the English poet Coventry Patmore's popular sequence of poems *The Angel in the House* (1854–62), which idealized the life of a devoted wife and mother, Woolf argued that 'Killing the Angel in the House' should be a central occupation of the female writer. And in *A Room of One's Own* (1929) she argued that dignity and creativity were 'the offsprings of luxury and privacy and space', which women writers and other professional types should be able to claim, as their male equivalents did.[8]

Woolf pursued Gilman's demand, arguing for emancipation from the stifling confines of aggregated private life within the family to obtain the freedom to pursue individual privacy in 'a room of one's own'. She saw that privacy had protective qualities that could create a space for women in which they could develop their ideas and their own sense of self. Woolf understood that the development of an inner life was necessary to art, and that it required solitude and space away from others. Her insights, informed by feminism and modernism highlighted the disparity between men's access to both public life and solitary introspection.

The concept of aggregated privacy to protect the family unit that had so enraged Gilman – and given the Supreme Court of North Carolina grounds to find in favour of a domestic abuser – was giving way to something more individuated. The 'right to be let alone' and the desire for 'a room of one's own' were no longer matters of freedom from state interference. They reflected the individual's need for a place of retreat and reflection, apart from a frenetic public existence.

As the nineteenth century gave way to the twentieth, the idealization of the private sphere would fade. Less than seventy years after the Mazzini letter scandal and the publication of 'The Right to Privacy', the cultural pendulum would swing away from the unmitigated value of privacy back towards an emphasis on the risks that it can pose.

PART IV:
Border Crossings

Chapter 13:

THE HIDDEN ROOTS
OF HUMAN BEHAVIOUR

In the ashes of the fallen Habsburg Empire, Vienna in the 1920s stood at a crossroads between the old world and a rapidly evolving new one. A city steeped in centuries of imperial grandeur, it was now a cauldron of intellectual fervour, artistic rebellion and political upheaval. It attracted some of the boldest thinkers of the time. Here, in this cultural ferment, Sigmund Freud delved into the deepest recesses of the human mind. Arnold Schoenberg shattered the conventions of classical music; dissonant and raw, his atonal compositions reflected a world on the brink of change. And Egon Schiele, with his jagged portraits, brimming with emotional and sexual frankness, mirrored the era's interest in the psyche.

From this charged atmosphere, three remarkable men emerged, each destined to revolutionize how Americans would view human behaviour: Paul Lazarsfeld, a brilliant social scientist, would become a pioneer in using statistics to decode the mysteries of human actions. Edward Bernays, the nephew of Freud, took insights from psychology and twisted them into the emerging field of public relations to mould public opinion in ways few had ever imagined. And Ernest Dichter, who sought to uncover the hidden desires of consumers, creating a roadmap for modern marketing and advertising. Their theories and methods would ripple through academia, government and corporate boardrooms, for ever changing how institutions engaged with the public. Aiming to understand people's deepest desires and fears, they delved into what was once the private and subjective world of the individual, striving to influence human actions.

Most intriguing of all was the warmth of their welcome and how they cleared a path for those who followed, including a most curious figure: a wasp expert named Alfred Kinsey. Kinsey, an American biologist, would later probe the most intimate corners of human behaviour, overstepping all earlier boundaries of propriety.

*

Paul Lazarsfeld, a mathematics postgraduate, came of age in a politically active Jewish family. His father, a lawyer, and his mother, a psychologist, were well connected with the leaders of the Social Democratic Workers Party. However, the crushing defeat of the German Revolution in 1919 dealt a blow to Lazarsfeld's aspirations. The revolutionary Socialist Student Movement, which he had hoped to influence, disintegrated. Lazarsfeld and his comrades were forced to reconsider their strategies and look elsewhere to make an impact.

Seeking to understand the underlying reasons behind the failure of their political movements, Lazarsfeld turned to the study of influence and persuasion. As he put it: 'A fighting revolution requires economics (Marx); a victorious revolution requires engineers (Russia); a defeated revolution calls for psychology (Vienna).'[1] He set up the Austrian Research Study for Economic Psychology in 1927 to undertake rigorous statistical analysis, which was his forte, and combined it with insights from psychoanalysis to address complex political, economic and social problems.

Lazarsfeld found that studying apparently trivial matters could be enlightening. A study of working-class radio listeners, which showed that they preferred sweet chocolate, strong perfume and coffee over more complex and subtle tastes, led him to surmise that poverty left people starved not just of the necessities of life, but of pleasure itself. He concluded that his research methods had uncovered what he described as the 'hidden dimensions' of decision-making. Before long, his insights attracted interest from businesses.[2]

When the owners of a failing laundry asked him to increase their trade, he interviewed housewives, discovering that they were reluctant to send their washing to the laundry because it didn't fit their image of what a housewife should do. They would only relent if there was an emergency, such as a sick child or extra guests. But once they did send in their washing, they didn't return to doing it themselves. Lazarsfeld suggested the owners write to families who had recently experienced a bereavement. Orders picked up overnight.

With the rise of the Nazis, life in Vienna became impossible. Fortunately, one of Lazarsfeld's studies, *Marienthal: The Sociography of an Unemployed Community* (1933), which examined the social and psychological effects of the economic depression in a village south-west of Vienna, was well received in the international research community. The Rockefeller Foundation awarded him a two-year travelling fellowship to the United States. Robert Lynd, a sociologist at Columbia University, helped him emigrate and settle for good.

The relationship between Lazarsfeld and the Lynds was a meeting of minds. Robert Lynd and his wife, Helen, shared an enthusiasm for Thorstein Veblen's foundational classic *The Theory of the Leisure Class* (1899) and were interested in the issues of social stratification, urbanization and the effects of industrialization. They had also conducted pioneering research, notably a study of Muncie, Indiana, which resulted in their hugely influential research report *Middletown: A Study in Modern American Culture* (1929).

Without revealing their purpose, the Lynds had moved to Muncie, which they had identified as a typical American town, and spoken with as many locals as they could: men on their way to work or nursing drinks at bars, women shopping or visiting the library, and high school students at diners. They then compared their qualitative findings with Census Bureau data.

In *Middletown*, the Lynds painted a vivid portrait of Muncie, as if chronicling a distant tribe. They noted that streetlights flickered on at 6 a.m. in the working-class neighbourhoods, ensuring factory and construction workers could start their day on time, while middle-class streets remained dark. Their findings revealed that public speeches were growing shorter and church attendance was on the decline. Women were entering the workforce, becoming less likely to bake their own bread, and opting for cotton stockings over silk. Homes sparkled with new consumer goods: flushing toilets, washing machines, refrigerators, telephones. Teenagers went to the movies without their parents, and boys picked up their dates in motorcars – much to the dismay of a local judge, who railed against the 'houses of prostitution on wheels'.[3]

Unexpectedly, the 500-page report was a hit. 'Nothing is so interesting as yourself, and this was like looking at yourself in the mirror,' was how *Good Housekeeping* magazine heralded the hulking tome.[4] 'Nothing like it has ever before been attempted; no such knowledge of how the average American community works and plays has ever been packed between the covers of one book,' enthused Stuart Chase in *The Nation*, claiming that 'Whoever touches the book touches the heart of America.'[5] The *Literary Digest* described *Middletown* as a 'peep through the keyhole' of American life.[6] And a journalist from Iowa promised, 'Here is the chance to look at yourself from the outside, to see what you and your neighbours are up to.'[7] Even the usually cynical essayist

H. L. Mencken was effusive: 'It reveals, in cold-blooded, scientific terms, the sort of lives millions of Americans are leading.' In Mencken's judgement, *Middletown* was 'as exhilarating as even the dirtiest of the new novels'.[8] The book went through six printings in its first year of publication. Librarians had to order extra copies. *Middletown* had found an audience who, it seemed, couldn't read enough about themselves.

Middletown was an early snowball in an avalanche of sociological research that encouraged Americans to answer questions about themselves and stimulated their interest in the results. In this respect it was followed by George Gallup, who founded his polling company in 1935 and soon became a household name. Dr Gallup always emphasized his scholarly credentials. He insisted that he was apolitical and indifferent to election outcomes, and focused solely on understanding the public mood. To achieve this, he argued, researchers needed a 'laboratory mindset' and training in the scientific method.[9]

The enthusiasm shown for studies like *Middletown* and Gallup's polling sharply contrasted with the scepticism that met government-led research. Efforts to conduct the national census in the 1940s ignited a firestorm of controversy, leading to Senate hearings on Capitol Hill. The census aimed to gather extensive demographic information to aid in national planning and resource allocation. It included not only basic information like age and sex but also detailed inquiries about income, education, occupation and home ownership. Testimonies during the hearings raised alarms about 'snoopers collecting statistics' and likened the fact-gathering process to the invasion of precious secrets.[10] They highlighted the fear of government overreach and the need for safeguards to protect individual privacy. Critics of the census raised questions about the ethical implications of collecting such detailed information.

The academic foundation and scientific presentation of studies like the Lynds' and Gallup's work gave them a legitimacy that government efforts lacked. As one commentator praised *Middletown*: 'No one who wishes a full understanding of American life today can afford to neglect this impartial, sincerely scientific effort to place it under the microscope slide.'[11] Or, as another reviewer put it: 'Scientists armed with questionnaires and statistical charts, have ... penetrated the inmost privacies of the town with patience and cunning.'[12]

Across the Atlantic in 1937, the UK also embarked on an ambitious research venture with the Mass-Observation project. It aimed to study the lives of ordinary people, using qualitative methods to achieve an 'anthropology of ourselves'. The project employed a combination of methods. It conducted surveys, and gathered diaries from the general population. It also included detailed written observations by volunteer 'observers' to note individuals' conversations and actions on the streets and during public meetings, religious gatherings and sporting events. The welcome it received was more tentative than any American counterpart.

The Mass-Observation study revealed a nation deeply protective of personal boundaries, finding: 'The desire for privacy, for keeping oneself to oneself, is a powerful motive in modern society.'[13] As the social reformer Margery Spring Rice noted, 'In England, alongside the fervent wish to protect the sanctity of the family, there is a resolute determination to keep it as isolated as possible from other families and external intrusion.'[14]

*

As Lazarsfeld introduced psychological insights combined with statistical methods into academia, Edward Bernays – whose family had travelled from Vienna to New York City at the turn of the century – applied behavioural science to political power. In the 1920s, he worked with the Woodrow Wilson administration, which had established the Committee on Public Information, a federal effort to influence public opinion in support of the war. He later helped the US government orchestrate propaganda during peacetime, rebranding it as 'public relations'.

In his book *Propaganda* (1929), Bernays argued that 'the conscious and intelligent manipulation of the organized habits and opinions of the masses' was essential in a modern mass society. He believed governments couldn't rely on logical arguments to win over a public with limited education, especially in times of crisis. Instead, leaders had to appeal to hidden desires.

Bernays developed a theory called 'the engineering of consent', which involved using insights from psychology and the natural sciences to direct the public. He believed that experts in human behaviour could enable leaders to 'control and regiment the masses according to our will without their knowing about it'.[15] To achieve this, he argued, it was essential to appeal to the unconscious mind rather than to reason.

The methods Bernays promoted were a departure from traditional democratic ideals. The nineteenth-century vision of the rational 'liberal subject', capable of informed consent, was being supplanted by an understanding of the public as targets for psychological manipulation. As Bernays himself put it, 'Those who manipulate this unseen mechanism of society constitute an invisible government which is the true ruling power of our country. We are governed, our minds are moulded, our tastes formed, and our ideas suggested, largely by men we have never heard of . . . It is they who pull the wires that control the public mind.'[16]

Bernays' methods did, however, echo the philosophy of nineteenth-century positivism, which emerged in the wake of the French philosopher Auguste Comte. Comte believed society could be understood and governed through scientific methods, much like the natural world. He framed his theory as a critique of liberal values and envisioned a technocratic society run by experts, where individual autonomy was dismissed as outdated. Henri de

Saint-Simon, Comte's mentor, encapsulated this vision: 'The government of people will be replaced by the administration of things.'[17] Comte had a great hold on certain Victorian intellectuals, but not John Stuart Mill. While Mill initially appreciated Comte's efforts to systematize the social sciences, he grew concerned with Comte's technocratic and authoritarian vision, fearing it would suppress individuality and freedom – values Mill saw as essential to human progress and societal flourishing.

In the twentieth century, positivism was always stronger in US academic and public institutions than in Britain. Britain's politics departments were closer to the discipline of history and an academic association called the Political Studies Association, whereas the US typically had departments of political science and political science associations.

Bernays' stark views on the public's deficiencies were far from unique in his time: terms like *mass society* were often used pejoratively, particularly in the early twentieth century, as voting rights began to expand. Influential thinkers such as Walter Lippmann and philosopher John Dewey engaged in heated debates over the public's capacity for meaningful, informed decision-making. Lippmann, who had led a propaganda unit during the First World War, argued that the ideal of the public as rational participants in democracy was fundamentally misguided. In *The Phantom Public* (1925), he asserted that the average citizen lacked the necessary knowledge to engage responsibly in politics: 'The public must be put in its place . . .' he wrote, 'so that each of us may live free of the trampling and the roar of a bewildered herd.'[18] In contrast, Dewey remained optimistic about the potential for ordinary people to engage effectively at the ballot box. He opposed the idea that experts and technology could replace genuine public deliberation, championing instead the belief that democracy thrives when citizens actively participate in discourse and decision-making.

But as Americans watched Hitler and Mussolini harness the

mass media to appeal to populations that seemed all too easily persuaded by Strong Men, febrile anxieties about the imperfections of democracy escalated. Serious discussions of the public's susceptibility to persuasion could be heard in many quarters. Explicitly critical of the old model of a democratic system and the rational citizen, psychological techniques and behaviourist theories dominated political discourse.

*

American businesses had largely ignored the importance of tracking consumer habits – until Paul Lazarsfeld's statistics student Ernest Dichter came along. (Although the Harvard Bureau of Business Research was opened in 1911, reluctant businesses didn't at first see the point of collecting such information.) Dichter's ideas would transform the landscape of marketing for ever.

'The thing about bathing,' he told executives at the New York Compton Advertising Agency, who were smirking in their grey flannel suits, in the summer of 1939, 'is that it is one of the few occasions when the puritanical American was allowed to caress himself or herself.'[19]

Only a year earlier, Dichter, a thirty-one-year-old with a striking head of red hair, had fled Vienna with his wife Hedy, a concert pianist. When they arrived in Manhattan, Lazarsfeld helped him secure a position in a market research firm, from where he wrote to companies: 'I am a young psychologist from Vienna . . . and I have some interesting new ideas which can help you be more successful, sell more and communicate better with your potential client.'[20]

Knowing that Freud's name opened cheque-books on Madison Avenue, Dichter bragged that he had lived on the same street as the master of psychoanalysis. Though they had never met, the name-drop was enough. Freud's ideas that subconscious urges and socialized inhibitions could be managed and harnessed seized the imagination of the corporate world. Dichter rode this wave of interest, receiving business account after business account.

The Compton Advertising Agency hired Dichter to help them sell Ivory soap. Traditional market research typically involved asking shoppers questions like, 'Why do you use this soap brand?' However, Dichter knew such questions were ineffective because people often couldn't articulate their true motivations. 'You would be amazed to find how often we mislead ourselves, regardless of how smart we think we are, when we attempt to explain why we are behaving the way we do,' he commented in his book *The Strategy of Desire* (1960).[21]

Dichter envisioned human motivation as an 'iceberg': two-thirds hidden from view, even to the decision-maker. He believed that to understand what motivated people, it was necessary to get them to talk at length about their everyday habits so they would inadvertently reveal lower parts of the iceberg. By burrowing deep beneath the surface and accessing consumers' hidden emotions, irrational behaviours and unconscious desires, it would become obvious how to market a product.

He ran in-depth psychoanalytical interviews for Compton in which he asked interviewees about their bathing experiences. He found that it was a ritual that afforded moments of fantasy and indulgence, particularly before a romantic date. Dichter often emphasized the erotic element in purchasing. He also worked out that it was women who usually made the key purchasing decisions in a family, which had previously been missed. As for why customers picked a particular brand, Dichter concluded that it wasn't just the price or even the look or feel of the soap, but the *gestalt* or 'personality' of the soap, which could be old or young, male or female, sexy or pure. Ivory, Dichter realized, carried utilitarian, purifying associations; it was a soap for mothers and their daughters. His work led to the slogans: 'Be Smart and Get a Fresh Start with Ivory Soap' and 'Wash Your Troubles Away'.[22]

Dichter amassed a fortune by leveraging psychological insights that revolutionized the advertising industry, turning corporations like Exxon, Chrysler, General Mills and DuPont into household names. His ideas transformed the marketing strategies of countless products. Convertibles became synonymous with mistresses, while a sedan represented the reliable comforts of a wife. Lipstick was reimagined as a bold phallic symbol. In an ingenious move, he adjusted cake mix instructions by calling for the addition of an unnecessary egg, purely as a way of encouraging women to feel as though they were still partaking in the home baking tradition.

Companies across the nation employed legions of psychoanalysts – known as 'the depth boys'– to delve into the nation's subconscious and sell them what they didn't realize they wanted. Marketing began to play with desire and indulgence, tapping into more emotional responses.

The extensive use of in-depth interviews, opinion polling and studies like *Middletown* accustomed Americans to sharing personal information. Gradually, no aspect of life remained too private to examine. As one commentator pointed out: 'In an age when opinion polls are taken on nearly every conceivable subject it was probably inevitable that a mass study would some day be made on the most intimate of all aspects of human behaviour.'[23]

*

The Indiana University gymnasium was packed to capacity as the autumn term of 1938 began. Students had gone to great lengths to secure a spot in the coveted 'Marriage and Family' course. Enrolment came with strict requirements – only those who were married, engaged or academically exceptional could apply. Yet the most crucial test was meeting the man at the helm: Alfred C. Kinsey, a charismatic scientist in a bow tie.

American campuses had been teaching courses on marriage since the 1930s, but this one was different. While earlier programmes were steeped in religious and moral teachings about family life, Kinsey stripped away the moralizing rhetoric and presented the unvarnished truths of biology. Here, love and relationships would be examined not through the lens of doctrine, but with the stark clarity of scientific enquiry.

Insects were Kinsey's initial objects of fascination. A trained biological taxonomist, he was an expert on gall wasps, having collected 7.5 million specimens and identified forty-eight new species. He took a similar approach to humans, starting with those close at hand. After each class he interviewed his students individually and in confidence about their sex 'histories'. That morphed into his big idea: apply the taxonomical methods of the zoologist to the human primate. He resigned as lead instructor of the marriage course to embark on a more ambitious research project.

In 1948, Kinsey published *Sexual Behavior in the Human Male*, which analysed 5,000 in-depth interviews with primarily white men about their sexual histories. (He would follow this up in 1953 with *Sexual Behavior in the Human Female*; both works were popularly known as the Kinsey Reports.) He concluded that there was more variety in sexual activity than had been thought: rates of premarital and extramarital sex among average Americans were high. Just under three-quarters of men said they had paid a prostitute at least once in their lives. Thirty-seven per cent of men had had some form of homosexual experience, and between 8 and 10 per cent were exclusively homosexual.

In advance of Kinsey's first report, *The New York Times* refused to carry advertising for it, considering the material too risqué. However, it soon found itself in the minority. Booksellers hadn't seen anything this popular since Margaret Mitchell's *Gone with the Wind* over a decade earlier. Kinsey's report, with 804 printed pages of data and graphs, kept two printing presses running twenty-four hours a day to meet demand. The publishers expected to sell

Alfred Kinsey on Time *magazine, 1953.*

10,000 copies, but it instead spent twenty-seven weeks on the *New York Times* bestseller list, selling 250,000 copies.[24]

Facts and insights from the Kinsey Report circulated widely through media channels, dominating news headlines and far beyond traditional press coverage. Kinsey himself became a celebrity, the only academic to have his research immortalized in a Cole Porter song. The chorus of 'Too Darn Hot' (1948), written for the musical *Kiss Me, Kate*, mentions the Kinsey Report in stating that the 'average man' prefers to court his 'lovely lovey' in cooler temperatures, rather than when it's 'too darn hot'. Kinsey's report had not, in fact, contained any statistics about the ideal temperature for romance, but it had evidently achieved the status of a cultural reference point. As *Life* magazine noted, the Kinsey Report was 'a phenomenal source of talk and controversy', achieving the status of a new American institution. By the middle of 1949, the New York Public Library stopped accepting reservations for the book due to an excessively long waiting list.[25]

Scientific candour shattered the public silence surrounding sex that had persisted throughout the early twentieth century. In the 1940s and 1950s, cultural and legal restrictions limited publications about sex. The Kinsey Report challenged these norms. By 1953, the softcore yet mainstream magazine *Playboy* was launched; by the mid-1960s, bans on many previously prohibited erotic novels were lifted.

Not everyone embraced the scientific approach. Moralists were shocked. One newspaper columnist complained: 'We have been so *statisticized* [emphasis original] in the United States that nothing is sacred anymore.'[26] Even Mae West, the film star known for razor-sharp double entendres, weighed in with an open letter to Alfred Kinsey, published in *Cosmopolitan*. The blonde bombshell, who in 1927 had been arrested for 'corrupting the nation's youth' with her controversial Broadway play *Sex* and who had been sentenced to ten days in prison for 'obscenity', challenged Kinsey's clinical perspective. She pointedly asked, 'Is man, then, to weigh all his emotions in test tubes and note down some kind of formula?'[27]

But Gallup polling suggested West was in a minority. The majority of the public judged the report a 'good thing'.[28] Readers were fascinated. As Kinsey himself concluded: 'Scientists have been uncertain whether any large portion of the population was willing that a thoroughly objective, fact finding investigation of sex should be made ... Even the scientist seems to have underestimated the faith of the man in the street in the scientific method.'[29]

Kinsey had discovered that the American people were more

than ready to discuss their own private lives. Individuals sought the chance to be interviewed, sending letters to express their interest. Those who had once been tight-lipped about their personal experiences now willingly shared intimate details of their sex lives with the surveyors. It was a new openness that marked a transformation in the American character.

Chapter 14:

PERSONALLY AUTHENTIC

For much of the 1950s, the clinking of cocktail glasses at parties often accompanied a spirited debate over whether one was 'inner-directed' or 'other-directed'. These terms, plucked from the research of academics David Riesman, Nathan Glazer and Reuel Denney, had infiltrated the parlance of America's middle classes. Their book, *The Lonely Crowd: A Study of the Changing American Character* (1950), had defied expectations to become a bestseller.

By the autumn of 1954, the book's impact was so electric that it propelled Riesman onto the cover of the 27 September edition of *Time* magazine, heralded with the strapline: 'What is the American Character?' He was the first social scientist to grace the cover of a major news magazine, an honour subsequently bestowed upon only a select few. The cover's bold query underscored the national fascination with understanding the evolving character of the American people.

Riesman, the team leader of the research project and an assistant professor at the University of Chicago, believed that different historical periods favoured different personality types. He argued that individuals are not uniformly shaped by their time and place; rather, they are born into specific economic, political and social conditions that influence their character. These conditions reward certain behaviours, encouraging traits advantageous to the era while discouraging others. For instance, times of war and conflict favour warriors, while an era of exploration requires risk-taking adventurers.

Riesman and his team were interested in understanding the personality types of Americans in the mid-twentieth century, a period of significant transition. Traditional sources of influence were in decline. Church attendance was falling, while the family hierarchy faced challenges from other sources of authority in education and the media. By the 1940s, television had become widespread in people's homes alongside the already established radio. Riesman viewed the media revolution as beneficial, but he also recognized that it would contribute to the erosion of established institutions.

The American economy was evolving from one based on agricultural and industrial production, derived from activities such as mining or farming, to one underpinned by services, sales and consumer goods. Rather than make things, companies needed employees who could sell products. As they bureaucratized, becoming larger and more centralized, they no longer needed entrepreneurs. Businesses, especially in finance, wanted team players: sharp-suited company men who could work and play together, instead of the risk-taking capitalists of the old school. They sought people who could wine and dine clients and ingratiate themselves with colleagues and customers.

The researchers wondered what kind of employee this society would cultivate. At the heart of their findings was a change in character type from what they called 'inner-directed' to 'other-directed'. Inner-directed individuals looked to traditional authorities for guidance and developed rich inner lives based on personal convictions. In contrast, other-directed individuals orientated themselves outward, using a 'social radar' to navigate their environments. They were highly attuned to the expectations and opinions of their peers, constantly seeking approval and validation from those around them. As Riesman noted, 'The other-directed

person wants to be loved rather than esteemed.'[1] He had anticipated the emergence of what he later described as the 'egocentric'
or 'narcissistic self': one that would become ever more comfortable with being open and invading their own privacy.[2]

In this evolving landscape, the old middle class – farmers, small
business owners, engineers – remained inner-directed, while the
new middle class – bureaucrats, salaried employees – were increasingly other-directed. Riesman argued that while inner-
directed individuals clung to outdated rules, other-directed
people thrived in the fluid, rapidly changing environment of
modern America, becoming indispensable to the burgeoning
service industries. In a few years' time, they would dominate.

For the student activist of the 1960s Todd Gitlin, *The Lonely
Crowd* was hugely perceptive. But he noticed that within decades
it had become baffling to others. While teaching the research at
Berkeley in the 1980s, Gitlin found that his university students
struggled to understand the distinction between inner-directed
and other-directed orientations; it made little to no intuitive
sense to them. He realized that these students found it difficult to
grasp this key distinction because they had been born into a world
that was fundamentally other-directed at every level.[3]

As with *Middletown* and the Kinsey Reports, *The Lonely
Crowd* was not just a sociological study, it was a cultural phenomenon. Published as one of the first high-quality paperbacks aimed
at a mass audience, it resonated deeply with readers, who saw
themselves reflected in its pages. The public's fascination with
identifying their own and others' character types fuelled its success, turning a complex sociological concept into a topic of
everyday conversation.

The Lonely Crowd quickly became understood in two con-
trasting ways. First, as a lament for past times; but Riesman and
his colleagues weren't arguing in favour of a return to tradition
or inner-directedness, even though the cover of their book

displayed a tightly massed flock of sheep. The design, like the title, was the responsibility of the publisher, as Riesman was keen to point out. Riesman praised the greater sensitivity and tolerance of a society that was becoming less respectful of traditional authorities. He cautioned that other-directed individuals could typically only identify themselves by reference to others. They were likely to be less self-reflective and to be limited in their ability to truly know themselves. Riesman also argued that because other-directed individuals would be crucial for the smooth functioning of the modern organization, there was a risk that the autonomous individual might become endangered, and that the new, open ways of being could become just as conformist as the older behaviour.[4]

Second, Riesman's exploration resonated with young activists who were beginning to challenge authority and social norms. *The Lonely Crowd* became a guidebook for what to reject: business degrees, the corporate ladder and societal expectations. The phrase 'the lonely crowd' entered the cultural lexicon, even making its way into Bob Dylan's 1967 song 'I Shall Be Released'. Alternative ways of living and being were being sought by the new generation.

*

In the summer of 1962, the air was thick with a heady sense of possibility. Along the shores of Lake Huron in Michigan, a group of young idealists gathered at camp, poised to adopt a manifesto that would shape their struggle for justice and equality.

For countless young Americans, life had evolved into an urgent cycle of protests and sit-ins. The Students for a Democratic Society (SDS) were mobilizing on university campuses across the country. Descended from the youth branch of a socialist educational organization known as the League for Industrial Democracy (LID), SDS was moving away from that form of trade-union orientated politics and embracing a vision of student activism that resonated with the disillusionment of their generation.

Tom Hayden, an aspiring journalist and student at the University of Michigan, drafted the Port Huron Statement.[5] It opened with the now famous line: 'We are people of this generation, bred in at least modest comfort, housed now in universities, looking uncomfortably at the world we inherit.'

The statement expressed how the students once believed in American values and their potential for positive global influence. However, that belief had faded. Peaceful intentions were overshadowed by the harsh realities of the Cold War and the economic and military investments fuelling it. Observing the racial bigotry in the South, they realized the declaration that 'all men are created equal' rang hollow. Meanwhile capitalism imposed 'meaningless work and idleness' on many while the upper classes revelled in 'superfluous abundance', leaving two-thirds of humanity undernourished.

Seeking an alternative to the apathy and absurdity they perceived in the world, the students rejected both the centrist Democratic Party and the rigid Marxist parties that had dominated the left. In a landmark speech, Hayden argued: '[T]he essential challenge . . . is to quit the acquiescence to political fate, cut the confidence in business-as-usual futures, and realize that in a time of mass organization, government by expertise, success through technical specialization, manipulation through the balancing of Official Secrecy with the Soft Sell Technique, incomprehensible destructiveness of two wars and a third which seems imminent, and a Cold War which has challenged man's relation to man: *the time has come for a reassertion of the personal* [emphasis added].'[6]

Port Huron promised a political project that was about 'men's unrealized potential for self-cultivation, self-direction, and creativity'. It continued: 'The goal of man and society should be human independence: a concern not with image or popularity, but with finding a meaning in life that is personally authentic.'[7]

As Hayden later recalled, 'the idea was that to become whole you had to participate in all the spheres of your life'.[8] This approach required total engagement in political life: participating in referendums, protests, recalls, non-violent civil disobedience, direct action, community organizing and union organizing. Simply casting a vote each year would not suffice and could hinder personal development. The envisioned path encouraged individuals to achieve greater personal growth and fulfilment by fully committing themselves to the cause. In Hayden's view, the alternative was to live like a zombie, a person without vitality.

SDS rejected the bureaucratic structures of traditional political institutions, believing they stifled individual agency and authentic expression. They instead advocated for participatory democracy, where individuals actively engaged in decision-making processes rather than relying on elite leaders. The SDS ethos emphasized living authentically as a form of resistance against societal norms that perpetuated inequality and injustice. They believed that personal integrity was essential in their fight against systemic oppression.

The students weren't alone in their quest to rethink the left-wing project. All over the Western world, leaders of the left were trying to distance themselves from the failures of Soviet communism. After the events of 1956, when Nikita Khrushchev revealed the crimes of Stalinism and the Soviet Union invaded Hungary to brutally crush the uprising, the left's confidence in the certainty of its mission was shaken to the core. British and French groups self-consciously adopted a description of themselves as the 'New Left', which suggested their search for a socialist path was distinct from the mainstream social democratic system. The traditional focus on class struggle had lost its appeal. Drawing on existential currents, the New Left rejected the impersonal, bureaucratic approaches of its predecessors, advocating instead for a politics deeply rooted in individual experience and personal growth. This ethos was about bridging the gap between public commitment and private values, striving to align one's external actions with inner beliefs.

Todd Gitlin, who succeeded Hayden as president of SDS, serving in 1963 and 1964, recalled how they were fuelled by a passion 'to bring political commitment into private life, and make private values count in public'. The aim was to overcome the 'treacherous liberal schism between public postures and private evasions and hierarchies'.[9] It was, in part, a crusade against hypocrisy. Rousseau had been a forerunner of this way of thinking, his influence extending beyond the Romantics to the existentialists and then to the anti-American, anti-capitalist sentiment of these times. Students rejected what they saw as artificial and fake public postures in favour of what was genuine. It felt like an exciting rupture with the past. And it fired up students on campus.

SDS would grow into the largest left-wing student organization in the United States and would prove highly influential to the political discourse. But as the 1960s progressed, its goals became less about social change and civic equality, to a greater emphasis on personal values and behaviour.

*

At the time of the Port Huron declaration, SDS had about 1,000 members. A couple of years later, the organization had mobilized thousands of students on American university campuses. Soon that number would increase beyond the founders' wildest dreams.

SDS had supported Lyndon B. Johnson's presidential campaign because of his pledge not to further escalate the conflict in Vietnam. So it was with a burning sense of injustice, that, on 7 February 1965, members watched as Johnson authorized the first air raids onto North Vietnam and, two weeks later, began daily bombings.

On 17 April 1965, the National Office of SDS organized a march in Washington against the war, co-sponsored by the group Women Strike for Peace. They expected a few thousand people to turn up. In the end, around 25,000 stunned and angry protesters thronged in the capital, an event that saw activism against the war spread across the country's universities. There were teach-ins and sit-ins, and students took to the streets to make their voices heard.

In October, anti-Vietnam War rallies were held in thirty American cities. One of the largest was in Berkeley. It began at 6 a.m. on 16 October, when around eighty protesters congregated around the Oakland Army Induction Centre to hand out anti-war leaflets to inductees who were entering the governmental processing hub. They were joined by more protesters who burnt their draft cards, an illegal act under a law passed by Congress two years earlier. 'We won't go!' they shouted, holding up placards that read 'Make Love Not War' and 'Kill for Peace' alongside pictures of dead Vietnamese children.

Two days later, the front page of the *San Francisco Chronicle* read: 'THE BIG DRAFT BATTLE' with a standfirst offering more detail: 'A bloody attack by police – clubs, tear gas and boots'. As the week progressed, thousands more joined the protests. As mainly students congregated around the entrance to the Induction Centre, riot-clad police emerged from underground parking lots to attack them. The protesters responded in kind to police brutality. The marchers, wearing helmets, had brought with them plywood shields. They threw rocks and let the air out of car tyres or set them on fire. The police, unprepared, lost control of the streets for hours.

The Stop the Draft Week in Oakland ushered in a new era of activism around the country. Many of those who took part found it exhilarating. As Todd Gitlin wrote of the events, which saw a new spirit of militancy: 'Of course the politics of the Oakland insurrection like those of the Mobilization are hazy. The point is that people have demonstrated their seriousness.'[10]

Momentum on the streets resulted in local SDS chapters springing up all over the country. The organizational structure and philosophy was initially flexible enough to encompass diverse political orientations and a variety of styles of activism. There were still the older leftists, who talked about class struggle and unions, those who wanted to withdraw their labour and strike; there were anarchists, who wanted to break up everything; and long-haired members of the counterculture who were practised in the art of tuning in and dropping out. Mixed in with them were Maoists, hippies, Wobblies (who advocated for the overthrow of the capitalist system and the establishment of a worker-run economy) and Diggers (community anarchists), civil rights activists and pacifists. This capacious group hung together loosely, bound by their hatred of the old system and the war in Vietnam, hoping to make something new. But it was a coalition that couldn't withstand even modest success.

In 1968, with an estimated 30,000 members and more than 300 campus chapters, the Students for a Democratic Society was the largest student organization in the history of the US.[11] But during 1968–9, a more radical tendency developed within the organization: the Weatherman (or Weathermen), after a Bob Dylan lyric. Terry Robbins, a small and wiry English major and poet, came up with the name – later shortened to the 'Weather', as the -man part of the title was deemed sexist. Robbins had had enough of the endless theorizing of the SDS leadership, who, it seemed to him, were afraid to act and scared of violence. He argued for more confrontation with the authorities to recruit members to the movement. It was obvious to him what needed to be done; he knew which way the wind was blowing.

Weather's leaders were some of the biggest stars of the SDS movement: Mark Rudd, who was world famous after appearing in the centre of the cover of *Newsweek*, having led demonstrations that had shut down Columbia University; Bernardine Dohrn, a determined lawyer and former SDS national secretary, usually seen wearing a black leather jacket over a black turtleneck, short skirt and high black boots; and Bill Ayers, a former University of Michigan student with long dirty blond hair, round glasses, and a talent for eye-catching initiatives. All three were attractive and radiated certainty.

The Weather faction gained control of SDS in the summer of 1969, after its national convention in June resulted in an acrimonious split between different factions. As SDS fragmented into various groups, it haemorrhaged members. What was left of the movement looked on in despair.

Several hundred Weathermen moved into collective houses in cities. Susan Stern, who joined the Seattle branch, described the split from SDS as akin to a rebirth, saying: 'I ceased to think of Susan Stern as woman; I saw myself as a revolutionary tool . . . my family, my past all faded into dreary insignificance. For the first time in my life that I would remember, I was happy.'[12]

The Weather leaders identified their own selves as the site of radical change. Bill Ayres was determined that there be 'harmony' between their actions, words and deeds, allowing them to be true to themselves. He urged them to live by the motto: 'Don't let your life make a mockery of your values.'[13]

They demanded the end of all monogamous relationships, believing that such exclusive partnerships reinforced outdated patterns of female subservience. Women, it was said, needed to end the relationships to achieve independence. The leaders also noted that, in self-criticism sessions modelled after Maoist struggle sessions – public confrontations in which individuals were forced to confess and criticize their own and others' ideological failings – couples often protected each other. As a result, these sessions became characterized by intense scrutiny and detailed regulation of each other's thoughts and conduct.

The members of former couples were sent to different cities. Everyone was encouraged to sleep around. There was a sex schedule. Many couples went their separate ways, but in Seattle a couple, Jay and Beverly, who stayed together, were reprimanded for displaying 'flagrant monogamy'.[14] According to Mark Rudd: 'It was a moment of extreme sexual experimentation. Group sex, homosexuality, casual sexual hook-ups were all tried as we attempted to break out of the repression of the past into the revolutionary future.'[15] The actions of the individual, whether rioting, or when engaged in violence, or during intimacy, were experienced as moments of self-revelation, of fusing with some deeper reality, of proving one's true political self.

The project came to a deadly end when SDS member Cathy Wilkerson accidentally blew up her parents' West Village home with a nail bomb intended for a non-commissioned officers' dance at Fort Dix, New Jersey, killing three members of the Weather: Ted Gold, Terry Robbins and Diana Oughton. The radical faction was forced into hiding, signalling the end of an era.

*

As Marshall Berman predicted in his 1971 work, *The Politics of Authenticity*, the New Left would leave a lasting cultural legacy through its politicization of the concept of authenticity. The groupings detoured away from traditional politics: away from the working class, away from material changes and collective action, towards self-realization. Or, as Abbie Hoffman, a leading figure in the Yippies – an organization of young activists who combined countercultural ideas with theatrical political protests – stated, it was 'more important to get your head together than to move the multitudes'.[16]

This focus on the personal ran in parallel with depoliticization.

Politics become more about showing your rage and how you felt; more about developing oneself. In the words of Elinor Langer, a teacher active in the civil rights movements in the 1960s, the New Left 'mistook revolution . . . for a moral choice'.[17] The fate of the student movement of the 1960s, she said, herself included, was determined when its leaders made the 'curiously apolitical' decision to start thinking of themselves as revolutionaries.[18]

The blurring of lines between the political and the personal led to intense introspection. Political activism was transformed: it was no longer just about changing laws or challenging institutions, but about defining one's own truth and confronting internalized oppressions that mirrored the external world. It led to the politicization of intimate life and the breaching of the private realm.

Chapter 15:

THE PERSONAL IS POLITICAL

Betty Friedan lived in Grand View-on-Hudson, a village in New York state, with her husband, Carl, and their three children. It was a good life, but she was concerned about the slow progress of women in public life and the constraints that faced them in their private lives. Her response was *The Feminine Mystique*, an instant bestseller on publication in 1963, selling 300,000 copies in its first year and speaking to millions of women around the world.

Forty years after the passage of the Nineteenth Amendment in 1920, which guaranteed American women the right to vote, the women's movement had stalled. More than 97 per cent of US senators and members of Congress were men. In the states of Alabama, Mississippi and South Carolina, women were not allowed to serve on juries. Men dominated the professions, and many still believed that the best place for women was in the home. Classified job ads were segregated by sex. There were no laws against sex discrimination. There was no maternity leave. Women couldn't apply for a credit card in their own name. Legal abortion was practically non-existent. And marital rape was not a crime.[1]

Material affluence had improved the lives of women, yet many were left disillusioned by the hollow promises of consumerism. Middle-class women, living in the suburbs, often felt isolated from the world. Friedan, a freelance writer in her early forties who had been fired from her job when she became pregnant with her second child, felt a burning sense of injustice. She described the condition of women – the self-hatred, demoralization and misery of those trapped in domestic life – as 'the problem that has no name': 'Each suburban [house]wife struggled with it alone. As she made the beds, shopped for groceries, matched slip-cover material . . . she was afraid to ask even of herself the silent question – "Is this all?"'[2]

Friedan tore into the 'new authorities', the psychologists and educators and the advertising men – singling out Ernest Dichter – for exploiting women's hopes and insecurities to keep them in the kitchen: 'Experts told them how to catch a man and keep him, how to breastfeed children and handle their toilet training, how to cope with sibling rivalry and adolescent rebellion; how to buy a dishwasher, bake bread, cook gourmet snails.'[3] She recognized that women who would once have wanted careers, or to play a part in public life, were instead making their family their life's work, which in turned left them unfulfilled.

With her chin-length brown hair, fondness for suit jackets and high-collared, frilly blouses, Friedan was self-consciously feminine. She wasn't calling for The System to be overturned. Rather, she was a liberal centrist who wanted the rights and ways of being in the public domain already claimed by men to be extended to women. She sought a future where women were not confined to the private domain as homemakers but were able to have careers and were no longer treated as second-class citizens: 'Why should women accept this picture of a half-life, instead of a share in the whole of human destiny?' she asked.[4]

On 30 June 1966, in a modest hotel room in Washington, DC, amid the Third Annual Conference of Commissions on the Status of Women, Betty Friedan and fifteen like-minded women pooled $135 from their handbags and founded NOW, the National Organization for Women. The founding statement committed NOW to integrating women into full participation in mainstream society. They campaigned for equal pay, fought against sexually segregated 'Help Wanted' ads, and advocated for maternity leave, childcare centres for working parents, and legal abortion.

Their efforts ignited a movement. Women across the country – and the world – soon joined the cause. *The New York Times* dubbed these activists 'second wave feminists': a term the women embraced, marking a new era in the fight for gender equality.[5]

*

Meanwhile, Carol Hanisch was twenty years old and working in New York at the Southern Conference Education Fund (SCEF), which campaigned for civil rights. She wanted to confront sex and racial discrimination but was harbouring serious doubts over whether the political movements of which she was part were making any progress. New Left groups tended to be run by men. Female activists felt patronized by their male comrades; the SDS leadership didn't seem to take gender equality seriously. Many women were dismayed to find themselves restricted to secretarial work, answering phones and typing up speeches that the men delivered. They could make coffee, it seemed, but not policy. They began to see their own cause as distinct.

But Hanisch didn't agree with Betty Friedan's diagnosis of the root of women's problems, and she wasn't alone. A stream of what came to be termed 'radical feminists' were coming together in organizations that included New York Radical Women, Red-stockings, Radical Mothers, Bread and Roses, Radicalesbians, Furies, and WITCH (Women's International Terrorist Conspiracy from Hell). They disagreed frequently with each other but were united by a belief that it was necessary to change things from the inside out.

At the heart of the conflict between these two feminist currents was a disagreement over the source of women's oppression.

For Friedan and many others, it derived from the social order – the public sphere. The solution was to extend full civil rights to women and enable them to enter public and social life so that they could, as Friedan put it, take their share of the full picture of human destiny. But for Hanisch and the radical feminists, the source was patriarchy itself, which constantly reinvented ways for men to dominate women through structural inequalities embedded in institutions like marriage, and even in language. Rights alone would not be enough to end women's oppression; they wanted to change the way people were brought up and how they thought. And to do this, they needed to tear down the boundary between the public and private spheres, to open up and reform private life.

The offices of the SCEF became a regular meeting place for the New York Radical Women (NYRW). Alongside Carol Hanisch were members Shulamith Firestone, who had studied fine arts, and Kate Millett, a humanities graduate. Firestone, who co-founded the NYRW and the Redstockings, would write the philosophy for the movement; Millett would catapult it into the mainstream.

They called Firestone 'the Fireball' because of the way she tore into and reinterpreted Marx, Engels and Freud. She was twenty-five and a little over five feet tall. In *The Dialectic of Sex: The Case for the Feminist Revolution* (1970) she argued that biology, rather than capitalism, was the true source of oppression. She dismissed traditional Marxist ideas about the domination of the bourgeoisie over the proletariat: the 'sexual class system', Firestone asserted, was more powerful and entrenched than any other social or economic division. She claimed that men oppressed women by limiting them to reproduction while freeing themselves to shape the world.

Rather than emphasizing the socialist argument for workers gaining control over economic production (such as factories and resources, etc.), Firestone proposed that women should seize control of reproductive technology to free themselves. In her envisioned future, sex distinctions would be eliminated, pregnancy would be replaced by artificial wombs, the nuclear family would be dismantled and children would be raised communally.

Kate Millett's *Sexual Politics* was published in the same year as Firestone's *The Dialectic of Sex*, making radical feminism front-page news. Millett asserted that to address women's oppression, feminists must 'redefine politics' away from the 'narrow and exclusive world' of 'chairmen and parties' and expand it to include 'power-structured relationships'.[6] She argued that the patriarchy socialized women to accept their lower social status by 'interior colonization'.[7] She identified the family as its 'chief institution', stating that it not only 'encourages its own members to adjust and conform, but acts as a unit [in the] patriarchal state which rules its citizens through its family heads'.[8]

Millett criticized romantic love as just 'a means of emotional manipulation which the male is free to exploit'. She argued that sex had political implications because it represented the exercise of men's power over women. Heterosexual intercourse, she wrote, was 'an assertion of mastery, one that announces his own higher caste and proves it upon a victim who is expected to surrender, serve, and be satisfied'.[9]

She drew on *The Authoritarian Personality* (1950), a seminal work in personality theory, in which thinkers in the Frankfurt School attributed authoritarian tendances to socialization. The social psychologist Else Frenkel-Brunswik, who had studied in Vienna, contended parenting shaped social outcomes, as evidenced in the type of family – strict, conformist and conventional – that typically created authoritarian personalities. This represented a generational change for those who regarded themselves on the political left. In the 1930s, Theodor Adorno had defended the family unit as a countervailing source of authority to that of the state. Twenty or thirty years on, the family was seen as the wellspring of oppression, repression and various social ills.

Sexual Politics became an immediate bestseller and received positive reviews far and wide. 'This book is supremely entertaining to read,' raved Christopher Lehmann-Haupt in *The New York Times*, and 'breathtaking in its command of history and literature'. He praised how it was 'written with such fierce intensity that all vestiges of male chauvinism ought by rights to melt and drip away like so much fat in the flame of a blow torch'.[10] Soon, Kate Millett and the radical feminists were part of the national conversation. The second wave 'liberal' feminism of Betty Friedan was old hat.

*

One rule of NYRW meetings was that members shouldn't generalize about oppression unless they preceded it with testimony from their own lives. Gatherings began by going around the room to listen to attendees talk about their day-to-day problems. One NYRW member, Robin Morgan, recalled: 'We were talking about sex one night. I admitted that on occasion in my marriage I had faked an orgasm. I was convinced that I was the only person in the world sick and perverse enough to have done this. Every woman in the room said, "Oh, you too?" It was an amazing moment.'[11]

For most of the women, it was the first time they had ever given voice to these feelings, and the first time their private yet shared experiences had ever been spoken about in any kind of public forum: illegal and dangerous abortions; difficult childbirth; the stultifying reality of full-time motherhood; unsatisfactory and often unwanted sex. This 'consciousness-raising', as it was called, was life-changing and politically necessary. It proved that the problems many women faced were bigger than them as individuals and potentially had social solutions. Soon it took on a life of its own.

On the evening of Friday, 21 March 1969 at the Washington

Square Methodist Church in New York's Greenwich Village, some 300 women, accompanied by a few supportive men, filled the wooden pews, ready to bear witness. In the soft glow of dimmed lights, twelve courageous women rose in turn to share their harrowing testimonies about a deeply controversial and illegal medical procedure: the termination of their pregnancies. For three long, emotionally charged hours they laid bare their struggles, fears and hopes, illuminating a hidden chapter of their lives.[12]

Abortion was illegal in the USA except in extreme circumstances. In New York state, it was permitted only if the doctor deemed the pregnant woman mentally unfit to raise a child. Women were put in a position where, if they didn't want to continue with a pregnancy, they had to either act as if they were unstable or procure an illegal and dangerous abortion. There was little discussion of the procedure. Women's magazines and daytime television hardly mentioned it, if at all; like many problems that had a major impact on millions of women's lives, it merited little public reflection or representation. It was as if it just didn't happen.

And at the level of discussion about state reform on these very issues, women were excluded. When, in February, the New York Joint Legislative Committee on the Problems of Public Health had convened a panel of fifteen experts to consider whether to make abortion legal in the state, fourteen were men. The only woman was a nun. 'Let's hear from the real experts: women!' shouted an activist from the Redstockings who stormed the meeting.[13]

In that context, one woman at the Greenwich Village abortion 'speakout' made the point that the speakers' own experiences gave them specialist knowledge: 'We are the ones that have had the abortions ... This is why we're here tonight. We are the only experts.' According to another, 'We discovered that by just talking about own experience, about our own lives, that by talking about this, all together, in our group, that we were able to find out a lot more about reality, than by talking about all those objective things.' As yet another woman at the church that night put it: 'Feelings are facts'.[14]

The sense that private experience was more authoritative than learned expertise reflected the sentiment in the Redstockings manifesto: 'We regard our personal experiences and feelings about experience as the basis for an analysis of our common situation . . . Our chief task is to develop female class consciousness through sharing experience and publicly exposing the sexist foundation of all our situations.'[15]

Feelings trumping objective facts was the idea of one of the era's towering psychotherapists, R. D. Laing: an alcoholic Glaswegian with a fondness for paisley shirts and a cadaverous stare that was as terrifying as his prose style. In *Sanity, Madness and the Family* (1964) he and his co-writer, Aaron Esterson, explored the dynamics of mental illness within the family context. The book argued that psychiatric disorders were deeply influenced by family interactions. Laing, who himself would have two wives, innumerable partners and ten children, demonized the nuclear family. In *The Politics of Experience* (1967), Laing argued that personal experience should become the accepted basis for understanding oneself and society: 'No one can begin to think, feel, or act now except from the starting point of his or her own alienation,' he wrote. 'Experience is the only evidence', while psychology 'is the key to the interpretation of experience in its political significance'.[16]

By 1973, at the height of their popularity, 100,000 women in the United States belonged to consciousness-raising groups, with the NYRW organizing them all over New York City. Up to 400 women might attend meetings on any one evening, which would go on into the early hours of the next day. That radical women seemed to spend so much of their time sitting in groups talking about relationships rapidly became the subject of derision in parts of the left. Carol Hanisch's colleagues at the SCEF ridiculed it as navel-gazing. In response, she wrote the article that gave radical feminists their credo: 'The Personal Is Political'. The title came from its editors, Shulamith Firestone and Anne Koedt, a New York-based feminist and author of *The Myth of the Vaginal Orgasm* (1970).

Carol Hanisch argued that consciousness-raising should be the main organizational strategy of the NYRW because: 'One of the first things we discover in these groups is that personal problems are political problems'.[17] Consciousness-raising groups weren't an end in themselves. She rejected the idea that they were a form of therapy, arguing instead that they were an essential means of forging solidarity and understanding in advance of the coming political struggle.

On the other side of the Atlantic, where consciousness-raising had also spread, an editorial in the British feminist magazine *Shrew* reinforced this point: 'Our first priority isn't to get over information, but to know what everyone in the room thinks. We believe in getting people to interact, not to listen to experts. We want them to listen to themselves and make an analysis of their situation, which will lead them to action.'[18] A member of the British Bristol Women's Liberation workshop reported that her group 'circled like seagulls afraid to dive and swoop onto our innermost secrets' before they too were talking about sex, orgasms, abortion, children and, of course, husbands.[19]

Consciousness-raising exposed to public view, and therefore understanding, many issues that were not addressed in political life or public policy. But the process also served to fetishize the individual voice and the private, individual experience. As the New York Radical Feminists' manifesto asserted: 'We do not challenge another woman's experience.'[20] Politics was becoming more about impulse, immediacy and subjectivity – and for many, personal experience was now the primary source of political legitimacy and the main way to understand society.

*

Towards the end of 1970, Kate Millett agreed to an interview with *Time* magazine for an issue about contemporary feminism. She told the editors that she didn't want to be on their prestigious cover because she didn't want to be regarded as the leader of the women's movement. Her celebrity status was a source of some resentment among her fellow radicals, who felt (as Millett herself did) that there should be no leaders because hierarchy was an oppressive patriarchal construct. Millett suggested a group shot, but the magazine ignored her and put her on the front of its December issue anyway, using a portrait painted by the artist Alice Neel. It called her 'the Mao Tse-tung of Women's Liberation'. Overnight, Millett had become the media-anointed figurehead of radical feminism. She hated the attention it brought.

Demonstrator at a women's rights march holding a copy of
Time *magazine with Kate Millett on the cover, 1970.*

'Has anyone gone mad from media before?' Millett asked in *Flying* (1974), her memoir chronicling the ferocious aftermath of the publication of *Sexual Politics*. Although she preferred being in the classroom to being on stage, she felt she had to accept speaking engagements – even though, as a natural introvert, she often vomited in terror beforehand. Worse, she quickly found herself the victim of radical feminism's central premise, which she, Firestone and Hanisch had helped to advance: that the personal is political.

Within months of the publication of *Sexual Politics*, her own sexuality became a matter of public debate. Millett – who was then married to a man, the artist Fumio Yoshimura, but who had also had relationships with women – was quoted (or, according to Millett, misquoted) in an interview for *Life* magazine distancing herself from lesbianism, saying that it was not her thing. The Radical Lesbians took issue with this, as they were sensitive to any suggestion that women should feel ashamed of their lesbianism.

Betty Friedan, concerned that lesbian activists would set back the mainstream feminist cause, had already unhelpfully described them as the 'lavender menace', while the lesbian and gay liberation movements believed that queer people needed to smash the social taboos that kept them persecuted, ashamed and in the closet. They argued that self-disclosure – coming out – could be a radical political action that defied the social forces that demeaned or silenced them. Many believed passionately that it was imperative for Millett to express pride in her sexuality. Millett, however, thought of herself as bisexual, which many lesbian activists saw as a lie and a betrayal.

On 12 November 1970, in front of 500 people at a packed public event at Columbia University, lesbian activists in the crowd vocally demanded that Millett publicly confess her sexuality. In *Flying*, Millett recounts the moment when a member of the Radical Lesbians heckled her: 'Time stops while Teresa Juarez's loud voice butches me from the floor mike center of the room, yelling at me from the audience, "Are you a Lesbian? Say it? Are you?"[21] Millett, feeling like she had been forced into a corner, gave in to the hecklers. She admitted to being a lesbian, describing Juarez as 'A bully for all the correct political reasons.'[22]

But it wasn't enough. It never would be. Even once Millett had come out and engaged with organizations that championed gay rights, activists turned on her for not having done so sooner. She also found that she couldn't be honest about the more nuanced aspects of her sexuality – that she was bisexual and married to a man, whom she loved – because that wouldn't fit the prescribed political template. Millett's most intimate choices were subjected to the inspection and judgement of others, leaving her feeling constrained and controlled.

*

'The personal is political' was understood to imply that large social problems could be addressed, or even solved, by individual transformation – by targeting the private individual as well as the private sphere. The politicization of the private sphere served to depoliticize the public sphere and opened private life to political scrutiny. Rather than targeting the social and economic structures of society, the New Left and radical feminists began to scrutinize personal relationships. Every aspect of intimate life was invaded by politics: someone's sexual identity, their relationships, whether they were gay or straight, had children or not, how they brought those children up. The books they read, the language they used – all came to be viewed as reflections of an individual's politics, and as factors in determining whether they were a good or a bad person.

This placed an intolerable burden on everyone committed to this political praxis. Within a decade, the radical feminist movement had collapsed amid internal divisions. Yet, the invasion of private life was only beginning. It soon became clear that sweeping political and cultural changes had blurred the lines between the public and private spheres, fundamentally reshaping the notion of privacy and leaving it vulnerable to an all-out assault.

Chapter 16:

AN UNDUE OBSESSION

The British Parliament had previously debated a right to privacy no fewer than thirteen times before, on 13 May 1970, the nation's first official inquiry into privacy was launched. Under its chairman, Sir Kenneth Younger – a lawyer, former Labour cabinet minister and campaigner for homosexual law reform – the Younger Commission on Privacy, made up of nineteen politicians and public figures, convened a series of nearly forty lengthy hearings to determine whether legislation was necessary to give protection to the citizen. Britain, a country long known for its culture of reserve and understatement, was finally considering legal remedies to privacy invasions.

Unlike in America, where Warren and Brandeis's 'The Right to Privacy' had sparked a national discussion in the late nineteenth century, the concept of privacy as a right was rarely talked about in Britain before the late 1950s. It was widely believed respect for privacy was inherent to the national character and embedded in cultural norms. In terms that David Riesman, author of *The Lonely Crowd*, would understand, the British were a reticent people, more 'inner-directed' than 'other-directed'.

As Erwin Schrödinger, an Austrian physicist living in Britain in the 1950s, surmised on the BBC: 'I consider the British spirit to be distinguished by a deep reluctance to intrude unnecessarily into a man's privacy, by a great respect towards a single personality, and by a complete understanding that it may be a valuable one in spite of – or even because of – its being an individual phenomenon, deviating strongly or even quaintly from all the others.'¹

But by the end of the decade, that quintessentially British spirit seemed to be fading. This was most evident in the public's approval of a news media that was abandoning all decorum in its competition for readers.

*

When in the early 1950s Princess Margaret, the Queen's sister, fell in love with Group Captain Peter Townsend, a divorced man who had been equerry to her father, King George VI, their relationship was known only to a select few. That changed when Margaret inadvertently revealed the affair during her sister's coronation at Westminster Abbey on 2 June 1953. While waiting for her carriage back to Buckingham Palace, the Princess absent-mindedly plucked a piece of fluff from Townsend's uniform. A tabloid reporter witnessed the gesture, understood its significance, and the rumours about their clandestine relationship, already flickering, spread like wildfire. The next day, the New York media flooded its pages with the news. Other international newspapers followed.

The more restrained British press refrained from printing anything, but couldn't keep silent for long. On 14 June, *The People*, a Sunday tabloid, broke the *omertà*, stating that it was 'high time for the British public to be made aware of the fact that scandalous rumours about Princess Margaret are racing around the world'. Tongue firmly in cheek, it said, 'The story is, of course, utterly untrue' – after all, a marriage between the two would fly in the face of royal and Christian tradition. The paper demanded the Palace should 'end the official silence': 'They must deny it now.'

Behind the scenes, a full-blown crisis was in play. Townsend had proposed to Margaret but, as a member of the royal family, her answer had to adhere to established rules. The prime minister, Winston Churchill, instructed the Attorney-General, Sir Lionel Herald, to examine the constitutional position and to discreetly gauge the British Cabinet's views on the match. Both the Church of England and Churchill himself were opposed to divorce. Furthermore, as Margaret was below the age of twenty-five, the Royal Marriages Act of 1772 stipulated that she could only marry with the permission of her sister, the Queen. While officials deliberated, Princess Margaret and the Queen Mother swiftly departed on a tour of Rhodesia. Meanwhile, palace advisers sent Townsend abroad, giving him seven days in which to remove himself to Brussels as air attaché at the British Embassy.

The British press reported on the romance with headlines that today seem tame but at the time caused a sensation. After the lovers were temporarily separated, the *Daily Mirror* splashed with: 'Princess Margaret's Friend Posted Abroad' and 'The Sad Princess'.[2] When it ran a poll headlined 'If Princess Margaret, now 22, so desires, should she be allowed to marry him?' it cast aside all pretence at deference. Dr Donald Soper, president of the Methodist Conference, complained that the poll was an 'unwarrantable and disgusting intrusion into the affairs of that royal personage'.[3] The *Daily Sketch*, a tabloid newspaper, was also affronted. Its leader, titled 'Private Lives', blustered, 'If the *Daily Sketch* launched a ballot on Never's [the editor of the *Daily Mirror*] private life he would be furious. And rightly so. He would be justified in howling blue against intrusion into private lives.'[4]

But the public didn't seem to feel the same way. The *Daily Mirror* reported that the questionnaire had broken the 'world record entry for newspaper polls'. The record number of 67,907 votes (to 2,235) in favour of allowing the marriage suggested that a large number of readers felt entitled to comment, and were tolerant and supportive of a young woman's search for love. The newspaper surmised as much: it 'had launched the poll in the belief that the views and feelings of the British people on the problem confronting a beloved Princess should be given expression' – and the response 'more than justified the holding of the poll'.[5]

The Times condemned the gossip surrounding Princess Margaret, but it rejected what some MPs had started to call for: restrictions on the press. A free press, it argued, was essential to democracy as part of a system of necessary checks and balances.

Princess Margaret on the front page of the Daily Mirror, *'Is She Sad?', 1955. The media coverage of Margaret's relationship with Captain Peter Townsend persisted for years and eventually shifted to focus on her later relationships and glamorous showbiz lifestyle.*

Others were unconvinced. In 1961, the Conservative peer Lord Mancroft called for a Right of Privacy Bill. Sounding not unlike Warren and Brandeis with their call for a 'right to be let alone', Mancroft argued that it was time to give 'every individual' protection against the invasion of his privacy 'for the maintenance of human dignity'.[6] Mancroft assured members of the House that this would not affect the workings of the press: 'My Bill is designed only to give the individual the right to protect himself from unwarranted prying into his personal affairs.' However, it would still ensure 'the right of the public to be kept informed in all matters in which the public may be concerned'. It was difficult, he acknowledged – 'But the line between public and private interests can, and I think should, be drawn.'[7] Mancroft's proposal gathered little support, and years would pass before a similar idea was again proposed in the House.

In 1967, Labour MP Alexander Lyon introduced his Right to Privacy Bill in the House of Commons, asserting: 'There ought to be in the law a right to be left alone if one wishes to be left alone.' Lyon sought protection for 'a person from any unreasonable and serious interference with his seclusion of himself, his family or his property from the public'.[8]

Lyon's concerns had in part been triggered by ongoing press interest in the infamous Profumo Affair. A political scandal that rocked the nation in 1963, it saw the downfall of British Secretary of State for War John Profumo after he lied to Parliament about his affair with Christine Keeler, a model who was also involved with a Soviet naval attaché. The revelation of Profumo's deception sparked a public outcry over national security implications and his attempt to mislead Parliament, causing considerable damage to the credibility of the Conservative government.

The story ignited questions that lingered – were Profumo's clandestine transgressions relevant to his public position? Could he, after he stood down, become a private person? Lyon disputed its relevance. He railed against the publication of Keeler's memoirs in the *News of the World* in the summer of 1969, for the 'offensive industries into the privacy of a man who is not now in public life',[9] and made a formal complaint to the Press Council. A government watchdog banned a TV commercial advertising the serialization, because 'the memoirs offended public feeling'.[10]

However, there was little real evidence of an offended public. The *News of the World* claimed that publishing the 'Confessions of Christine' increased its circulation by 150,000. Its editorial was unrepentant: 'in the belief that the public is entitled to know what is going on, and to know authentically, we have discharged our prime duty of giving the news. A prodigious and mounting readership tacitly acknowledges the rightness of the course we have followed.'[11]

The *Daily Sketch*, which had condemned the poll on Princess Margaret and Peter Townsend a decade earlier, strongly supported the publishing of Keeler's memoirs: 'No good will come of pretending that how a Cabinet Minister behaves in private can be separated from his job as one of the country's leaders. For a man's character does not change when he goes out of one door and goes into another.'[12] Slowly, an individual's private doings were becoming relevant to their public position.

Notably, Lyon's bill was also driven by his concern over the privacy risks posed by new technologies, specifically covert surveillance. He cited a troubling divorce case where agents had secretly recorded a hotel room to collect evidence, underscoring the urgent need for legal safeguards against such invasive practices.

The Times trembled that privacy was 'threatened by new techniques of mass communication and concealed observation, such as bugging devices, electronic surveillance, and subliminal persuasion'.[13] 'No Private Conversation Left in Great Britain That Cannot be Overheard', ran a headline in the *Sunday Graphic*.

Worries spread as the Midlands Electricity Board announced it would place more than 1.5 million records onto a computer and British Rail started using computers for its timetables. The *Daily Sketch* warned of proposals to run London's traffic by computer, with the headline: 'Motorists Are to Be Controlled by Big Brother Traffic Computers'.[14]

A disconcerting report published in the *Illustrated London News* amplified these fears, highlighting the alarming prospect of bugging devices that might be found in a sugar cube, cufflinks, even a matchbox. 'Bugging's Got to Stop' was the take of the *Daily Mirror* – the paper that had proudly published the poll about Prince Margaret's relationship. It seemed worried only about the threat to individual privacy presented by technology.

Lyon's proposed privacy bill brought a new perspective to these ongoing discussions. Although he called for a 'right to be let alone', the focus of concern was shifting away from Victorian ideas of privacy and individual dignity, as set out earlier by Lord Mancroft, and onto the challenges posed to individuals of surveillance by electronic bugging and computer databanks.

It was in this context – as the definition of privacy was bifurcating – that the Younger Commission was assembled.

*

The Younger Report, released in July 1972, had little impact on legislation, but it did amount to an evolution in the concept of privacy. 'We have conceived of the right of privacy as having two main aspects,' it began. 'The first of these is freedom from intrusion upon oneself, one's home, family, and relationships. The second is privacy of information, that is, the right to determine for oneself how and to what extent information about oneself is communicated to others.'[15] In other words, it made a distinction between the right to be let alone and the newer idea of the right to informational privacy, which was in the ascendency.

That demarcation was influenced in part by public opinion. The Younger Commission had invited comments from the public but was surprised to receive only 214 letters, which it considered 'a very small response'.[16] As a result, the commission conducted a survey to gauge public attitudes. This research revealed a generational divide in how privacy was defined. Those aged forty-five and over described privacy as 'keeping your own private affairs to yourself', 'other people minding their own business' and 'freedom from nosy parkers'.[17] The home, for them, was still a castle. However, people who had come of age in the 1960s and 1970s were much more likely to define privacy as 'leading your life as you want to lead it', 'doing what you like at home' and 'living as you want to'.[18] There was no mention of a right to be let alone for this cohort. As with young Americans, who were, in the words of a popular album and cultural touchstone from 1972, 'Free to Be . . . You and Me', for young Brits, privacy was about self-actualization and being themselves, rather than a defence against unwelcome intrusion or interference and scrutiny. It was about the freedom to do things they wanted to do, not freedom from the state or the oversight of their peers. They sought affirmation and recognition, not dignity or the right to be let alone.

All this was happening at a time when people were pursuing diverse lifestyles much more openly. Indeed, the word *lifestyle* only became common usage in the 1960s and 1970s. For this generation, constraints on intimate relationships were already noticeably looser. The contraceptive pill had been introduced in Britain in 1961. The Abortion Act of 1967 legalized the termination of a pregnancy on certain grounds by registered doctors. Women had greater control over their bodies, and sex was demarcated from reproduction. In 1967 the British Parliament passed the Sexual Offences Act, which decriminalized private homosexual acts between men in England aged over twenty-one – bringing an end, it was hoped, to moralism in the bedroom, as well as prostitution on the street. What had once been closely guarded information – sexual, emotional and autobiographical – was moving out into the open. Activities that had previously been forbidden or considered shameful no longer had to be hidden quite so carefully. It was a step towards liberation, although there was still some way to go before people could truly be 'out and proud'.

Malcolm Bradbury's bestselling novel *The History Man* (1971) satirized this new era. Its hero, Howard Kirk, a radical sociology lecturer, sits with his lover Myra and his wife Barbara, with whom he has an open marriage, and describes his new book: 'It is called *The Defeat of Privacy* . . . It's about the fact that there are no more private selves, no more private corners in society, no more private properties, no more private acts . . . There are no concealments any longer, no mysterious dark places of the soul. We're all right there in front of the entire audience of the universe, in a state of exposure. We're all nude and available.'[19]

In the end, most of the Younger Commission's recommendations concerned the second definition: 'informational privacy'. Its proposals were confined to legislation on credit rating agencies, the licensing of private detectives, and restrictions on the use of electronic surveillance devices. As for placing limitations on the press, the report found the balance between the protection of the individual and freedom of the press 'difficult'. It half-heartedly recommended that non-members of the press should be appointed to the Press Council, a voluntary organization that aimed to maintain ethical standards in journalism.

The 207 pages of the Younger Report barely addressed the first part of its definition of privacy: 'freedom from intrusion upon oneself, one's home, family and relationships'. Family privacy was hardly mentioned. One of the few references came from the submitted testimony of the British Council of Churches, but this was not to defend it. Instead, the BCC criticized the 'undue obsession with personal or family privacy' in the earlier part of the century, because community participation required some 'surrender' of privacy. Religious bodies, it noted, 'are positively encouraging more openness and less privacy in meeting contemporary needs' and 'social responsibility'.[20]

The Younger Committee concluded that excessive privacy could be 'damaging': 'The result is likely to be loneliness, estrangement from society and the growth of secretiveness and introversion.'[21] Keeping one's business to oneself, formerly seen as a British virtue and part of the national character, was now regarded in certain quarters as suspect.

*

In 1967 the eminent anthropologist Edmund Leach, then Provost of King's College, Cambridge, delivered the prestigious Reith Lectures on BBC Radio 4 on the hot-button issue of teenage rebellion. The London School of Economics had recently experienced a student sit-in protesting at fees for overseas students, and there was considerable soul-searching about the cause. In a crowded lecture hall, wearing a dishevelled pinstripe suit and with hair flying all over his face, Leach rejected the conventional explanations: that either economic problems or young people themselves were to blame. Instead, he pointed his finger at the home. Rather than 'soppy propaganda about the virtue of a united family life', the reality was markedly different: 'Far from being the basis of the good society, the family, with its narrow privacy and tawdry secrets, is the source of all our discontents.'[22]

What went on behind closed doors and was protected by, in Leach's words, 'narrow privacy' was a threat. One approving female correspondent wrote to Edmund Leach after his lecture: 'I clapped my hands when I heard your statement regarding the family as the unit in society . . . I questioned it long ago, but only voice my opinion in private and that in a limited way.'[23]

This sentiment, then controversial, was relatively new. Though in the 1950s it was seen as plausible that parents could negatively impact their children, it was not a commonplace assumption. Even patients who visited the Tavistock Institute in London – a pioneering mental health clinic known for its contributions to psychotherapy, psychological research and social psychiatry – tended not to blame their mothers or fathers. Most people left blank the first question on the clinic's application form: 'Did you experience any special difficulties or changes in the home during your early years?'[24] But when patients described their family life as 'happy' or 'united', pioneering psychiatrist R. D. Laing dismissed that as a 'stereotyped idealisation'.[25] As far as he was concerned, the family was a fundamental source of mental illness.

In 1971, Penguin published David Cooper's *The Death of the Family*, a scathing critique of the traditional family structure aimed at the mass market. Cooper, a colleague of Laing's, argued that, rather than being a source of stability and moral virtue, the family was a source of repression and social dysfunction. He posited that the family unit upholds social norms that restrict individual freedom and contribute to psychological and social problems. The 'age of relatives is over', he said, 'because the relative invades the absolute centre of ourselves'.[26] The family was also the maidservant of 'imperializing capitalism'.[27] Cooper proposed that dismantling the traditional family structure could lead to a more liberated and equitable society. The book was reprinted in paperback three times between 1972 and 1978.

By the early 1970s, the notion that the family repressed its members had become a prevailing theme in cultural output, as noted by a theatre critic from *The Times*; many productions suggested that 'Behind the comfortable veneer of family life, a sulphurous and barely containable turmoil of frustrated ambitions simmers.'[28]

Hitherto, the notion of privacy had primarily been related to dignity and solitude – the freedom to retreat from public view, the right to be let alone. Whole areas of life, including one's personal and lifestyle decisions and the family unit, were to be respected as separate from others and protected from scrutiny and intervention. But by the mid-1970s, the idea of a private life as freedom from interference, forged over centuries, was evaporating.

Rather than a 'death of privacy', as the alarmist headlines of newspapers and the anxious tones of magazines suggested when reporting on new surveillance devices such as bugging, what was truly unfolding was something more profound and transformative: the 'death of private life'. The once hallowed sanctity of private life had been stained. The value of the family was no longer obvious, nor privacy for it assumed. The concept of privacy had shifted from being associated with the tarnished private sphere to being linked directly to the individual. A preoccupation with individual privacy and 'informational privacy' (what would later be called 'data privacy') replaced broader discussions of the virtues of the private sphere. It also co-existed more comfortably with the personally expressive culture of the times. This development had a parallel across the Atlantic.

Chapter 17:

THE RIGHT TO PRIVACY

On 12 August 1974, three days after he was sworn in as US president, Gerald Ford made his first speech to Congress. Dressed in a dark-blue suit, paired with a white shirt featuring extended collars, all pulled together by a thick striped tie, the former Republican House minority leader from Michigan projected a commanding presence. 'My fellow Americans, we have a lot of work to do,' he began.[1]

Domestic enemy number one was a recession characterized by high inflation and low employment. The federal budget needed balancing. Defence capabilities had to be secured. Ford's government would continue the foreign policy of his predecessor, Richard Nixon, and honour the Paris Agreement, which committed the US to withdraw from the war in Vietnam and welcome home American prisoners of war.

The one issue Ford did not address directly was also the reason he was now commander-in-chief: the Watergate scandal – the Nixon administration's attempts to conceal its involvement in a break-in at the Democratic National Committee offices. However, towards the end of his thirty-minute address, Ford reaffirmed his commitment to privacy, declaring: 'There will be no illegal tappings, eavesdropping, buggings, or break-ins by my administration.' He paused for emphasis, raising his voice above the cheers: 'There will be hot pursuit of tough laws to prevent illegal invasions of privacy in both government and private activities.'

Illegal wiretapping, break-ins and intrusion into personal records were the very rights violated by Nixon, the only US president ever to have resigned from office. Five months later, Ford signed the Privacy Act of 1974, calling it 'an initial advance in protecting a right precious to every American – the right of individual privacy'.[2]

*

Watergate had confirmed fears that the US was becoming a surveillance society, but it didn't give rise to them. Gerald Ford was following up on the commitment he had made as vice president and chair of the Domestic Council Committee on the Right of Privacy, before scandal had engulfed the White House.

Nixon had once championed the cause of privacy. In February 1974, during a national radio address as president, he asserted that privacy was 'the most basic of all individual rights', and that 'A system that fails to respect its citizens' right to privacy fails to respect the citizens themselves.' He continued, referencing Warren and Brandeis's 'Right to Privacy' article, 'In the first half of this century, Mr Justice Brandeis called privacy "the right most valued by civilized men". In the last half of this century, we must also make it the right that is most protected.'[3] It was Nixon who established the Domestic Council Committee on the Right of Privacy, which he said would be 'primed for high-level action' and would devise direct, enforceable measures. He appointed Ford as its head.[4]

Nixon was responding to a rising tide of privacy fears that swept through the 1960s. Thanks to revolutionary changes in computer chip technology, wiretaps had shrunk to a size that allowed them to be hidden with startling ease, slipping unnoticed into the fabric of daily life. *Life* magazine painted a chilling picture: a martini spiked with olive transmitters and a toothpick antenna, a woman's dress concealing a device taped to her back, and even the cavity of a tooth of a close associate being used for wiretapping.[5]

When *Time* magazine published an article titled 'Bug Thy Neighbor', which alleged that the US government was spending more than $20 million per year on electronic surveillance operations,[6] it seemed as if everyone was listening in to everyone else. 'Bugging is so shockingly widespread and so increasingly insidious,' one article despaired, 'that no one can be certain any longer that his home is his castle, free from intrusion.'[7] America seemed to be in the grip of an epidemic of bugging. It was a terrifying problem depicted in Francis Ford Coppola's 1974 film *The Conversation*, in which Gene Hackman's surveillance expert Harry Caul becomes ensnared in the very web of secrecy and paranoia he has helped to weave.

Cover of Life *magazine, 'The Big Snoop', May 1966.*

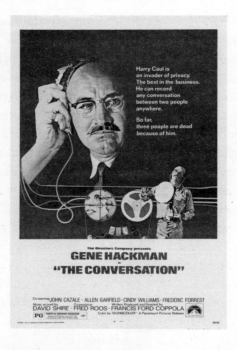

Film poster to The Conversation, *directed by Francis Ford Coppola, 1974.*

America was entering an era where privacy became a focal point of public concern and political debate, sparking intense controversy. Concurrently, the very concept of privacy was evolving. Though Nixon invoked the Victorian idea of privacy, 'the right to be let alone' and the ability to retreat into the private sphere, what crystallized during the 1960s and 1970s was a significant departure from this traditional view. By the time of Ford's Privacy Act of 1974, it had become clear that privacy of the old sort wasn't being protected at all. While the Privacy Act was a hinge moment, it was the landmark Supreme Court ruling on privacy, *Griswold* v. *Connecticut* (1965), that fundamentally reshaped both the landscape of privacy rights and the notion of privacy itself.

*

Griswold v. *Connecticut* was set in motion in the autumn of 1961, when detectives Blazi and Berg knocked on the door of a Planned Parenthood centre in New Haven. The clinic, which had only just been opened, was in flagrant contravention of a dusty statute. Under the Connecticut Comstock Act of 1873, the state had made the use of contraceptives a crime, punishable by jail or a fine or both. A later statute applied the same penalties to anyone who assisted the practice. It was openly contravened and often overlooked, but formally, legally, anyone who wanted contraception had to travel out of state lines to obtain it.

During a ninety-minute police interview, Estelle Griswold, executive director of Planned Parenthood Connecticut, who was in her early sixties, pressed pamphlets advertising the clinic's services into the detectives' hands. She explained in detail that the clinic's doctors advised women how to insert a diaphragm and how they should use contraceptive jelly. She also informed them that she knew the clinic was in violation of the law.[8]

Griswold and the clinic's medical director, Charles Lee Buxton, were convicted of aiding and abetting the criminal offence of supplying contraception and each fined $100. When they appealed to the Connecticut Supreme Court, the court upheld their convictions. Griswold then escalated the battle by taking it to the United States Supreme Court.

On 7 June 1965, the court under Justice William O. Douglas ruled seven to two that the Connecticut law was unconstitutional because a married couple had a right to privacy. He asked: 'Would we allow the police to search the sacred precincts of marital bedrooms for telltale signs of the use of contraceptives? The very idea is repulsive to the notions of privacy surrounding the marriage relationship.'[9] Estelle Griswold had won, allowing Planned Parenthood to open clinics throughout the state. Finally, couples could obtain contraception locally. It was a long overdue change.

But before *Griswold* v. *Connecticut*, birth control activists had not described the fight for access to contraception in terms of privacy. For Estelle Griswold, the issue was simple: 'We merely desire freedom in this most intimate of all our practices.'[10] The American Civil Liberties Union framed contraception as an issue of public health and equality, arguing that bodily autonomy was essential for women to fully participate in public life. However, recognizing an opportunity, campaigners and lawyers began to tap into widespread anxieties about privacy that were coursing through society, including those about wiretapping, to advance their cause

This case marked a significant legal shift, as prior to Griswold, the law had not recognized a marital right to privacy. In fact, it was the first time the Supreme Court identified a right to privacy, full stop. As Warren and Brandeis had noted with some dismay, the word *privacy* does not appear in the original US Constitution. Nor does it appear in any of its amendments. To rule that privacy is a constitutional right, Justice Douglas argued that the Bill of Rights' specific guarantees have 'penumbras' which, when drawn together, add up to a de facto right to privacy. The spirit of the First Amendment (free speech), Third Amendment (prohibition of the forced quartering of troops), Fourth Amendment (freedom from searches and seizures); Fifth Amendment (freedom from self-incrimination) and Ninth Amendment (other rights, as applied against the states by the Fourteenth Amendment) all add up to a general 'right to privacy'.

Overnight, the Supreme Court's historic ruling raised privacy to the status of a constitutional right. Douglas's ruling was an opportunistic legal fudge: 'one of the most idiosyncratic opinions in the two centuries of Supreme Court history', according to one commentator.[11] Even so, its impact would endure. As *Time* magazine predicted: 'Lawyers can now spend years happily fighting over just what else the new right of privacy covers.'[12]

*

On Tuesday, 26 July 1966, one year after the Supreme Court had identified that Americans had a constitutional right to privacy, Neil Gallagher, New Jersey Democrat and decorated war hero, ruffled his papers and looked at the clock. It was 10.10 a.m. and Gallagher was sitting in room 2247 of the Rayburn House Office Building, a vast edifice on Capitol Hill in Washington, DC. He called the Special Subcommittee on the Invasion of Privacy, of which he was chairman, to order. To the five other men seated around the table – Democratic congressman Benjamin S. Rosenthal, Republican Frank Horton, and a sprinkling of suited officials – Gallagher explained that the object of their scrutiny was a disturbing federal government proposal: President Johnson's National Data Center.

The intention was that the National Data Center would make the Great Society – a collection of ambitious domestic programmes that LBJ vowed would bring an end to poverty and racial injustice – easier to administer. It would consolidate information from twenty government agencies, including the Census Bureau and Social Security, into a single national database. No new information would be collected; rather, the database would serve as a centralized repository, functioning like a library to store and access existing data more efficiently. The administration didn't expect any hostility to the proposal.

Immediately, civil rights leaders criticized the plan to consolidate numerous federal databases into a single centralized data centre, viewing it as suspicious. They were already concerned about being under surveillance. Those on the political right warned of creeping totalitarianism, suggesting comparisons to communist Russia. From church pulpits, sermons denounced the plan; nuns wrote to their congressmen, and the patriotic non-profit organization Daughters of the American Revolution passed a resolution in strong opposition. Jerry Rosenberg, a psychologist who would go on to publish *The Death of Privacy* a few years later, summed up the tenor of what quickly became a furious national debate: '[A] national computer system is planned that will have an almost limitless capability to store, intermingle and, at the push of a button, retrieve information on persons, organizations and a variety of their activities without the knowledge of those involved.'[13] In a rare moment of consensus, disparate factions were united. An editorial in *The New York Times* titled 'To Preserve Privacy' encapsulated the sentiment, arguing that to approve the National Data Center would lead to an 'Orwellian nightmare'.[14]

Congress reacted quickly. The proposed database came at a time when numerous privacy-related hearings were under way – on wiretapping, lie detectors, psychological testing. Members of Congress seized on the data centre concept as confirmation of their worst fears. The mere presence of government files, Neil Gallagher said to his subcommittee on that Tuesday morning in July, was 'frightening enough', but the thought of them 'bundled together in one compact package is appalling'. Gallagher acknowledged the value of efficiency, but not at the cost of individual privacy. The subcommittee's task was to find the right balance between the two.

He called the first witness: Vance Packard, a prominent social critic known for *The Hidden Persuaders* (1957). In this work Packard criticized the psychological manipulation tactics used by advertisers, particularly Ernest Dichter's 'depth boys', to influence consumer behaviour. Packard's critique exposed how advertisers tapped into subconscious desires, warning of the ethical implications: Americans, he claimed, had become 'the most manipulated people outside the Iron Curtain', with advertisers exploiting hidden weaknesses to control their behaviour.[15]

But today, Packard was being called to discuss his book *The Naked Society* (1964), which had spent twenty-three weeks on the *New York Times* bestseller list. It joined many other related privacy titles on the bookshelves. In *The Privacy Invaders* (1964), former private detective Myron Brenton revealed that a complete record of a man's life could soon be compiled from his Internal Revenue file, bank statements, credit card receipts and telephone bills. That same year, *The FBI Nobody Knows* by the investigative journalist Fred J. Cook exposed the prying of J. Edgar Hoover and the FBI. Missouri senator Edward V. Long had just published *The Intruders: The Invasion of Privacy by Government and Industry* and pledged to eradicate government eavesdropping for good. Robert M. Brown's *The Electronic Invasion* (1967), on the eavesdropping industry, would go through three editions.

In Packard's *The Naked Society*, the cover of which featured an image of a man with headphones connected to a telephone, the social critic warned that big business, big government and big education were using a range of invasive techniques – wiretapping, undercover agents, lie detectors, night-vision cameras and highly intrusive questionnaires – to invade the privacy of ordinary Americans. He also expressed concern about dolls equipped with tape recorders listening to children. Most alarmingly, he highlighted the dangers of 'banks of giant memory machines that conceivably could recall in a few seconds every pertinent action – including failures, embarrassments or possibly incriminating acts – from the lifetime of each citizen'.[16]

These were the colossal mainframe computers, invented in the 1940s: behemoths that filled entire rooms with humming circuitry and flashing lights. Two decades on, they had become the backbone of a data empire, processing staggering amounts of information about the everyday lives of Americans. There were no rules governing what data could be collected or who could do the collecting. Corporations hungrily amassed details about consumer behaviour, from the cereals people ate to the brands they favoured, all in the pursuit of effective marketing strategies. But Packard fixed his gaze on the entity that had become the largest consumer of mainframe computing power: the United States government.

He solemnly informed the Special Subcommittee that more than three million government records were already stored on punch cards and magnetic tape, housed in more than twenty buildings. The proposed database would go a step further and consolidate them all – a huge amount of personal information – giving the government capacities akin to the 'all-seeing eye of totalitarian states'. Though Packard ponderously added that he didn't know anything about computers, he was confident about the threat they posed. At stake was the 'depersonalization of the American way of life'. And what he meant could be explained with the example of canned fruit: 'I am reminded of a description given me of some of the new automated food canneries. A truck brings baskets of peaches up to the automated building. Once the peaches are unloaded automated machinery takes over. The peaches are washed, peeled, sliced, pitted, sirruped, canned, packed in cartons entirely by machines. The cartons, properly labelled, emerge out the other end of the building. Most of us applaud the automated processing of peaches. But does it follow that we should applaud the automated processing of people? I think not.'[17]

Chairman Gallagher, unfazed by the confusing analogy, agreed. The database, he explained to the subcommittee, could lead to 'The Computerized Man', stripped of individuality and privacy as well as personal identity. 'His life, his talent, and his earning capacity would be reduced to a tape with very few alternatives available.'

Packard pointed to the free speech protests at Berkeley two years earlier as evidence of widespread suspicion of computers. The Berkeley Free Speech Movement had ignited in 1964 when University of California students were barred from fundraising for civil rights causes on campus, with such activities allowed only

for Democrat and Republican clubs. Protesters demanded an end
to this ban and called for recognition of their rights to free speech
and academic freedom. As the movement grew, activists criticized
the university's pro-business and pro-war stances. The University
of California was closely linked to defence research, housing labs
that developed thermonuclear weapons.

On 2 December 1964, thousands of students had streamed
into an open-air space in front of Sproul Hall and lain down.
They hung computer punch cards around their necks, perforated
to spell out 'FSM' (free speech matters) and 'Strike'. One parroted
the cards' instructions: 'I am a UC student. Please do not fold,
bend, spindle or mutilate me.'[18]

Mario Savio, leader of the Free Speech Movement, invoked a
striking technological metaphor in a speech that would capture
the zeitgeist: 'We're human beings! . . . There's a time when the
operation of the machine becomes so odious, it makes you so sick

Free Speech marchers at Berkeley wearing computer cards
as a sign of protest, December 1964.

at heart, that . . . you've got to put your bodies upon the gears and upon wheels . . . and you've got to make it stop. And you've got to indicate to the people who run it, to the people who own it, that unless you're free, the machine will be prevented from working at all.'[19]

Computer punch cards represented the university's bureaucratic systems and its complicity in war. They also served as a general symbol of alienation from a dehumanizing system that turned people into mere cogs. The machine – the computer, the government, the military, war and the university – were all connected.

As well as gesturing to those student protests, Vance Packard peppered his testimony to Gallagher's subcommittee with reference to communist and Nazi totalitarianism: 'We should all be scared stiff about the possibility that these giant machines would be fed data about individual Americans . . . I think it would clearly create the preconditions for a totalitarian system.'[20]

Totalitarian regimes claim the right of unlimited interference in the lives of their citizens. Under such a regime, there is no border between the political and the private, as it tries to extinguish the private realm completely. No sphere of life was outside their control. The Nazi politician Robert Ley boasted that in the Third Reich, the only 'private person' was someone 'asleep'.[21] 'The so-called sphere of private life cannot slip away from us,' said Anatoly Lunacharsky, head of the People's Commissariat for Education for the Soviet State, in 1927, 'because it is precisely here that the final goal of the revolution is to be reached.'[22] In reaction to these events, the 1948 Universal Declaration of Human Rights included a global commitment to individual privacy. George Orwell's novel *Nineteen Eighty-Four* was published a year later.[23]

The spectre of totalitarianism loomed large in US discussions about privacy. In the epochal conflict between totalitarian dictatorship and liberal democracy, privacy was deployed as a sign of progress or its absence: America did not invade the privacy of its citizens.

Vance Packard then veered to Senator Joe McCarthy's witch-hunting House Committee on Un-American Activities of the 1950s. These cases from recent history, he argued, showed that the threat to privacy posed by the National Data Center was 'very real'. Congressman Gallagher agreed. Vance Packard's testimony was 'hair-raising', he said. But Packard wasn't finished.

Dialling down the alarm, he acknowledged that computers are useful. The problem, he said, was linking the stored information to the individual. If the proposed National Data Center could ensure that the name of the person was 'sanitized', unidentifiable, then the threat to privacy would be minimized. Packard concluded his testimony, which had ranged from a discussion of canned peaches to student protests and totalitarianism, by advocating for a law that would grant individuals the right to review and correct the information the government held about them. Notably, though confident of the multiple threats the data project posed, Packard did not suggest abandoning it altogether.

Another witness before the Special Subcommittee was Charles A. Reich, a Yale Law School professor known for his long, beaded necklaces and floppy bell bottoms. Reich's law students would, in future, include the young Bill Clinton and Hillary Rodham; but all that was still ahead of him.

On the matter of Johnson's database, he was unequivocal. It had to be stopped. Regulation or transparency, as Packard had proposed, wasn't enough. The 'evil' of the database, Reich told the subcommittee, was that the information held on it would define the individual yet he would have no say over it, or right of reply.

Reich advocated for new laws that would prevent the government from soliciting certain types of personal information altogether. He argued that aspects of personal life such as one's religion or private family matters were not within the government's purview and should remain beyond its scrutiny. 'Things that go on between a man and a wife and his children are nobody's business,' he said.[24]

*

The Special Subcommittee reconvened on 28 July. Finally, they were to hear evidence from a 'computer man' (the term *computer scientist* did not yet exist): Paul Baran, a forty-year-old Polish-born engineer with the Rand Corporation, the Santa Monica think tank that offered research to the US Armed Forces. What he said surprised and confused them. Baran dismissed the concerns about databases: 'Whether the information is centralized in one central data bank or whether it is spread around the country doesn't make a darn bit of difference,' he asserted. 'The result is the same.' One way or another, data would be linked up.

Baran explained that both the government and private sector were already developing individual data systems that would eventually be linked together in a network. One day, there would be a computer in the air – what we now call the cloud. He predicted that centralized computers would provide information processing as a public utility. People would even have computers in their own homes that could send and receive messages across the networks.

He patiently outlined that it wasn't possible to stop the collection of data, which was happening at great pace, but that it had to be regulated: there were, so far, no restrictions on who could collect what. He also recommended that the US government encrypt all sensitive data to protect individual privacy.

The subcommittee did not follow up on any of Paul Baran's recommendations. With the attention of Congress focused on the national database, the Rand expert's talk about a new kind of computer in the air seemed unfathomable to congressmen, whose understanding of technology was primitive, to say the least.

But Baran knew what he was talking about, because he was part of a team developing a communications network designed to function even in the event of a nuclear war. This network would contribute to the creation of ARPANET (the Advanced Research Projects Agency Network), the direct precursor to the modern internet. In 1966, the groundbreaking concept of packet switching – breaking data into small, manageable chunks – was introduced. This innovation became the backbone of the new network, enabling communication between distant computers while ensuring resilience against potential attacks, a pressing concern during the Cold War. ARPANET's capabilities would be publicly demonstrated in 1972 at the International Computer Communication Conference, held in the ballroom of the Washington Hilton. Advancements such as email and remote access were showcased, though they went largely unnoticed outside of the specialized community of computer enthusiasts.

The testimonies of Vance Packard, Charles Reich and Paul Baran expressed subtly different views of what privacy was and how it was threatened by computers. For Packard, when governments held important information on the individual over which they had no say or redress, individuality was at risk. Privacy amounted to a right to control sensitive information about oneself so as not to be turned, as he put it, into a can of peaches. He accepted the need for the database but wanted information-gathering to be regulated, transparent and anonymized. Packard's view of privacy was more in line with the informational view which would come to dominate.

Reich opposed it, full stop. In his, more Victorian, view the government should not ask the individual personal questions at all: some things were no one's business. For Paul Baran, however, technology was already threatening privacy – and because some of that data was sensitive, safeguards were urgently needed. Baran understood that the problem wasn't President Johnson's proposed national database, but rather the networked computers and unregulated data collection. Since data was being collected without restrictions, by government and corporations, there wasn't much time left to protect privacy. As he put it in an article for the policy journal *Public Interest*, 'We may to think of this as tomorrow's problem; but it is already here.'[25]

In August 1968, the House Special Subcommittee on Invasion of Privacy recommended the National Data Center be postponed until the technical requirements for protecting privacy could be fully explored. The following year, with the disastrous war in Vietnam, Lyndon Johnson stepped down. All plans for the national database were shelved. It seemed to be a big win for privacy.

*

Since the days of Warren and Brandeis, privacy advocates had decried a glaring omission in the Constitution. While the Fourth Amendment protected citizens from unreasonable searches and seizures by the government, it left the private sphere vulnerable to the lenses of portable cameras, the penmanship of the press, and the encroachment of wiretapping technologies that could breach the sanctity of the home without ever physically crossing property lines. All of these innovations evaded the constitutional shield designed to protect against unreasonable searches and seizures.

With the *Griswold* v. *Connecticut* judgment establishing privacy as a constitutional right, lawyers seized the moment to advocate for new legislation on wiretapping, with an unlikely figure as a gamechanger: Charles Katz, an enterprising Los Angeles gambler who used a public phone booth down the road from his boarding house to place his bets. The FBI taped the phone booth and used the recordings to obtain a search warrant, which enabled agents to search Katz's home and seize further evidence that he violated a federal law banning wagering by telephone across state lines. During his trial, Katz filed a motion to suppress all evidence stemming from the recorded phone calls, but the motion was denied. He was convicted and fined $300.

Katz appealed his case all the way to the Supreme Court, challenging the legality of the FBI's methods. His lawyers built upon the principles established in *Griswold*, arguing that his privacy had been violated by the government's surreptitious eavesdropping, even though he was using a public phone booth. In *Katz* v. *United States* (1967), the Supreme Court addressed the critical question of whether the Fourth Amendment's protection could apply to the privacy of bugged phone conversations outside the home. The court ruled in Katz's favour, marking a watershed moment.

Justice Potter Stewart extended the Fourth Amendment to protect individuals, ruling: 'The traditional standard to determine whether the protections of the Fourth Amendment apply in this case, referred to as "trespass" doctrine, is inadequate. The Fourth Amendment protects people, not areas, from government intrusion. It does not matter that the microphones were not actually inside the phone booths. The microphones recorded Katz's statements, which he justifiably believed were made in privacy.' In a resounding phrase, Stewart said that Katz had a 'reasonable expectation' of privacy in the phone booth and, as a result, what the FBI did was unlawful.[26]

Katz v. *United States* had huge implications for privacy. It formally and decisively decoupled privacy rights from property and applied them to the person. The court also held that the Fourth Amendment applied to oral statements just as it did to tangible objects.

In one respect, this strengthened privacy rights. The ruling reflected the fact that with technology allowing telephone calls to be made on the street, privacy rights should reside with the person. In the twenty-first century of networked digital technology, the principle that the Fourth Amendment protects people, not places, is more consequential than ever.

The subtle yet significant development that went largely unnoticed at the time was that the Supreme Court decision did not make electronic eavesdropping illegal. Instead, it made it constitutionally permissible – as long as the police obtained a judicial warrant, they could tap telephone lines. This nuance was lost on many privacy advocates.

The ruling actually normalized wiretapping surveillance as a tool of law and order. Subsequent decisions, building on the Katz precedent, expanded the scope of wiretapping, most notably through Title III of the Omnibus Crime Control and Safe Streets Act of 1968. This legislation outlawed private wiretapping, while government wiretapping with judicial approval was authorized. It was passed at the height of social disorder on the streets and was shaped by racial politics.[27] It remains in effect today and is widely used, as viewers of the acclaimed TV series *The Wire* may recognize.

*

In 1972, *Griswold* v. *Connecticut* (1965) was extended to unmarried couples in the case *Eisenstadt* v. *Baird*. Then, in *Roe* v. *Wade* (1973), the Supreme Court held that the right to privacy 'was broad enough to encompass a woman's individual decision, taken with her doctor, to terminate her pregnancy'.[28] The defining legislation on a woman's right to have an abortion was achieved by expanding the constitutionally deemed right to privacy.

Millions of women who had campaigned for abortion to be legalized were overjoyed and relieved. But most activists had argued for abortion based on the right of a woman to control and to choose what happened to her body, rather than as a privacy issue. As Betty Friedan told the First National Conference on Abortion Laws in Chicago in 1969, there was: 'no full human dignity and personhood possible for women unless we demand the control over our own bodies.'[29]

Some pro-choice activists later criticized the privacy framing of the ruling. In the 1980s, radical feminist Catharine MacKinnon argued that abortion should be a public right rather than a private privilege. She noted that many women, especially poor and minority women, required government support to access rights like healthcare, which privacy laws did not address. MacKinnon called for 'abortion on demand' and free access to abortion. She also opposed the concept of privacy rights, believing that privacy served male supremacy and that limiting intervention into the private sphere would harm women.[30]

Granting abortion on the basis of privacy rights was also an error in the eyes of Justice Ruth Bader Ginsburg, who was nominated to the Supreme Court in 1993 – a nomination that was controversial because she had criticized *Roe* v. *Wade*. As a staunch advocate for abortion rights, Ginsburg believed that the right to abortion should be framed as a matter of equal rights: to achieve gender equality, women needed control over their fertility. She would have preferred that the court provide state legislatures with limited guidance, allowing them to gradually develop new policies for abortion. Ginsburg also warned that linking the right to abortion solely to a constitutional right could elevate its prominence and exacerbate the conflict surrounding it, while leaving feminists relying on a less convincing privacy argument. She felt that a privacy-based justification would not strengthen the moral argument for abortion but instead weaken it. Her observations have proven to be highly prescient.

*

'Privacy' was not the key issue for those whose private lives remained criminalized. Sodomy was illegal. Gay and lesbian rights groups, including the Mattachine Society and the

Daughters of Bilitis, were more concerned with seeking civil rights. They demanded the freedom to enjoy same-sex relations in private and to be themselves. Members of the Gay Liberation Front, which formed in New York in 1969 after the Stonewall riots, prioritized visibility. Only by rejecting silence could one live honestly and be oneself.

The riots had begun on the night of 28 June 1969, when patrons of the Stonewall Inn, a gay bar in Manhattan's Greenwich Village, resisted a police raid with unprecedented defiance. What followed was a series of clashes that galvanized a movement, inspiring the creation of organizations which championed visibility and demanded recognition. On 28 June 1970, thousands of people marched from the Stonewall Inn to Central Park, New York, in America's first gay pride parade, which they called 'Christopher Street Liberation Day'. The official chant was: 'Say it loud, gay is proud.'

And yet, with the language of privacy in the air and being written into law, campaigners for sexual freedom seized the momentum to advance their causes. In 1973, the American Civil Liberties Union launched the Sexual Privacy Project to advance gay and lesbian rights. The ACLU's lawyer, Marilyn Haft, broadened the project's scope to include all consensual sex, partly to maintain the support of *Playboy*, which was funding the initiative. (Despite *Playboy*'s favourable coverage of gay liberation, Haft believed this broader focus would help keep publisher Hugh Hefner engaged.) A team of ACLU lawyers worked with sex workers, cross-dressers and porn stars as well as gay and lesbian people to challenge laws on sexual orientation and to advance people's right to make their own choices in sexual matters. They argued that laws against sodomy, cross-dressing and prostitution violated privacy rights.[31]

Mary Ann Larger, leader of the National Organization for Women's task force on rape law reform, then argued that rape violated women's 'sexual privacy' by compromising bodily integrity and publicly shaming them. Patient groups including the Network Against Psychiatric Assault suggested that the right to privacy meant patients could refuse unwanted treatment.[32] Privacy was increasingly framed as the freedom to do something, or to gain attention for a problem, rather than the freedom *from* something, as it had formerly been.

*

Just four months after President Ford's inaugural address, he signed into law the Privacy Act 1974, championing it as 'an initial advance in protecting a right precious to every American – the right of individual privacy'.[33] The legislation opened: 'The increasing use of computers and sophisticated information technology, while essential to the efficient operations of the Government, has greatly magnified the harm to individual privacy that can occur . . .'

The Privacy Act regulated what the government could do with data. It prohibited federal agencies from disclosing information without an individual's consent, gave individuals the right to access government records, and permitted them to pursue claims against government actors who breached the statute. It focused on an individual's right to know about the information government databases held on them, rather than addressing the question of whether the information should have been gathered in the first place. (Charles Reich would have been displeased.) An individual could enquire about information the government held on them, but not challenge the government's right to obtain and retain that information. Furthermore, exceptions were made for significant government agencies, including law enforcement.

Even though private companies were gathering acres of data about people's spending habits and shopping choices, Congress voted not to include the private sector in the Privacy Act. Instead, it created a commission to decide whether the private sector should be covered by federal privacy guidelines. This came to nothing. Congress never passed legislation to apply the guidelines to private businesses, although all major European nations would later do so. American companies were left free to gather whatever data they liked on the people who used their products. This would enable the as-yet-unborn giants of Silicon Valley to become some of the largest and most valuable companies in history.

One month after President Gerald Ford made his first speech to Congress, his wife, Betty Ford, found a lump in her right breast. She knew what she had to do. 'There had been so much cover-up during Watergate that we wanted to be sure there would be no cover-up in the Ford administration,' she told the feminist activist Gloria Steinem. 'So rather than continue this

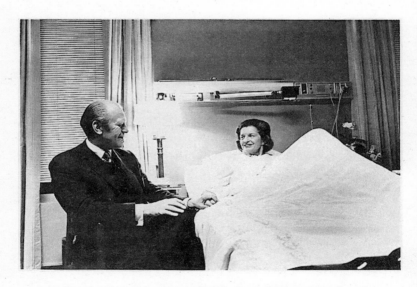

President Ford sits at Betty's bedside at Bethesda Naval Hospital on 2 October 1974 as she recovers from her mastectomy.

traditional silence about breast cancer, we felt we had to be very public.'[34]

Ford's senior advisers were unconvinced, believing that the revelation would cost them conservative votes. But Gerald and Betty Ford went ahead anyway and gave a press conference. No public figure had ever discussed their treatment, which included a radical mastectomy, in public, or in such detail. On CBS's news programme *60 Minutes*, the First Lady explained her decision: 'I thought, there are women all over the country like me. And if I don't make this public, then their lives will be gone or in jeopardy.' Millions of women began performing self-examinations and going for screenings.[35]

Until the 1950s, *The New York Times* wouldn't even publish the words *breast* and *cancer* together, and Betty Ford's candid approach was not universally embraced. The *Boston Globe* columnist Ellen Goodman complained that 'one of the worst things about being a public person – by marriage and not by choice – must be having a private problem. When the removal of your breast becomes a media event, you've had the ultimate invasion of privacy.'[36] But the Fords' popularity, and especially Betty's, rose.

Betty Ford didn't stop there. She held regular press conferences – the first First Lady since Eleanor Roosevelt to do so – and talked freely and openly about her private life. When journalist Morley Safer pressed her on *60 Minutes* about whether her kids had smoked cannabis, she said she assumed they had experimented with it. She also admitted that she and her husband slept in separate beds, and that she'd had a face-lift.

Betty Ford confronted her own struggles with striking honesty. She disclosed her alcoholism and her struggle with dependence on prescription drugs. In 1978, lacking a suitable rehab clinic and following a family intervention, she sought help at a naval hospital. Four years later, she established the Betty Ford Center, a facility dedicated to addiction recovery.

In her memoir, *A Glad Awakening*, Ford shared her thoughts on why she was so popular: 'I do think people relate to someone who has the same problems they have, and who overcomes them. And I think God has allowed me – along with thousands of others – to carry a message that says, there's help out there, and you too can be a survivor. Look at us. Look at me.'[37] The authentic self had arrived in the White House.

Chapter 18:

RELIGION COMES OUT OF THE CLOSET

In October 1976, George Gallup Jr, president of the American Institute of Public Opinion, stood before a congregation of Episcopalians in Minneapolis. The atmosphere was charged with anticipation. Gallup, who had broadened the scope of public opinion surveys to include the realm of religion, proclaimed that this year would for ever be etched in history as the 'Year of the Evangelical'.[1]

This statement was not made lightly. A nationwide Gallup poll had revealed a remarkable change in the religious landscape of America. Of the 1,500 Americans interviewed, one in three said they had had a 'born again' experience, a figure that *Time* estimated as amounting to fifty million Americans over the age of eighteen. Forty per cent of respondents said that the Bible was to be taken literally. The pews in evangelical churches were loud and full, while mainstream Protestant churches were hushed and losing members.[2]

Gallup was an active member of the Episcopalian denomination. He criticized them for being 'curiously restrained' and noted with dismay that 'we try very hard to keep our religious emotions in check'. It was time to end the silence, he suggested, asking rhetorically, what did they have to hide? He ended with a call to arms: 'Isn't it time for us to bring our religious feelings out of the closet?'[3]

The Gallup poll was conducted amid a heated campaign pitting Democrat Jimmy Carter, a third-generation Southern Baptist and devout born-again Christian who was comfortable talking about his beliefs, against the incumbent Republican president Gerald Ford, who mostly kept schtum about his Episcopalian faith. Religion had been broadly viewed as a private matter, to be kept out of the political sphere. However, in the course of his campaign, Carter discovered that this was no longer necessary or beneficial. His ability to talk about his beliefs struck a chord with millions of Americans who found resonance in his faith-driven narrative.

But when Carter spoke too openly about his religious beliefs and private matters in an infamous article in *Playboy* magazine, he almost cost himself the election. Distancing himself from the 'lying, cheating and distorting' of the truth of previous presidents, the Democratic nominee explained that he 'hoped' that his 'religious beliefs alone would prevent that from happening to me'. And, in a reckless case of a man invading his own privacy, he spoke about his own human failings. While explaining the Christian concept of sin and redemption, he said that he knew God had forgiven him, even though: 'I've looked on a lot of women with lust. I've committed adultery in my heart many times.'[4]

The soft pornography magazine promoted its interview with the Democratic candidate on the cover with the strapline: 'Now, the Real Jimmy Carter on Politics, Religion, the Press and Sex in an Incredible Playboy Interview'.[5] To the right of the text was an image of 'Playmate' Patti McGuire smouldering into the camera, her hands poised to undo the final button of a flimsy white top. The image took up most of the page.

Unsurprisingly, Carter's imagined infidelity was all anyone could talk about. Carter dropped fifteen percentage points and it looked for a moment like he would lose the election. He tried to dig himself out of the hole, by saying his comments were 'just part of being a human being', and that *Playboy* magazine was 'just another forum', but many voters were unconvinced. One man puzzled, 'It's weird that he's saying things like this.' The man's wife was more emphatic: 'It's not the kind of thing that a President ought to be talking about.' The vice president, Nelson Rockefeller, campaigning for Gerald Ford, practically cheered as he told an audience: 'I never thought I'd see the day when Christ's teachings were discussed in *Playboy* – and I am a Baptist, ladies and gentlemen!'[6]

Despite his gaffe, Carter had tapped into a powerful new force in American politics: private faith. Evangelical Christians were usually ignored or taken for granted. For over a century, they had steered clear of party politics. But now they were waking up, determined to protect both the family and their faith, which they feared were under threat from liberalization and feminism. They pushed their beliefs into the political arena and demanded their concerns be addressed. 'They've got an underground communications network,' the pollster Robert Teeter warned Gerald Ford's campaign, and Carter was 'plugged right into it'.[7] Ford's reticence about religion, his son Mike suggested, was a virtue: 'Jimmy Carter wears his religion on his sleeve but Jerry Ford wears it in his heart,' he said.[8] But after noting the mounting significance of the evangelical vote, Ford invited twenty-three evangelical leaders to the White House for a special conference.

This surge of religious fervour signalled a transformative moment in American politics. Historically, the church was viewed as responsible for preserving the soul and the family, not the state. However, various groups on the right were beginning to challenge this perspective, advocating for the family to become a central focus of government policy. They crossed the boundaries between the public and private spheres, challenging the traditional separation of the two. Their primary concerns included promoting family values, restricting reproductive rights, opposing abortion and resisting the expansion of gay rights.

*

On the morning of Saturday, 19 November 1977, Congresswoman Barbara Jordan, the first African American woman elected to the United States House of Representatives, opened the 1977 National Women's Conference in Houston, Texas, with a powerful speech: 'The call of equal and human rights will reap what is sown,' she began. 'What will you reap? What will you sow?'⁹ Huge cheers went up from the floor. There were around 2,000 delegates and 15,000 to 20,000 observers in attendance.

Jordan tamped down the applause with a note of caution. She reminded the women of the differences of opinion and experiences among the delegates, which, she said, should not be ignored. But she also called for humility in the quest for a larger cause: 'No one person and no subgroup has the right answer.' With a wry flash of humour, she joked: 'Wonder Woman is not in the hall.' Jordan assured the audience that there was plenty of room for disagreement, but they needed to be united in their aim. The National Women's Conference must focus on the prize, she said. Congress had approved $5 million for them to spend: 'If we do nothing here productive, constructive or healing, we will have wasted much more than money.'

They aimed to develop a plan of action and compile it into a report titled *The Spirit of Houston*, which they intended to present to the Carter administration and Congress. The report would address key issues like reproductive rights, childcare funding, sexual orientation, education reform and the rights of minority, disabled and elderly women. Most importantly of all, the resolutions up for vote at conference that year included a landmark piece of legislation: the Equal Rights Amendment (ERA). Introduced to Congress as early as 1923, the ERA sought to outlaw discrimination based on sex. Despite its promising start, the amendment had stalled for decades, failing to secure the necessary support for ratification. Yet it now appeared on the verge of success. Thirty-five states had already ratified the amendment, leaving just three more needed to enshrine gender equality into the Constitution.

Resolving this matter had been a long time coming, but both major parties appeared united in their support for women's rights. Standing behind Jordan on stage were Lady Bird Johnson, Rosalynn Carter and Betty Ford – First Ladies representing both Democrats and Republicans, presenting a powerful front. Apart from Jordan, who foresaw potential fractures within the feminist movement, they all believed victory was assured. However, they had underestimated the sheer force and passion of the women offstage, who felt very differently. An undercurrent of dissent would soon make itself impossible to ignore, challenging the very assumptions of those who thought the battle was already won.

Within the hall, the women's movement was fragmenting. It was here that women of colour formed their own minority caucus. Informed by the work of Black feminists from Boston, who developed a theory that would later become known as intersectionality, theirs was a perspective which departed from that of the white women who dominated the feminist movement. They argued that a person's social and political identities combined to create discrimination and privilege, and that white feminists didn't fully acknowledge the role race played in their oppression.

Two days after Barbara Jordan's opening address, as the policies on reproductive freedom were finalized, including the endorsement of *Roe* v. *Wade*, a group of women surged onto the stage, holding a large photograph of a fetus. They were protesters, deeply opposed to abortion. Some sobbed, while others sang, 'All we are saying is give life a chance.' Nearby, the conservative Mississippi delegation knelt in prayer. Many of the demonstrators wore long

white ribbons emblazoned with the word MAJORITY, a clear nod
to Nixon's invocation of the 'silent majority' – the Americans who
supported his policies but rarely voiced their opinions publicly.
During a discussion about freedom of sexual preference, a delegate
from Texas raised a homemade sign that read, 'Keep 'em in the
closet'. Hundreds of women inside the hall – and beyond it – were
opposed to equal rights. They were self-described 'anti-feminists'.
And they weren't going to be silent any more.

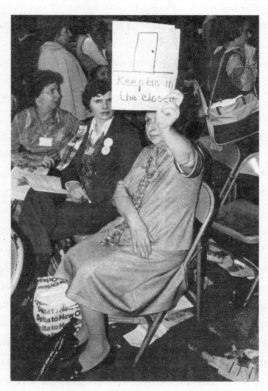

A delegate at the First National Women's Conference in Houston, Texas,
expresses her displeasure with the views aired during the discussion on
freedom of sexual preference.

On the other side of the city, on the same day, a counter-event to the National Women's Conference took place. 'I would like to thank my husband Frank for letting me come today,' the conservative activist Phyllis Stewart Schlafly said with a bright smile to the women congregated before her. 'I like to say that because it irritates the women's libbers more than anything else I say.'[10]

Schlafly, a mother of six with a blonde bouffant, always had a sparkle in her eye and steel in her spine. As a loud and proud conservative, she declared, 'I am not ashamed or afraid to ask for God's blessing,' earning cheers and applause at the 'Pro-God, Pro-Life, Pro-Family' rally she had organized.

She told the assembled crowd that she had been banned from the NWC and asserted that several thousand other women who shared her feelings had also been turned away and ignored (both claims seemed unlikely). She announced that her goal was to defeat the ERA, calling it a threat that would entrench abortion and grant homosexuals the same rights as married couples. Addressing the crowd and the surrounding media, she declared, 'By coming here today, you have shown that this is not what women want.' She and her acolytes cannily adopted the language of radical feminism, referring to ideas like 'the personal is political' that had suffused the political culture and the women's movement. 'We are raising the consciousness of the public all over America. We are in the business of raising the consciousness of our lawmakers in Washington,' said one speaker.[11]

With an eye for media opportunities and a knack for soundbites, Schlafly leveraged grassroots support to unite three separate single-issue campaigns – anti-ERA, anti-abortion and anti-homosexual rights – into a vocal and cohesive pro-family and pro-life movement. She and her expanding network argued that the ERA would undermine traditional family values, remove legal protections for women and instigate social changes they opposed.

By consolidating these diverse groups, Schlafly also made a significant impact on the politics of the Republican Party.

*

Until the mid-1970s, both Democrats and Republicans had generally supported the women's rights movement. Women's issues were divisive, of course, but that division did not necessarily align with party lines. In 1967 the Republican governor of California, Ronald Reagan, signed a bill liberalizing abortion laws. In August 1972, a year before *Roe* v. *Wade* legalized abortion, a Gallup poll revealed that 68 per cent of Republicans and 58 per cent of Democrats agreed 'the decision to have an abortion should be made solely by a woman and her physician'.[12]

At the time of Jimmy Carter's election victory in 1976, abortion was still relatively uncontroversial. Although a few evangelical voices, including the journal *Christianity Today*, were critical of *Roe* v. *Wade*, most were silent on the issue. Southern Baptists, including Carter, viewed the decision as a proper expression of the separation of church and state. Or they advocated for the liberalization of abortion laws – in 1971, the Southern Baptist Convention had passed a resolution supporting liberalization in certain cases, including rape.[13] But this perspective was in flux.

A growing anti-abortion movement was mobilizing, drawing support primarily from grassroots activists, though it also received backing from the Catholic Church. This cause engaged ordinary people in the political arena for the first time, driven by strong convictions about abortion as a moral evil. As Ellen McCormack, a New York homemaker who ran for the Democratic presidential nomination on a right-to-life platform in 1976, told *Newsday*, she was a 'very contented housewife, happy with my family'. But then, she continued: 'the feminist movement had become the darling of the media and they were pressuring the legislatures around the country to legalize abortions. And they were winning'.[14]

Right-to-life advocates saw 'state-sanctioned' abortion as an intrusion by government into the private sphere of the family. In their view, the secular state was imposing its values on families and violating the rights of parents. They invoked their own concept of 'privacy' as a way of protecting the rights of parents to shape the moral content of family life; of guarding themselves against the ERA, abortion, gay and lesbian rights, and pornography. But at the same time, they also argued that these issues were no longer solely matters for the church or the family; instead, they were political questions: the personal was for them political.

By the end of the Carter years, the religious right had gelled, in part due to Schlafly's focus and energy. Ronald Reagan realized that to win the votes of this new movement, he too needed to take these deeply personal and increasingly divisive issues seriously. He understood that the voters he aimed to attract were angry about the situation and that he had to appeal to their concerns. By 1976, the year Carter was elected, Regan had jumped on the bandwagon and claimed that it had been a mistake to liberalize abortion in California. By the 1980s, he had declared the Grand Old Party the party of 'family values'.

Political strategist Paul Weyrich, of the conservative Heritage Foundation, and Republican Richard Viguerie worked to mobilize the agitating evangelicals as a political force. In 1979 they enlisted Jerry Falwell, a Baptist pastor, to establish an organization called the Moral Majority. Coined by Weyrich, the name was reminiscent of Nixon's 'silent majority', and the movement aimed to combat secular humanism.

Falwell pulled together supporters around the issues that Schlafly had already highlighted and energized: opposition to abortion, gay rights, sexual freedom, women's liberation and the ERA. The Moral Majority's main purpose was to mobilize evangelical Christians and other religious conservatives into political action, with a focus on promoting traditional family values, conservative social policies and Christian moral principles in government. Notably, those Falwell rallied to his political congregation were not all evangelical believers, but the movement sought to integrate conservative Christian values into public policy and politics. By pushing private issues into the public arena, they helped to erode the boundary between private religious morality and behaviour in the secular political realm.

Across the political spectrum, deeply personal and private issues became subjects of significant interest, with both the left and right politicizing the private realm. Radical feminists sought to dismantle traditional family structures, organizing to liberate women and children from patriarchal oppression. In contrast, conservative proponents of the traditional family criticized the prevailing emphasis on individual choice and rights, advocating instead for a renewed focus on moral discipline and the preservation of the traditional nuclear family. By the end of the 1970s, each had adopted a political and a cultural style animated by indictment and indignation, focused on fighting over deeply personal matters. Both factions had developed political and cultural styles characterized by indictment and indignation, focused on the debate over the best version and purpose of private life. But while the New Left faced internal divisions, the right gained momentum.

Chapter 19:

'A SPECTATORIAL STATE OF MIND'

On Thursday, 11 January 1973, ten million Americans gathered around their televisions at 9 p.m. to watch a household self-destruct. *An American Family* was a twelve-hour documentary series on PBS, the publicly funded broadcasting service, chronicling seven months in the lives of the William C. Louds: an attractive, upper-middle-class family living on a mountain drive in Santa Barbara, California. Pat was forty-seven years old and Bill fifty-one. Their children were Lance, twenty; Kevin, eighteen; Grant, seventeen; Delilah, sixteen; and Michele, fourteen.

The Louds were prosperous, with four cars, three dogs, two cats and a horse. They had a sumptuous ranch-style home. Bill owned a successful manufacturing business; Pat was a hip housewife who wore mini-skirts and polo necks. Their sons sloped about with shoulder-length hair, their slim hips wrapped in flared trousers. The family held huge parties, surrounded by precious antiques and modern art, and stretched out by their pool. On the face of it, this modern family was living the American dream.

The producer, Craig Gilbert, had deliberately chosen a family, from the many who volunteered, whose lifestyle seemed most similar to those portrayed in popular sitcoms like *The Brady Bunch*. He hoped to get underneath that affluent veneer, to show a 'real view' of the ideal middle-class lifestyle to which people were supposed to aspire.[1]

In a radical departure from other documentaries, there would
be no script and no presenter. Instead, viewers would be able to
witness the unvarnished truth in the subjects' own words. Writing
in *TV Guide*, the eminent anthropologist Margaret Mead called
An American Family 'as new and significant as the invention of
drama or the novel – a new way in which people can look at life,
by seeing the real life of others interpreted by the camera'.[2]

To create Gilbert's 'real' view of family life, he and his crew
filmed 300 hours of raw footage, capturing all the messiness of what
goes on in a family behind closed doors. The life of the Louds may
have seemed perfect from the outside, but in reality the family was
as complicated as any other, working life out as they went along –
only they were doing so in front of millions of people. In the ninth
episode, Pat told her womanizing husband to move out. She and
Bill would go on to divorce after two decades of marriage. Lance,
their twenty-year-old son, lived a hedonistic lifestyle in Manhattan's Chelsea neighbourhood and was the first openly gay person to
be portrayed in a family context on American television.

Overnight, all of America seemed to be talking about the Louds,
examining their lives and dissecting their shortcomings. In *Newsweek*, the journalist Shana Alexander described them as 'affluent
zombies'. Their 'shopping carts overflow', she sneered, 'but their
minds are empty'.[3] In *The New York Times*, Anne Roiphe pulled each
member apart. She likened Lance Loud to an 'evil flower', 'camping
and queening about like a pathetic court jester, a Goyaesque emotional dwarf', with his 'flamboyant, leechlike homosexuality'. She
conceded that Grant had a 'charming but disturbing indolence', but
Delilah possessed no saving graces: 'like the rest of the Louds', the
teenage girl 'never grieved for the migrant workers, the lettuce pick-
ers, the war dead; never thought of philosophy or poetry, was not
obsessed by adolescent idealism'.[4] It was brutal.

The Louds were the first TV stars to become famous simply for
being themselves, and the experience changed them for ever.

'Television ate my family,' Lance Loud said in the aftermath.[5] They each felt compelled to keep on performing. Pat Loud wrote an auto-biography, prefiguring the memoir boom of the 1990s. Bill modelled in his bathrobe for *Esquire*. Delilah appeared as a 'bachelorette' on *The Dating Game*, and all five children performed as a rock band on *The Dick Cavett Show*. Lance posed naked for *Screw* magazine.

The cameras never turned off for good. As the years passed, the producers came back to them for updates in documentaries that included *An American Family Revisited: The Louds 10 Years Later*. Even in 2001, when Lance was dying from an AIDS-related illness, filmmakers Susan and Alan Raymond filmed his final two months in *Lance Loud! A Death in an American Family*. At the end of his life, at its most tragic and private moment, Lance invited a TV camera to his hospice bedside. According to the Raymonds, he wanted to be filmed one last time to show the bonds of affection that survived in his family. His dying wish was to prove to the American people that the Loud family was not broken.

On 3 April 1974, one year after the airing of *An American Family*, the BBC ran its own twelve-part observational series, *The Family*, credited as Britain's first fly-on-the-wall documentary. As many as ten million people, about a quarter of the adult popula-tion, sat down at 9.25 p.m. to watch the first episode.

In this case the intention of the producer, Paul Watson, was to make a film about the kind of people who never normally got onto television. Each episode began with the camera panning across the rooftops of terraced houses before zooming in through a window and focusing on the photograph of a family on the mantelpiece, framed by knick-knacks – a grey china dog and a white plastic poodle. The camera pulled back to show the family themselves standing in front of their photo: Margaret Wilkins, thirty-seven; her husband Terry, forty, a bus driver, and their four children: Marion, nineteen; Gary, eighteen; Heather, fifteen; and Christopher, nine. Squeezed into a rented flat in Reading above the greengrocer's shop where Margaret worked part time, they were struggling to get by.

The documentary-makers spent two months with the Wilkins family before starting to film them, which they did for eighteen hours a day over three months. They even had their own key to the front door. In the very first episode, Watson warned Margaret Wilkins that the series would be 'a tremendous intrusion into your privacy . . . We will film everything.' Across a blue Formica table, surrounded by her brood, Margaret replied that the family had talked it over and they had all agreed to proceed. Between mouthfuls of fish and chips and bread and butter, she elaborated: 'It gives us a chance to portray ordinary people, if you like, instead of actors and actresses on the screen . . . with beautiful kitchens, nothing out of place . . . no dirty pans . . . all sparkling – well, people's kitchens aren't like that.' Giving up their privacy would reveal the authentic truth behind glossy appearances. It would be real life.

The Wilkins family, filmed at home during morning coffee, 25 March 1974. From left to right: Marian, Karen and her boyfriend Tom, and Margaret with her grandson Scott.

But 'real life' was not to every viewer's liking. By the standards of the day, the Wilkinses had an unconventional – and for some, immoral – set-up. Of the children, nineteen-year-old Marian was living with her boyfriend Tom, who didn't see the point of getting married. Eighteen-year-old Gary had fathered a child two years earlier and, together with his young wife Karen, was living with Margaret and Terry until they could secure council accommodation. Heather's boyfriend, Melvin, was from the Caribbean. In the early 1970s, mixed relationships were met with societal resistance as racial prejudices remained ingrained, further exacerbated by negative sentiments towards recently arrived Black immigrants. The family received hate mail about the relationship. The youngest of the children, nine-year-old Christopher, was not Terry's biological son but the result of an affair, although Terry accepted him as his own. The family talked about their difficulties as if they were in a dark corner of the local pub and the camera was a close friend in whom they could confide – except their conversations were broadcast to the nation.

The Christian art teacher Mary Whitehouse, a well-known critic of the 'permissive society', lambasted the programme and the Wilkinses for their 'vulgarity'.[6] Other outraged commentators, including five MPs, called for *The Family* to be banned in case its millions of viewers began to emulate their behaviour. The family were vilified by the press. Their use of profane language and willingness to talk about taboo subjects were reported as definitive evidence of social breakdown. Eventually they removed their number from the phone book to avoid the hundreds of telephone callers wanting to condemn or congratulate them for challenging social mores.

To say that the Wilkins family found the attention a strain would be an understatement. Within a few years of filming, their personal lives had imploded. 'When you see your life through other people's eyes, it does change things,' reflected Margaret

Wilkins in one of her many subsequent interviews.[7] In the years following the show, three of the marriages – Margaret's, Gary's and Marian's (as she had eventually married Tom) – broke up. 'I might never have divorced and married again if it hadn't been for the programme because Terry and I were getting along fine before *The Family* went out,' Margaret remarked. 'Things change, though, when you wash your dirty laundry in public. That's what made us different – other people didn't do that sort of thing, then, but we did.'[8]

Margaret Wilkins was right. Back then, most people didn't expose the minutiae of their family life and its inevitable entanglements to millions of strangers on national television. The nature and scale of that disclosure was unprecedented, and the Wilkinses, who were entirely unprepared for life in the spotlight, were burnt by the glare of publicity. They remained a kind of public property for decades, with the press continuing to follow them on and off for the rest of their lives.

While Margaret expressed mixed feelings about having taken part in the documentary, her American counterpart Pat Loud was sanguine. In the years after *An American Family* was broadcast, she conceded that they had been naive but stood by their decision to take part. She advocated greater openness in everyday life to dispel romantic and outdated notions of what domestic life was really like. In her 1974 autobiography, she wrote that she hoped their experience would inspire others: 'We opened the doors in a lot of houses and blew out a lot of dust and I'll bet we started a thousand arguments of the kind Bill and I never had. If families are going to make it, that's how. Not with secrets, or little slots to fit into, or a lot of propaganda from parents.'[9]

The making of *An American Family* and *The Family* signalled a revolution in our understanding of private life. By taking television cameras deep inside the home and pointing them into the nooks and crannies of family relationships, the programme-makers stepped across the residual historical border between the public and private spheres. The Louds and the Wilkinses became famous for who they were rather than what they had achieved; for their private doings rather than their public acts.

The responsibility for this intrusion lay with documentary-makers at PBS and the BBC, but also with the two families themselves. They were eager participants. It is inconceivable that a family from an earlier period would have countenanced inviting millions of strangers into the home to poke about and pass judgement on how they lived. The family unit had been a fortress of privacy; the Louds and the Wilkinses lowered the drawbridge and welcomed everyone in.

They were not the only ones exposing the intimate details of their lives to strangers. Ideas and feelings about what should be public and what should be private, as well as privacy itself – what it was and what it was for – were in flux. The right to be let alone had been transformed into being seen or known, and the revealing of one's inner self. This was a development that three influential thinkers – Tom Wolfe, a daring writer with keen insights into American culture; sociologist Richard Sennett, author of a landmark study of the public sphere; and historian Christopher Lasch – were poised to illuminate.

*

Tom Wolfe strode through the bustling streets of New York City in 1976, his signature cream linen suit gleaming in the afternoon sun. Known for his sharp eye and even sharper pen, Wolfe had become a literary sensation, capturing the essence of American society with unparalleled flair. It was in this metropolis that Wolfe wrote his epoch-defining article for *New York Magazine*, provocatively titled 'The "Me" Decade and the Third Great Awakening'.[10]

The magazine's cover was a striking tableau of cheerful men

and women adorned in bright yellow T-shirts, each emblazoned with the word 'Me'. Each person in that jubilant crowd pointed at themselves, an illustration of the self-obsession Wolfe sought to lampoon. Within the pages of his report, he dissected 'The "Me Decade"' with merciless wit, skewering the legions of individuals spending small fortunes on psychoanalysis, indulging in endless conversations about their own psyches.

Wolfe ridiculed the 'est' movement, a popular programme of self-actualization founded in 1971 San Francisco by a former encyclopedia salesman named Werner Erhard. Erhard ran courses enabling people to find out how to be themselves, asserting that there was no fixed, innate self, meaning a person could become anything they desired. Equally worthy of Wolfe's scorn was the Human Potential Movement, which emerged along the scenic coastline of Big Sur in California. This movement sought to counter the stultifying psychological and social conditioning of modern life using hallucinogenic drugs. To Wolfe, the whole endeavour reeked of self-importance and a desperate yearning for transcendence that bordered on the absurd.

Wolfe masterfully encapsulated the social movements and trends of the 1960s and early 1970s into one quasi-religious mantra: 'Let's talk about Me.' He observed that the self-realization movement's influence stretched far beyond the picturesque confines of Big Sur, permeating every corner of American society. No group or fashion, he declared, was immune to the mania for 'me'.

Wolfe did not hesitate to include feminism. He noted with a touch of sardonic humour, 'The great unexpected dividend of the feminist movement has been to elevate an ordinary status – woman, housewife – to the level of drama.' Wolfe characterized the Me Generation's narcissism as a millenarian awakening – 'the greatest age of individualism in American history', as he described it. Richard Sennett and Christopher Lasch observed the same trend but attributed it to different causes.

Sennett's seminal *The Fall of Public Man* (1974) regarded an obsession with the self as the dominant social and cultural phenomenon of the late twentieth century. But unlike Wolfe, he argued that changes in the public and private realm were decisive to the rise of the me-obsessed self. Sennett described how the 'Public Man' of the Enlightenment era had inhabited an impersonal, theatrical space in which he had acted out public roles. Private men had donned public personas meticulously governed by elaborate rituals and conventions, such as formal terms of address and the handshake. This was the world of the flourishing metropolises of London and Paris, the spectatorship of Joseph Addison, coffee-houses, the thundering presses and stinging criticism, the French salon, the beauty spots and long wigs decried by Rousseau. It was where new rituals of engagement were fashioned. Physical public spaces had expanded, and the concept of public opinion had emerged as a critical arbiter of values.

The men of that world did not typically reveal their inner, private selves in this public sphere, where they were known for their deeds rather than their identities. The realm of the Public Man was one where private identity remained discreetly behind the curtain; public performance was what mattered. That theatricality allowed for a separation between public persona and private self, and for freedom in private life.

Sennett argued that this carefully constructed public sphere had been overwhelmed by what he called the 'intimate society'. Public life had become dry and regarded as phoney. In this new paradigm, individuals began to treat public matters as extensions of their personal lives. Social relations were no longer about communal engagement but, rather, opportunities for self-disclosure and personal revelation. The public square, once a stage for collective discourse and shared rituals, had been transformed into a platform for the inner lives and private selves of its inhabitants. As he put it: 'Intimate society has entirely reversed [Henry]

Fielding's dictum that praise or censure should apply to actions rather than actors; now what matters is not what you have done but how you feel about it.'[11]

But rather than, as Sennett's argument holds, the private realm *overtaking* the public, it might be more accurate to understand it as the erosion of any meaningful border between the two. As the two spheres collapsed into each other, the once-distinct boundary between public and private realms effectively vanished.

For Sennett, the fading of the public, theatrical man and the valorization of feelings marked a sharp and unfortunate turn inward. It meant that the private self was everything, effacing the public. 'The world of intimate feeling loses any boundaries,' he wrote; and 'the private overspills its boundaries and overtakes the vitality and importance of the public.'[12] Sennett's analysis underlined the destructive social consequences: diminished public engagement and community life but also a shallow individual: to know oneself had become an end in itself rather than a way of knowing the world.

Almost as soon as *The Fall of Public Man* hit the bookshelves, and as Tom Wolfe was tearing into the Me Generation, another voice emerged, offering one of the most prescient analyses of the era.

*

On the evening of 30 May 1979, Christopher Lasch, a professor of history at the University of Rochester, stood in the White House lobby. The disenchanted man of the left, then in his late forties, was questioning whether he should really be there. Daniel Bell, a Harvard sociologist known for *The End of Ideology* (1960), a sober attempt to come to terms with the exhaustion of political ideologies, joined him. Bell, then sixty, had recently published *The Coming of the Post-Industrial Society* (1976). He stood, relaxed, as they waited. The Reverend Jesse Jackson strode in, too.

In his late thirties, the self-appointed heir to Martin Luther King was in no doubt about what he was doing there. He had been invited to dinner with President Jimmy Carter to discuss America's problems.

The energy crisis dominated the news. There were massive fuel shortages. Purchasing petrol was regulated. Long lines of people, including on one day a woman with a pillow stuffed in her dress to suggest a pregnancy, queued down the streets to buy what they were permitted on their allotted day. Prices had doubled.[13] Carter's approval ratings were plummeting.

The evening began with drinks, followed by a simple dinner and ice cream. Carter's pollster Patrick Caddell, a twenty-nine-year-old tasked with presenting top intellectual ideas to the President, introduced the night's topic. Caddell noted that the country faced a deep moral crisis and a loss of confidence in the system, with rising pessimism about the future, cynicism towards politics and declining public interest. He asked the experts for advice on what the administration should do.

Christopher Lasch shifted uncomfortably in his seat. He didn't think of himself as a government adviser and had criticized public intellectuals who gave up detachment for influence. He was also sceptical of Carter's approach. The first president to call himself a born-again Christian seemed to think that what the downbeat American people needed was a chastening lecture. Lasch stayed silent for most of the discussion.

Eventually, he made a clumsy contribution. The crisis of confidence, he said, sitting up in his chair, wasn't just a spiritual or psychological condition. It had a basis in reality. Americans, he said, had a realistic awareness of the economic and political climate. The public were right to be worried – he certainly was. Once he started, Lasch didn't hold back. Calling for civil responsibility, as the President had suggested, was one thing; but he advised Carter not to ask the public to make minor personal sacrifices, which would hit the least well off. Individual solutions wouldn't be distributed fairly. Lasch warned Carter that his approach would benefit the professional classes and elites while penalizing ordinary people.

But when Carter asked him what *he* would do, Lasch replied that he had no idea. At that point, he later recalled, 'I realized that my career as a presidential adviser was destined to be a short one.' When the group met again, Lasch wasn't invited.[14]

Even so, Lasch had a big impact on the understanding of the times. Over pre-dinner drinks, Jimmy Carter had boasted that he had speed-read all the guests' works. With his broad white smile and folksy manner, Carter explained that it was Lasch's book *The Culture of Narcissism: American Life in an Age of Diminishing Expectations* (1979) that had particularly hit a nerve inside the White House, as well as far beyond it.

Despite his hopeless dinner performance, Lasch was the go-to public intellectual of his time, known for his ability to diagnose the problems of the age. His book spent seven weeks on the *New York Times* bestseller list, propelling the droll social critic into the limelight. He wasn't as flamboyant or as impeccably dressed as Tom Wolfe, but his book had the word *narcissism* in its title – a ringing term of the era, and one that would continue to resonate for decades. *Time* magazine described him as a 'biblical prophet'.[15]

While Tom Wolfe thought the narcissistic self was a consequence of aggressive individualism, in Lasch's crucial insight it was an expression of a 'fragile self', or what he later characterized as a 'minimal self'.[16] A narcissist, according to Lasch, wasn't just an individual with a huge ego. And he didn't think that individualism had come to dominate society. For Lasch, the self being shaped in this period was a weak self: anxious and needy rather than egotistical and hedonistic, and perpetually seeking recognition that it existed.

Lasch's overarching metaphor was inspired by Ovid's myth of Narcissus, the beautiful boy who becomes so absorbed in his own image that he forgets the water in which it is reflected is separate from himself. Narcissus drowns in the pool, not because he's in love with himself but because he doesn't understand that what is before him is a reflection. Lasch argued that the narcissistic individual is diminished, unable to differentiate between what goes on in their own mind and what happens in the outside world. A narcissist sees no boundary between how they feel and the reality around them.

For Lasch, narcissistic culture was not a product of the rise of social liberalism, as the right argued; nor was it the consequence of rampant and empty consumerism, at which Tom Wolfe pointed the finger of blame. Instead, Lasch saw the self-expressive, self-obsessed individual of the 1970s as a product of deeper long-term social and political trends that had eroded solidarity. As David Riesman had identified, religion and tradition, once sturdy pillars of communal life, lay shattered. Lasch also pointed to the disintegration of a shared historical continuity which fostered an unsettling alienation from the past. The individual was adrift in the present, with their uncertain gaze fixed upon an elusive future.

Pervasive pessimism gripped the zeitgeist, manifesting in apocalyptic visions that permeated the cultural consciousness. Environmentalists, epitomized by Rachel Carson's watershed work *Silent Spring* (1962), prophesied the imminent extinction of life on Earth. The Cuban Missile Crisis further underscored humanity's predicament, casting doubt on its ability to alter its inexorable fate. In this context, wrote Lasch, it made sense 'to live only for the moment' and to fix our eyes on our own 'private performance'; to become 'connoisseurs of our own decadence, to cultivate transcendental self-attention'.[17]

Lasch noted that collective politics had responded to these

issues by retreating inward and focusing on the private realm. The New Left had shifted its emphasis from broader social change towards developing the self and personalizing politics. This combination of pessimism about the future and the retreat from collective politics to the self, Lasch argued, created a 'spectatorial' state of mind in which people became observers rather than agents of their own lives and required constant affirmation. In an age long before selfies, social media and live-streaming, Lasch observed that 'we cannot help responding to others as if their actions – and our own – were being recorded and simultaneously transmitted to an unseen audience'.[18]

*

In the course of the twentieth century, psychology and behaviourism had crossed into the private realm with social research and Edward Bernays' 'engineering of consent'. Rather than leave individuals alone or improve them for their own good, there was a sense that they should be manipulated or reengineered. That meant going into their heads – the private sphere.

The public sphere, once a vibrant arena for political engagement and social ritual, had come to be understood as a place of falsity and inauthenticity. Disenchanted with its potential to foster genuine social change, various political groups and movements had turned away from it and gone inwards. Their private selves were what they viewed as important, not their public personas or collective politics. The optimism that had once fuelled public activism gave way to a retreat into the private realm, which now held a privileged position in the social consciousness.

While the private realm was revered as a sanctuary from the perceived insincerity of public life, it simultaneously became public property and the focus of intense politicking. The intimate details of individual lives, once shielded from the public gaze, were exposed and scrutinized. A culture of disclosure evolved in which people exposed their private lives to public view more readily and more completely than ever before, and sought to be affirmed for their private selves.

As people became ever more open in public about their private selves, they were also being held to more demanding political standards by the guardians of progressive thinking. In other words, just as the public was experimenting with greater openness about private life, the private domain itself was being politicized. The private sphere was left unprotected, and separated from privacy, while the self was projected further and further outwards. In turn, the right began to focus its political energy on realizing the best version of the private domain, and questions of faith and private matters were pushed into the public realm. By the end of the 1970s, the separation between public and private that had been forged in the eighteenth century had dissolved.

PART V:
Blurred Lines

Chapter 20:

REALMS BEYOND OUR DREAMS

In the autumn of 1983, a twenty-eight-year-old man with feathered brown hair walked across the stage at a hotel in Hawaii to a spotlit podium fronted with the Apple logo. He stood, bouncing lightly on the balls of his feet in time to Irene Cara's uplifting 'What a Feeling', from the hit film *Flashdance*. As the music faded, he started to speak.

'Hi,' he said casually to the 900-strong crowd of Apple sales executives. 'I'm Steve Jobs.'[1]

The audience erupted into laughter. Jobs, after all, alongside his partner Steve Wozniak, had achieved the near-impossible. From their humble beginnings in the early 1970s as a two-man operation tinkering away in the confines of Jobs' father's garage, they had transformed the Apple Computer Company into a 300-million-dollar enterprise, the fastest-growing corporation in American business history. Jobs was practically a god.

He proceeded to deliver a brief and somewhat tendentious history of computing, focused on arch-competitor IBM's failures. At first, he explained, IBM had dismissed the personal computer as 'too small to do serious computing and therefore unimportant to their business'. It was left to Apple to develop 'the first personal computer as we know it today'. IBM – Jobs recounted, with a shake of his head – had only entered the personal computing market in 1981, when it brought out its first PC, lagging behind as the market took off. The crowd lapped this up, incredulous at the lack of foresight that had plagued their rivals.

But by 1983, Big Blue, IBM's nickname, had caught up with Apple. Which was why Jobs now stood on the stage with news of the Next Big Thing.

'It is now 1984,' Jobs said, envisaging the year ahead. 'IBM wants it all and is aiming its guns on its last obstacle to industry control: Apple. Will Big Blue dominate the entire computer industry? The entire information age? Was George Orwell right about 1984?'

The spotlight on Jobs faded as an advertisement for the next product launch took over the stage. Directed by Ridley Scott, it was as well produced as a Hollywood blockbuster.

Bald men in grey prison uniforms marched through a tunnel and filtered into a hall, taking their seats in neat rows. Their faces were expressionless as they faced a giant TV screen, where a large male head droned on. The scene was shot entirely in monochrome, except for one striking figure: a blonde athlete in red shorts. Pursued by police, she raced into the hall, clutching a long hammer in her hand. With a powerful leap and a graceful spin, she hurled the weapon at the talking head, shattering the screen into a thousand fragments. As the glass rained down, a male voiceover intoned: 'On January 24th, Apple Computer will introduce Macintosh. And you'll see why 1984 won't be like *1984*.'

With flashes of camera bulbs lighting up his face, Jobs rallied the crowd: 'Let's go do it again. Let's show 'em . . . why 1984 won't be like *1984*.'

Back in the late 1960s, computers – what Vance Packard called 'giant memory machines' – had been the stuff of nightmares. These colossal devices evoked visions of a future where humanity might be subjugated by the very technology it had created. A mere two decades later, the technological behemoths had been miniaturized into sleek desktop boxes, readily accessible to businesses and individuals alike. No longer monstrous and intimidating, they were symbols of innovation, creativity and boundless potential.

The advert showcasing the Macintosh as a tool for challenging conformity ran during the Super Bowl of 1983 and was wildly successful, generating sales of 50,000 over the following seventy-four days.[2] Although it was only broadcast once, it ranks high on lists of the most influential commercials of all time.

Steve Jobs was a visionary who realized long before anyone else that the invention of the computer would be more important than the introduction of TV. When he predicted that people would spend more time interacting with personal computers than with their cars, few believed him. He was also broadly correct that the future world of personal computing would not be like George Orwell's dystopian novel *Nineteen Eighty-Four*, and that it would be bound up with dreams of liberation. But even Jobs didn't foresee that, rather than a dictatorial Big Brother figure installing surveillance cameras in every home, hundreds of millions of people would voluntarily admit the all-seeing camera into their lives and invite the world to watch them in real time.

This is the paradox of the digital age. What was marketed as a revolt against conformity and authority became the means by which people's lives were more observed than in Jeremy Bentham's Panopticon vision. How this happened is a story of seismic changes in economics, politics and ideas about the self that came together just as the digital world was taking shape.

*

At the time of the Macintosh anti-conformity advert, Silicon Valley, which had led the world in defence technology and semi-conductors since the 1950s, had grown, making this corner of California the wealthiest real estate in the US. And in 1988, in a speech to students and faculty at Moscow State University, President Ronald Reagan heralded the beginning of economic revolution: 'Like a chrysalis, we're emerging from the economy of the Industrial Revolution – an economy confined to and limited by the Earth's physical resources . . . In the new economy, human invention increasingly makes physical resources obsolete. We're breaking through the material conditions of existence to a world where man creates his own destiny.'[3]

Reagan celebrated the shift from manufacturing to technology as evidence of a weightless New Economy, a sign that capitalism could extract value from knowledge and creativity. The rise in the mid-1990s of the 'dot com' or web-based company only seemed to confirm that giant leap into the future.

The enthusiasm for the New Economy initially came out of a turn to the right in American political and corporate life. Alvin Toffler, a libertarian and author of the giant 1970 bestseller *Future Shock*, argued that America was entering an era of accelerated and destabilizing change in which technology would do away with the need for bureaucratic oversight of markets and politics. Deregulation would free markets to become the engine of economic, political and social progress. The House of Representatives, led by Republican Newt Gingrich, pushed for smaller government and deregulation of the telecommunications sector.

Thinkers from the political right and libertarian circles also found common ground with a distinct subset of the political left. While conservatives viewed computers as tools for economic growth, innovation and efficiency, liberals saw them as instruments for democratization and individual empowerment. This intriguing alliance was reflected in a magazine that captured the spirit of the time and was well read, not only by computer nerds, but also by CEOs, politicians and journalists.

'We're trying to make a magazine that feels as if it has been mailed back from the future.' That was the elevator pitch of *Wired* according to libertarian Louis Rossetto, the founder and editor-in-chief, when the magazine was launched in 1993. 'We were

Jane Metcalfe, co-founder of Wired, *2 September 1993.*

trying to merge words and images to communicate ideas, to make the magazine one that McLuhan would look at and say, "Well, finally,'" Rossetto recalled in an oral history of the magazine.[4] He was referring to the Canadian philosopher Marshall McLuhan, who in the mid-1960s had famously declared 'The medium is the message' – by which he meant that the form, whether it be print, television or digital technology, embedded itself in the message it conveyed. 'The whole experience', Rossetto continued, 'had to convey what it was like to be in this revolution. It had to look as jangly and electric as the times.'

The *Wired* project had begun after Rossetto and Jane Metcalfe, the magazine's co-founder and his life partner, met the director of MIT's Media Lab, Nicholas Negroponte, who was brimming with optimism about the future of networked computers. Negroponte funded *Wired* with the aim of joining Rossetto and Metcalfe along with his longtime associate Stewart Brand, the impresario of a group of technologists and anti-authoritarian entrepreneurs who had grown up in the communal wave of the late 1960s.

Back in the early days of computing – when many on the right feared that projects like Lyndon B. Johnson's national database would lead to a totalitarian state, and those on the left saw them as symbols of government, military and corporate power – Stewart Brand believed computers could be a tool of liberation. A visionary who coined the term 'personal computer', Brand saw in this technology a reflection of his anti-authoritarian ideals and a world of bottom-up possibilities.

In 1968 Brand had founded *The Whole Earth Catalog*, a publication that was part magazine, part product guide. With its strapline 'Access to Tools', the catalog became a touchstone of the counterculture movement. Aimed at hippies yearning for agrarian self-sufficiency, it was notable for its eclectic approach, featuring everything from computational physics and synthesizers to Hewlett-Packard's latest calculators, to gardening and farming tools. It offered guidance on building geodesic domes – huge spherical structures for living in – and concocting home remedies for crabs. It celebrated the empowering potential of new technologies, encouraging readers to seize control of their own lives and futures. *The Whole Earth Catalog* was a roadmap for what was come. Steve Jobs later praised it as the 'conceptual forerunner of the Internet'. 'It was sort of like Google in paperback form, thirty-five years before Google came along,' he said. 'It was idealistic, and overflowing with neat tools and great notions.'[5] The final issue, in 1971, sold a million copies and won the National Book Award.

Stewart Brand had anticipated the coming technological revolution and was determined to be in the vanguard. 'Ready or not, computers are coming to the people,' he proclaimed in *Rolling Stone* magazine on 7 December 1972, cheering, 'That's good news, maybe the best since psychedelics.' Computers would create a world that was like a big commune.

By 1984, as Jobs released the Macintosh, Brand had initiated the first Hacker's Conference, celebrating hackers as anti-authoritarians who used computers to do good. A year later he co-founded the Whole Earth 'Lectronic Link, or WELL, an early and influential online discussion forum and social network where people connected online. Brand had essentially come up with the idea of the internet before the internet, and the idea of social networking before social media.

Brand and his followers embraced computers because they thought the technology would disrupt old authorities and usher in direct democracy; that digital networks would stir things up, give power to the people and transform consciousness. As he said upon founding the WELL: 'psychedelic drugs, communes, and Buckminster Fuller domes were a dead end, but computers were an avenue to realms beyond our dreams.'[6] His optimism knew no bounds. Life would be better under the machines, he told a magazine about the San Francisco Bay Area: 'Computers suppress our animal presence. When you communicate through a computer, you communicate like an angel.'[7]

Brand contributed to *Wired* magazine, encouraged in no small part by Kevin Kelly, the founding executive editor who had previously worked on the *Whole Earth Catalog* and *Whole Earth Review*. Brand's and Kelly's involvement lent *Wired* a sense of cool, positioning computers as both countercultural and futuristic. This fusion of libertarian politics and countercultural aesthetics was labelled the 'Californian ideology' by scholars Richard Barbrook and Andy Cameron. It was a mash-up of Sixties ideas of self-expression with Eighties free-market economics and technological utopianism.[8]

*

It was no coincidence that the embrace of technology as *the* driver of social change came at a key moment in history. *Wired* hit the shelves two years after the dissolution of the Soviet Union and four years after the fall of the Berlin Wall. The Cold War was over, and with it, the prospect of instantaneous nuclear oblivion. In this new social and political context, old authorities and certainties were tumbling down.

In one of the most famous pronouncements of the times, American political scientist Francis Fukuyama made the case in *The End of History and the Last Man* (1992) that without the counterbalancing power or ideological threat to Western liberalism, there would be no more meaningful political struggles over basic questions of social organization and human freedom. It was an understanding encapsulated in the slogan associated with the British prime minister, Margaret Thatcher: 'There is no alternative.'[9] The big political questions about how to organize society were off the table. History was over, and capitalism was the only viable system. Both left and right had to accept the market and accept liberalism.

This historic moment propelled the technological idealism behind *Wired*. In the magazine's first edition, Rossetto heralded the coming digital revolution, 'whipping through our lives like a Bengali typhoon – while the mainstream media is still groping for the snooze button'. He predicted that it would foment 'a revolution without violence that embraces a new, nonpolitical way to improve the future based on economics beyond macro control, consensus beyond the ballot box, civics beyond government and communities beyond the confines of time and geography'.[10] With the end of traditional politics, Rossetto was sure that the digital revolution would bring about social changes 'so profound that their only parallel is probably the discovery of fire'. It would 'flatten organizations, globalize society, decentralize control, and help harmonize people'.[11]

The libertarian right and the New Communal Left were convinced that technology would solve social problems, stimulate economic prosperity, give people a voice and set them free. They outsourced their vision of progress to the machines. But just three years after *Wired* launched, the utopian vision quickly gave way to a more unsettling reality. Instead of liberating society, technology began to facilitate self-surveillance, allowing others to peer into the most private moments of people's lives.

*

On a September day in 1997, four visionaries convened at the headquarters of the Dutch production company Endemol. Their mission: to brainstorm a new television show. They had had their heads turned by the runaway success of consumer programmes like the British *Changing Rooms*, where ordinary homes were transformed with decorative makeovers, drawing millions of viewers. They were intrigued by the 1991 Biosphere 2 project in the Arizona desert, which involved eight individuals living within a geodesic dome made of glass and steel designed to simulate Earth's environment, exploring alternative ways of living. But what truly ignited their imagination was an experiment by an American college student with a new communications medium called the internet.

In the spring of the previous year, Jennifer Ringley, a nineteen-year-old computer science major at Dickinson College, had set up a webcam on her dorm room computer. The webcam streamed live, 24/7, to a website. In an era of slow internet speeds, her set-up transmitted a series of grainy black-and-white images, each replacing the last. But what started as a personal challenge – Ringley didn't expect anyone to watch – quickly became a sensation she called Jennicam.

At the time, the number of people with home computers was skyrocketing, yet the internet remained largely uncharted territory. It was the adult entertainment industry that first recognized the web's potential, driving massive traffic to adult sites. Jennicam, however, was different. It offered raw, unfiltered life in real time, without staged performances or curated content. Ringley's stream was one picture of an ordinary student's everyday life replaced by another: Ringley sleeping, eating, dressing, reading, writing, sometimes an empty room. In no time at all, hundreds and then thousands were watching. At its peak the site had three to four million viewers. When Ringley threw a party, her student friends mooned the camera. The first time she kissed a boy, the site crashed within minutes from too many viewers.[12]

Ringley was one of the first individuals to broadcast her life online. Jennicam was a natural extension of *An American Family* – but with no third parties, and unedited. Viewers interacted with her as if they knew her personally, offering unsolicited advice like, 'That toothpaste you use doesn't work,' or abusive comments such as, 'You're fat and ugly. Get off camera.' Despite, or perhaps because of, this constant scrutiny, she became a significant topic of discussion offline, gaining widespread recognition and even fame.

On 31 July 1998, Ringley appeared on the TV show of the king

Jennifer Ringley, creator of Jennicam, in 1999.

of celebrity interviewers, David Letterman. In a revealing and prophetic exchange, she articulated the allure of displaying one's private life to strangers and foresaw the transformative potential of the internet. 'If you look at the internet,' she observed, 'it's mostly TV programmes ... What was needed was something made for the medium.' Letterman agreed, saying, 'This is the best idea I've heard for that silly internet thing.' He elaborated: 'People are lonely and desperate. They want to see life somewhere else. It's comforting.' Despite the potential threat to his own profession, he concluded with a striking prediction: 'This will replace television.'[13] Watching someone else's ordinary life was what this revolutionary technology appeared to offer, providing a new kind of connection and voyeuristic comfort that traditional media could not match.

Ringley ventured that it was more 'authentic' and 'natural' to put private matters online in front of strangers than to keep them to herself. Echoing the ancient Greek cynic Diogenes, who ate and masturbated in the marketplace as a challenge to the rarefied public realm of ancient Athens, Ringley saw little point in distinguishing between public and private. If it was natural and normal to do something, why not do it in front of strangers? Animals, she pointed out, weren't concerned about performing private acts in front of others; why should humans feel any different? 'Just look at zoos!' she said.

Ringley explained that being without a disguise, being her true private self in public, and not a fake, was empowering for herself and others: 'I'm just glad I give permission for somebody to just be themselves and to be OK with that.'[14]

'What about "intimate moments"?' Letterman asked, testing her boundaries.

'Sure,' she responded without hesitation. 'If I am trying to portray real life, then that's a part of it.' She then made an important clarification: *portray* was the wrong word. What happened online was 'real life'. Living your life online in front of others wasn't a performance or for show – it was reality.

The TV execs from Endemol, looking for the next big thing, took inspiration from Jennicam. They came up with the idea of putting a group of complete strangers into a house and filming them for twenty-four hours a day. This was the original version of what became the hit British TV show *Big Brother*. In the first series, which began at 11 p.m. on 18 July 2000, Anna Nolan, an Irish lesbian and former nun, won the heart of *Big Brother* viewers but ultimately came second to the builder Craig Phillips. Nicholas Bateman, dubbed 'Nasty Nick' by the tabloids, was the pantomime villain after he become known for his duplicity, and was thrown out due to his scheming. They were three of the 40,000 people who had applied to be a part of the entertainment, which was also a social experiment.

As with Jennicam, participants spoke about how being on camera, living in front of others, was a 'personal journey' that helped them better understand who they were. But 'who they were' was reduced to how they lived in a restrictive private space, with others, in front of an audience. The contestants were totally isolated from the outside world; all news was banned from the *Big Brother* house. They had no access to public life: no books, no radio, no outside connections, just the bare necessities of food, sleep and sex. The action and drama of *Big Brother* was all about minute personal interactions under constant surveillance.

Inevitably, there was a sexual undertone; what else was there to think about or do? Who fancied whom, and who was under the bedsheets with whom, became the focus of national conversation as old media, especially salacious British tabloids, realized that reality TV could sell papers. The broadsheet media did not ignore it, either. Far from it. *Big Brother* launched a thousand think pieces about the state of the nation.

Initially, the show followed the traditional television format of being scheduled at a specific time on a particular day, on a set channel, for a designated length. However, a visionary proposed airing it on the web as well, an idea so novel that Channel 4 executives, accustomed to their fixed time slots and television boxes, tried to veto it. They thought no one would be interested and that the experiment would be a failure. Contrary to their expectations, the online stream sent viewing figures through the roof. TV executives had discovered how to harness the internet, and online viewing began to take off.

The format revolutionized television. By empowering viewers to vote on whether to keep or evict a housemate, *Big Brother*'s audience became integral to the unfolding narrative. It was a dynamic that made the housemates acutely aware of their actions, blurring the lines between television drama and real-life interaction.

Big Brother was a transformative moment in the creation of a surveillance culture. The programme was a godsend for television and the press. Glossy magazines like *HELLO!*, which launched in 1998, were paying a fortune for celebrity interviews and photographing the famous in their extravagantly decorated mansions; newspapers had been priced out of the market. Reality TV stars were just what the papers needed to fill their pages, and they kept on giving copy, knowing that they needed the coverage for their profile. A new economic model was born, and reality TV shows proliferated around the globe.

*

As the popularity of *Big Brother* increased, social commentators concerned about political apathy began to take notice, speculating whether the show's format might offer valuable lessons. There were widespread concerns about record-low election turnouts, the average age of political party members being sixty-seven, and political parties losing members at an alarming rate. Additionally, civic and community involvement was on the wane, reflecting a broader trend of disengagement in society. In the US, social scientist Robert Putnam highlighted the decreasing participation in communal activities in his 2000 book, *Bowling Alone*. He noted that people were bowling alone more often than with others, drawing attention to the weakening of social ties.

In a report published by the Hansard Society, Oxford University law professor Stephen Coleman proposed that politicians could learn valuable lessons from reality TV. An opinion poll of 2,000 people revealed that a majority of *Big Brother* viewers found politicians 'inauthentic' and thought that they should adopt a more relaxed, informal and less 'stiff' demeanour. In contrast, these viewers found members of the *Big Brother* household 'lively' and felt they better represented 'the main bulk of the electorate'.[15]

Instead of finding negative associations with the constant surveillance in the *Big Brother* house, Coleman found the opposite: 'Surveillance was regarded as the highest form of political accountability, not only in terms of procedures and policies, but personalities, principles and integrity.' Transparency was viewed as a social good. Coleman concluded that politicians needed to be more 'real' and 'authentic', 'open' and 'transparent'. He argued that liberating 'political democracy from its current cultural ghetto' required 'a new conception of two-way accountability; a creative and exciting use of the new technologies of interactivity'.[16]

The prevailing trend in political circles was that combining authenticity, openness and interactive technology could help rekindle interest in politics. In 2000, Prime Minister Tony Blair, a pioneer of centrist 'Third Way' politics, introduced the Freedom of Information Act (FOI), which granted the public the right to access information held by public authorities, promoting transparency and accountability in government. Blair also adopted a more informal style in his communications, often appearing in open-collared shirts without a tie, and emphasizing his connection with the public.

Eventually, however, Jennifer Ringley had enough. She no longer wanted to live in a virtual zoo, and she shut off her webcam on 31 December 2003. She disappeared completely from public life and no longer maintains a presence on the web.

*

Despite early optimism, the economic revolution promised by new technology did not materialize as expected. When the dotcom bubble burst in 2000, the search engine Google was burning through millions. Its two biggest venture capital investors, John Doerr of Kleiner Perkins and Michael Moritz of Sequoia Capital, pushed its founders, Larry Page and Sergey Brin, to find a business model. Their breakthrough came in 2001: harnessing the trove of data from user searches to power algorithms that accurately predicted consumer interests proved an invaluable resource for online advertisers. What had previously been dismissed as mere 'data exhaust' was suddenly a lucrative commodity.

The digital landscape churns out vast amounts of data daily – searches, purchases, likes, dislikes, passive observations. Internet engineers soon discovered that controversy and anger were more effective at keeping people's attention than the more mundane stuff. Complex algorithms were devised to push people's buttons, grab emotions and keep their attention, giving rise to a new business model that the scholar Shoshana Zuboff christened 'surveillance capitalism': an economic order that claims human experience as the raw material for hidden commercial practices of extraction, prediction and sales. 'With so little left that could be commodified,' Zuboff wrote, 'the last virgin territory was private human experience.'[17]

While internet users are essential for surveillance capitalism, they are not its paying customers. That role is reserved for advertisers. The relationship of platform to user is essentially manipulative. Platforms encourage users to provide as much data as possible, which advertisers then use to sell them products.

*

Just under twenty years after Steve Jobs heralded the Macintosh as a tool to challenge conformity, voluntary surveillance had been normalized for entertainment, as a way of living and being authentic, and become the business model of the internet. Then, after the 9/11 attacks in 2001, the American state turned to mass surveillance as a tool to fight terrorism.

The Bush administration appointed Reagan's former National Security Adviser, John Poindexter, to direct the Total Information Awareness programme, the logo for which was a pyramid with an all-seeing eye overlooking the Earth. Poindexter was convinced that mass electronic data collection would help prevent more attacks. The idea was that a potential terrorist would leave a digital trail that could be traced, as all digital information was collected in vast silos derived from the internet companies.

Congress hesitated due to privacy concerns, with politicians from both parties worrying that programme treated *everyone* in America as a potential terror suspect. As a result, Congress ended the proposal and used the 2004 Defense Appropriations bill to defund Total Information Awareness. But that was not the end of the matter. In 2013, Edward Snowden, a computer intelligence consultant who was working for the National Security Agency, exposed the US government's vast covert global surveillance programmes. Snowden showed that the state was secretly constructing a '*potential* panopticon'. 'The construction of the system *was* itself the abuse,' he told *Wired*. 'We've been forced to live naked before power for a generation.'[18]

The encroachment of technology on privacy faced minimal resistance, bolstered by a belief in technology's transformative power amid political stagnation. As digital technology pervaded society, it ingrained itself into its frameworks during what was considered the 'end of history', a time when politics centred on technocratic governance rather than ideological battles or revolutionary change. This elevated technology as the primary catalyst of societal evolution, driving individuals deeper into their private realms at a time when distinctions between public and private were increasingly blurred. People became both performers and voyeurs in this new digital arena. Perhaps as life offline was duller, more narrowly material in comparison, life online was attractive. There had, after all, always been a strain of disenchantment with the politics and the physical world among those that initially embraced the internet: 'Life will be happier for the on-line individual', J. C. R. Licklider, one of the visionaries behind ARPANET, had predicted in 1968, 'because the people with whom one interacts most strongly will be selected more by commonality of interests and goals rather than by accidents of proximity'.[19]

Those using the technology soon found that privacy concerns were residual and could be brushed aside. The idea that some acts should be kept private, and not for the eyes of strangers, seemed almost perverse in an age when keeping something out of sight was seen as weird, conformist, or inauthentic.

*

In the twenty-first century, technology is frequently identified as the primary threat to privacy. But by understanding the historical circumstances in which digital technology was introduced, it becomes clear that this context was as important to its development as the technology itself.

That is, if the right and left had not outsourced social progress – and their authority – to technology; if public life hadn't already been diminished, with a retreat into the private realm underway; if the divide between public and private life hadn't been crossed by the political movements of the New Left, radical feminism and the New Right; if personal and private life hadn't been deemed political; and if the concept of the authentic, more open and emotive individual hadn't already entered the mainstream, then the online world might not have evolved into a virtual playground of self-surveillance.

Had there been a strict separation between the public and private worlds when the worldwide web took off, had we been less interested in displaying our private lives and more interested in the world outside our own front doors, then the online world today would be very different. While digital technology amplifies and facilitates a culture of self-surveillance – allowing individuals to perform and observe from anywhere, and thereby accelerating the development of a borderless world – it did not create that culture. A particular form of technology that can go anywhere and be used anywhere was introduced at a point when, in Western society, the separation between the public domain and the private world had blurred.

Back at the turn of the millennium, while Jennifer Ringley was switching on her webcam and Anna and Nick were entering the Big Brother house, other significant changes were occurring in public and private life. The intimate life of the president of the world's most powerful country became an international scandal, an incident that prompted the American people to grapple with questions about where, or if, a line should be drawn between the two domains.

Chapter 21:

LOVE LETTERS NEVER SENT

When she looked back at the fireball that had engulfed her, Monica Lewinsky realized it was the retrieval of her love letters – the ones she'd drafted just before Christmas, but never sent – that had been most invasive. She recalled screaming, in tears, at her inquisitors: 'This is so *wrong*! Do you not understand that no one else is supposed to read this?'[1]

From the moment she lifted her jacket and offered Bill Clinton a glimpse of her thong underwear, Lewinsky had embraced the President with enthusiasm. She had never expected their relationship to become the focus of an FBI investigation or a national discussion. 'It was nobody's business what the President and I did. I was never harassed. I lost my job because I was his girlfriend and the bottom line is that it's not their business,' she told her colleague and the woman she thought of as her friend, Linda Tripp.[2]

The affair was exposed shortly after midnight, Washington time, on Saturday, 17 January 1998, when the *Drudge Report*, an online political gossip magazine, published an explosive story headlined: '*Newsweek* kills story on White House intern; Blockbuster Report: 23-year-old, former White House intern, sex relationship with President'. The next day, the creator and editor of the website, Matt Drudge, followed up with a longer post. He alleged that Michael Isikoff, a journalist for *Newsweek*, one of his old-media rivals, had been tipped off about Clinton's infidelity with a young intern. Drudge also revealed her name: Monica Lewinsky.

It was the first time a massive news story broke online. The scoop set off an international media storm that would rage for sixteen months. The scandal became part of a lengthy investigation which saw federal officials investigating the private life of the leader of the Western world. This ultimately resulted in Clinton becoming the second president in American history to be impeached.

That the scandal had erupted at all was thanks to rolling changes in public and private life. While the ideal of a private life separate from public affairs was still defended, especially by Clinton's Democrat supporters, it was not the firm principle it had once been. It no longer seemed *that* important. After all, public figures were increasingly open about private matters, as was the culture. People no longer felt the same need to hide their private predilections.

Historical legal protections for private life were also being eroded. There remained the belief, advanced by radical feminists in the mid-seventies, that the private sphere was a paramount site of reform, combined with the idea that male sexual misconduct had for too long been protected by privacy. These ideas had gained traction, not least in Republican circles.

*

The origins of Bill Clinton's impeachment lie not with Monica Lewinsky and her calamitous relationship with the President, but with his adversaries, who had spent years trying to bring him down for a failed real-estate deal. In the run-up to his presidential election in 1992, all kinds of accusations were thrown at Clinton, including that he had avoided the Vietnam draft. His now infamous admission that he briefly experimented with marijuana in the 1960s, but didn't inhale, was seized upon by opponents. They painted a portrait of a man with questionable integrity and a dubious relationship with the truth. Clinton, with a mixture of frustration and resolve, refused to be drawn into the quagmire of personal attacks. He asserted that these distractions were orchestrated by George H. W. Bush and the Republicans, diverting attention from the urgent issues plaguing the nation.

Once elected, the new administration was beset by scandal. One rumour snowballed: 'Whitewater' was a tangle of allegations involving investments by the Clintons, while Bill was governor of Arkansas, into a real-estate company called the Whitewater Development Corporation. The cloud of suspicion around the Clintons grew.

Then, on 23 July 1993, something happened that sent the conspiracy theorists into overdrive. Vince Foster, the deputy White House counsel of the Clinton administration, shot and killed himself under a tree in Fort Marcy Park in Fairfax County, Virginia. Republicans on Capitol Hill, fuelled by suspicion and political intrigue, wasted no time in questioning the official account and casting doubt on the investigation that followed. In a bizarre spectacle aimed at challenging the narrative of suicide, Congressman Dan Burton shot a melon in his own backyard to try to prove that Foster couldn't have killed himself. Some political opponents suggested that he may have been murdered; others said the Clintons were involved in the cover-up.

Amid mounting pressure and swirling controversy, Bill Clinton, ever pragmatic and mindful of public perception, took a decisive step. He asked Attorney-General Janet Reno to appoint a special prosecutor to investigate whether there had been financial irregularities at the Whitewater property company, which, in January 1994, she did.

That same month, the conservative monthly magazine *The American Spectator* published an 11,000-word exposé of Clinton's extramarital affairs by journalist David Brock, headlined 'His

Cheatin' Heart'. Brock had been tipped off about the story by Cliff Jackson, a lawyer from Arkansas, a onetime Clinton friend who had become a longtime Clinton hater. Based on interviews with four state troopers who had worked for Clinton when he was state governor, the piece described how they had arranged sexual encounters for their boss in hotel rooms and parking lots; sneaked women into the gubernatorial mansion while Hillary and their daughter, Chelsea, slept; and, afterwards, wiped make-up off his shirt collar.

The impact of the article belied the difficulty Brock had in placing it. Members of the broadsheet media had been sceptical that it was a story worth covering, believing it lacked interest, so no one picked it up. When it finally ran, Brock went out of his way to justify writing it at all. He conceded that rumours of extramarital dalliances had swirled around many presidents before Clinton, but said that the scale of his indiscretions appeared to exceed that of any of his predecessors, with the possible exception of John F. Kennedy. Even more important, Brock argued, was that many of his sources had described how Clinton's private activities had caused lies to be told, threats to be made, and cover-ups – especially by the Democrats – to be undertaken. This turned his infidelities into an issue of public integrity. Brock concluded that the public's right to know about the cover-ups outweighed Clinton's claim to a private life.

The revelations came as no surprise to the Democratic Party. When Clinton had started his run for the presidency in 1992, his aide Betsey Wright had spent the majority of her time trying to quell what she memorably described as 'bimbo eruptions': reports of sexual liaisons between Bill Clinton and, by her reckoning, at least twenty-six women, including a rumour about a twelve-year affair with an Arkansas state employee and cabaret singer, Gennifer Flowers.[3]

The huge public interest in the story prompted Bill and Hillary Clinton to confront the swirling rumours head on in an interview with Steve Kroft on *60 Minutes*. Kroft, a seasoned journalist known for his incisive questions, didn't shy away from probing the matter. Repeatedly, he pressed Clinton on whether he had engaged in extramarital affairs. Clinton, navigating the treacherous waters of personal scrutiny, acknowledged there had been 'problems' in his marriage to Hillary, but chose not to delve into specifics. He defended the sanctity of marital privacy, asserting that discussions about infidelity should remain within the confines of the relationship itself.

Hillary Clinton, equally steadfast in her stance, pushed back against Kroft's line of questioning, highlighting the broader implications of invading personal privacy. 'I think it's real dangerous in this country if we don't have some zone of privacy for everybody,' she asserted.[4]

Battle lines drawn, the Democratic Party dismissed the *American Spectator* article as a politically motivated smear. Despite these efforts, the public's curiosity soared, driving unprecedented demand. The special 'His Cheatin' Heart' edition flew off the shelves, selling a staggering 300,000 copies – nearly double the magazine's typical circulation. Its ultimate effects would be beyond David Brock's wildest imagination.

In the mountain of stories Brock recounts, one details how, in 1991, state troopers had approached a woman named Paula at an event and invited her to join Clinton in a hotel room in Little Rock, which she did. They were alone together for no more than an hour. The trooper said that Paula had told him afterwards that if Clinton so desired, she was available to be his regular girlfriend. When Paula Jones, the twenty-seven-year-old daughter of an evangelical preacher, read the article, she knew that she was the woman concerned – and that her friends and family would too. Two months after the article was published, and after encouragement from Cliff Jackson, who had tipped off David Brock in the first place, she went public.

First, Jones spoke via a press conference at the annual Conservative Political Action Conference in Washington, DC. On stage, accompanied by her husband Steve and her attorney, she briefly addressed what had happened: 'It is wrong that a woman can't work in the workplace – and be harassed by a figure that high, and, um, it's just humiliating what he did to me . . . I would just put it this way. He presented himself to me in a very unprofessional manner and, I would call it sexual harassment. And that's all.'

The journalists pushed for more: 'Will you tell us in your own words something about what really happened in that room? Everybody has been vague,' said one.

'Did he ask you to have sex with him?' asked another.

'A type of sex, yes,' she replied.

'You mentioned that he asked you to perform a sexual act,' was the follow up. 'Is it something that could have been performed without your taking your clothes off?'

Her answer was yes.

Back and forth they went, with the journalists speculating on what type of sex they had, and Paula Jones struggling to find the words to confirm or elaborate.

Finally, the question was put to her: 'Did the governor ask you to perform fellatio?'

'Excuse me?' said Jones.

'Fellatio?' he asked again.

With the question unanswered, Cliff Jackson brought the press conference to an end. It was deemed a failure. There was nothing to report; the story was a dud.[5]

Frustrated with the lack of media coverage, Paula Jones gave an interview to Patrick Matrisciana, a fringe filmmaker funded by the religious right. When the footage appeared in *The Clinton Chronicles*, a conspiratorial film that circulated only on VHS and portrayed the Clintons as murderers and drug dealers, no one took her seriously.

'Quite simply,' Bob Bennett, Bill Clinton's attorney, announced at a press conference, 'the incident did not occur.'

'The president has no recollection of ever meeting this woman,' he continued, with a rhetorical flourish: 'Do the American people really want the president of the United States to be spending his time with lawyers, rather than solving the problems of the times?'[6]

On 6 May 1994, Jones filed a civil lawsuit against Clinton for sexual harassment, and the state trooper who had allegedly led her to the hotel room where, she said, Clinton had exposed himself to her. She wanted $700,000 for emotional damages. But she didn't exactly receive a sympathetic hearing. Jones was ridiculed and smeared in popular culture. *New York Magazine* ran as its August 1994 cover story, 'White Trash Nation', a piece about how the Nineties were the 'alarming decade' of the 'white underclass'. Jones was exhibit number one: she wore too much make-up, used too much hairspray, and didn't always wear a bra. Although the magazine didn't explicitly accuse her of 'asking for it', those interviewed for the article edged close. According to her brother-in-law: 'Paula dressed – shit, *provocative* ain't even the word for it. You could see the crease of her ass, and at least two lips, maybe three. If a woman dresses to where a man is almost *seeing* it . . .' After highlighting the fact that Jones had accepted $50,000 to model for No Excuses jeans, the magazine implied she was politically and financially motivated to make her allegations.

*

In September 1994, Bill Clinton signed into law the landmark Violence Against Women Act, which was introduced by Democratic Senator Joe Biden. This comprehensive federal legislative package aimed to combat violence against women by increasing penalties for such crimes, funding law enforcement and supporting women's shelters. Republican congresswoman Susan Molinari also introduced an amendment allowing juries hearing cases of sexual harassment, assault and child molestation to consider evidence that the accused had committed similar crimes in the past. Without realizing it, Clinton had installed a trapdoor under his own desk in the Oval Office.

Legal scholars had debated the implications of the Molinari amendment. The Federal Judicial Center voiced apprehensions, fearing that allowing prosecutors to introduce past accusations – regardless of whether the defendant had been prosecuted – could spawn mini-trials within court proceedings. Miguel Méndez, a respected law professor, cautioned against the potential fallout, arguing that presenting inflammatory and salacious evidence about a defendant's past behaviour would undoubtedly prejudice the court.

Shortly after the President passed the Violence Against Women Act, Paula Jones's lawyers amended their complaint to allege that Clinton had put his hand on her leg and tried to reach her pelvic area, strengthening their sexual harassment case. Under Molinari's amendment, Jones's lawyers could trawl through the President's private life for other episodes that proved a pattern of behaviour. In Clinton's case, it wouldn't be difficult.

In November 1995, on the eve of a government shutdown, the activities of the White House slowed to a standstill. Monica Lewinsky and the President had been flirting for some time. After a surprise party thrown for him by White House staffers, she upped the stakes and showed him her thong. 'It was unnoticeable to anyone else in the room. But he noticed,' she said.[7] Their intimate relationship began that day.

But when, a year on, she was moved by a White House staffer to the Pentagon – and out of Clinton's immediate field of vision – Lewinsky was distraught. Though he was still in touch, she was uncertain about the direction of their on-off relationship as well as her career. He had promised to get her back to work at the White House, but hadn't. Seeking advice, Lewinsky confided in her colleague, Linda Tripp. Unfortunately, Tripp was the wrong person to trust. What Tripp did with Lewinsky's secret set in motion a national crisis and tied together all its threads.

Tripp had worked for, and was loyal to, the previous White House administration under George H. W. Bush. Vince Foster had been a colleague. She had also been in ongoing conversations with a literary agent, Lucianne Goldberg, about a potential book, but the idea stalled. Suddenly, with Lewinsky's secret entrusted to her, that changed. Tripp called Goldberg with the news that she knew Clinton was having an affair with a former White House intern, and Goldberg advised her to get proof on tape. She warned Tripp that it would harm Lewinsky and end their friendship if she ever used it. 'I have already made this decision,' Tripp confirmed.[8]

Tripp surreptitiously recorded twenty-two hours of her private telephone conversations with Monica Lewinsky, calls in which Lewinsky disclosed explicit details about her sexual encounters with Clinton in the White House and her emotional distress, frustrations and feelings of being used by him. With a trove of potentially incriminating material at hand, Goldberg, her confidante and strategist, made two phone calls. The first was to the lawyers representing Paula Jones. Goldberg unveiled the affair, suggesting that if Monica Lewinsky were to confess that her entanglement with President Clinton began while she was employed at the White House, it would undeniably establish a damning pattern of Clinton's behaviour – pursuing subordinates – and would significantly strengthen Jones's sexual harassment claim.

Her second call was to Michael Isikoff, the intrepid journalist who thought he was on the verge of breaking the story for *Newsweek*. Goldberg's tip-off was delivered with the finesse of a seasoned insider, setting the stage for a media firestorm.

In December 1997, Paula Jones's legal team served both Tripp and Lewinsky with subpoenas, and then the President himself.

Determined to protect him, Lewinsky signed a sworn affidavit
that she had never had a sexual relationship with the President,
and that she did not have any information relevant to the allegations made by Paula Jones. Despite that lie, the Paula Jones case
and Monica Lewinsky were now intertwined. All that was needed
for everything to fall into place was Kenneth Starr.

For three years, Kenneth Starr, the Independent Counsel, had
investigated allegations of financial corruption around Whitewater with little success. In February 1997, he announced that
he would step down from the investigation to become dean of
Pepperdine University Law School in California. Within days, he
found himself subjected to stinging criticism from conservative
pundits. In *The New York Times*, columnist William Safire lambasted Starr as a 'wimp' who had brought 'shame on the legal
profession'. Torn, he stayed, ditching the Pepperdine job.[9] But he
realized he had to get creative.

Starr shifted the focus of his investigation from finances into a
new direction: Bill Clinton and women. On 25 June 1997, in a
front-page article titled 'Starr Probes Clinton Personal Life', *The
Washington Post* reported that FBI agents were questioning
troopers about extramarital relationships Clinton may have had
with twelve to fifteen women while governor of Arkansas. David
Kendall, a lawyer for the President, slammed the investigation as
'out of control', declaring that 'no one's personal life should be
subjected to a desperate dragnet by a prosecutor with unlimited
resources'.[10] But Starr's team was just getting started.

On 16 January 1998, Lewinsky, on her way to meet Linda Tripp
for lunch in the Pentagon City Mall, was stopped and apprehended by the FBI. She had been betrayed. Tripp had informed
Starr's investigators about the tapes she had recorded with Lewinsky and had made a deal with Starr to entrap her. Tripp's
crowning piece of evidence was a blue dress, a garment Lewinsky
had tucked away in her closet. The dress bore the damning

evidence of her liaisons with President Clinton: traces of his semen, preserved in the fabric like a keepsake. Tripp, under the guise of friendship, had slyly advised her against cleaning it. When Lewinsky questioned her about why, Tripp had feigned a sisterly concern. 'I don't know, Monica,' Tripp had said. 'It's just this nagging awful feeling I have in the back of my head.'[11]

The FBI escorted Monica Lewinsky to a room in the nearby Ritz-Carlton Hotel. The opulent surroundings stood in contrast to the intense interrogation that awaited her. Agents pressed her about the sworn affidavit in which she had denied any affair with President Clinton. For twelve gruelling hours, they bombarded her with questions. They threatened her with twenty-seven years of jail time if she didn't confess and cooperate with their investigation. But she didn't give in or betray Clinton. Despite the immense pressure placed on her, their negotiations reached an impasse, and Lewinsky went home.

The next day, lawyers involved in the Paula Jones sexual harassment case questioned Bill Clinton under oath about his sexual history. Unbeknownst to him, the interviewers had been briefed on his relationship with Monica Lewinsky and were aware of the tapes made by Linda Tripp.

'Have you ever had sexual relations with Gennifer Flowers?' they asked.

'Yes,' he answered.

Other women were named. Then, Lewinsky. Were they alone together in the Oval Office at any time? He couldn't recall, Clinton said. Finally, the killer question came. 'Have you ever had sexual relations with Monica Lewinsky, as that term is defined in Deposition Exhibit 1?'

Clinton was firm: 'I have never had sexual relations with Monica Lewinsky.'[12]

That statement would cost him, and Lewinsky.

After Michael Isikoff's story at *Newsweek* about the affair was spiked, Lucianne Goldberg contacted Matt Drudge, whose online *Drudge Report* splashed it, a site barely known outside Washington. Within the hour, every other national newspaper had grabbed it.

*

Between 1963 and his assassination in April 1968, Martin Luther King Jr lived under the relentless scrutiny of the FBI, overseen by J. Edgar Hoover. The Bureau bugged his hotel rooms and tapped his telephones, gathering evidence of his extramarital affairs. Hoover's goal was clear: to uncover and exploit King's sexual transgressions, using them as weapons to tarnish the revered civil rights leader's image.

The FBI circulated these damning tapes as a way of humiliating, harassing and intimidating King and undermining his influence among other civil rights leaders, as well as putting his marriage to Coretta Scott King under strain. The Bureau pressured media outlets to release the material, hoping to destroy King's public persona. However, the press stood firm, refusing to support Hoover's vendetta and declined to publish the story.

The media knew about the multiple extramarital affairs of John F. Kennedy and Lyndon B. Johnson, but did not report on them because they were not, at the time, considered newsworthy, as the journalist Johnny Apple found out early in his career. When he was a young reporter assigned to cover JFK's visit to New York in 1963, he saw a beautiful woman being escorted to Kennedy's suite. Excited that he might have a story, he dashed back to the *New York Times* office and told Sheldon Binn, chief assignment editor of the Metro desk. Binn brushed him aside. 'Apple,' he said, 'you're supposed to report on political and diplomatic policies, not girlfriends. No story.'[13]

The media's respect for the wall between the political and private man also covered much more serious acts that went far beyond consenting extramarital liaisons. In his memoir, *Reporter* (2018), investigative journalist Seymour Hersh recounts how in 1974, a few weeks after Richard Nixon resigned the presidency in disgrace, he was told by a source at a Californian hospital that Nixon had assaulted his wife Pat so badly that she was hospitalized. Hersh confirmed the story with Nixon's former adviser, John Ehrlichman, who told him of other occasions when Nixon had beaten up his wife.

Hersh, who was a fierce critic of Nixon's, never wrote about what he had learned. Only later did he ask himself why. In 1998, at the height of the Clinton–Lewinsky scandal, when giving a talk at Harvard's Nieman Foundation for Journalism, he tried to explain why he hadn't thought to report that Nixon had assaulted his wife. 'The issue [of the talk] was the merging of private life and public life, and I explained that I would have written about the attacks if they were an example of why his personal life impinges on policy, but there was no evidence of such a link . . . I added that it was not a case where Nixon had gone looking for his wife with an intent to hit her, could not find her, and bombed Cambodia instead.'[14]

Hersh records the ferocity of his audience's response: 'I was taken aback by the anger my decision generated among some of the female fellows, who noted that battery is a crime in many jurisdictions.' He reflects that he had not, 'in his ignorance', viewed the incident as a crime, nor as newsworthy.[15]

In January 1998, Bill Clinton's private life dominated the news media and talk shows, the Lewinsky affair feeding a public hungry for supposedly genuine testimony. Emotional narratives of family strife and confessions of personal indiscretion had already become mainstays of daytime TV schedules. *The Oprah Winfrey Show*, which had debuted in 1986, was the highest-rated programme of its genre in television history. Jennifer Ringley of Jennicam fame was soon to make her appearance on David

Letterman's late-night talk show. Peter Weir's film *The Truman Show* would be released in the spring, starring Jim Carrey as a man whose entire existence was being secretly filmed by 5,000 hidden cameras.

The revelations about the President and the intern added to the existing accounts of private life, making headlines and sparking reports and commentary worldwide. From the *Toronto Star* to the German *Frankfurter Allgemeine Zeitung*, the British *Daily Mirror* and even the local *Coventry Gazette*, leaped on the story. Newspapers in Mumbai and Hong Kong speculated on how Clinton's sexual misconduct might impact the global economy. It seemed as if the whole world was involved in a conversation about the relevance of the President's sex life to his public position.

According to conservative commentator William Bennett, a president's public effectiveness alone did not suffice; private conduct was equally crucial. Bennett argued, 'A man's character is not only relevant to his mode of governance, it is inseparable from it.' He asserted that Clinton's 'seamless web of deceit', intertwining his public and private lives, necessitated his removal from public office.[16]

Evangelical Christians seized the moment. For James Dobson, campaigner and founder of non-profit organization Focus on the Family, Americans were facing a 'profound moral crisis'.[17] Clinton epitomized all that was wrong with public life. Senator John Ashcroft, the Missouri Republican and lay preacher, called for Clinton to resign. The President was discredited and could no longer be trusted, Ashcroft said.[18]

Conservative politicians and evangelical Christians found themselves once again in a curious alliance. On 26 January 1998, on the PSB radio talk show *Democracy Now!*, Linda Hirshman, a professor of philosophy and women's studies at Brandeis University, reflected on how she found herself 'unexpectedly . . . in bed' with Republicans. Hirshman said that the power imbalance between the President and a young woman two months out of college meant that what Clinton had done was wrong, and he should resign.

On the same radio show, Catharine MacKinnon, the influential legal scholar and pioneer in sexual harassment law, agreed: the age difference and power imbalance between Clinton and Lewinsky was so great that it raised questions about the relationship. MacKinnon was known for her view that 'feminism has to explode the private' and for being deeply critical of privacy rights, arguing that the right of privacy was 'a right of men "to be let alone" to oppress women one at a time'.[19] She strongly criticized the divide between the public and private spheres in her writing.

Linda Hirshman also expressed her scepticism about the distinction between the public and private domains, particularly regarding privacy, in response to a female caller to *Democracy Now!* who contended that the President's affair was not anyone else's concern and discussing sex was 'tawdry'. Hirshman repudiated that position. 'Keeping quiet about sex,' she said, was 'one of the most anti-women attitudes that we can have'. She continued: 'For centuries, sex was confined to the secrecy and privacy of the private home. And within that home, we know, enormous amounts of wrongdoing occurred: domestic violence and so forth, as well as happy, loving sexuality . . . It hurts women to draw that curtain. We need to bring sex out into the light, as Catharine MacKinnon has done so ably, and look at it as a matter of moral theory, and political theory. It's not tawdry to do this. We need to be concerned about this, and the harm that will befall Monica Lewinsky is an example of that.'[20]

The agreement between Clinton's Republican critics and radical feminists like Hirshman and MacKinnon was the latest expression of a political alignment that had begun in the 1980s, when President Ronald Reagan had tried to take on *Playboy* magazine and its pornographer-in-chief, Hugh Hefner. In 1983, *Playboy*, *Penthouse* and *Hustler* had a combined circulation of nine million. They were, respectively, the fourteenth, seventeenth and fifty-seventh largest magazines in America. Reagan described them as a 'form of pollution' and established a commission to investigate their social impact. Attorney-General Edwin Meese was appointed to lead this initiative, with Reagan promising Bible-belt conservatives that he would clean up America.

Reagan was channelling a familiar and reliable rallying theme among American conservatives: the belief that the nation had lost its moral direction. He was appealing to the vocal 'pro-family' movement that had emerged in response to radical and liberal feminism and had played a significant role in his election to the White House and revitalized the Republican Party.

Catharine MacKinnon, alongside Andrea Dworkin and Susan Brownmiller, co-founders of Women Against Pornography in 1979, aligned themselves with Reagan's campaign. However, while the campaign focused on moral questions, they asserted that pornography degraded women and contributed to sexual violence. Dworkin and MacKinnon contended that pornographic material, both in words and images, caused harm, and suggested that the victims should be able to sue publishers.

Mainstream feminist groups rejected this idea. In *The New York Times*, the National Organization for Women, founded by Betty Friedan, defended free expression: 'A great many feminist leaders are opposed to Prof. Catharine A. MacKinnon's proposed legislation allowing persons "harmed" by written or printed materials to sue writers, publishers and retailers of literature and art ... Whether or not dominance-orientated erotica inspires negative attitudes and actions toward women (a thesis still very much at issue among professionals), pictures and

words about violent acts are not acts themselves . . . Censorship
has been, throughout history, the single most widely used patriarchal tool for "protecting" women – from birth control,
abortion, sexual satisfaction and non-heterosexual relationships. Without free speech we can have no feminist movement.
And if the anti-porn censorship is enacted, it is the right-wing-
packed courts . . . who will decide what materials are printable
in the United States.'[21]

Feminists for Free Expression, including the writer Nora
Ephron, the librarian Judith Krug and the law professor Nadine
Strossen, argued that women's autonomy and agency was at stake.
Women, these feminists asserted, did not need intervention from
the state for their own good, and they did not require protection
from sexually explicit material.

The resulting 2,000-page report by the Meese Commission
claimed that non-violent sexual material *did* harm society, but to
no one's great surprise it concluded that the Justice Department
could not engage in any censorship that violated the First
Amendment. Republicans and radical feminists lost the war
against pornography, but they had formed a compact that would
strengthen during the Clinton–Lewinsky scandal.

Hillary Clinton refused to comment on specific allegations
about Clinton's relationship with Lewinsky, saying the 'truth will
come out' and describing the media 'feeding frenzy' and the Starr
investigation as 'political', the result of a 'vast right-wing conspiracy'. She said that she worried that the 'criminal justice system'
was being used for 'political ends'. On a personal note, she
described feeling 'hollowed out' by the erosion of the boundaries
between public and private life.[22]

Most of Clinton's supporters argued that it was the Clintons'
business what Bill did in private. Public opinion polls suggested
that most people thought he was lying about the affair, but didn't
care; his job approval rating was at a record high. Looking back,

it is notable that Bill Clinton's supporters included many high-profile liberal, 'sex-positive' feminists.

*

On the last Friday in January 1998, ten influential American women, all involved in the very public debate about sex, met in a cosy private room at Le Bernardin, a French seafood restaurant in midtown Manhattan. They were brought together by the *New York Observer* magazine to discuss the Clinton–Lewinsky liaison. On the Monday of that week, the evening of his State of the Union address, Clinton had appeared on television to deny reports of the affair, uttering one of the most memorable lines of the era: 'I did not have sexual relations with that woman, Miss Lewinsky.'[23] Everyone quoted in the piece took it for granted that the President was lying.

The ten women at Le Bernardin included Erica Jong, whose 1973 book *Fear of Flying* (1973) had coined the celebratory term 'zipless fuck', a sexual encounter with no commitment or emotional involvement. Nancy Friday, author of the bestselling *My Secret Garden*, about female sexual fantasy, was also at the table. The retired dominatrix and writer Susan Shellogg was there, as were the fashion designer Nicole Miller; Marisa Bowe, editor of online magazine *Word*; and Patricia Marx, former *Saturday Night Live* writer and author of *How to Regain Your Virginity* (1983). The restaurateur Maguy Le Coze, owner of Le Bernardin, and Elizabeth Benedict, author of *The Joy of Writing Sex* (1996), attended. Katie Roiphe, author of *The Morning After: Sex, Fear and Feminism on Campus* (1993), also joined them.

Roiphe was a twenty-five-year-old graduate student in the English department at Princeton and a national figure. In *The Morning After*, which had propelled her into the limelight, she warned that a new 'bedroom politics had entered the university' and that 'feminist preoccupations with rape and sexual harassment' epitomized by a concern on campus around 'date rape' were reintroducing older ideas of women as victims, which did them no favours. Roiphe pointed to new, all-encompassing definitions of sexual misconduct which combined serious crimes like rape with regretted, sometimes messy sex, giving the false impression of a widespread problem. Female students, she argued, were being encouraged to view 'everyday experience' – leery passes and jokes – as harmful assaults, which in Roiphe's view disempowered them. 'This image,' she wrote, 'of a delicate woman . . . offended by a professor's dirty joke, pressured into sex by peers . . . bears a striking resemblance to that fifties ideal my mother and the other women of her generation fought so hard to get away from.'[24]

'Proclaiming victimhood doesn't help project strength,' she believed. The ideas about female fragility and the need for a protector, Roiphe elaborated, had in the past kept women out of public life and sheltered in the private sphere: 'myths surrounding female innocence have been used to keep women inside and behind veils. They have been used to keep them out of work and in labor.' She cautioned against a situation where 'The rhetoric of feminists and conservatives blurs and overlaps in this desire to keep our youth safe and pure.'[25] Roiphe's argument was fiercely debated, but it resonated. She was one of the most prominent feminist voices of her generation.

The journalist and novelist Francine Prose, who interviewed the eminent guests, described the subject of their gathering with worldly disdain. They had been brought together to discuss 'the telltale stains on a White House intern's dress, to debate the Clinton Doctrine (does oral sex constitute infidelity?) and to decide which is worse, fucking a humble intern or secretly tape-recording your friend'. The breezy headline in the resulting article said it all: 'New York Supergals Love that Naughty Prez'.[26]

When Prose asked the assembled women, 'Do we want a President who has sex or a President who has no sex? Or only married sex?' Jong parried, 'I want him alive from the waist down.' They joked about Clinton's sexual appetites, finding his infelicities thrilling. Patricia Marx was delighted: 'I, for some strange reason, like Clinton even more because of this . . . I'm not sure what happened. But I don't care.' The consensus, expressed by Erica Jong, was that a presidential 'fuckabout' was better than someone like the investigator Kenneth Starr, a 'fascist pig'.

Gloria Steinem, campaigner and co-founder of the pioneering *Ms* magazine, opined in *The New York Times* that feminists were right to resist the pressure from the right wing for the President's resignation or impeachment. Clinton wasn't guilty of harassment, but consensual sex. 'Whatever it was, [Lewinsky's] relationship with President Clinton has never been called unwelcome, coerced or other than something she sought.' Twenty-one-year-olds, she observed, were old enough to say 'yes or no'. Steinem said that the 'real violators of her will' were Linda Tripp, the FBI and Kenneth Starr. As for Paula Jones: 'Mr Clinton seems to have made a clumsy sexual pass, then accepted rejection.'[27]

Paula Jones's case was dismissed in April, on the grounds that even if her allegations were true, she still didn't have a case. The judge found that Jones hadn't proved she was harmed, either personally or in her career, by the incident. By then, however, her lawyers had already questioned Clinton about his contact with other women.

In July 1998, a federal grand jury started to call witnesses in the Starr Inquiry. First up was the Clintons' personal secretary, Betty Currie, a regular at the Community United Methodist Church. 'How is this relevant to Whitewater?' journalists asked. 'Our job is to get to the truth,' replied Kenneth Starr. Monica Lewinsky's friends were called to testify about their knowledge of her sex life, as was her mother, who left agitated and in tears. Finally, Lewinsky too was indicted.

In her biography, she recalls with horror the nature of her

questioning: 'It was too violating and humiliating to talk about such private issues with a roomful of strangers, most of them men. It was very difficult to talk openly about a private sexual moment. Quite frankly, I thought the level of detail they wanted was sick.'[28] She had to turn over all items of evidence of their relationship, including the love letters she had drafted to the President but never sent.

The prohibition of such searches was once fundamental to the US Constitution. The concept of officials breaking into someone's home and rifling through their papers and private diaries was exactly the kind of unreasonable search that the framers of the Bill of Rights intended to prohibit. Protected by the Fourth Amendment, which guarantees 'the right of the people to be secure in their persons, houses, papers, and effects, against unreasonable searches and seizures', a person's private residence and personal correspondence were considered inviolable. In 1886, the US Supreme Court explicitly ruled that compelling the production of a defendant's private papers to be used against them was tantamount to forcing that person to incriminate themselves.

But by the late twentieth century, that constitutional principle had waned. The legal scholar Jeffrey Rosen documents that starting from the late 1960s, laws preventing the subpoenaing of private diaries as evidence in civil or white-collar criminal cases had gradually eroded. Subsequently, through a series of rulings, the Supreme Court narrowed the definition of prohibited searches while broadening the scope of permissible searches and warrants. As a result, constitutional protections for privacy were progressively undermined.[29]

Monica Lewinsky also had to hand over all her gifts from the President, and the blue dress that she had worn on one fateful encounter. The FBI laboratory took it for DNA testing. That proved, independently of other evidence, that Clinton had been sexually involved with her.

Starr's investigators subpoenaed a Washington bookstore for receipts of all Lewinsky's purchases over a three-year period and closely examined every book. *The Washington Post* gleefully reported that she had bought *Vox*, a 1992 novel by Nicholson Baker, the subject of which is telephone sex.

Lewinsky described the bookstore subpoenas and the reading of her love letters as 'a violation'. 'It seemed that everyone in America had rights except for Monica Lewinsky,' she reflected.[30] As well as having her personal life raked over and her private love letters read, she was subjected to global mockery, becoming the butt of grotesque innuendo, jokes and savage satirical songs. Writing in the British *Daily Mirror*, the cultural commentator Tony Parsons reflected that Clinton was merely behaving as men have 'since the dawn of time'. 'If the President of the United States can't have a bit on the side, then who can?' However, when it came to Lewinsky, Parsons took a different tone: 'The poor cow has been treated like a cheap groupie, but that is only because she has acted like a cheap groupie.'[31]

*

On 17 August 1998, Bill Clinton became the first sitting president to testify before a grand jury. One of the prosecutors on the team, Brett Kavanaugh, wrote a memo to Judge Starr and the other attorneys, urging them to be relentless: 'The idea of going easy on him at the questioning is abhorrent,' he said, listing ten sample questions that Starr's team should ask, including: 'If Monica Lewinsky says that you ejaculated into her mouth on two occasions in the Oval Office area, would she be lying?' and 'If Monica Lewinsky says that you masturbated into a trashcan in your secretary's office, would she be lying?'[32]

Clinton began with a prepared opening statement, in which he finally admitted to the relationship: 'When I was alone with Ms Lewinsky on certain occasions in early 1996 and once in 1997, I engaged in conduct that was wrong. These encounters did not consist of sexual intercourse . . . But they did involve inappropriate intimate contact.' He said that he was prepared to answer questions but that 'because of privacy considerations' and in an effort 'to preserve the dignity of the office I hold', the written statement was 'all I will say about the specifics of these particular matters'.

During four hours of questioning, Clinton admitted to intimate acts, but refused to concede that they amounted to 'sexual relations'. 'My recollection is that I did not have sexual relations with Ms Lewinsky and I am staying on my former statement about that,' he said.[33]

That same evening at 10 p.m., Clinton spoke to the nation in a televised statement. He confessed to having engaged in a relationship with Monica Lewinsky that was 'not appropriate. In fact it was wrong . . . I know that my public comments and my silence about this matter gave a false impression. I misled people, including even my wife. I deeply regret that.'

After a pause, he reminded viewers how all this had come about. That the investigators into the Whitewater land deal had spiralled out into unrelated issues. It had 'gone on too long, cost too much and hurt too many innocent people'. Finally, he tried to draw a line under the matter. 'Even presidents have private lives. It is time to stop the pursuit of personal destruction and the prying into private lives and get on with our national life.'[34]

The Office of the Independent Counsel delivered the 453-page report – officially called *Referral from Independent Counsel Kenneth W. Starr in Conformity with the Requirements of Title 28, United States Code, Section 595(c)* – to Congress on 9 September 1998. The accompanying thirty-six sealed boxes of supporting evidence required two FBI vans to transport. The bulky envelopes were stamped with warnings that they contained material of a deeply personal nature.

*A photograph showing former White House intern Monica Lewinsky
meeting President Bill Clinton at a White House function submitted as
evidence in documents by the Starr investigation and released by the
House Judiciary Committee, 21 September 1998.*

Two days later, the House voted to release the entire report, sight
unseen, to the public – and on the internet. The House Speaker,
Republican Newt Gingrich, said that this was done as a gesture of
'transparency'. To ensure against any biased framing of the report,
Congress would read it at the same time as the nation.[35]

Journalists scrambled to obtain copies of Starr's report, an
urgency shared by millions of Americans. Even Congress had not
anticipated the scale of online demand. The three government
websites hosting the report crashed under the surge of traffic.
CNN.com notably became the first news site to publish the
report in its entirety. Within minutes, its homepage was receiving
300,000 hits per minute. Other sites uploaded as much of the
report as quickly as the computer modems of the day allowed.

Within just forty-eight hours of its release, an estimated twenty million Americans had accessed parts of the report online. Overnight, journalism was transformed. The internet overtook old media in setting the news agenda.

The report was a global story. *The Indian Express* led with the headline 'Clinton Adrift in a Sea of Smut' and revelled in the lurid details. *The Pioneer*, a Delhi-based paper that had defended India's acquisition of nuclear devices, ran an editorial stating that few would mourn the departure of a president (which they assumed would follow) whose administration had acted 'like an outraged bully' over the nuclear tests in Pokhran that May. One website provided a Hebrew translation of the entire report.

The Chinese press, though avoiding explicit details, still reported extensively on the story. The *People's Daily*, the main communist newspaper, published a comparatively short article on page 2, giving more space to the White House rebuttal than to descriptions of sexual encounters. In Iran, headlines were also restrained, with the most eye-catching reading: 'The Report on Clinton's Moral Case Shocked Americans'. In Mexico City, the Starr Report led in five of the most prominent papers. Meanwhile, newspapers in Cambodia and Indonesia complained that the scandal overshadowed their own political crises.[36]

In the Starr Report, Whitewater is mentioned just four times. Ostensibly to prove that Bill Clinton lied (and committed perjury, obstructed justice, tampered with witnesses and abused his constitutional powers), the report details all of his and Lewinsky's intimate relations in a graphic 'narrative section'. The extent of the specificity, the report coyly admits, is 'unfortunate, but it is essential'. The word *sex* and its variations are mentioned 548 times. The term *oral sex* appears eighty-five times, including, 'the President initiated the oral sex by unzipping his pants and exposing his genitals'. The word *breasts* appears fifty-one times, as in, 'The President fondled Ms Lewinsky's bare breasts with his hands and

mouth and fondled her genitalia directly by pulling her underwear out of the way. In addition, the President inserted a cigar
into Ms Lewinsky's vagina.'[37]

*

The whole prurient circus took place at a time when ideas about
the relevance of the private lives of public figures and the place of
sex in public life were in rapid flux. Clinton's critics saw the whole
episode as conclusive evidence of his immorality and poor character. They included an alliance of Republicans and a number of
radical feminists who were outside the mainstream: for them, the
President's private life was pertinent to his fitness for office and a
sufficient reason to remove him. Although some of Clinton's
supporters appeared to relish the detailed revelations about his
sex life and others were appalled, most shrugged off his indiscretions, arguing that what he did in the bedroom (or even in sexual
encounters in the Oval Office) was his own business. Liberal
feminists defended the President's right to a private life. They saw
the private domain as somewhere separate from the public world
and had a more permissive and 'sex-positive' attitude towards sex
and sexuality. They also had a robust sense of a woman's autonomy and her capacity, even as a young woman, to make her own
decisions. Though some of this was down to partisanship, no
doubt, there was also a commitment to the ideal of privacy and
the right to private life, even for public figures. Although they
were uncharitable and unsisterly about Monica Lewinsky, they
also defended a woman's freedom to have private relationships.

In the following decades, the residual separation between
public and private matters in public life, the defence of private
life – and the capacity of men and women to make their own
choices within it – would be washed away. Private life would
become both more exposed in public and more regulated in
private.

Chapter 22:

PARENTAL GUIDANCE

In 2007, Alan Johnson, the then governing Labour Party's Education Secretary, launched the policy document *Every Parent Matters*, setting out a more interventionist family policy for the British state. 'Traditionally,' he wrote, 'parenting and the home environment' had been a 'no-go' area for government: 'But now, more than ever, government needs to be supportive of parents who are themselves increasingly seeking help.'[1]

Johnson noted that parents were increasingly turning to popular reality television programmes like Channel 4's *Supernanny*, where professional nanny Jo Frost devoted each episode to helping a family where the parents were struggling with child-rearing. It was so successful that it spawned an American version. The British government must respond to this need, Johnson said, because 'although parenting is an intensely private matter, it has immense public consequences'. Parenting, he wrote, is the 'single most important factor' in shaping a child's 'well-being, achievements, and prospects'.[2]

More than anyone else on the Labour front bench, Johnson understood the significance of the party's change in approach.

*

Born five years after the Second World War, Alan Johnson grew up in West London in grinding poverty with his mother Lily, father Steve, and sister Linda. They lived in a two-room tenement that had been declared unfit for habitation. There was no indoor toilet, and the kitchen was a stove on the landing. Johnson's abiding memory of the time is of always being hungry.[3] Lily worked as a charlady. Steve played the piano in pubs and clubs, when he wasn't lying in bed or beating his wife. The family were relieved when Steve went off with a barmaid, after which his only contact with them was sending the occasional postal order. Johnson often said that his biggest fear growing up wasn't the absence of a dad but having one.[4]

Lily had a heart condition and was constantly in and out of hospital. She was terrified that, like her own mother and grandmother, she would die at forty-two. Tragically, she did. That left Alan, aged thirteen, and his sister Linda, sixteen, on their own. Linda, who had taken jobs from the age of twelve and helped around the home, was mature for her age. She organized their mother's funeral and fended off offers from their Liverpudlian extended family who thought they should move in with them. Linda felt that she and Alan could manage quite well by themselves, thank you. Her plan was met with resistance.

Their social worker wanted to place them both in care. But that would have meant separating them, and Linda would not accept that. After much discussion and reflection, the social worker decided that Linda was capable of caring for them both and that it would be wrong to sever the sibling bond. They could live on their own. He did not abandon them and visited every week for dinner, cooked by Linda – but effectively, she raised her brother.

As Alan Johnson himself said, this arrangement was a testament to the broad-minded approach taken by social work agencies in the 1950s. By the time New Labour came into power in 1997, such an arrangement would have been inconceivable.

Until the 1970s, the British state supported the family at a distance. The family model that underpinned child welfare policy in the post-war period was based on the traditional institution of marriage, where both parents lived in the same household as their biological children. The extended family and community were relied upon for support. Social workers acted as intermediaries between the state and the family. When they intervened with the full force of the law, it was generally in circumstances where families were clearly failing – cases of repeated and serious physical abuse, or when a child was left with no parents. But even then, as with Alan Johnson and his sister, there was room for individual discretion.

That began to change after the tragic death of Maria Colwell at the hands of her violent stepfather in 1973, while she was under the supervision of the local authority and social workers. Thereafter, interventions happened more frequently. So much so that the removal of 121 children from their parents in Cleveland in 1987, based on later disproven allegations of sexual and Satanic abuse, showed that the authorities could step in too early, with destructive consequences.

In 1993, the murder of two-year-old James Bulger by Jon Venables and Robert Thompson, both just ten years old, sent shockwaves through the nation. The public was outraged, demanding better protection for the most vulnerable. It seemed as though neither the family nor the community could be trusted to keep children safe. The tragic case appeared to underscore that children were at risk from their peers as well as from their parents.

In a defining moment, Tony Blair, then Labour's Shadow Home Secretary, cast a stark light on the Bulger case as emblematic of a society teetering on the brink of chaos. His words reverberated through the pages of the *New Statesman*, where he accused the incumbent Conservative government of abandoning the fight against crime. Blair seized this moment to redefine Labour, soon to be reborn as New Labour, as the uncompromising voice of law and order, promising to be 'tough on crime, tough on the causes of crime'. He had parenting in his sights.[5]

As soon as New Labour was elected to power in 1997, it published the Green Paper 'Supporting Families', signalling a change in social policy in two key ways. First, it announced that the government would no longer interfere in the personal relationship choices made by adults. Second, it was interested in assisting all families, not just intervening in at-risk situations.

The Home Secretary, Jack Straw, emphasized that while marriage was considered the 'preferred arrangement', the government would refrain from lecturing single parents, unmarried parents or gay couples about their lifestyles.[6] This was an explicit departure from the Tory party's attempt to claim the moral high ground, exemplified in 1993 when Prime Minister John Major delivered his 'Back to Basics' speech to the party at their annual conference praising 'traditional values'.

Major was trying to draw a line under party squabbles over Europe and the economic disaster of 'Black Wednesday', when a collapse in the pound sterling forced Britain to withdraw from the European Exchange Rate Mechanism, plunging the nation into financial chaos. 'It is time to return to core values,' he told delegates: 'time to get back to basics, to self-discipline and respect for the law, to consideration for the others [sic], to accepting responsibility for yourself and your family and not shuffling it off on other people and the state.'[7]

But as Major soon found out, attempting to advocate for family values when MPs' own houses were not in order was a perilous enterprise. Back to Basics was ridiculed as 'back to my place' after several Tory MPs were associated with highly publicized sleaze scandals: Tim Yeo's extramarital affair and his 'love child'; Michael Brown's involvement with an underage man; and Stephen Milligan's accidental death by auto-erotic asphyxiation. Perhaps the only sex scandal not uncovered at the time was the

Prime Minister's own extramarital affair with fellow Conservative MP Edwina Currie. (Currie herself revealed all in her *Diaries*, published with a splash in 2002.) Never again would a prime minister dare to set himself up as an arbiter of public morality, at least not when it came to sexual relations.

When New Labour swept into power after eighteen years of Conservative rule, they discarded the Conservatives' 'back to basics' moralizing and their emphasis on 'family values'. Instead, New Labour dismantled the married families tax allowance, replacing it with tax credits for all families with children, irrespective of marital status. This was a statement of inclusivity, culminating in the landmark Civil Partnerships Act of 2004, which set the stage for same-sex marriage.

New Labour's vision was also revolutionary in its commitment to intervene in the lives of families, not just for those deemed 'at risk'. 'Good parenting', as the Home Secretary Jack Straw outlined in 'Supporting Families', was now a priority. The government would assist parents in managing the everyday challenges and stresses of raising children. As he wrote: '[W]hat families – all families – have a right to expect from government is support . . . [They] want clear advice to be available when they need it on everything from their children's health to their own role as parents.'[8]

It was the dawn of a more expansive approach to intervention that gave new powers to courts and local authorities to mandate Parenting Orders, compulsory classes for parents of children deemed antisocial or dysfunctional. The children themselves were enrolled in literacy or numeracy clubs and programmes addressing anger management and substance abuse. The orders restricted their movements, barring them from places like shopping centres and ensuring they were supervised at home.

Parenting classes resulted in the creation of a whole new cadre of 'parent trainers', who were given official status in 2007 with the launch of the government's £30 million National Academy for Parenting Practitioners. Additionally, there was the Sure Start programme, a flagship policy aimed at children from birth to five years old in disadvantaged areas, which offered a suite of services to bolster children's health, well-being and social development. Tony Blair would later reflect on Sure Start as one of his proudest achievements.

In a speech on improving parenting, Blair encapsulated his government's vision with his usual relaxed delivery. He acknowledged that just a few years earlier, the idea of Parenting Orders, classes and support might have seemed 'bizarre or dangerous', dismissed as 'nanny state' interference. Now, he argued, it was essential to offer this support – especially when failing to do so could harm the wider community. 'How people parent,' Blair emphasized, 'makes a difference to the lives of others.'[9]

At the heart of these initiatives was a belief in concepts of 'well-being' and 'inclusion', driven by the ascendant notion of 'early intervention'. This idea, popular on both sides of the Atlantic in the 1990s, posited that giving children a strong start in life would combat social exclusion and social issues.[10]

In the United States, Senator John Vasconcellos had championed the cause in the late 1980s with the California Task Force to Promote Self-Esteem and Personal and Social Responsibility. Vasconcellos argued that low self-esteem was at the root of crime, drug addiction and teenage pregnancy, and that good self-esteem functioned as a 'social vaccine'. British psychologist Terri Apter pursued this idea in her 1997 book *The Confident Child: Raising Children to Believe in Themselves*, asserting that self-esteem was even more crucial to successful development than intelligence or ability.

British social policy reflected these ideas. The Department of Health for Wales, for example, identified low self-esteem as a common factor among children involved in prostitution.[11]

Richard Layard, an influential economist and social policy analyst, further argued that 'well-being' and 'happiness' should be explicit political goals. He advocated for a culture where people openly discussed their feelings, citing Princes William and Harry as role models for their public expressions of grief after Princess Diana's death in 1997. Layard urged governments to measure subjective well-being and take steps to improve it, a recommendation heeded by the UK's Office for National Statistics starting in 2011–12.[12]

This approach, linking parenting and self-esteem to social issues, was a departure for the Labour Party. Having previously focused on material deprivation and inequality as the root causes of social ills, the party now emphasized therapeutic concepts, parenting and intervention in family life. This shift from addressing broad social causes to engaging with personal issues, feelings and emotions would lead to greater governmental involvement in citizens' private lives. It introduced a vision of the citizen in which personal affairs and emotional well-being were a persistent concern to be monitored and addressed through ongoing support, even on everyday matters such as eating or reading books. This model treated individuals almost like patients needing ongoing care or children requiring constant guidance. It represented not just a policy shift but a fundamental reconceptualization of human agency and autonomy, reshaping the relationship between the individual and the state.

*

When the Conservative–Liberal Democrat coalition ascended to power in the UK in 2010, David Cameron, the Conservative prime minister, eschewed the old 'back to basics' moralism. Instead he championed a progressive stance on social issues, most notably with the legalization of same-sex marriage. On 10 December 2013, the Marriage (Same Sex Couples) Act was passed in England and Wales, marking a monumental step forward in the fight for equality – a legislative achievement Cameron held in high regard.

Cameron embraced New Labour's more expansive interventionist approach, believing in the power of the family. 'Families,' he proclaimed, 'are the best anti-poverty measure we have.' His vision was clear: to fortify the family unit as a means of enhancing life chances across the nation and shaping the adults of the future. His government rolled out an array of initiatives in support of this goal, bolstering childcare provisions, introducing shared parental leave and providing relationship support. Often, however, these initiatives were less about money or tax breaks, more about a nebulous sense that the family, whatever shape it took, required extra support. In this vein, Cameron articulated a bold ambition: 'I believe we now need to think about how to make it normal – even aspirational – to attend parenting classes,' he declared.[13]

Initially, concerns about the invasion of privacy were minimal regarding the government's expansive support for families, which could seem more rhetorical than consequential. However, the continuing encroachment of the state into family life eventually sparked a momentous legal privacy challenge north of the border.

*

In April 2014, James and Rhianwen McIntosh of Falkirk, Scotland, received an alarming letter. After they had taken two of their four children to a routine doctor's appointment, the paediatric consultant followed up: 'We are now required to inform the Named Person for your child if your child fails to attend an appointment . . . In addition we may also send them copies of future relevant reports.'[14]

Ahead of its implementation across Scotland in 2016, the McIntosh family had been swept into an early rollout of the 'Named Person scheme' – a key component of the Scottish

National Party's Children and Young People (Scotland) Act 2014. This legislation mandated the appointment of a 'named person', such as a teacher or health visitor, for every child in Scotland from birth until the age of eighteen. Neither parents nor children had the option to refuse this appointed individual.[15]

The Named Person scheme was not solely about responding to suspicions of abuse or harm. Instead, it was grounded in a broad concept of well-being, aiming to ensure a comprehensive support system for every child in Scotland. The Named Person was to serve as a single point of contact with social and other services. They were responsible for entering 'notable' information into a database whenever they deemed it relevant, unless doing so might prejudice a criminal investigation. This information would then be shared with relevant bodies and officials. The Named Person was also tasked with exercising specified statutory functions to 'promote, secure, or safeguard the wellbeing of the child or young person'.

This scheme was a central part of the Scottish government's broader programme, GIRFEC – 'Getting It Right For Every Child'. Within this framework, the Named Person was instructed to monitor the child's progress and needs using a 'wellbeing wheel' comprised of seven indicators known as SHANARRI: safe, healthy, achieving, nurtured, active, respected, responsible and included.[16]

The Scottish National Party (SNP) government argued that the Named Person scheme would yield three benefits. First, the Named Person would serve as a source of help when no other source was available. Second, the scheme would ensure that children did not 'fall through the cracks'.[17] Third, a Named Person would be able to identify the need for early intervention in the lives of children who required support *before* it was obvious. This was why the scheme was designed to apply to all children, not just those identified as being at risk. Numerous reviews into the horrendous deaths of children at the hands of their parents or carers had identified two key contributing factors: failure to act soon enough, and a lack of communication between agencies. As underlined by Alison Todd, chief executive of the Scottish charity Children 1st, the Named Person scheme was to support *all* families *all* the time, because 'No one knows when they might need support.'[18] This comprehensive approach, coupled with the broad definition of responsibilities for a Named Person, provoked a furious response.

'Safety is one thing,' *The Courier*, a newspaper based in Dundee and published in six regions, queried, 'but how would the Named Person decide if a child is not being "respected" or "included"?' It warned that the Named Person could intervene 'merely where there are concerns about a child's happiness'. The editorial continued: 'It authorizes the invasion of privacy according to a government checklist, which is administered by a stranger approved by another government checklist. It sanctions intrusion into every aspect of a child's life, from interfering in personal issues to checking if children get a say in how their room is decorated and what they watch on TV . . . All parents will be in the dock.'[19]

James and Rhianwen McIntosh, who went to the press, were 'concerned as parents that our role is being undermined, that there is an implicit lack of trust that we are the best people to bring our children up'. James continued: 'It does seem to be a little bit Big Brother and our concern is that it could be the beginning of a real slippery slope where a lot more is undermined and that if families, if couples, if parents disagree with what the state decides is right, where does that leave us?'[20] Rhianwen said: 'I love my child better than anyone else and so for the Government to tell me that I needed someone who knew better about my child to see to their wellbeing, that was really quite belittling to me as a parent.'[21]

Two months after the McIntosh family received their letter, they emerged as key figures in a campaign group known as

NO2NP (No to Named Person), spearheaded by the Christian Institute. Their rallying cry resonated deeply: they feared the Named Person scheme would encroach upon their cherished vision of family life. Home schoolers, concerned about the possibility of being demonized under the scheme, joined the cause. Across Scotland, in town halls and community centres alike, voices multiplied as parents, educators and concerned citizens gathered to voice their dissent.

A fierce debate erupted. Maggie Mellon, vice chair of the British Association of Social Workers, highlighted the risk of diverting scarce resources towards monitoring all children without evident need for state intervention, even as beleaguered social work departments struggled to fulfil their existing duties to at-risk children already under their watchful gaze.[22] Those tasked with potentially serving as named persons added their voices to the growing concern. They wanted to know where their jurisdiction would begin and, crucially, where it would end.

The Scottish Parent Teacher Council joined the chorus, arguing that the policy failed to honour the sanctity of the parent–child bond. Legal minds, too, sounded alarms. The Faculty of Advocates, guardians of Scotland's legal integrity, cautioned that the Named Person concept risked diluting parental authority, potentially paving the way for 'indiscriminate provision for possible interference in the lives of all children', and that such a move could amount to an 'assumption by the state of functions that have historically in Scotland been the responsibility of parents'.[23]

Politicians found they had to grapple with mounting discontent. Ruth Davidson, leader of the Scottish Conservatives, opposed the scheme. Kezia Dugdale, leader of Scottish Labour, made a bold about-face, calling for an immediate halt to the scheme, despite her party's earlier endorsement of the legislation.

Nicola Sturgeon, leader of the SNP, found herself on uncertain ground. Confronted by mounting criticism and a groundswell of public concern, she sought to placate detractors by rebranding the Named Person not as a mandatory imposition, but rather as an optional entitlement, a semantic manoeuvre that only served to deepen the confusion surrounding the policy's true nature and implementation.[24] Any remaining support for the scheme evaporated.

Critics had noted the scant mention of 'family' in the extensive legislative documentation accompanying the Act, viewing this omission as indicative of a broader oversight. The Act's implications for family autonomy came under fire, with concerns that it might breach the European Convention on Human Rights (ECHR). The Law Society of Scotland warned of potential conflicts with European law regarding the sanctity of private and family life. This raised the possibility of a legal challenge.

*

In January 2015, NO2NP took the SNP to the Court of Session in Edinburgh. The seven petitioners were James and Rhianwen McIntosh; the Christian Institute; Family Education Trust (an English charity that researches the causes and consequences of family breakdown); the Young ME Sufferers Trust; Care (Christian Action Research and Education) and Deborah Thomas, a parent from Perthshire. They argued that the Named Person was a 'state snooper's charter' that would undermine parents and 'breach privacy'.[25] The group argued that the legislation would lead to 'unjustified and unjustifiable state interference with family rights' and that responsibility for monitoring a child's well-being should be the role of parents, not the state.

The Court of Session in Edinburgh dismissed their case as 'hyperbole'. It said the Named Person did not diminish the role of parents and had 'no effect whatsoever on the legal, moral or social relationships within the family'. Undeterred, NO2NP escalated

Parents James (41) and Rhianwen McIntosh (38) stand victorious outside the Supreme Court in London on 28 July 2016 after judges ruled against the Scottish government's Named Person scheme. They were informed in April 2014 that their four children – Caleb (9), Joel (6), Charis (4) and Micah (2) – had been assigned Named Persons before the scheme was scheduled to be implemented.

their challenge to the highest judicial authority in the United Kingdom – the Supreme Court. This decision marked a critical juncture.

On 26 July 2016, the Supreme Court of the United Kingdom ruled that the Scottish government's Named Person scheme risked breaching rights to privacy and a family life. The five judges ruled that the information-sharing provisions could result in disproportionate interference with article 8 rights under the ECHR, which guarantees everyone's 'right to a private and family life'.

It was a defence of informational privacy, but not necessarily private life. The Supreme Court ruled that the Scottish government had 'exceeded' its powers by making a law that allowed public bodies to share sensitive private information about children and parents without proper consent. The court stated: 'The sharing of personal data between relevant public authorities is central to the role of the Named Person . . . the operation of the information sharing provisions will result in interferences with the rights protected by article 8 of the ECHR.'[26] And because of the lack of safeguards, 'the overriding of confidentiality is likely often to be disproportionate.'[27]

The Supreme Court's decision to strike down the Named Person scheme centred primarily on concerns over inadequate safeguards for data sharing. Had the scheme avoided such sweeping data collection, or at least imposed rigorous confidentiality measures, it might have survived judicial scrutiny. This decision highlights a critical facet of our modern debate over privacy. Today, threats to privacy are almost exclusively framed in terms of data and digital security, while deeper encroachments into our private lives go largely unnoticed. It's in that blind spot where privacy truly erodes.

Chapter 23:

LET'S TALK ABOUT SEX

In 2014, Joe Gow, a professor of communications studies and chancellor of the University of Wisconsin-La Crosse, and his wife, Carmen Wilson, an associate professor of psychology, began filming themselves having sex. The recordings were solely for their own use, part of what they called their 'private collection'. But as their library grew, so did their ambition. They invited 'adult content stars' to take part. Not content with recording these explicit encounters, Gow and Wilson sought to humanize the performers, to peel back the layers of their on-screen personas and discuss the reality of their lives off camera.[1] They also introduced one of Wilson's passions into the mix: vegan cookery. Each film became a blend of conversation, culinary demonstration, and sex.

The couple were proud of their films, describing them as 'genuine' and comparing them favourably to conventional, 'impersonal' pornography.[2] But they wondered, much as they might if they had recorded a song or written a book, what other people might think about them. Curious, they shared some of the videos via the online platforms OnlyFans and LoyalFans.

Both websites are well known for hosting adult content and require users to be over eighteen to access them. They are also famous for hosting non 'adult content' created by YouTubers, fitness trainers, Olympic athletes, models, musicians, reality TV stars, and other well-known public figures who use them to monetize their work. As subscription-based social media sites, they allow content creators to set a monthly subscription price, typically ranging from $5 to $50.

Despite their efforts, Gow and Wilson found themselves trailing far behind more prominent content creators. Hardly anyone subscribed to their channel. Viewers were scarce and 'fans' even rarer. Frustrated, their video editor offered a suggestion: 'Try posting them on the free sites – Pornhub and X-Hamster. See what happens.' So in 2023, they did.

Gow and Wilson didn't expect their videos with titles like 'Juicy Anniversary' and 'Vacation Sex' to stand out among the millions already online. Pornhub, a giant site owned by tech behemoth MindGeek, reported forty-two billion visitors and thirty-nine billion searches in its 2019 annual report. By 2024, it had ascended to become the thirteenth most visited website in the United States, boasting over 100 million daily visitors – figures rivalling the giants of e-commerce and social media.[3] It has a larger audience than Netflix.

Although they did nothing to promote their videos, to their surprise, the views started rolling in – first hundreds, then thousands, soon millions. Their content was ranked number two in America and Oceania on X-Hamster. The comments were overwhelmingly positive. One viewer noted, 'These videos are hot, but in a wholesome way.'[4]

Before long, a lawyer from his university's HR department contacted Joe Gow for a Zoom meeting about a 'personnel issue'. The university had become aware of the videos – a fact Gow found surprising, given the vast sea of content online. He still doesn't know who alerted them. Soon after, he received an email informing him that he had been fired as chancellor. In a public statement, the Universities of Wisconsin President Jay Rothman described Gow's actions as 'appalling' and claimed he inflicted 'substantial reputational damage' on the university, a sentiment echoed by the Board of Regents.[5]

In September 2024 the university stripped Gow of his faculty position and tenure. In response, he called the regents a 'Board of Hypocrites.'[6] He accused them of breaching the university's commitment to academic freedom and of caving in to pressure. The regents, Gow said, 'are willing to fire me for the short-term goodwill they get with the far right.'[7] From his perspective, he and his wife had done nothing wrong and had nothing to apologize for.

Yet explaining the situation to their families who did not know about their filmmaking was difficult. Wilson's daughter initially refused to speak to her, and it took a long, heartfelt conversation to work through a family history with which Wilson had not wanted to burden her. The conversation with her mother was slightly easier – they ended up discussing sex in a way they never had before.

*

Over the past few decades, pornography has emerged from the shadows to become a billion-dollar industry managed by up-front digital capitalists. It even has a new name: 'adult content'. Equally significant is the rise of amateur pornographers who carve out lucrative careers. Platforms like OnlyFans and Pornhub's user-generated content place everyday individuals alongside seasoned professionals and are a far cry from the discreet 'readers' wives' sections of traditional adult magazines. Advances in technology have undeniably pushed pornography into the public realm. By enabling anyone with a smartphone to film and be filmed, production has moved away from studios and professionals, making it accessible for more people to be participants. But there is more to the wider availability of pornography than would first appear.

Historically, technological revolutions have tended to make the consumption of pornography more private. Samuel Pepys, the seventeenth-century diarist, is the first known Englishman to document his purchase of written pornography. He discovered *L'Escole des Filles* (*The School for Girls*), an erotic French text with no pictures, in a bookshop on the Strand. Initially thinking it might interest his French-speaking wife, he soon found it to be the 'most lewd book' he had ever read. Pepys decided to burn it, reflecting the shame associated with consuming such material.[8] While pornography flourished in the eighteenth century, its circulation was limited by legal, social and technological constraints.

With the invention of the camera, nineteenth-century pornographic photographs were printed for private viewing. As the twentieth century dawned, specialized film houses screened pornography exclusively, distinct from mainstream cinemas. They were often located in designated red-light districts. 'Private shops' discreetly sold adult material, or it was kept on the 'top shelf' at newsagents, separated from other printed material. Mail-order pornography was unobtrusively delivered in anonymous brown envelopes. The advent of video cameras and cassette players further facilitated private consumption of pornography at home.

Private shop, Nottingham, 1988.

The migration of pornography to the internet marked a profound shift in social attitudes and cultural norms surrounding sex. What was once discreetly purchased and consumed in secret is now showcased prominently in the online public square alongside content about sport or cooking, readily available at the click of a mouse. People who participate in making it aren't just porn stars, but ordinary people who have day jobs. Sex, for so long a private matter, is increasingly performed for audiences on computer screens, with more and more individuals opting to share intimate acts with strangers.

OnlyFans experienced a massive rise in both posts and sign-ups during the Covid pandemic. The online platform was already growing when, in 2020, Beyoncé name-dropped it in the remix of the song 'Savage', after which it experienced a further 15 per cent increase in traffic.[9] *Time* magazine included OnlyFans in its 100 Most Influential Companies of 2021, alongside Tesla and Twitter/X. Since launching in 2016, the platform had already attracted 120 million subscribers and hosted more than a million creators. *Time* applauded its role in 'boosting the creator economy' and 'monetizing human connection'.[10]

The mainstream acceptance of OnlyFans meant that in August 2021, when it announced its intention to block sexually explicit photographs and videos, the reaction in some established quarters was one of outrage. Amid the uproar, the BBC conducted comprehensive interviews with site users who were dismayed by the decision. The national broadcaster spoke to Tezza Williams, a twenty-two-year-old from Birmingham, who explained that he had started making explicit videos with his boyfriend that summer to pay off debts. It was more than an economic lifeline, he raged: 'If you're not allowed to post really explicit content it's going to be a massive kick in the teeth.' He continued: 'There's this massive stigma on sex workers that just should not be a thing. We're doing it from the comfort of our own bedrooms, it's given us a living – it could be getting people off drugs, off the streets. [Making porn] is helping people and they still want to put bans on it, and [that's] disgusting.'[11]

BBC Newsbeat, a TV programme tailored for young people, spoke with Liv McClelland, a twenty-two-year-old creator from Birmingham, who expressed frustration with the new restrictions. She was concerned about finding an alternative platform to sell her explicit content. McClelland described the platform as a 'safety blanket' for many sex workers, particularly when dealing with intimate content. She said she wouldn't meet any of her subscribers in person because 'you could be meeting a psycho' and 'anything could happen'. She added: 'I worry about the people that have to now go out and do this stuff in person.'[12]

Less than ten years after *The Sun* stopped publishing images of topless glamour models on page 3, the curtailing of explicit material on OnlyFans was met with consternation, even in parts of the broadsheet press. The 'sanitization' of the site is 'the latest in a long line of instances of internet censorship pushing sex workers to the margins', despaired *The Guardian*.[13] In an interview with the *Financial Times*, Tim Stokely, the thirty-seven-year-old founder and CEO of OnlyFans, clarified that the decision to restrict hardcore content had been made under pressure exerted by banking partners who had clamped down on the kinds of products that could be paid for on the site. Stokely reassured readers and users of the platform that some nudity would remain permissible, and criticized banks for imposing these restrictions based on perceived reputational risks. He affirmed that OnlyFans would unequivocally reinstate pornography if banking regulations were to evolve favourably: 'We obviously do not want to lose our most loyal creators,' he emphasized.[14]

Such was the overriding negative response to the move that in a matter of days, OnlyFans was able to reverse its decision. It issued a statement on Twitter/X: 'We have secured assurances necessary to support our diverse creator community and have suspended the planned October 1 policy change.' It explained that the change was in part because of the backlash from creators, who were beginning to leave the platform in numbers. 'Thank you to everyone for making your voices heard,' it said.[15]

Yet, intriguingly, as sexual content becomes more publicly available alongside other types of 'creative' output, private sexual interaction is also facing increased regulation and scrutiny. There is growing mistrust of the idea of being in private with another person.

*

In the early 1990s, Antioch College, a small, private liberal arts college in Ohio, introduced the first Sexual Offense Prevention Policy on an American campus. At the time, this development was regarded as eccentric and widely mocked. The policy required students to obtain explicit affirmative consent for sexual activity. *The New York Times* commended the intention, but suggested implementation would be impossible since 'adolescence, particularly the college years, is a time for experimentation, and experimentation means making mistakes'. It added that 'legislating kisses won't save [young people] from themselves'.[16]

Satirists seized on the policy as a rich source of humour. The long-running sketch show *Saturday Night Live* featured a skit sending it up, implying that the very concept of asking for consent was itself absurd:

UNIDENTIFIED ACTOR: May I kiss you on the mouth?

UNIDENTIFIED ACTRESS: Yes, I would like you to kiss me on the mouth.

UNIDENTIFIED ACTOR: May I elevate the level of sexual intimacy by feeling your buttocks?

UNIDENTIFIED ACTRESS: Yes, you have my permission.[17]

The overwhelmingly derisive response prompted Alan E. Guskin, the president of Antioch College, to write a defence in *The Washington Post*. He clarified that the decision was not imposed from above; rather, it had been requested by students two years earlier, as they grappled with ongoing abuse on campus. The consent policy, he explained, aimed to educate individuals about healthy human relationships. And he ventured that the overblown reaction was perhaps a result of their 'breaking the taboo' on speaking openly about sexual behaviour.[18]

As of 2024, Antioch College is no longer an outlier. To date, most federally funded US colleges and universities mandate that affirmative consent is required for all sexual activity on campus. California's Student Affirmative Consent law, passed in 2014, for instance, requires that *all* university students obtain verifiable and ongoing consent before having sexual relations, and that the initiator is responsible for doing so. Yale University describes consent in its policy as 'positive, unambiguous, and voluntary agreement to engage in specific sexual activities'.[19]

One driving force behind these policies is Title IX, the 1972 federal law that prohibits sex discrimination in federally funded educational institutions. Title IX's regulations have evolved over time to address sexual harassment and assault and all sexual activity. In 2011, the Department of Education warned universities that failing to ensure a sexual violence-free environment would be a violation of students' civil rights. By 2014, the White House Task Force to Protect Students from Sexual Assault had issued a sexual misconduct checklist. At a minimum, it advised, the definition of consent in university consent policies should recognize that:

consent is a voluntary agreement to engage in sexual activity;
someone who is incapacitated cannot consent;
past consent does not imply future consent;

silence or an absence of resistance does not imply consent;
consent to engage in sexual activity with one person does
not imply consent to engage in sexual activity with another;
consent can be withdrawn at any time; and
coercion, force, or threat of either invalidates consent.

Although they were initially developed to address sexual
assault, many university consent policies regulate every sexual
encounter. As the 2022 Antioch College policy puts it: 'each new
level of sexual activity requires affirmative consent . . . regardless
of the parties' relationship, prior sexual history, or current activity
(eg. grinding on the dance floor is not consent for further sexual
activity)'.[20] This bureaucratic approach is very explicitly an intervention into the private sphere of students.

Harvard law professor Jeannie Suk has been a vocal critic of
what she terms 'sex bureaucracy': the complex regulations and
policies that have emerged in response to issues of sex on US college campuses, particularly under Title IX. Suk argues that these
well-intentioned policies have created a bureaucratic overreach
that often serves to undermine due process and leads to overreg-
ulation of consensual sexual behaviour. In her view, the sex
bureaucracy blurs the lines between genuine misconduct and
ordinary human interactions, fostering an environment in which
students, especially men, live in fear of being accused, and where
'protection' severely restricts sexual autonomy. For Suk, the system's paternalistic approach infantilizes students, who are not
permitted privacy for their sexual encounters.[21]

For now, these polices are confined to American universities.
Although in Britain consent policies are not mandatory, universities across the UK host consent classes during freshers' week. In
2021, a survey by the British Higher Education Policy Institute
found that 58 per cent of students believe they should have to pass
a test on sexual consent before entering university. In addition,

51 per cent wanted compulsory sex and relationship education at the start of term.[22]

As for adults, most employers have policies requiring the disclosure of workplace relationships to HR, even in the early stages. In 2023, the television network ITV implemented new, stringent guidelines mandating that employees disclose all relationships with co-workers – including friendships – following TV presenter Phillip Schofield's resignation over what was reported as a workplace affair. Schofield, a co-presenter of *This Morning*, stepped down after admitting to an 'unwise, but not illegal' affair that he had kept quiet, with claims that ITV executives had ignored the relationship. The network's Personal Relationships at Work Policy now requires any relationships between colleagues to be reported. This extends beyond partners to include 'a person living in the same household' and 'anyone engaged in a sexual, romantic, or close relationship or friendship (whether brief or long-term)'.[23]

In *Tomorrow Sex Will Be Good Again* (2021), the academic Katherine Angel details her reservations about the concept of 'consent culture', arguing that it has become widespread but with deleterious effects. Her primary concern is its impact on women. She contends that requiring formal consent presumes women can easily articulate their desires, but that this doesn't reflect the reality of sexual experiences. Desire is not always clear-cut or predictable; it can be messy, unruly and spontaneous. Angel criticizes the affirmative consent approach for turning sex into something contractual. She also warns that insisting that women should always know and be able to clearly state what they want could lead to them being blamed if sexual encounters fail to go well or if abuse occurs. Consent culture, Angel argues, creates an ever more transactional approach to sex, making it less about freedom than about minute regulation. It discourages the taking of risks, which is essential in all intimate interactions. 'We need to be vulnerable,' she writes, 'to take risks, to be open to the unknown – if we are to experience joy and transformation.'[24] Other critics have characterized the new sexual regulations as 'neo-puritan'. Parallels are often drawn with the Victorians. Writing in the online magazine *Quillette*, American attorneys Samantha Harris and Michael Thad Allen note that college administrators dissecting the minutiae of students' sex lives are following in the footsteps of nineteenth-century administrators of Victorian universities. They cite a 1923 rule at Yale University: 'Ladies may not be entertained in college dormitories except by the written permission of the Dean.'[25] They observe that 'university surveillance of the student body has, in some ways, come full circle'.[26]

While these comparisons lend a rhetorical flourish, they don't capture current trends. The Puritans enforced strict moral codes: sex was only permitted within marriage, it had to be heterosexual, and it was intended solely for procreation. The Victorians had them too: men and women were meant to be married, divorce was practically impossible until the 1850s, and homosexuality was a capital offence until 1828 (throughout the rest of the nineteenth century, it was punishable by imprisonment).

Contemporary culture discusses and portrays sex differently. The old moralizing is largely gone. At the same time, sex is no longer a purely private activity, but is widely depicted in the public sphere. Companies and institutions like universities have started to play an overseeing role.

Every year, Antioch College runs a programme of events called 'Sex Month', in which students attend classes to learn about sex. These classes are very different from the ones held by Alfred Kinsey in the 1940s, which confined themselves to biological facts, or the 'marriage courses' that were common a decade earlier. Antioch's Sex Month classes have covered ethical pornography, 'Dildo Bingo' (with sex toys for prizes), ropes-and-bondage workshops, and events that students were invited to attend dressed in ways that expressed their identity along the gender continuum. Other American universities run similar events. In 2023, students at the University of Wisconsin-La Crosse (where Joe Gow was formerly chancellor, but nothing to do with him) organized a five-day Sexual Health Week. It offered a variety of workshops, including 'Breakfast and Birth Control', where students received free sexual health supplies, and 'Condom Bingo', which allowed participants to win prizes by showcasing their sexual health knowledge. Another event encouraged students to discuss consent by challenging the 'sex is like baseball' metaphor and exploring how sex can be compared to pizza. One 'teach-in' was on 'Clitoral Masturbation' and featured a free sex toy giveaway.[27]

*

In seventeenth-century England, sexual activity was heavily regulated, and any sex outside of marriage was forbidden. The eighteenth century saw the first sexual revolution and the rise of bawdy popular culture, while sex as an activity became a comparatively private matter. The Kinsey Reports in the mid-twentieth century brought discussion of human sexuality into the mainstream, but approached it with the same detachment used to study wasps. This scientific perspective – shared by Desmond Morris in his bestselling *Naked Ape* books – emphasized our fundamental biological instincts and behaviours, challenging traditional views of human sexuality rooted in morality or social norms. The twentieth century saw a welcome liberalization and, in the 1960s and 1970s, a second sexual revolution, in which the women's liberation movement called for women – like men – to be free to have sex without fear of either pregnancy or moral disapproval.

These feminists demanded access to contraception and legal abortion so that they could control their own fertility. They successfully challenged regulations and restrictions and over-turned the double standard that dictated only men could enjoy sex. Second-wave feminists like Germaine Greer in *The Female Eunuch* (1970) rejected chaperones, curfews and social conventions and instead celebrated women's sexual agency. Greer would have regarded the idea of a university regulating her sexual activity as absurd. She would have challenged the paternalism and championed the ability of women's agency and ability to take risks.

That's not to say that most factions within the feminist movement didn't argue vigorously for sexual assault to be taken more seriously by the police and courts and for urgent reform of rape laws. Feminists have also argued for the regulation of private life in certain circumstances. Just over a generation ago, British courts accepted that marriage granted conjugal rights to a spouse and that since a spouse could not withdraw consent, there could be no rape. In fact, it wasn't until 1991 that the marital rape exemption was finally abolished in the UK. Up until the 1980s, the legal commission advising government on rape law said that 'the criminal law should keep out of the marital relationships between cohabiting partners – especially the marriage bed'.[28]

But even while fighting sexual harassment and assault, setting up rape crisis centres and advocating for changes in law, most feminists were reluctant to call on the state or other authorities, especially universities or companies, to oversee *all* of their sexual relationships. Indeed, Black feminists such as bell hooks and Patricia Hill Collins rejected any move towards an 'uncritical alliance' between feminism and the state in relation to sexual relationships and beyond.[29]

In the 1980s and 1990s, what has been called 'liberal feminism' and later 'sex-positive feminism' confidently asserted the capability of women to oversee their own sexual activities. American feminists like Betty Friedan, the writer and filmmaker Nora

Ephron, the librarian Judith Krug and the law professor Nadine Strossen promoted women's autonomy and defended women's agency over their private lives. Women, they said, did not need the intervention of the state for their own good. They did not require protection from explicit sexual materials. They didn't want differential treatment from men. They trusted themselves and each other more than they trusted the authorities. When the Clinton–Lewinsky scandal broke in the 1990s, liberal feminists defended Clinton's right to a private life, arguing it was separate from his public position. They treated Monica Lewinsky unsympathetically (to say the least), but they defended the principle that she – like all adult females – had the capacity to make informed decisions about her sexual life.

Today, the liberal feminists who argued that women do not always require additional protection have retreated. They have been overtaken by the idea, first advocated by radical feminists in the late 1970s and early 1980s, that all sexual and intimate relationships are potentially risky and in need of oversight. As Katie Roiphe discussed in *The Morning After* (1993), during the 1990s mainstream discussion, especially on university campuses, moved from celebrating 'free love' to a preoccupation with risk: with 'date rape' and 'bad sex' on campus which triggered a proliferation of protocols designed to ensure there was active consent at all times. Roiphe argued that the blurring of the line between rape, a serious and devastating act, and 'bad sex' was especially detrimental for women as it encouraged them to see themselves as intrinsically vulnerable and as victims. For Roiphe, it was a rehabilitation of older tropes that suggested women always needed the protection of men.

As of the mid-2020s, sexual acts and preferences are no longer confined to the private sphere. They have become increasingly public, much like any other activity, and are now woven into mainstream popular culture. At the same time, sexual relationships face greater regulation. The first shift seems to be the result of a feeling that there is no need for sexual relationships to be private, while the second is linked to a sense that we, everyday people – women and men – probably can't handle such relationships for ourselves, and that taking them out of the private sphere is almost necessary for our own protection. Private encounters are considered too risky and dangerous to leave unmonitored. With the increasingly public nature of sex and the proliferation of sexual consent policies, sexual conduct that does not align with institutional guidelines or oversight is viewed as inherently suspicious, dangerous and potentially criminal. 'Problematic sex' is increasingly regarded as any unregulated intimate encounter that occurs without oversight. In other words, something that happens in private.

Chapter 24:

BIG DATA IS WATCHING YOU

In December 2019, *The New York Times* issued a blazing warning through a series of articles called 'The Privacy Project' – an exhaustive probe that had begun as a month-long endeavour but swelled into a year-long investigation. Its message was stark: 'You Should Be Freaking Out About Privacy', one headline warned, underlined by the strapline: 'Nothing to Hide, Nothing to Fear? Think Again.' Another stated: 'Be Paranoid About Privacy', and yet another: 'You Are Now Remotely Controlled'.[1]

The seeds of the project had been sown that spring, an editorial revealed, by a growing unease over the expanding reach of companies and governments. These entities had acquired unprecedented power to track individuals across the internet and the globe, prompting an urgent reevaluation of risks to privacy. It noted the benefits of technological innovation but painted a disquieting picture: privacy was under siege, its future in doubt.

The year-long investigation alerted readers to the problems of surveillance capitalism. It also examined what the era of big data meant for state bodies: how loopholes in the law meant that data, usually constitutionally protected, lost its protections when in the hands of private companies. Governments – such as those of the United States and the United Kingdom – as well as non-governmental organizations, could purchase this data from brokers. Some of it would be highly sensitive, including financial details, location, DNA and medical data. Such practices can be particularly alarming in contexts like insurance, where access to personal data could lead to discriminatory pricing, denied coverage, or invasive profiling. Insurers, for example, might use data on individuals' health, behaviour and even genetic predispositions to determine premiums, potentially penalizing customers. Furthermore, real-time monitoring through apps and wearable devices could lead to constant surveillance, making privacy increasingly elusive.

There is a concerning overlap between the state's surveillance ambitions and the data-harvesting powers of corporations. A striking example emerged during the Covid-19 lockdown, when the Public Health Agency of Canada (PHAC) purchased location data for thirty-three million phones from Canadian telecom giant Telus to secretly monitor the movements of its citizens. An agency spokesperson explained that the intention was to better understand possible links between the movement of populations within Canada and the spread of the Covid virus. But PHAC also disclosed plans to continue tracking population movement for at least the next five years, citing concerns about 'other infectious diseases, chronic disease prevention, and mental health'.[2] This highlights serious questions about the long-term implications of such surveillance practices, particularly regarding citizens' privacy rights and the potential normalization of large-scale government tracking, both during and beyond emergencies.

Governments need to collect data to save lives and address global problems. However, data revealing individuals' identities is sensitive. Companies' and the state's retention and use of such information should be transparent and closely controlled. While tech companies, governments and lawmakers are taking steps to protect data, there are difficulties. It's hard to restrict internet companies that are embedded in all areas of life and that operate across multiple continents and jurisdictions. There are grey areas about who can do what, with what data.

There is a battle in play between who has possession of and control over data on what grounds. Such as that between tech companies and governments over access to mobile phones. In 2016, the FBI sought access to encrypted data on a locked iPhone following the San Bernardino terrorist attack, believing it could contain critical information. The Bureau asked Apple to create a special version of its iOS software that would disable security features, allowing them to unlock the phone. Apple refused on the basis that complying would set a dangerous precedent, compromising the security and privacy of all iPhone users by creating a 'back door' into the device that could be exploited by hackers or other governments.

The case went to court, but before a legal resolution was reached, the FBI announced that it had successfully accessed the iPhone without Apple's assistance by using a third-party tool. This vaguely technical description disguises the fact that a small Australian hacking firm that sells its cyber wares to democratic governments crafted a solution that the FBI used to gain access.[3] That effectively ended the immediate legal battle, although the broader debate over encryption, privacy and law enforcement's need for access to digital data continues.

As of now, the issue remains unresolved on a broader scale. A fundamental conflict persists between tech companies, who at least rhetorically prioritize user privacy and security, and government agencies seeking access to encrypted information for national security or criminal investigations. Occasionally, new cases arise in which law enforcement agencies request access to encrypted data, reigniting the debate. But no definitive legal precedent or legislation has been established to resolve this ongoing conflict.

And then there is the privacy paradox.

The term 'privacy paradox' refers to the disconnect between individuals' concerns about privacy and their actual behaviours online. Despite voicing worries about data security and the misuse of personal information, people frequently engage in activities that compromise their privacy. This includes sharing extensive personal details on social media, using easy-to-remember but less secure passwords, and consenting to terms and conditions online without fully understanding their implications. As opinion columnist Jennifer Senior observed in *The New York Times*, 'it seems safe to say that most of us harbour inconsistent – if not neurotically contradictory – notions about our personal privacy'.[4]

Indeed, just weeks after the launch of 'The Privacy Project', security cameras appeared almost overnight in the newsroom of *The New York Times*. When the journalists arrived at work, they were alarmed to see them fastened on ceiling tiles, in corridors and in the newsroom. Some questioned the timing. The editor, Eric Nagourney, wondered if the cameras were part of a privacy-related experiment; perhaps the journalists involved in 'The Privacy Project' wanted to chronicle how people would react to the introduction of workplace surveillance?

It was nothing of the sort. Anticipating the possibility of a terrorist attack, the company had installed cameras throughout the building to 'shorten incident response time'. Nagourney realized that he felt resigned to it; that people are used to CCTV, and have been for some time. And the journalists were unable to stop the destruction of their privacy: 'I think people have just been a little beaten down when it comes to privacy,' he wrote. 'Just look at me, the failed rabble-rouser. Here I am back at my desk, writing this. I am surrounded by cameras. And I am meekly going about my work.'[5]

*

In the 1960s, 'giant memory machines' loomed large, their presence stirring fears of a dystopian future where privacy was under siege. They became synonymous with governmental overreach, representing a threat to individuality. Fast-forward to the 1990s, and the personal computer and new technology were heralded as catalysts of positive social change.

Entering the age of big data, we find ourselves once again in a nightmare. Commentators repeatedly warn that big tech possesses omniscient powers, that it knows everything about us and can influence our actions in unseen, pervasive ways. Sensitive personal information appears vulnerable, inadequately protected from prying eyes and potential misuse. At the same time as privacy is threatened, society seems resigned to it.

However, while new technology does pose privacy-related threats, there are limits to the current analysis of the problem, with much of the discourse surrounding big data and privacy myopic in focus and veering into apocalyptic territory.

When *The New York Times* launched 'The Privacy Project', opinion editor James Bennet posed the ominous question: 'Do you know what you have given up?' He highlighted the trade-offs between sacrificing anonymity and privacy for convenience, suggesting that the stakes had never been higher. Bennet urged readers to consider whether 'corporations and politicians', through their access to detailed personal information, had gained 'dangerous power' to 'manipulate our perceptions'.[6]

Under the headline 'This Is Why You Should Care About Privacy', Shoshana Zuboff, author of *Surveillance Capitalism*, urged *New York Times* readers to be alarmed: 'The last 20 years have seen, especially the last decade, the wholesale destruction of privacy.' She warned that big tech's vast knowledge of individuals, stemming from their massive accumulation of data, allows them to do more than just target advertising; they can create sophisticated targeting mechanisms. She provided several examples, including subliminal cues, psychological microtargeting, real-time rewards and punishments, algorithmic recommendation tools, and engineered social comparison dynamics. All of these tactics are designed to capture users' attention, maximize their time on platforms and keep them engaged in order to influence their decisions.

Zuboff emphasized the dire consequences of such omniscient power, linking it to the spreading of disinformation on social media, unnecessary Covid deaths and the storming of the United States Capitol on 6 January 2021 by supporters of the Republican president Donald Trump. 'These are all connected points in one process,' Zuboff asserted, 'and the process is called "how knowledge becomes power."'[7]

In a similar tone and with a similar message, in *Privacy Is Power: Why and How You Should Take Back Control of Your Data* (2020), the philosophy and ethics scholar Carissa Véliz states: 'They are watching us. They know I am writing these words. They know you are reading them. Governments and hundreds of corporations are spying on you and me, and everyone we know. Every minute of every day.' Véliz highlights that these entities are not just passive observers: 'They want to know who we are, what we think, where we hurt. They want to predict and influence our behaviour.'[8]

All of which sounds like the hyperbolic claims advanced by the tech giants themselves, such as when Eric Schmidt, then Google CEO, said that Google 'more or less' knows what people are thinking: 'With your permission, you give us more information about you, about your friends, and we can improve the quality of our searches. We don't need you to type at all. We know where you are. We know where you've been. We can more or less know what you're thinking about.'[9]

These warnings encapsulate the flavour of the contemporary discussion about privacy. Through accessing our data, corporations and governments can know what we are thinking and feeling, and even change our minds. Elections are fought and lost, democracies die, and so do people. There is a lot at stake.

But many of the claims don't stand up.

*

Before he became a whistleblower, Christopher Wylie was a data consultant working for the British political consulting firm Cambridge Analytica. By using personal data mined from millions of Facebook profiles, the company advised the 2016 presidential campaigns of Ted Cruz and Donald Trump on how to engage with the electorate in their political advertising. It also gave advice to the British campaign group Leave EU during the 2016 Brexit referendum.

Cambridge Analytica claimed that their 'psychographic profiling' could be used to target and persuade people through digital marketing. This profiling would reveal personal information about individuals and indicate which political messages they would be receptive to. Wylie described it as 'Steve Bannon's psychological warfare mindfuck tool' and asserted that it had tipped the Trump vote in 2016.[10] Similar claims were made about the Brexit vote. In the words of the *Observer* reporter Carole Cadwalladr, the company 'hijacked democracy' to deliver Brexit.[11]

Wylie revealed that Cambridge Analytica had obtained data through a privacy violation, with the data collected by Aleksandr Kogan, an academic at Cambridge University, via a fake personality test on Facebook. This test not only gathered personal information from the test-takers but also accessed data from their friends, who were unaware of the breach.

But while Cambridge Analytica had committed a privacy violation, claiming that the consequence of their work was to sway the vote in one direction is an exaggeration. The idea that digital marketing changes minds, and that some digital Svengali tells people how to vote, is highly questionable. Politicians have always sought to persuade voters to mark their ballots. In the past, they employed pamphlets, radio and TV campaigns, psychological tactics, public meetings and door-to-door canvassing. Today, they utilize behavioural science, propaganda and digital advertising.

The data was acquired unlawfully and violated privacy, but the allegations of successful manipulation are overstated. Using big data to find, understand, and try to communicate with voters is a strategy that has been employed by all political parties in the US since at least 2008. When, in 2012, Democratic Party campaigners used online data to build up large potential audiences for political messaging in Barack Obama's presidential campaign, no one was concerned about voter manipulation; instead, politicos and commenters celebrated the use of Facebook and data to tailor messages to individuals on social media. When it brought results that they found agreeable, such tactics were lauded.

Indeed, the conclusion of the UK Information Commissioner Elizabeth Denham's investigation into Cambridge Analytica was that the self-publicists of Cambridge Analytica used online data in a standard way. 'On examination,' it concluded, Cambridge Analytica's methods were 'well-recognized processes using commonly available technology'.[12]

The reaction to Cambridge Analytica's actions is just one example in a long history of elite anxieties about the masses being influenced by technology – whether through advertising that, in Ernest Dichter's words, targets the public's 'hidden desires', or through television and political propaganda, which, as Edward Bernays believed, can be used to 'manufacture consent'. Faced with outcomes they find hard to accept – the Brexit referendum result, or the election of Donald Trump – governing elites have leaned towards external factors like digital influencers as an explanation because, as their thinking goes, why else would anyone in their right mind vote that way?

The ongoing discussion over digital privacy echoes past fears, such as the outcry over Lyndon B. Johnson's National Data Center in the 1960s. These fears often focused narrowly on specific technologies: databases, 'giant memory machines', wiretaps the size of an olive, while missing the broader societal shifts that blurred the line between public and private life. They also over-look the gradual narrowing of the concept of privacy as it became detached from the private sphere.

Amid the death throes of private and public life, contemporary public debate and policy concentrate on partial, technical and superficial solutions rather than addressing the root issues. But if the notion of a protected private life, separate from the public sphere, has been largely abandoned – if privacy is now more about agreeing to terms of service rather than the right to be left alone – why should anyone care? When the very idea of private life loses meaning, it's not surprising that many people are indifferent about protecting it.

While concerns about data privacy are justified – corporations and governments do infringe on people's privacy, and digital tools can indeed be used to try to exert control over individuals – the nature of the discussion around these issues is often misguided. The core issue facing the West is not merely technological but lies in the blurred boundaries between corporate power, state authority and the rights of citizens. To address privacy violations, we need to go beyond talking about technology and instead focus on the relationship between power and the individual. Much of the current anxiety around digital surveillance focuses too heavily on platforms and apps, without adequately addressing the actions of the authorities themselves.

One key problem is the tendency towards technological determinism. Many commentators warn of technology's increasingly sophisticated ability to surveil, influence and control populations. For example, historian Yuval Noah Harari warned in the *Financial Times* that surveillance technology capable of harvesting biometric data could be used by corporations and governments not only to monitor citizens but also to 'manipulate feelings' and sell them 'anything' from products to politicians.[13] However, when privacy advocates echo big tech's narrative – that algorithms and artificial intelligence are so powerful they will dominate our lives regardless of human will – they create a sense of helplessness. The narrative shifts responsibility away from governments and corporations, who are the ones invading privacy. It reduces the possibilities for democratic accountability, while placing the responsibility for action in the hands of legal or technical experts.

Another problem is the lack of faith in individual agency. Pro-privacy advocates often exaggerate the power of technology to manipulate the public, reinforcing a cynical view of human nature that portrays individuals as easily influenced. This view, shared by tech executives, politicians and some privacy advocates, undermines the case for protecting privacy. It also fuels a broader distrust of private life itself, suggesting that ordinary people cannot be trusted with their private decisions or actions. Ultimately, the protection of individual privacy, while sometimes aided by technology, depends on a clear boundary between the private and public domains. This border must be erected and defended not only online but also in the offline world.

Chapter 25:

THE SOUND OF SILENCE

In the early hours of Friday, 21 June 2019, the neighbours of Carrie Symonds and Boris Johnson, who was then campaigning to be the leader of the Conservative Party and British prime minister, overheard a heated argument between the couple, which they recorded. After knocking on the door without receiving an answer, they also called 999. Within minutes, two police cars and a van arrived. Officers visited the couple, determined that they were safe and well and concluded that there was no need for further investigation.

Despite this, *The Guardian* published the transcript of the recording on its front page. Under the headline 'Boris Johnson: Police Called to Loud Altercation at Potential PM's Home' the article, splashed as 'an exclusive', reported that a woman could be heard complaining that a white sofa had been damaged with red wine: 'You just don't care for anything because you're spoilt. You have no care for money or anything.' She was also heard saying, 'Get out of my flat.' Johnson was heard refusing to leave and telling Symonds to 'Get off my fucking laptop.'[1]

The newspaper's coverage, along with the neighbours' recording of the couple's argument, amounted to an invasion of privacy intended to discredit Johnson, whose character was often criticized as unreliable. Johnson was an easy target, as people tend to behave differently – and sometimes poorly – when in private. It was also easy because violating the boundary between public and private life has become acceptable.

Invasions of privacy – especially regarding private conversations – have become normalized. But at the same time, privacy is increasingly demanded for political discussions that should be in the public realm. Information that ought to be public is becoming more private; while private conversations are increasingly being exposed to public scrutiny. Nowhere is the blurring of boundaries between public and private – and its topsy-turvy impact – more evident than in conversation, with significant implications for both realms.

*

A few days into the UK Cabinet Office's 2023 legal case against the Covid-19 Inquiry, Sir James Eadie KC argued in the High Court in London that thousands of WhatsApp messages exchanged between Prime Minister Boris Johnson and his colleagues during the pandemic were irrelevant. Eadie's position was that the inquiry, established to assess the UK's pandemic response and draw lessons for the future, did not require every message exchanged by senior politicians over the two-year period. The government had already provided 55,000 documents, twenty-four personal witness statements and eight corporate statements. Eadie suggested that the government should not be compelled to supply material that was 'unambiguously irrelevant'. He noted that WhatsApp chats, being private, encrypted and informal, would inevitably include content not pertinent to the inquiry, giving examples of personal matters like a child's schooling arrangements or details of an illness.[2]

Baroness Heather Hallett, chair of the inquiry, responded that WhatsApp messaging was central to decision-making in Britain during the pandemic and therefore relevant. 'So much government decision-making happens on WhatsApp,' one government aide told *The Times* when interviewed about the inquiry's case. 'It's faster to use WhatsApp to ask questions than wait to arrange a meeting. It's very efficient.' Another concurred: 'Government could not run without it.'[3]

The Public Records Act of 1958 requires the government to review and retain all written records related to policy formation. Messages exchanged during a crisis or as part of routine governmental work – whether in the form of minutes, documents, papers, briefings or letters – are typically scrutinized later in an effort to understand how decisions have been made. This is a crucial aspect of accountability. Additionally, the Freedom of Information Act (FOI) 2000, introduced by Tony Blair when he was leader of the Labour Party and prime minister, grants the public the right to access information held by public authorities – with some exemptions for sensitive data – promoting transparency and accountability in government.

When Tony Blair first proposed the FOI Act while in opposition, he stated that it would 'signal a new relationship between government and people', viewing the public as 'legitimate stakeholders in the running of the country'.[4] He argued that effective government required greater transparency in decision-making, lamenting the prevailing 'addiction to secrecy' and the tendency to conduct government business 'behind closed doors'. However, after becoming prime minister and witnessing the law's effects, Blair reconsidered, describing it as 'utterly undermining of sensible government' and admitting forcefully, 'There is really no description of stupidity, no matter how vivid, that is adequate. I quake at the imbecility of it.' In his memoirs, he called it a 'dangerous act', emphasizing that governments need to debate and decide issues in confidence.[5]

All governments need privacy in their decision-making processes to allow officials to discuss ideas, criticisms and concerns freely, without constraint. Without this confidentiality, participants may be reluctant to engage in open and honest dialogue, leading to less effective decision-making and potentially hindering the development of well-considered policies. Officials need the freedom to explore unconventional, difficult or sensitive ideas and test them before they are scrutinized by their professional peers. This process helps ensure that policies are robustly challenged and refined before implementation.

At the same time, for the sake of accountability and full understanding of events that have taken place, democratic governments must be subject to scrutiny. From ancient Greece to Jeremy Bentham's paean to open government, *Of Publicity*, democracies have valued public accountability. Given the gravity of Covid-19, which led to millions of deaths, economic shutdowns and unprecedented restrictions on public and private life, it is crucial that these measures undergo thorough open examination to assess what worked, what didn't, how decisions were made, why and by whom.

And yet, many British political leaders failed to provide their WhatsApp messages to the inquiry. Although in July 2023 the Cabinet Office lost its challenge against the inquiry's request for Boris Johnson's unredacted WhatsApp messages, notebooks and diaries, many of these records were never retrieved, ostensibly due to technical issues. Johnson and other politicians, including Rishi Sunak, who was chancellor during the pandemic, were unable to contribute their messages, claiming they had been 'lost' or 'deleted'.[6]

Welsh ministers and members of the SNP, Scotland's ruling party, also failed to provide their messages. Despite First Minister Nicola Sturgeon's assurance that she would supply them, most of her messages had been deleted. Her deputy, John Swinney, set messages to auto-delete. When questioned by the inquiry, the SNP dismissed the deletion of messages as 'routine management', citing the high volume of messages exchanged and claiming that much of it was just 'banter'. Retired civil servant Ken Thomson

explained that electronic messaging had increased rapidly during
the pandemic. He stated that while the policy was to retain
formal records of decision-making, many messages were simply
informational exchanges and not relevant. Thomson denied any
attempt to circumvent FOI laws, suggesting that private information might be disclosed in such chats, with salient information
being transferred to the public record as policy. However, the
WhatsApp messages that have been retrieved suggest otherwise.

Thomson was questioned about an August 2020 group chat
during a Covid outbreak, which included the deputy chief medical officer and national clinical director Professor Jason Leitch. In
the chat, he reminded participants that the messages were 'FOI
discoverable' and urged them to use the 'clear chat' button,
adding, 'Plausible deniability is my middle name.' In another
WhatsApp group message from May 2021, he wrote, 'I feel moved
at this point to tell you that this chat is FOI-recoverable,' accompanied by a zipped-mouth emoji. Two minutes later, Leitch
responded, 'WhatsApp deletion is a pre-bed ritual.'[7]

While these actions appear to be a deliberate attempt by politicians to avoid accountability, it was Boris Johnson himself who
had appointed Baroness Hallett chair of the inquiry and, on
doing so, empowered her to requisition any WhatsApp messages,
diaries and notebooks as she deemed fit. Johnson's personal
mobile phone number had been freely available on the internet
for the previous fifteen years, throughout his tenures as foreign
secretary and prime minister – a careless oversight fraught with
potential security vulnerabilities. These actions suggest that the
Prime Minister had, to put it mildly, at best an inconsistent sense
of what information should be kept private or made public. Nor
is he the only one.

Around 100,000 WhatsApp messages sent during the pandemic, including one by Matt Hancock, Secretary of State for
Health and Social Care, stating the government should 'frighten

the pants off everyone', were leaked to *The Telegraph* by journalist Isabel Oakeshott. 'We cannot wait any longer for answers,' she told readers of *The Telegraph*'s 'Lockdown Files' in February 2023. 'These texts are a vital historical record at a time when we need urgent answers.'[8]

In leaking the messages, Oakeshott violated a non-disclosure agreement – another recent attempt to control information and keep it secret – but Hancock had willingly shared them with her. He did so while they were collaborating on his *Pandemic Diaries*, an autobiographical account of the pandemic and his role in its mitigation. The book was published in December 2022, one month after Hancock appeared on the reality TV programme *I'm a Celebrity . . . Get Me Out of Here!* and six months after he resigned as health secretary after breaching social distancing guidance by kissing a colleague, Gina Coladangelo, inside the Department of Health, despite both being married at the time.

It's hard to believe that the former health secretary, with an eye always on the TV cameras, would not have contemplated the possibility of Oakeshott, a seasoned journalist and vocal critic of the lockdown measures, exposing the contents of the messages. By the time Hancock handed them over to her, he had already been brought down by the leaked CCTV footage that showed him in an office cheating on his wife.

Many journalists now spend much of their working life making FOI requests, while politicians have resorted to alternative means of communication that try to circumvent its parameters: Post-it notes and emerging technologies that sit within a nebulous realm, much like WhatsApp.

Meanwhile, leaking has emerged as a political stratagem employed by journalists, civil servants and politicians themselves. The British public were only made aware of the parties hosted within the confines of No. 10 during lockdown, triggering a political scandal that brought down Boris Johnson's premiership,

because attendees and colleagues leaked the information to journalists – some of whom were also partying. Exposure of hypocrisy
and bad behaviour has become an end in itself, bypassing other
more rigorous, and indeed political, forms of accountability.

The extensive use of WhatsApp by government ministers
during such a grave crisis raises the question of what senior politicians thought they were doing, conducting so much of their
business on the platform? It's true that they were dealing with a
highly contagious new disease and needed to be contactable at all
times, but WhatsApp is fundamentally a quick-fire messaging
service unsuited to complex policy discussions about matters of
life and death. As health secretary, Matt Hancock took a while to
read a message informing him that excess care-home deaths had
risen to a staggering 10,000. When he finally did, his response
was: 'Aargh sorry – just got this.'[9]

Decisions of the magnitude taken by UK government officials,
such as implementing nationwide lockdown measures and
attempting to protect the vulnerable, are far too important to be
handled while multitasking with household chores. Such pivotal
choices deserve a singular focus, from all involved, untangled
from the distractions of day-to-day life. There also need to be
clear lines of accountability and an unambiguous sense of what
should and should not be public and private.

*

The same governments that attempted to keep their own
WhatsApp messages private were simultaneously working to
erode the privacy of conversations for citizens. In March 2021, the
Scottish National Party ended the sanctity of conversations in
the home with the Hate Crime and Public Order (Scotland)
Act. The Act abolished the common-law offence of blasphemy. It
also criminalized speech deemed to incite hatred against individuals or groups based on protected characteristics: age, disability,

religion, sexual orientation, transgender identity and variations in sex characteristics. Unlike other regulations of speech in the West, which govern public discourse, this Act uniquely extends its reach into the private sphere.

The defining feature of the Act is its removal of the 'dwelling defence', which was present in the Public Order Act of 1986. This defence exempted people from prosecution for what they said in the privacy of their homes. With its removal, statements made within one's own home – whether during a heated argument about something like white sofas and red wine, or at a dinner party – were no longer considered off limits and are now subject to legal penalties. Offenders could face up to seven years in prison, an unlimited fine, or both.

Humza Yousaf, then Scotland's Justice Secretary, defended this radical departure by emphasizing the need to protect children, family members and houseguests from hate speech. Introducing the bill to the Scottish Parliament's Justice Committee, he challenged MSPs: 'Are we comfortable giving a defence to somebody whose behaviour is threatening or abusive and is intentionally stirring up hatred against, for example, Muslims? Are we saying that that is justified because that is in the home? . . . If your intention was to stir up hatred against Jews . . . then I think that deserves criminal sanction.' Yousaf further argued that a dwelling defence would draw an 'entirely artificial distinction' between public and private speech.[10]

Scotland is the only country in the Western world where the state has the power to police speech in the privacy of the home. The Law Commission of England and Wales, a non-departmental public body which reviews law, recommended something similar, momentarily, but decided against it so as not to criminalize private comments in a person's home. As it stands, in Scotland, not even the privacy of home will be a refuge from the ears of the state.

This is a historic change. Since the seventeenth century, it has been accepted that there is a crucial distinction between what a person says or thinks in private and their public speech, a demarcation between private life and public life. Only totalitarian governments ignored that. But in certain ways and certain places, private speech is in the sight of the state.

Governments around the world are in conflict with tech companies over access to private messages on digital platforms. Apps like WhatsApp, iMessage and Signal maintain end-to-end encryption: only the sender and recipient can read the messages, as they are encrypted on the sender's device and only decrypted on the recipient's device. Even the companies providing these services cannot access the content of the messages. This keeps

The introductory page for the Signal app arranged on a smartphone in Sydney, New South Wales, Australia, on 20 January 2021. Messaging apps like Signal, Element, Session, Threema, Viber, WhatsApp and Wire all claim to protect user privacy through encryption, careful data handling and user transparency – though these claims are contested.

conversations confidential and prevents unauthorized access by hackers, corporations or governments. In fact, it is often governments that seek to bypass the encryption, while technology companies resist attempts to violate their users' privacy.

In the UK, the British government targeted encryption in 2023 during the early stages of its Online Safety Bill. This bill aimed to give Ofcom, the communications regulator, the power to mandate that messaging platforms use 'accredited technology' to detect, block and report illegal images. Its stated goals were to protect children from abuse and prevent terror attacks. These were admirable objectives, but ones that could also lead to the infringement of privacy. If implemented, the bill would allow authorities to compel communication providers like WhatsApp to scan all messages sent within the UK to identify criminal activity.

Apple protested that the bill posed a 'serious threat' to end-to-end encryption, which it described as 'a critical capability protection'.[11] Seven tech companies – Signal, WhatsApp, Element, Session, Threema, Viber and Wire – warned that the Online Safety Bill and breaking encryption posed 'an unprecedented threat to the privacy, safety and security of every citizen and the people with whom they communicate around the world, while emboldening hostile governments who may seek to draft copy-cat laws'. They made the point that if governments could scan private messages, so could hostile actors.

That part of the bill didn't succeed and was dropped by the time it was given royal assent in October 2023. But the Communications Act 2003 already makes it a crime in the UK to post anything 'grossly offensive' on a 'communications system'. Consequently, people have been prosecuted – even jailed – for sharing posts on what they thought were private WhatsApp groups (a messaging group within WhatsApp where only invited members can join and participate). The cases in question are not straightforward legal battles of 'good people versus bad laws'. They are difficult cases that raise important questions about the privacy of conversations that are assumed to be confidential. They don't concern the criminal acts of sharing child pornography or criminal conspiracy, but what is termed 'offensive' speech.

On 6 November 2023, a retired police officer was convicted of sending a 'grossly offensive' message on WhatsApp. Sixty-two-year-old Michael Chadwell had shared messages, including one about a parrot, with five former Met officers in a private WhatsApp group established for the officers to remain in contact after retirement. The bird-related message was a meme that someone else had created, and which had already been widely shared over social media before Chadwell sent it to his mates in the 'Old Boys Beer Meet – Wales' group chat. It shows different coloured parrots above a picture of children of different races. The text says: 'Why do we cherish the variety of colour in every species . . . but our own?' underneath which a comment read: 'because I have never had a bike stolen out of my front yard by a parrot'.

This was obviously a racist joke. But – in what, in future, will likely be called the Dead Parrot Defence – Chadwell reached for art history and claimed that this and the other messages he sent were deliberately 'silly'. As he explained in court: 'My reason for (posting) it into the group was because of what the person had written on Facebook underneath, which I felt was Dadaist, surreal and a little bit Monty Python.'[12]

Deputy Magistrate Tanweer Ikram found Chadwell guilty under Section 127 of the Communications Act 2003. This law criminalizes anyone who 'sends by means of a public electronic communications network' – that is, a private message over the internet or a mobile network – anything 'grossly offensive or of an indecent, obscene or menacing character'. It is a summary offence with no right to a trial by jury. The judge alone decides if the message sent is abhorrent or threatening. Ikram ruled: 'He [Chadwell] posted the whole thing. He thought it was funny but it was grossly offensive and he was aware of that at the time. That is why I find the defendant guilty of this offence.'[13] Chadwell and the five other former police officers were sentenced to between six and fourteen weeks' imprisonment, suspended for twelve months.[14]

The racist parrot joke is far from the only instance of a private group message landing someone in court. Another involves Paul Bussetti, whose own video footage, filmed at a private party, of a cardboard model of the Grenfell Tower being burnt on a bonfire on 5 November, with appalling jibes and laughter in the background from guests, was sent to a private WhatsApp group. It was subsequently leaked, to understandable public outrage. Chief Magistrate Paul Goldspring said he was 'horrified' when he saw it. Bussetti himself acknowledged: 'It was terrible, definitely offensive to people, it was just complete stupidness, one of those stupid moments.' He received a ten-week suspended jail sentence under the 2003 Communications Act.

In another case in 2022, James Watts, an ex-police officer, was jailed for twenty weeks over racist messages sent to a private WhatsApp group. Watts was a probationary constable with West Mercia police in 2020 when he shared 'grossly offensive' material. He sent ten memes to a group of former colleagues from HMP Rye Hill, where he had been a prison guard. One featured a white dog wearing Ku Klux Klan clothing, and another showed a prayer mat with George Floyd's face printed on it.

One of the group found the messages offensive. Rather than confronting the members and countering the content exchanged among them himself, he went straight to the public forum of Twitter/X to make sure thousands of other people could read them: 'Former work colleague now serving police officer sent these in group chat' he tweeted, with all the details. 'What hope is there in police in the UK sharing these.' A public uproar, inevitably, ensued.

Watts quit before he was dismissed. In police interviews, he admitted to the racist nature of the messages. In addition to the twenty-week prison sentence, he was banned for life from holding any policing role.

It's understandable that people saying racist or offensive things should not go unchallenged, particularly when they are involved in upholding the law and maintaining social order. But it's important to think this law through, as it applies to any British citizen sending a message over a mobile phone or online.

The British writer Ed West has drawn attention to the relative severity of the Watts sentence, arguing that it 'jars' with the usual standards of British justice.[15] He compares the twenty weeks' jail time for Watts's WhatsApp messages to the case of two men in Lancashire who were spared prison for an attack that left a stranger in intensive care. West notes that offensive speech is increasingly being treated as a more serious crime than actual violence; tweeting can lead to longer sentences than inflicting grievous bodily harm. The Watts sentence, he writes, is 'a quite extraordinarily harsh sentence in a country where violent offenders regularly avoid prison'. His conclusion is that Britain, in effect, has two sets of blasphemy laws.

The Watts case also raises a different question: people are being prosecuted and jailed for things they have said in what they regarded as a private space. This isn't clear-cut. Some of the men in the WhatsApp group were connected in a semi-professional capacity, in positions where public trust is essential, and the group nature of the chat makes it more akin to a conversation in a pub than a private home. Additionally, the leaked nature of these private exchanges suggests poor judgement in choosing friends and speaking unwisely. Without question they should have been, and rightly were, professionally disciplined.

But these incidents reveal an evolving social landscape in which divulging private conversations is incentivized, rather than stigmatized as reprehensible snitching. It's tempting to argue that people shouldn't send messages online or via apps if they don't want them to become public, and there's some truth to that. It's also the case that unlike spoken words, which are as ephemeral as breath, digital conversations last for ever and therefore have some affinity with published material.

The individuals involved in these cases were indeed foolish; in some instances, their behaviour was deplorable. However, given that most people communicate online through apps, the principle that private messages should remain private should be upheld. The messages concerned were not intended for everyone; only for a select group of people. Additionally, the phrase 'anything grossly offensive or of an indecent, obscene or menacing character', as used in Section 127 of the Communications Act 2003, has a highly subjective quality. One judge could easily disagree with another about what they find 'indecent' or 'offensive' in a conversation that was not intended to include them.

*

Across time and place, from Thomas More to Monica Lewinsky, the private words of public and private figures have frequently been wielded against them – precisely because everyone knows that we act differently when we believe no one else is watching or listening. In private, among friends or colleagues, words and images can take on different meanings than they do when expressed in the bright light of day. If there are layers of history and shared understanding between speaker and listener, they alter the meaning and significance of what is said.

But while a person may show their playful, experimental side in private, they also show the worst aspects of who they are when they think no one else outside a select group can hear them. Everyone says things in private that they wouldn't want other people to read or hear, because they are messing around, joking, releasing frustration – or, indeed, being a bigot. The liberty to behave in this way in private is important, and its loss undermines autonomy and freedom.

Private speech is a way of testing out what you think, of seeing what it sounds like out loud among people you trust. It's a chance to be a bit transgressive, perhaps, before you behave better – maybe, as a consequence, even rethinking things. Or maybe not. Ultimately, though, privacy does protect people with abhorrent views that they normally hide from public view. And so it should: we all need a space of private release, a backstage area where we can safely mouth off. Even scumbags need privacy.

*

In his investigation of life in Stalin's Russia, the historian Orlando Figes documents the impact of totalitarian regimes in Russia on the lives of ordinary people. The regime encouraged friends and lovers, neighbours and strangers, parents and children to denounce each other. Any private remark or act could be labelled subversive. A doctor recalls how his family were forced to behave at home: '[Y]ou were afraid to drop any kind of unguarded word, even in front of your own son, because he might inadvertently mention it in school, the directorate would report it, and they would ask the boy, "Where did you hear that?" and the boy would answer, "Papa says so and Papa is always right," and before you knew it, you'd be in serious trouble.'[16]

Figes describes how the sense of being under permanent surveillance seeped into people's innermost thoughts. It was difficult for individuals even to think outside the terms defined by the state discourse of Soviet politics. Any other thoughts or emotions were likely to be felt as a 'crisis of the self' – something dangerous, to be purged from the personality. As a result, it was almost impossible to undergo any kind of self-reflection. Figes concludes that the lasting consequence of Stalin's murderous dictatorship in Russia is a silent and conformist population.[17]

The contemporary drive to eliminate controversial or anti-social opinions and speech from the private realm, forcing them into the light, encourages people to conduct themselves as if they are being permanently surveilled. It leads to a society in which we must filter everything we say through a kind of internalized show trial, which inevitably encourages conformity and uniformity. Since everyone has the capacity to say awful, silly, strange or stupid things, this destroys social trust and leads to a never-ending crusade against hypocrites. Ultimately – in the words of Thomas Wentworth, seventeenth-century aide to Charles I – the outcome could be 'a silent world'.

Chapter 26:

SAVING PRIVATE LIFE

Until the late 1960s, privacy was so highly esteemed in the West that its erosion was the subject of numerous dystopian works, such as *Nineteen Eighty-Four* and *Brave New World*. The prevailing view was that Western societies preserved privacy, while totalitarian regimes sought to destroy it. Warnings about the consequences of privacy erosion were plentiful and powerful. But no longer.

The private realm is now under assault from both indifference – where private matters are seen as no different from public ones – and from a growing suspicion of privacy itself. We are revisiting an era when the seventeenth-century adage 'Do nothing publicly that you wouldn't do privately' and the observation 'Privacy is for adulterers and murderers' resonate strongly.

Many blame this situation on narcissistic individuals who broadcast their lives online or on tech companies that devour personal data, but this overlooks the deeper changes at play. The divide between public and private, established in the eighteenth century, has dissolved. The two realms have become indistinguishable, leading to confusion about the rules governing each and preventing the realization of their respective benefits. Moving forward, it is essential to recognize the importance of maintaining a distinct boundary between the two. This entails both reinvigorating public life and defending private life.

It's essential to have a private space shielded from corporate, state and public scrutiny – a place where we can be alone. This solitude enables us to develop an inner life and a sense of self without constant external pressures. Originality begins in private, shaded from the conformity of social pressures, long before it is made public. Permanent visibility can hinder our ability to think, reflect and concentrate. The ongoing externalization of the self threatens our capacity for introspection and contemplation.

In the twenty-first century, those who don't comply with the culture of exposure are often seen as old-fashioned, quaint, even odd. But when private matters are flooded with light, their very nature changes – this is true of relationships, birth, even death. Experiencing them through the eyes of others whom we do not know strips them of their power. It's not that they are embarrassing or wrong. It's that they are weighty, have a particular context, and are specific to the individual.

The private sphere is where we make personal commitments. It's where we have freedom to discriminate; to be with whom we wish to be with, say what we want to say. It's where we take off our public masks and turn away from the world. Private life is where we can make mistakes with those we trust. It's where our secrets, our vices and our faults, which make us unique and which are wrapped up with being human, can breathe. It is the necessary grounding of the personality.

Privacy is required for love and sex, not because they are shameful, but because they are so powerful. We should give ourselves to them without thinking of how we appear to others we do not know. Privacy is required to remove ourselves from the everyday and lose ourselves in another person; to let go and to focus on the moment; to feel everything with abandon.

In safeguarding the private realm, we not only protect our individual freedoms but also enrich the public domain. A private life guards the public from the intrusion of private matters, and thus opens a realm of common judgement. But at present, our public life is dominated by personality, emotion and private affairs. Politicians and public figures are judged on their character and claims to 'lived experience'. Personal experience can, of course, be informative. However, to generalize and apply it to a larger group requires moving beyond individual perspective. And yet, revelations and scandal about private lives, identities, personal troubles and foibles dominate public debate. Politics appears obsessed with personality or concerned with fighting over the best version of the private world. Our democratic and social existence is debased.

The political and the non-political have merged. Today, engaging in politics often requires revealing personal aspects of life, which is intrusive and compromising. Private matters, especially intimate ones, are increasingly exposed to political pressures. However, not all personal matters are political, nor should they be bound by such constraints. Similarly, politics need not be so personal; it benefits from broader perspectives that look beyond individual concerns and focus on the bigger picture. Without the divide between the two realms, the public arena of contestation is much reduced. It is not political enough.

The public sphere should be a place in which to transact human affairs that we have in common and outside the boundaries of the family, loved ones and friends, and to realize the promise of democratic life. It is where we work with people with whom we may disagree in a civilized manner. Rituals of politeness, agreed social terms, formalities like rules of rational debate, are now regarded with suspicion if not actual contempt, rather than being valued for giving us a common culture and a shared understanding of reality. This is one reason why it must be open to scrutiny. Privacy laws that limit reporting and the use of super injunctions, a legal order that not only prohibits the disclosure of certain information but also prevents the reporting or even mentioning that the injunction exists, are a threat to accountability, open justice and civic engagement.

Accusations of hypocrisy and criticisms of people's public personas as not reflecting their 'true selves' miss an essential understanding of human behaviour. It is important to recognize and accept that we naturally present ourselves differently in public and in private. Both modes of behaviour are authentic; neither is fake. Each domain – public and private – requires a different form of expression and serves a distinct purpose.

There is nothing phoney in having a public self; indeed, it is what makes society, politics and collective identity possible. Public behaviour, where our actions and words are shaped by social norms and tailored to the context, is real and valid. It is not deceptive, but a necessary adaptation that allows us to navigate the complex social landscape we inhabit. In private, conversely, we are free from the external pressures and expectations that influence our public selves. This domain allows for a different kind of being, one that is often more introspective and personal. Here, we can express thoughts and emotions without the filter required in public settings. Understanding this distinction helps us to appreciate that both public and private behaviour are genuine facets of who we are, and that they complement each other. Embracing this duality enriches our understanding of being human and underscores the complexity of our interactions in various spheres.

Private life is double edged – it protects us from certain kinds of public accountability and interference, but it can hide wrongdoing. It can stultify and be mind-numbingly boring. But while it is not an unmitigated good, it is unquestionably necessary.

Towards the end of the second decade of the twenty-first century, the dividing line between our public and private lives has blurred. But it is essential for human flourishing that we conduct substantial parts of our lives unobserved. To best achieve that, we must resurrect a meaningful divide between the public and private domains. Men and women need to be able to present their best selves in public and participate as equals in civil society, but still be able to withdraw, separately and together, to a protected private sphere.

In its defence, there's no wish to return to the servitude of the ancients or the restrictive and stultifying privacy of the Victorians. The private realm must be validated and respected as equal to the public. Ultimately, we need to shape a private realm and restore vitality to the public realm; the key is not to insist on the primacy of either sphere, but on their interdependence and the crucial importance of the boundary between them.

In tracing the origins of the private sphere, we see that the concept of individual conscience laid the groundwork for distinguishing between public and private life. The emergence of these two realms, and the value placed on the private, demanded that individuals be granted respect and autonomy to manage their own lives and influence the world. This historical development implies that safeguarding private life and revitalizing public engagement require both a confidence in our humanity and a bold vision for our potential achievements. We need to think bigger and, once again, find the determination to set ourselves apart.

Acknowledgements

Books are never the work of one person alone. They are the result of the assistance, support and expertise of many. I am deeply grateful to my editor, Andrea Henry, whose dedication and boundless energy were crucial in shaping this manuscript, and ensured I wouldn't be writing it for ever. My thanks also go to the amazing team at Picador for their professionalism and infectious enthusiasm. In particular, I owe a debt to Lewis Russell and John Sugar for their invaluable assistance. And none of this would have been possible without my agent, Toby Mundy, whose insights and ambition helped bring this project to life.

I would also like to thank Mette Birkedal Bruun, Anni Haahr Henriksen, Johannes Ljungberg, Frank Ejby Poulsen, Maj Riis Poulsen and the brilliant team at the Centre for Privacy Studies at the University of Copenhagen. Their invigorating engagement and wonderful hospitality on a research trip were invaluable to this project. Many other amazing scholars generously shared their knowledge, addressed my seemingly endless questions and queries, and gently corrected errors. These include Elisabeth Lasch-Quinn, David Vincent, Jeffrey Rosen, Rochelle Gurstein, Roger Berkowitz, Teresa M. Bejan, James Panton, John Fitzpatrick, Alan Hudson, Jonathan Healey, Erica Longfellow, Brian Cummings, Neil Richards, Ronald Huebert, Sean Lang, Daniel Jutte, Josh Cohen, Andrew Orlowski, Sam Rubenstein and Paul Lay.

The eagle-eyed Felice Basboll provided thoughtful insights and constructive criticism, as did Nancy McDermott, Aruna Vasudevan, Sue Armstrong, Timandra Harkness and Emily Waterfield. Endless thanks go to Iain Macwhirter for putting up with this writer's life and helping to simplify the task and get the words on the page.

Notes

INTRODUCTION

1. *ITV News*, 10 May 2023, www.itv.com/news/2023-05-10/mirror-tabloid-group-admits-it-unlawfully-gathered-info-on-prince-harry.

2. Meghan Markle, 'The Losses We Share', *The New York Times*, 25 November 2020.

3. 'The Worldwide Privacy Tour', *South Park*, season 26, episode 2, Comedy Central, 15 February 2023.

4. 'Julia Hartley-Brewer Clashes With Rupert Bell', TalkTV, 8 June 2023, www.youtube.com/watch?v=bZT39fhmPRE.

5. *Dan Wootton Show*, GB News, 8 September 2022.

6. 'Oprah Defends Harry and Meghan Amid Criticism: "Privacy Doesn't Mean Silence"', *Today*, 21 May 2021.

7. 'Google CEO Eric Schmidt on Privacy', *CNBC*, 9 December 2009, www.youtube.com/watch?v=A6e7wfDHzew.

8. Quoted in Sir Brian Leveson, *An Inquiry Into the Culture, Practices and Ethics of the Press* [Leveson Report] (London: Stationery Office, 2011), vol. II, p. 505.

9. Catharine A. MacKinnon, *Feminism Unmodified: Discourses on Life and Law* (Cambridge, MA: Harvard University Press, 1988).

10. Mitchell Cohen (ed.), *Princeton Readings in Political Thought: Essential Texts since Plato* (Princeton, NJ: Princeton University Press, 1996), p. 81.

11. Ibid., p. 258.

12. Keith Thomas, 'Behind Closed Doors', *New York Review of Books*, 9 November 1989.
13. Erving Goffman, *The Presentation of the Self in Everyday Life* (New York: Doubleday, 1959).
14. Brian Cummings, *Mortal Thoughts: Religion, Secularity and Identity in Shakespeare and Early Modern Culture* (Oxford: Oxford University Press, 2013), p. 139.

CHAPTER I

1. Brian Cummings, 'Conscience and the Law in Thomas More', *Journal for Renaissance Studies*, 24.4 (2009), p. 474.
2. Diarmaid MacCulloch, *The Reformation: A History* (London: Penguin, 2003), p. 131.
3. Tom Holland, *Dominion: The Making of the Western World* (London: Little, Brown, 2019), p. 364.
4. MacCulloch, *Reformation*, p. 131.
5. Holland, *Dominion*, p. 364.
6. Louis L. Snyder, *A Survey of European Civilization, Vol. II: Since 1660* (New York: Houghton Mifflin, 1947), p. 104.
7. Martin Luther, *Letters of Spiritual Counsel*, trans. and ed. by Theodore G. Tappert (Vancouver, BC: Regent College Publishing, 2003 [1960]), p. 85.
8. Peter Marshall, *Heretics and Believers: A History of the English Reformation* (New Haven, CT: Yale University Press, 2017), p. 127.
9. G. R. Elton, *Policy and Police: The Enforcement of the Reformation in the Age of Thomas Cromwell* (Cambridge: Cambridge University Press, 1972), pp. 222–4.
10. Marshall, *Heretics*, p. 212.
11. Jonathan Michael Gray, *Oaths and the English Reformation* (Cambridge: Cambridge University Press, 2013), p. 132.
12. Perez Zagorin, *Ways of Lying: Dissimulation, Persecution and Conformity in Early Modern Europe* (Cambridge, MA: Harvard University Press, 1990).
13. Gray, *Oaths*, p. 141.
14. Marshall, *Heretics*, p. 212.

15. Peter Ackroyd, 'More and Theology', *Mercer Law Review*, 53.3 (2002), p. 1060.

16. Peter Ackroyd, *The Life of Thomas More* (London: Vintage, 1999), p. 351.

17. Alvaro de Silva (ed.), *The Last Letters of Thomas More* (Cambridge: Eerdmans, 2000), p. 87.

18. Keith Thomas, 'Cases of Conscience in Seventeenth-Century England', in John Morrill, Paul Slack and Daniel Woolf (eds), *Public Duty and Private Conscience in Seventeenth-Century England: Essays Presented to G. E. Aylmer* (Oxford: Clarendon Press, 1993), pp. 29–56.

19. Cummings, 'Conscience and the Law', p. 477.

20. Joanna Paul, 'Thomas More: Saint or Sinner?', *History Extra, BBC History Magazine*, 26 October 2020.

21. Michael W. Bruening, *A Reformation Sourcebook: Documents from an Age of Debate* (Toronto: University of Toronto Press, 2017), p. 146.

22. Ackroyd, *The Life of Thomas More*, p. 383.

23. Ibid., p. 389.

24. Cummings, 'Conscience and the Law', p. 474; De Silva, *Last Letters*.

25. Brian Cummings, *Mortal Thoughts: Religion, Secularity and Identity in Shakespeare and Early Modern Culture* (Oxford: Oxford University Press, 2013), p. 146.

26. Ackroyd, *The Life of Thomas More*, p. 385.

27. De Silva, *Last Letters*, p. 90.

28. Gray, *Oaths*, p. 132.

29. Cummings, *Mortal Thoughts*, p. 88.

CHAPTER 2

1. Frances Bacon, *Early Writings 1584–1596*, ed. Alan Steward and Harriet Knight (Oxford: Oxford University Press, 2012), p. 228.

2. Peter Marshall, *A History of the English Reformation* (New Haven, CT: Yale University Press, 2017), p. 482.

3. Diarmaid MacCulloch, *The Reformation: A History* (London: Penguin, 2003), p. 392.

4. Todd Butler, 'The Cognitive Politics of Writing in Jacobean

England: Bacon, Coke, and the Case of Edmund Peacham', *Huntington Library Quarterly*, 78.1 (2015).

5. Ibid., p. 22.

6. Catherine Drinker Bowen, *The Lion and the Throne: The Life and Times of Sir Edward Coke* (Boston, MA: Little, Brown, 1957), p. 411.

7. Semayne's Case. See www.commonlii.org/int/cases/EngR/1572/333.pdf.

8. Ibid.

9. J. Baker, 'Sir Edward Coke and Magna Carta 1606–1615', in *The Reinvention of Magna Carta 1216–1616* (Cambridge: Cambridge University Press, 2017), pp. 335–409.

10. Brian Cummings, *Mortal Thoughts: Religion, Secularity and Identity in Shakespeare and Early Modern Culture* (Oxford: Oxford University Press, 2013), p. 88.

11. Joanna Moody, *The Private Life of an Elizabethan Lady: The Diary of Lady Margaret Hoby 1599–1605* (Stroud: Sutton Publishing, 1998).

12. Ibid.

13. Quoted in David Vincent, *Privacy: A Short History* (Cambridge: Polity, 2016), p. 44.

14. Alec Ryrie, 'Alone with God: The Practice of "Public" "Private" and "Secret" Prayer in Reformation England', paper presented to the conference Early Modern Notions of Privacy and Private, June 2021, Centre for Privacy Studies, Copenhagen University. https://teol.ku.dk/privacy/privacy-conference-2021-archive-early-modern-notions-of-privacy- and-the-private/ at 14.40 mins.

15. David Booy (ed.), *The Notebooks of Nehemiah Wallington, 1618–1644: A Selection* (London: Routledge, 2017), p. 18.

16. Lena Cowen Orlin, *Locating Privacy in Tudor London* (New York: Oxford University Press, 2007), pp. 325–6.

17. Erica Longfellow, 'Public, Private, and the Household in Early Seventeenth-Century England', *Journal of British Studies*, 45.2 (2006), p. 329.

18. Thomas Adams, 'The Sinners Passing Bell' (1614), in *The Works of Thomas Adams* (London, 1629), p. 249.

19. Martin Ingram, *Carnal Knowledge: Regulating Sex in England, 1470–1600* (Cambridge: Cambridge University Press, 2017); Martin

Ingram, *Church Courts, Sex and Marriage in England, 1570–1640* (Cambridge: Cambridge University Press, 1987).

20. Gloucester Diocesan Records: GDR/109, 820, *Henry Jones v. Michael Paine and Joan Anslett* (1610), p. 256.

21. Faramerz Dabhoiwala, *The Origins of Sex: A History of the First Sexual Revolution* (London: Allen Lane, 2012), pp. 42–3.

22. Jonathan Healey, 'In the Shadow of the Bum Courts', *Social Historian*, 13 April 2016.

23. Dabhoiwala, *Origins*, p. 29.

24. Laura Gowing, *Common Bodies: Women, Touch and Power in Seventeenth-Century England* (New Haven, CT: Yale University Press, 2003).

25. Healey, 'In the Shadow'.

26. Dabhoiwala, *Origins*, p. 41.

27. Ibid., p. 29.

28. Ibid., p. 41.

29. Bowen, *The Lion*.

30. Harry Potter, *Law, Liberty and the Constitution: A Brief History of the Common Law* (Martlesham: Boydell, 2015), p. 120.

CHAPTER 3

1. Jonathan Healey, *The Blazing World: A New History of Revolutionary England* (London: Bloomsbury, 2023), p. 27.

2. Jonathan Healey, 'What Sparked the Civil War?', *History Today*, 12 July 2018.

3. @SocialHistoryOx (Jonathan Healey), twitter.com/SocialHistory Ox/status/860855614712537094, 6 May 2017.

4. David Como, *Radical Parliamentarians and the English Civil War* (Oxford: Oxford University Press, 2018), p. 61.

5. While Geddes is probably a mythical figure, the presence of women is confirmed in contemporary accountsts

6. Michael Braddick, *God's Fury, England's Fire: A New History of the English Civil Wars* (London: Penguin, 2008), p. 135.

7. Robert Baillie, *The Letters and Journals of Robert Baillie*, ed. David Laing, vol. 1 (Bannatyne Club, Edinburgh 1841–2), p. 64.

8. Braddick, *God's Fury*, p. 135.
9. John Timmis, *Thine is the Kingdom: The Trial of Thomas Wentworth, Earl of Strafford, First Minister to King Charles, and the Last Hope of the English Crown* (Tuscaloosa: University of Alabama Press, 1974), pp. 115–16.
10. Braddick, *God's Fury*, p. 138.
11. Ibid.
12. Blair Worden, *The English Civil Wars 1640–1660* (London: Weidenfeld & Nicolson, 2009), p. 73.
13. Norman Davies, *The Isles: A History* (London: Pan Macmillan, 2008), p. 671.
14. Geoffrey Robertson, *The Levellers: The Putney Debates* (London: Verso, 2007, 2018).
15. Ibid., p. 84.
16. Ibid., p. 69.
17. Ibid., p. 87.
18. Keith Thomas, 'Cases of Conscience in Seventeenth-Century England', in John Morrill, Paul Slack and Daniel Woolf (eds), *Public Duty and Private Conscience in Seventeenth-Century England: Essays Presented to G. E. Aylmer* (Oxford: Clarendon Press, 1993), pp. 29–56.
19. Worden, *English Civil Wars*; Como, *Radical Parliamentarians*. Though most of the voices arguing for liberty of conscience came first from within Puritan circles, they weren't the only ones advocating for toleration. Jeremy Taylor, a Royalist and a cleric in the Church of England who had been close to the King and a fierce defender of Anglican prerogatives, penned *A Discourse of the Liberty of Prophesying* (1646). In it, he discussed the iniquity of persecuting differing opinions and argued that as truth is uncertain, the desire for it ought to yield to the necessity of peace and charity. However, he also noted that someone needed to draw a line, or there would be anarchy. This was a departure from his earlier staunch Anglican views and demonstrated his evolving thoughts on religious liberty.
20. Como, *Radical Parliamentarians*.
21. Christopher Hill, *Intellectual Origins of the English Revolution – Revisited* (Oxford: Oxford University Press, 2001), p. 7.

22. Paul Lay, *Providence Lost: The Rise and Fall of Cromwell's Protectorate* (London: Head of Zeus, 2020), p. 68.

23. Noel Malcolm (ed.), *Thomas Hobbes: Leviathan* (Oxford: Oxford University Press, 1996), 3 vols, iii.37.696. See also Teresa M. Bejan, *Mere Civility: Disagreement and the Limits of Toleration* (Cambridge, MA: Harvard University Press, 2017), p. 94.

24. Faramerz Dabhoiwala, *The Origins of Sex: A History of the First Sexual Revolution* (London: Allen Lane, 2012), p. 47.

25. Lay, *Providence Lost*, p. 167.

26. Dabhoiwala, *Origins*, p. 50.

27. Ibid., p. 47.

28. Bernard Capp, *England's Culture Wars: Puritan Reformation and Its Enemies in the Interregnum, 1649–1660* (Oxford: Oxford University Press, 2012); Dabhoiwala, *Origins*, p. 47.

29. Keith Thomas, 'The Puritans and Adultery: The Act of 1650 Reconsidered', in Donald Pennington and Keith Thomas (eds), *Puritans and Revolutionaries: Essays in Seventeenth-Century History Presented to Christopher Hill* (Oxford: Clarendon Press, 1978), p. 258.

30. Ian Harris, *The Mind of John Locke: A Study of Political Theatre in Its Intellectual Setting* (Cambridge: Cambridge University Press, 1998), p. 59.

31. John Locke, *Locke: Political Essays*, ed. Mark Goldie (Cambridge: Cambridge University Press, 1997), p. 144.

32. Raymond Martin and John Barresi, *The Rise and Fall of Soul and Self: An Intellectual History of Personal Identity* (New York: Columbia University Press, 2006), p. 92.

CHAPTER 4

1. *The Spectator*, 12 March 1711.

2. David Taylor, 'The Coal Industry 1700–1850', in *Mastering Economic and Social History* (London: Palgrave, 1988), p. 80.

3. Linda Coley, *Britons: Forging the Nation, 1707–1837* (New Haven, CT: Yale University Press, 1992), p. 69.

4. Ibid., p. 69.

5. Jürgen Habermas, *The Structural Transformation of the Public Sphere: An Inquiry into a Category of Bourgeois Society*, trans. T. Burger and F. Lawrence (Cambridge: Polity, 1989).

6. Henry Fielding, *The Works of Henry Fielding: Complete in One Volume, with Memoir of the Author* (London: W. Clowes and Sons, 1840), p. 765.

7. Matthew Green, 'The Lost World of the London Coffeehouse', *Public Domain Review*, 7 August 2013.

8. Larry Stewart, 'Other Centres of Calculation, or, Where the Royal Society Didn't Count: Commerce, Coffee-Houses and Natural Philosophy in Early Modern London', *British Journal for the History of Science*, 32.2 (1999), p. 149.

9. Keith Thomas, 'Cases of Conscience in Seventeenth-Century England', in John Morrill, Paul Slack and Daniel Woolf (eds), *Public Duty and Private Conscience in Seventeenth-Century England* (Oxford: Clarendon Press, 1993), p. 52.

10. Ibid.

11. Barbara Taylor, 'Philosophical Solitude: David Hume versus Jean-Jacques Rousseau', *History Workshop Journal*, 89 (2020), pp. 1–21.

12. James Van Horn Melton, *The Rise of the Public in Enlightenment Europe* (Cambridge: Cambridge University Press, 2001), p. 28.

13. Ibid., p. 2.

14. Ibid.

15. Habermas, *Structural Transformation*.

16. Leo Damrosch, *Jonathan Swift: His Life and His World* (New Haven, CT: Yale University Press, 2013), p. 178.

17. Michael McKeon, *The Secret History of Domesticity* (Baltimore: Johns Hopkins University Press, 2005), p. 170.

18. Roy Porter, *English Society in the Eighteenth Century* (London: Penguin, 1991), p. 85.

19. Barbara H. Rosenwein, *Negotiating Space: Power, Restraint, and Privileges of Immunity in Early Medieval Europe* (Ithaca, NY: Cornell University Press, 1999), p. 184.

20. David Vincent, *Privacy: A Short History* (Cambridge: Polity, 2016), p. 34.

21. Mark Girouard, *Life in the English Country House: A Social and*

Architectural History (New Haven, CT: Yale University Press, 1993 [1978]), p. 138.

22. Roger Luckhurst, *Passages of Modernity* (London: Reaktion Books, 2019), p. 24.

23. Carter L. Hudgins and Elizabeth Collins Cromley (eds), *Shaping Communities. Perspectives in Vernacular Architecture, Vol. 1* (Knoxville: University of Tennessee Press), p. 144.

24. Amanda Vickery, *Behind Closed Doors: At Home in Georgian London* (New Haven and London: Yale University Press, 2009), p. 38.

25. Peter Clark, *British Clubs and Societies 1580–1800: The Origins of an Associational World* (Oxford: Oxford University Press, 2000), p. 192.

26. Ibid.

27. Ibid.

28. Melton, *Rise of the Public*, p. 29.

29. Victoria Gardner, 'Liberty, Licence and Levenson', *History Today*, 63.2 (2013), www.historytoday.com/archive/liberty-licence-and-leveson.

30. Melton, *Rise of the Public*, p. 29.

31. Ibid., p. 20.

32. Faramerz Dabhoiwala, *The Origins of Sex: A History of the First Sexual Revolution* (London: Allen Lane, 2012), p. 315.

33. Melton, *Rise of the Public*, p. 28.

34. Janette Seaton Lewis, 'A Turn of Thinking: The Long Shadow of the *Spectator* on Franklin's *Autobiography*', *Early American Literature*, 13.3 (1978), pp. 268–77.

35. Markman Ellis, *The Coffee-House: A Cultural History* (London: Weidenfeld & Nicolson, 2014), p. 192.

36. John Brewer, 'This, That and the Other: Public, Social and Private in the Seventeenth and Eighteenth Centuries', in Dario Castiglione and Lesley Sharpe (eds), *Shifting the Boundaries: Transformation of the Languages of Public and Private in the Eighteenth Century* (Exeter: University of Exeter Press, 1995), p. 34.

37. John Mullan, 'The Labour of Being at Ease', *London Review of Books*, 28 October 1999.

38. Keith Thomas, *In Pursuit of Civility: Manners and Civilization in Early Modern England* (New Haven, CT: Yale University Press, 2018).

39. Penelope J. Corfield, *The Georgians: The Deeds and Misdeeds of 18th-Century Britain* (New Haven, CT: Yale University Press, 2022), p. 637.

40. Thomas, *In Pursuit*, p. 234.

41. Ibid.

42. Soile Ylivuori, *Women and Politeness in Eighteenth-Century England: Bodies, Identities, and Power* (London: Routledge, 2009), p. 41.

43. Brewer, 'This, That', pp. 8–9.

CHAPTER 5

1. James Boswell, *London Journal 1762–1763*, int. by Gordon Turnbull (London: Penguin Classics, 2010), p. 215.

2. Ibid., p. 272.

3. Ibid., p. 215.

4. Ibid., p. 272.

5. Faramerz Dabhoiwala, *The Origins of Sex: A History of the First Sexual Revolution* (London: Allen Lane, 2012), p. 51. A contributing factor was probably a stricter definition of illegitimacy following Hardwicke's Marriage Act (1753), after which marriage had to follow formal procedures, putting an end to the informal pledge between couples. See also, Laurence Stone, *The Family, Sex and Marriage in England, 1500–1800* (New York: Harper & Row, 1977).

6. Dabhoiwala, *Origins*, p. 92.

7. Ibid., p. 81.

8. Ibid., p. 87.

9. Ibid., p. 79.

10. Andre C. Willis, *Towards a Humean True Religion: Genuine Theism, Moderate Hope, and Practical Morality* (University Park, PA: Penn State University Press, 2015), p. 83.

11. Kndu Haakonsses (ed.), *Hume: Political Essays* (Cambridge: Cambridge University Press, 1994), p. 73.

12. Peter Martin, *A Life of James Boswell* (London: Weidenfeld & Nicolson, 1999), p. 94.

13. Anna Clark, 'Anne Lister's Construction of Lesbian Identity', *Journal of the History of Sexuality*, 7 (1996), p. 35.

14. Dabhoiwala, *Origins*, p. 154.
15. Francis Pearson Walesby, *The Works of Samuel Johnson: 'The Rambler'* (London: Legare Street Press, 1825), p. 113.
16. Matt Cook with Robert Mills, Randolph Trumbach and H. G. Cocks, *A Gay History of Britain: Love and Sex Between Men Since the Middle Ages* (Oxford: Greenwood World Publishing, 2007).
17. Penelope Corfield, *The Georgians: The Deeds and Misdeeds of 18th-Century Britain* (New Haven, CT: Yale University Press, 2022), p. 147.
18. William Brown trial record, 11 July 1726. See www.oldbaileyonline.org/record/t17260711-77.
19. Chris Bryant, *James and John: A True Story of Prejudice and Murder* (London: Bloomsbury, 2024).
20. Roy Porter, *English Society in the Eighteenth Century* (London: Penguin, 1991), p. 264–5.
21. Malcolm, *Forbidden Desire*.

CHAPTER 6

1. Peter Sabor and Betty A. Schellenberg (eds), *Samuel Richardson in Context* (Cambridge: Cambridge University Press, 2017), pp. 21, 46.
2. Quoted on *In Our Time*, 'Epistolary Literature', BBC Radio 4, 15 March 2007. Available at www.bbc.co.uk/programmes/b00775dh.
3. John Mullan, 'High-Meriting, Low-Descended', *London Review of Books,* 12 December 2002.
4. James Grantham Turner, 'Novel Panic: Picture and Performance in the Reception of Richardson's *Pamela*', *Representations*, 48 (1994), pp. 70–96.
5. Judith Flanders, *The Making of Home: The 500-Year Story of How Our Houses Became Homes* (London: Atlantic Books, 2015), p. 3.
6. John Brewer, *The Pleasures of the Imagination: English Culture in the Eighteenth Century* (New York: Farrar, Straus and Giroux, 1997), pp. 96–7.
7. Will and Ariel Durant, *The Story of Civilization, vol. 10: Rousseau and Revolution* (New York: Simon & Schuster, 1967), p. 170.
8. Robert Darnton, *The Great Cat Massacre and Other Episodes in French Cultural History* (New York: Basic Books, 1999), p. 242.

9. Ibid., pp. 242–3.
10. Ibid.
11. Ibid.
12. Jean-Jacques Rousseau, *Julie, or the New Heloise*, trans. Jean Vache (Hanover, NH: Dartmouth College Press, 1997), p. 193.
13. Leopold Damrosch, *Jean-Jacques Rousseau: Restless Genius* (Boston, MA: Houghton Mifflin, 2005), p. 164.
14. Robert Zaretsky and John T. Scott, *The Philosophers' Quarrel: Rousseau, Hume, and the Limits of Human Understanding* (New Haven, CT: Yale University Press, 2009), p. 27.

CHAPTER 7

1. Amanda Foreman, *Georgiana, Duchess of Devonshire* (London: Harper Collins, 1998), p. 140.
2. Ibid., p. 141.
3. Ibid., p. 136.
4. Linda Coley, *Britons: Forging the Nation 1707–1837* (London: Vintage, 1992), p. 238.
5. Roy Porter, *English Society in the Eighteenth Century* (London: Penguin, 1991), p. 22.
6. Coley, *Britons*, p. 254.
7. Michael McKeon, *The Secret History of Domesticity: Public, Private, and the Division of Knowledge* (Baltimore: John Hopkins University Press, 2005), p. 170.
8. Amanda Vickery, 'Golden Age to Separate Spheres? A Review of the Categories and Chronology of English Women's History', *Historical Journal*, 36 (1993), pp. 383–414.
9. Mary Astell, 'Some Reflections on Marriage', in Hannah Dawson (ed.), *The Penguin Book of Feminist Writing* (London: Penguin, 2021), p. 14.
10. Ibid.
11. McKeon, *Secret History*, p. 189.
12. Mary Wollstonecraft, *'A Vindication of the Rights of Woman' and 'A Vindication of the Rights of Men'*, ed. Janet Todd (Oxford: Oxford University Press, 2008), p. 230.

CHAPTER 8

1. Hansard, 14 June 1844, api.parliament.uk/historic-hansard/commons/1844/jun/14/opening-letters-post-office.

2. Ibid.

3. Letter from Thomas Carlyle, *The Times*, 19 June 1844, p. 6.

4. 'A Discussion Took Place Last Night on Mr. DUN', *The Times*, 25 June 1844, p. 5.

5. Jeremy Bentham, *Of Publicity*, in J. Bowring (ed.), *The Works of Jeremy Bentham* (London, 1843), p. 310.

6. Hansard, Parliamentary Reform—The Ballot, 15 February 1838, hansard.parliament.uk/Lords/1832-04-13/debates/714122bd-ec59-4d56-a313-c99d91558595/ParliamentaryReform—BillForEngland—SecondReading—FourthDay.

7. 'A Discussion Took Place Last Night on Mr. DUN', *The Times*, 25 June 1844, p. 5.

8. Hansard, 20 February 1845, hansard.parliament.uk/Commons/1845-02-20/debates/bfebc7a6-a8d6-41b2-a34d-e52e14a32317/OpeningLettersAtThePostOffice%E2%80%94AdjournedDebate.

9. Kate Lawson, 'Personal Privacy, Letter Mail, and the Post Office Espionage Scandal, 1844', *Branch Collective*, March 2013, branchcollective.org/?ps_articles=kate-lawson-personal-privacy-letter-mail-and-the-post-office-espionage-scandal-1844.

10. Debra N. Mancoff, *Love's Messenger: Tokens of Affection in the Victorian Age* (Chicago: Art Institute of Chicago, 1997), p. 46.

11. Dominic Sandbrook, 'The Last Post: The Shameful Betrayal of the Royal Mail', *Daily Mail*, 3 December 2011.

12. Hansard, 20 February 1845.

13. David Vincent, *The Culture of Secrecy: Britain 1832–1998* (Oxford: Oxford University Press, 1998), p. 1.

14. Ibid., p. 19.

15. Marjorie Stone, 'Joseph Mazzini, English Writers, and the Post Office Espionage Scandal: Politics, Privacy, and Twenty-First Century Parallels', *Branch Collective*, August 2012, branchcollective.org/?ps_articles=marjorie-stone-on-the-post-office-espionage-scandal-1844.

16. Lawson, 'Personal Privacy'.

17. 'Government Post-Office Espionage in England', *New-York Daily Tribune*, 10 July 1844.

18. David Vincent, *I Hope I Don't Intrude: Privacy and Its Dilemmas in Nineteenth-Century Britain* (Oxford: Oxford University Press, 2015), p. 209.

19. Samuel Johnson, *A Dictionary of the English Language* (London: Times Books, 1979 [1755]).

20. Bentham, *Of Publicity*, p. 310.

21. Georg Simmel, 'The Sociology of Secrecy and of Secret Societies', *American Journal of Sociology*, 11 (1906), p. 454.

CHAPTER 9

1. *Prince Albert* v. *Strange*, www.bailii.org/ew/cases/EWHC/Ch/1849/J20.html.

2. 'Etchings by Her Majesty and the Prince Albert', *Lady's Newspaper & Pictorial Times*, 3 February 1849, p. 59. See also Megan Richardson, *The Right to Privacy: Origins and Influence of a Nineteenth-Century Idea* (Cambridge: Cambridge University Press, 2017), p. 48.

3. *Prince Albert* v. *Strange*.

4. James Baldwin Brown, *The Home Life: In the Light of Its Divine Idea* (London: Smith, Elder & Company, 1866), p. 8.

5. David Vincent, *Privacy: A Short History* (Cambridge: Polity, 2016), p. 53.

6. James Vernon, *Distant Strangers: How Britain Became Modern* (Berkeley: University of California Press, 2014).

7. Roger Hutchinson, *The Butcher, the Baker, the Candlestick-Maker: The Story of Britain Through Its Census Since 1801* (London: Little, Brown, 2017), Kindle loc. 284.

8. Frederic J. Mouat, 'History of the Statistical Society of London', *Journal of the Statistical Society of London* (1885), p. 16.

9. Karen Chase and Michael Levenson, *The Spectacle of Intimacy: A Public Life for the Victorian Family* (Princeton, NJ: Princeton University Press, 2000), p. 65.

10. Samuel Beeton, *The Book of Garden Management* (London: Ward Lock, 1871), pp. 83–4.

11. Vincent, *Privacy*, p. 61.

12. Roger Luckhurst, *Passages of Modernity* (London: Reaktion Books, 2019), p. 24.

13. Robert Kerr, *The Gentleman's House; Or, How to Plan English Residences, from the Parsonage to the Palace* (London: John Murray, 1864), p. 73.

14. Chase and Levenson, *Spectacle of Intimacy*, p. 215.

15. Sarah Stickney Ellis, *The Daughters of England: Their Position in Society, Character and Responsibilities* (New York: D. Appleton, 1842), p. 193.

16. Deborah Cohen, *Family Secrets: The Things We Used to Hide* (London: Penguin, 2013), p. 73.

17. Herbert F. Tucker, *A New Companion to Victorian Literature and Culture* (Malden, MA: Wiley, 2014), p. 270.

18. J. A. Yelling, *Slum Clearance in Victorian London* (London: Taylor & Francis, 2012), p. 20.

19. Chase and Levenson, *Spectacle of Intimacy*, p. 147.

20. Ibid., p. 149.

CHAPTER 10

1. John Stuart Mill, 'Wordsworth and Byron', 20 January 1829, in *Collected Works*, vol. 26 (Toronto: University of Toronto Press, 1985), pp. 434–42.

2. Ibid.

3. Richard Reeves, *John Stuart Mill: Victorian Firebrand* (London: Atlantic Books, 2007), p. 20.

4. Mill, 'Wordsworth and Byron', p. 435.

5. Reeves, *John Stuart Mill*, p. 63.

6. Ibid., p. 65.

7. Ibid., p. 90.

8. Ibid., p. 100.

9. Ibid., p. 98.

10. Ibid., p. 228.

11. Ibid., p. 264.

12. Ibid., p. 10.

13. Ibid., p. 86.

14. Ibid., p. 278.

15. Ibid., p. 414.

16. Hansard, 20 May 1867, api.parliament.uk/historic-hansard/
     commons/1867/may/20/clauses-3-4-progress-may-17.

17. Reeves, *John Stuart Mill*, p. 414.

CHAPTER 11

1.   Sarah Igo, *The Known Citizen: A History of Privacy in Modern
     America* (Cambridge, MA: Harvard University Press, 2018), p. 30.

2.   Lowry Pressly, *The Right to Oblivion: Privacy and the Good Life*
     (Cambridge, MA Harvard University Press, 2024), p. 45.

3.   Robert E. Mensel, 'Kodakers Lying in Wait: Amateur Photography
     and the Right of Privacy in New York, 1885–1915', *American
     Quarterly*, 43.1 (1991), pp. 24–45, at p. 29.

4.   Sarah Igo, *The Known Citizen*, p. 41.

5.   'The Rights and Tights of an Actress', *The Baltimore Sun*, 19 June
     1890, p. 3; Jessica Lake, *The Face That Launched a Thousand Law-
     suits: The American Women Who Forged a Right to Privacy* (New
     Haven, CT: Yale University Press, 2016), p. 33.

6.   Ibid.

7.   Henry James, *The Notebooks of Henry James*, ed. F. O. Matthiessen
     and Kenneth B. Murdock (New York: Oxford University Press,
     1961), p. 82.

8.   Samuel D. Warren and Louis D. Brandeis, 'The Right to Privacy',
     Harvard Law Review, 4.5 (1890), pp. 193–220.

9.   Ibid.

10. Ibid.

11. 'Rights and Tights', *The Baltimore Sun*.

12. 'The Right to Be Let Alone', *The Atlantic Monthly*, 67 (1891),
     pp. 428–9.

13. Frederick S. Lane, *American Privacy: The 400-Year History of Our
     Most Contested Right* (Boston, MA: Beacon Press, 2009), p. 63.

14. Thomas Mason, *Brandeis: A Free Man's Life* (New York: Viking, 1946).

15. Rosen, *Louis D. Brandeis*, p. 42.

16. Brian Hochman, *The Listeners: A History of Wiretapping in the United States* (Cambridge, MA: Harvard University Press, 2021), p. 34.

17. Ibid.

18. Philippa Strum, *Brandeis: Beyond Progressivism*, 'American Political Thought' (Lawrence: University Press of Kansas, 1993), p. 137.

CHAPTER 12

1. Jill Bergman, *Charlotte Perkins Gilman and a Woman's Place in America* (Tuscaloosa: University of Alabama Press, 2017), p. 35.

2. Charlotte Perkins Gilman, *Women and Economics: A Study of the Economic Relation Between Men and Women as a Factor in Social Evolution* (Small, Maynard, 1898), p. 258.

3. Sarah Igo, *The Known Citizen: A History of Privacy in Modern America* (Cambridge, MA: Harvard University Press, 2018), p. 23.

4. Sarah Igo, 'Defining Privacy—and Then Getting Rid of It: The Beginnings of the End of Private Life in the Late Nineteenth Century', *Lapham's Quarterly*, 15 May 2018.

5. *State* v. *A. B. Rhodes*, Supreme Court of North Carolina, faculty. uml.edu/sgallagher/StatevRhodes.htm.

6. Ibid.

7. Ibid.

8. Virginia Woolf, *'A Room of One's Own' and 'Three Guineas'* (Oxford: Oxford University Press, 2015), p. 18.

CHAPTER 13

1. Paul F. Lazarsfeld, 'An Episode in the History of Social Research: A Memoire', in Donald Fleming and Bernard Bailyn (eds), *The Intellectual Migration 1930–1960* (Cambridge, MA: Harvard University Press, 1969), p. 272.

2. Ibid., p. 272.

3. Robert S. Lynd and Helen M. Lynd, *Middletown: A Study in*

Contemporary American Culture (New York: Harcourt, Brace and Company, 1929), pp. 163–4.

4. Sarah E. Igo, 'From Main Street to Mainstream: Middletown, Muncie, and "Typical America"', *Indiana Magazine of History*, 101.3 (2005), p. 241.

5. Ibid., p. 239.

6. Sarah E. Igo, *The Averaged American: Surveys, Citizens, and the Making of a Mass Public* (Cambridge, MA: Harvard University Press, 2008), p. 76.

7. Igo, 'From Main Street', p. 239.

8. Ibid.

9. Igo, *Averaged American*, p. 119.

10. Arthur Krock, 'The New Deal Resists Criticisms on Three Fronts', *The New York Times*, 17 March 1940.

11. Igo, 'From Main Street', p. 239.

12. Igo, *Averaged American*, p. 76.

13. David Vincent, *Privacy: A Short History* (Cambridge: Polity, 2016), p. 84.

14. Margery Spring Rice, *Working-Class Wives* (London: Penguin, 1939), p. 47.

15. Edward Bernays, *Propaganda* (New York: Ig, 2004 [1928]), p. 33.

16. Ibid., p. 51.

17. John Gray, 'The New Tech Totalitarianism', *New Statesman*, 6 February 2019, www.newstatesman.com/culture/2019/02/the-new-tech-totalitarianism.

18. Walter Lippmann, *The Phantom Public* (New York: Harcourt, Brace and Company, 1922), p. 145.

19. Lawrence Samuel, *Freud on Madison Avenue: Motivation Research and Subliminal Advertising in America* (Philadelphia: University of Pennsylvania Press, 2013), p. 33.

20. Ernest Dichter, *Getting Motivated by Ernest Dichter: The Secret Behind Individual Motivations by the Man Who Was Not Afraid to Ask 'Why'?* (Oxford: Pergamon Press, 1979), p. 33.

21. Ernest Dichter, *The Strategy of Desire* (London and New York: Routledge, 2017), p. 45.

22. Dichter, *Getting Motivated*, p. 35.

23. Igo, *Averaged American*, p. 193.

24. John D'Emilio and Estelle B. Freedman, *Intimate Matters: A History of Sexuality in America* (Chicago: University of Chicago Press, 1988), p. 687.

25. Francis Sill Wickware, 'Report on Kinsey', *Life*, 2 August 1948, p. 87.

26. Igo, *Averaged American*, p. 250.

27. 'An Open Letter to Dr. Kinsey from Mae West', *Cosmopolitan*, March 1949, pp. 42–3.

28. Igo, *Averaged American*, p. 238.

29. Ibid., p. 191. See also David Shneer and Caryn Aviv, *American Queer, Now and Then* (New York: Routledge, 2006), p. 12.

CHAPTER 14

1. David Riesman, Nathan Glazer and Reuel Denney, *The Lonely Crowd: A Study of the Changing American Character* (New Haven, CT: Yale University Press, 2001 [1961]), p. xxxvi.

2. David Riesman, 'Comments on "Dennis Wrong: *The Lonely Crowd* Revisited" Review Essay', *Sociological Forum*, 7.2 (1992).

3. Todd Gitlin, 'Foreword' to Riesman et al., *Lonely Crowd*, p. xiii.

4. Ibid.

5. James Miller (ed.), *Democracy Is in the Streets from Port Huron to the Siege of Chicago* (Cambridge, MA: Harvard University Press, 1987), pp. 329–75.

6. Tom Hayden, 'Student Social Action', *SDS Papers*, reel 37, series 4.B, no. 160 (March 1962), 1–10.

7. Miller (ed.), *Democracy Is in the Streets*, p. 14.

8. Quoted at www.rollingstone.com/politics/politics-news/tom-hayden-on-port-huron-at-50-204200/.

9. Todd Gitlin, *The Sixties: Years of Hope, Days of Rage* (New York: Bantam, 1987), p. 352.

10. Ibid., p. 242.

11. 'SDS Chapters 1962–1969 – Mapping American Social Movements Project', Civil Rights and Labor History Consortium, University of Washington, https://depts.washington.edu/moves/

sds_map.shtml. See also, Sale Kirpatrick, *SDS: The Rise and Development of the Students for a Democratic Society* (New York: Random House, 1997).

12. Susan Stern, *With the Weathermen: The Personal Journal of a Revolutionary Woman* (New Brunswick, NJ: Rutgers University Press, 2017), p. 72.

13. Bill Ayers, *Fugitive Days: Memoirs of an American Dissident* (Boston: Beacon Press 2009). p. 111.

14. Stern, *With the Weathermen*, p. 121.

15. Mark Rudd, *Underground: My Life with SDS and the Weathermen* (New York: William Morrow & Company, 2009), p. 164.

16. Frank Furedi, *100 Years of Identity Crisis: Culture War over Socialisation* (Berlin: Walter de Gruyter, 2021), p. 204.

17. Elinor Langer, 'Notes for Next Time: A Memoir of the 1960s', in *Working Papers for a New Society*, reprinted in R. David Myers, *Towards a History of the New Left* (New York: Carlson Publishing, 1989), p. 72.

18. Ibid.

CHAPTER 15

1. Betty Friedan, *The Feminine Mystique* (New York: Dell Publishing, 1974 [1963]), p. 11.

2. Ibid., p. 19.

3. Ibid.

4. Ibid., p. 60.

5. Martha Weinman Lear, 'The Second Feminist Wave', *The New York Times Magazine*, 10 March 1968, p. 24.

6. Kate Millett, *Sexual Politics* (Urbana: University of Illinois Press, 2000 [1969]), p. 59.

7. Ibid., p. 61.

8. Ibid., p. 72.

9. Ibid., p. 51.

10. Christopher Lehmann-Haupt, 'Books of the Times', *The New York Times*, 5 August 1970.

11. Joy Press, 'The Life and Death of a Radical Sisterhood', *New York*

Magazine, 15 November 2017, longreads.com/2017/11/19/
the-life-and-death-of-a-radical-sisterhood/.

12. Redstockings Abortion Speakout, New York, 21 March 1969,
archive.org/details/
RedstockingsAbortionSpeakoutNewYork1969March21.

13. Edith Evans Asbury, 'Women Break Up Abortion Hearing', *The
New York Times*, 14 February 1969.

14. Redstockings Abortion Speakout.

15. James Innes-Smith, 'A Brief History of Lived Experience',
The Spectator, 3 April 2021.

16. R. D. Laing, *'The Politics of Experience' and 'The Bird of Paradise'*
(Harmondsworth: Penguin, 1967), p. 16.

17. Carol Hanish, 'The Personal Is Political', in: Shulamith Firestone
and Anne Koedt (eds), *Notes from the Second Year: Women's Liberation: Major Writings of the Radical Feminists* (New York: Radical
Feminism, 1970), pp. 76–8.

18. Imelda Whelehan, *Modern Feminist Thought: From the Second
Wave to 'Post-Feminism'* (New York: NYU Press, 1995), p. 15.

19. Deborah Cohen, *Family Secrets: The Things We Tried to Hide*
(London: Penguin, 2013), p. 231.

20. Noreen Connell and Cassandra Wilson (eds), *Rape: The First
Sourcebook for Women by New York Radical Feminists* (New York:
New American Library, 1974), pp. 5–6.

21. Kate Millett, *Flying* (New York: Knopf, 1974), p. 328.

22. Ibid.

CHAPTER 16

1. Walter F. Pratt, *Privacy in Britain* (Lewisburg, PA: Bucknell University Press, Associated Universities Press, 1979), p. 16.

2. Ibid., p. 102.

3. Ibid.

4. Ibid., p. 103.

5. Ibid.

6. Ibid., p. 138.

7. Ibid.

8.　Ibid., p. 161.
9.　Ibid., p. 176.
10.　Ibid.
11.　Ibid., p. 152.
12.　Ibid.
13.　Ibid., p. 163.
14.　Ibid., pp. 132, 155.
15.　*The Younger Committee Report on Privacy* (London: HMSO, 1972), p. 10.
16.　Ibid., p. 3.
17.　Ibid, p. 228.
18.　Ibid., pp. 229, 235.
19.　Malcolm Bradbury, *The History Man* (London: Picador, 2000 [1975]), p. 78.
20.　*The Younger Committee Report on Privacy*, p. 33.
21.　Ibid.
22.　Deborah Cohen, *Family Secrets: The Things We Tried to Hide* (London: Penguin, 2013), pp 212–13.
23.　Ibid., p. 235.
24.　Ibid, p. 217.
25.　Ibid.
26.　David Cooper, *The Death of the Family* (London: Allen Lane, Penguin, 1971), p. 151.
27.　Ibid., p. 150.
28.　Cohen, *Family Secrets*, p. 225.

CHAPTER 17

1.　Gerald Ford, 'Address to a Joint Session of the Congress', 12 August 1974.
2.　Gerald Ford, 'Statement on Signing the Privacy Act of 1974', *Public Papers of the Presidents of the United States 1956–1992*, Book 1.
3.　Richard Nixon, 'Radio Address About the American Right of Privacy', 23 February 1974.
4.　Lesley Oelsner, 'President Picks Ford to Head Panel to Guard Citizens' Privacy', *The New York Times*, 24 February 1974.

5. John Neary, 'The Big Snoop: Insidious Invasions of Privacy', *Life*, 20 May 1966, p. 38.

6. 'Electronics: Bug Thy Neighbor', *Time*, 6 March 1964, pp. 61–3.

7. Neary, 'The Big Snoop', p. 38.

8. David J. Garrow, *Liberty and Sexuality: The Right to Privacy and the Making of Roe v. Wade* (New York: Prentice Hall & IBD, 1994), p. 204.

9. *Griswold v. Connecticut*, 381 U.S. 479 (1965).

10. Garrow, *Liberty and Sexuality*, p. 195.

11. Sarah Igo, *The Unknown Citizen: A History of Privacy in Modern America* (Cambridge, MA: Harvard University Press, 2018), p. 148.

12. Ibid., p. 160.

13. Jerry Rosenberg, *The Death of Privacy* (New York: Random House, 1969), p. 4.

14. 'To Preserve Privacy', editorial, *The New York Times*, 9 August 1966.

15. Vance Packard, *The Hidden Persuaders* (London: Pelican, 1963), p. 9.

16. Vance Packard, *The Naked Society: A Study of Privacy in America* (Brooklyn: Ig Publishing, 1964), p. 57.

17. United States Congress, House Committee on Government Operations, Special Subcommittee on Invasion of Privacy (1966), *The Computer and Invasion of Privacy: Hearings, Eighty-ninth Congress, Second Session*.

18. Fred Turner, *From Counterculture to Cyberculture: Stewart Brand, the Whole Earth Network, and the Rise of Digital Utopianism* (Chicago: University of Chicago Press, 2008), p. 2.

19. Ibid., p. 11.

20. United States Congress, House Committee on Government Operations, *The Computer and Invasion of Privacy*.

21. Andreas Wirsching, Elizabeth Harvey, Johannes Hürter and Maiken Umbach, *Private Life and Privacy in Nazi Germany* (Cambridge: Cambridge University Press, 2019), p. 49.

22. Orlando Figes, *The Whisperers: Private Life in Stalin's Russia* (London: Allen Lane, 2007), p. 9.

23. George Orwell, *Nineteen Eighty-Four* (New York: Harcourt, Inc., 1949).

24. States Congress, House Committee on Government Operations, *The Computer and Invasion of Privacy*.

25. Paul Baran, 'The Future Computer Utility', *Public Interest* (Summer 1967), p. 87.

26. *Katz v. United States*. See also Igo, *Unknown Citizen*, p. 167.

27. Brian Hochman, *The Listeners: A History of Wiretapping in the United States* (Cambridge, MA: Harvard University Press, 2021).

28. *Roe v. Wade*, 410 U.S. 113, 130–48 (1973).

29. Robert O. Self, *All in the Family: The Realignment of American Democracy Since the 1960s* (New York: Hill and Wang, 2012), p. 138.

30. Catharine MacKinnon, *Feminism Unmodified: Discourses on Life and Law* (Cambridge, MA: Harvard University Press, 1988).

31. Mary Ziegler, *Beyond Abortion: Roe. v. Wade and the Battle for Privacy* (Cambridge, MA: Harvard University Press, 2018), p. 48.

32. Ibid., p. 93.

33. Ford, 'Statement'.

34. Michael Schudson, *The Rise of the Right to Know: Politics and the Culture of Transparency* (Cambridge, MA: Harvard University Press, 2015), p. 10.

35. Lisa McCubbin Hill, *Betty Ford: First Lady, Women's Advocate, Survivor, Trailblazer* (New York City: Gallery Books, 2019), p. 206.

36. Igo, *Unknown Citizen*, p. 273.

37. Betty Ford and Chris Chase, *Betty: A Glad Awakening* (New York: Doubleday, 1987), Preface.

CHAPTER 18

1. 'Religious Fervour High, Gallup Poll Indicates', *St Louis Post-Dispatch*, 8 October 1976.

2. 'Religion: Counting Souls', *Time*, 4 October 1976, time.com/archive/6852182/religion-counting-souls/.

3. 'Religious Fervour High'.

4. Jimmy Carter interview, *Playboy*, November 1976, pp. 48–62.

5. Ibid.

6. Lee Dembart, 'Carter's Comments on Sex Cause Concern', *The New York Times*, 23 September 1976.

7. Rick Perlstein, 'An Interview with *Playboy* Magazine Nearly Torpe-doed Jimmy Carter's Presidential Campaign', *Smithsonian Magazine*, 17 August 2020.

8. Ibid.

9. *The Spirit of Houston: The First National Women's Conference: An Official Report to the President, the Congress and the People of the United States* (Washington, DC: National Commission on the Observance of International Women's Year, 1978).

10. Quoted in Ben Naddaff-Hafrey and Jill Lepore, 'She Said, She Said', *The Last Archive* podcast, pushkin.fm/podcasts/the-last-archive/she-said-she-said.

11. Ibid.

12. Jack Rosenthal, 'Survey Finds Majority, in Shift, Now Favors Liberal-ized Laws, *The New York Times*, 25 August 1972; Linda Greenhouse and Reva B. Siegel, 'Before (and After) Roe v. Wade: New Questions About Backlash', *Yale Law Journal*, 120 (2011), p. 2031.

13. Southern Baptist Convention, 'Resolution on Abortion' (1971), https://www.sbc.net/resource-library/resolutions/resolution-on-abortion-2/.

14. Robert O. Self, *All In the Family: The Realignment of American Democracy Since the 1960s* (New York: Hill and and Wang, 2012), p. 284.

CHAPTER 19

1. Jeffrey Ruoff, *An American Family: A Televised Life* (Minneapolis: University of Minnesota Press, 2002), p. 17.

2. Ibid., p. vii.

3. Ibid., p. 100.

4. Anne Roiphe, 'An American Family', *The New York Times*, 18 February 1973.

5. Elizabeth Jensen, 'Lance Loud's Last Testament', *Los Angeles Times*, 6 January 2003.

6. Peter Lee-Wright, *The Documentary Handbook* (London: Taylor & Francis, 2009), p. 100.

7. 'Paul Watson, Fly-on-the-Wall Documentary-maker Known as the

God-father of Reality TV – Obituary', *The Telegraph*, 23 November 2023, www.telegraph.co.uk/obituaries/2023/11/28/paul-watson-documentary-godfather-reality-television-bbc/9

8. 'The Family's Margaret Wilkins, "First Lady" of Reality TV, Is Dead', *Daily Mail*, 19 August 2008.

9. Pat Loud, *Pat Loud: A Woman's Story* (New York: Coward, McCann & Geoghegan, 1974), p. 168.

10. Tom Wolfe, 'The "Me" Decade and the Third Great Awakening', *New York Magazine*, 23 August 1976.

11. Richard Sennett, *The Fall of Public Man* (New York: Knopf, 1974), p. 263.

12. Ibid., p. 6

13. 'Revisiting Jimmy Carter's Truth-Telling Sermon to Americans', *The Conversation*, 13 July 2018, theconversation.com/revisiting-jimmy-carters-truth-telling-sermon-to-americans-97241.

14. Natasha Zaretsky, *No Direction Home: The American Family and the Fear of National Decline, 1968–1980* (Chapel Hill: University of North Carolina Press, 2010), p. 217.

15 'The Pursuit of Happiness', *Time*, 8 January 1979, pp. 38–9.

16. Christopher Lasch, *The Minimal Self: Psychic Survival in Troubled Times* (New York: Picador, 1984), p. 15.

17. Christopher Lasch, *The Culture of Narcissism: American Life in an Age of Diminishing Expectations* (New York: W. W. Norton & Company, 1979), p. 6.

18. Ibid., p. 47.

CHAPTER 20

1. Jean-Louis Gassée, 'Steve Jobs' perfect pitch: The Macintosh launch', CNET, 23 January 2014, footage available here: www.youtube.com/watch?v=XlovhiLUIxk.

2. Ibid.

3. Ronald Reagan, 'Remarks and a Question-and-Answer Session with the Students and Faculty at Moscow State University', 31 May 1988, Ronald Reagan Presidential Library and Museum.

4. Ted Greenwald, 'Step Behind the Scenes of the Frantic, Madcap Birth of *Wired*', www.wired.com/2013/04/wired0101/.

5. John Naughton, 'Steve Jobs: Stanford Commencement Address, June 2005', *The Guardian*, 9 October 2011.

6. Ed Rothstein, 'A Crunchy-Granola Path From Macramé and LSD to Wikipedia and Google', *The New York Times*, 25 September 2006.

7. John Markoff, *Whole Earth: The Many Lives of Stewart Brand* (Penguin, 2022), p. 606.

8. Richard Barbrook and Andy Cameron, *The Californian Ideology* (1995), first published online by the authors.

9. Thatcher never used this phrase word for word, but it was closely associated with her and her political outlook.

10. Louis Rossetto, 'Why Wired?', *Wired*, 1 (1993).

11. Ibid.

12. 'Jennicam: The First Woman to Stream Her Life on the Internet', *BBC News*, 18 October 2016, www.bbc.co.uk/news/magazine-37681006.

13. 'Jennicam', *Reply All* podcast, 14 December 2014, gimletmedia.com/shows/reply-all/8whoja.

14. Ibid.

15. Stephen Coleman, *Tale of Two Houses: The House of Commons, the Big Brother House and the People at Home* (London: Hansard Society, 2003), p. 25.

16. Ibid., p. 38.

17. Shoshana Zuboff, 'Surveillance Capitalism is an Assault on Human Autonomy', *The Guardian*, 4 October 2019.

18. Andy Greenberg, 'After 6 Years in Exile, Edward Snowden Explains Himself', *Wired*, 16 September 2019.

19. Howard Rheingold, *The Virtual Community: Homesteading on the Electronic Frontier* (Revised Edition), (Cambridge, MA: MIT Edition, 2000), p. 9.

CHAPTER 21

1. Andrew Motion, *Monica's Story* (London: Michael O'Mara Books, 1999), p. 257.

2. Ibid., p. 160.

3. Jim Twombly, *Political Scandal and American Pop Culture: Sex, Power, and Cover-ups* (New York: Palgrave, 2018), p. 46.

4. 'Governor and Mrs. Bill Clinton Discuss Adultery', *60 Minutes*, NBC, 26 January 1992.

5. 'Allegations of Clinton Marital Infidelity', 27 January 1992, www.c-span.org/video/?23995-1/allegations-clinton-marital-infidelity#.

6. 'Clinton Sexual Harassment Charges', 6 May 1994, www.c-span.org/video/?56632-1/clinton-sexual-harrassment-charges.

7. Blair Foster (dir.), *The Clinton Affair* (Jigsaw Productions, 2018).

8. Ibid.

9. Ken Gormley, *The Death of American Virtue: Clinton vs. Starr* (New York: Crown, 2010), p. 246.

10. Jonathan Peterson, 'Critics Rip Counsel's Probe into Clinton's Private Life', *Los Angeles Times*, 26 June 1997.

11. Foster, *The Clinton Affair*.

12. William J. Clinton, Deposition Statement, 9 September 1998, https://www.govinfo.gov/content/pkg/CDOC-105hdoc310/pdf/CDOC-105hdoc310.pdf.

13. Marvin Kalb, *One Scandalous Story: Clinton, Lewinsky, and Thirteen Days That Tarnished American Journalism* (New York Free Press, 2001), p. 8.

14. Seymour Hersh, *Reporter: A Memoir* (London: Allen Lane, 2018), p. 202.

15. Ibid.

16. William J. Bennett, *The Death of Outrage: Bill Clinton and the Assault on American Ideas* (New York: Free Press, 1998), p. 44.

17. Ibid.

18. Harry Jaffe, 'Hellfire from the Right', *Salon*, 20 August 1998.

19. Catharine A. MacKinnon, *Toward a Feminist Theory of the State* (Cambridge, MA: Harvard University Press, 1989), p. 118.

20. 'Clinton Scandal: A Feminist Issue?' *Democracy Now!*, PBS, 26 January 1998, www.democracynow.org/shows/1998/1/26?autostart_audio=true#.

21. Marilyn Fitterman, *Why I Marched* (Atlanta: Firebrand, 2020), n.p.

22. *Today Show*, NBC, 27 January 1998, www.c-span.org/video/?99377-1/today-tuesday.

23. Bill Clinton, press conference at the White House, 26 January 1998,

millercenter.org/the-presidency/presidential-speeches/
january-26-1998-response-lewinsky-allegations.

24. Katie Roiphe, 'Date Rape's Other Victim', *The New York Times*, 13
June 1993.

25. Ibid.

26. Francine Prose, 'New York Supergals Love that Naughty Prez', *New York Observer*, 9 February 1998.

27. Bob Herbert, 'In America; The Feminist Dilemma', *The New York Times*, 29 January 1998.

28. Motion, *Monica's Story*, p. 248.

29. Jeffrey Rosen, *The Unwanted Gaze: The Destruction of Privacy in America* (New York: Vintage, 2001), p. 35.

30. Motion, *Monica's Story*, p. 215.

31. Tony Parsons column, *Daily Mirror*, 24 August 1991, p. 10.

32. Brett M. Kavanaugh, 'Memorandum to Judge Starr/All Attorneys', Office of the Independent Counsel, 15 August 1998.

33. Grand Jury Testimony of President William Jefferson Clinton, www.govinfo.gov/content/pkg/GPO-CDOC-106sdoc3/pdf/GPO-CDOC-106sdoc3-3-3.pdf.

34. Bill Clinton, 'Transcript', CNN, 17 August 1998, https://edition. cnn.com/ALLPOLITICS/1998/08/17/speech/transcript.html

35. 'Bedfellows', *Slow Burn: The Clinton Impeachment* podcast, 28 September 2018, slate.com/podcasts/slow-burn/s2/clinton/e7/bedfellows.

36. Somini Sengupta, 'Testing of a President: The View Abroad; World's Press Reflects Itself in Coverage of Clinton Affair', *The New York Times*, 14 September 1998.

37. Kenneth W. Starr, *Referral from Independent Counsel Kenneth W. Starr in Conformity with the Requirements of Title 28, United States Code, Section 595(c)* (Washington, DC: United States Congress, 1998).

CHAPTER 22

1. Alan Johnson, *Every Parent Matters* (London: Department of Education and Skills, 2007), p. 1.

2. 'Parents Must Do Better – Johnson', *BBC News*, 8 November 2006, news.bbc.co.uk/1/hi/education/6128084.stm.

3. Alan Johnson, *This Boy: A Memoir of a Childhood* (London: Corgi, 2014), p. 184.
4. Ibid., p. 87.
5. 'From the Archive: Tony Blair is Tough on Crime, Tough on the Causes of Crime', *New Statesman*, 28 December 2015, www.newstatesman.com/uncategorized/2015/12/archive-tony-blair-tough-crime-tough-causes-crime.
6. 'Straw Sets Out Policy to Support Families Without Interference', *The Irish Times*, 5 November 1998.
7. 'Major Goes Back to the Old Values', *The Guardian*, 9 October 1993.
8. 'Straw Sets Out Policy'.
9. Tony Blair, 'Speech on Improving Parenting', Watford, 2005, www.britishpoliticalspeech.org/speech-archive.htm?speech=291.
10. Tony Blair, 'Our Nation's Future – Social Inclusion', York, 2006, www.britishpoliticalspeech.org/speech-archive.htm?speech=291.
11. 'Safeguarding Children Involved in Prostitution: Supplementary Guidance to Working Together to Safeguard Children' (Wales: Department of Health, 2000), p. 3.
12. Richard Layard, 'How to Make the World Happier – and Why It Should Be Our First Priority', *The Guardian*, 19 January 2020.
13. Prime Minister's speech on life chances, Prime Minister's Office, 10 Downing Street, 11 January 2016, www.gov.uk/government/speeches/prime-ministers-speech-on-life-chances.
14. 'Outraged Parents Undermined by "State Guardian" Speak Up', *Christian Institute*, 7 June 2014.
15. Scottish Parliament Policy Memorandum on the Children and Young People (Scotland) Bill (2013), para. 68.
16. Children and Young People Act 2014, s. 19(5).
17. Scottish Parliament Policy Memorandum on the Children and Young People (Scotland) Bill (2013).
18. 'Revealed: What Can Happen When a Named Person Reports on Your Children', *The Scotsman*, 3 April 2016.
19. 'Propaganda Being Used in Our Schools to Sell Named Person Scheme', *The Courier*, 11 November 2015.
20. 'Outraged Parents'.

21. Ibid.

22. Maggie Mellon, 'The "Named Person" debate: The case against', *Scottish Journal of Residential Child Care*, December 2015, vol. 14, no. 3, pp. 69–73.

23. Faculty of Advocates, 'Scottish Government's New Child Law Has "Potentially Insidious Aspects"', *The Herald*, 14 August 2013.

24. BBC interview with Nicola Sturgeon, 11 March 2016, www.youtube.com/watch?v=OHyAqeKY7Oo.

25. 'Petition of the Christian Institute and Others for Judicial Review of the Children and Young People (Scotland) Act 2014', 2015.

26. *The Christian Institute and others (Appellants) v. The Lord Advocate (Respondent) (Scotland)*, 28 July 2016, www.bailii.org/uk/cases/UKSC/2016/51.html.

27. Ibid.

CHAPTER 23

1. Author interview with the Gows, 23 August 2024.

2. Ibid.

3. 'Top 100: The Most Visited Websites in the US', www.semrush.com/blog/most-visited-websites/.

4. Author interview with the Gows, 23 August 2024.

5. 'Statements on the Termination of Joe Gow as Chancellor of UW-La Crosse', *News,* Universities of Wisconsin, 27 December 2023, https://www.wisconsin.edu/news/archive/statements-on-the-termination-of-joe-gow-as-chancellor-of-uw-la-crosse/.

6. 'Universities of Wisconsin Fires Joe Gow Again', Insidehighered.com, 27 September 2024, www.insidehighered.com/news/governance/executive-leadership/2024/09/27/universities-wisconsin-fires-joe-gow-again.

7. 'The Professor Fired for Making Porn', *Business Insider,* 13 October 2024.

8. Hal Gladfelder, 'Early Modern Porn Wars', OUPblog, 21 August 2014, https://blog.oup.com/2014/08/early-modern-porn-wars/.

9. Nicole Casperson, 'OnlyFans CEO Is on a Mission to Set the Record Straight', *Fintech*, 1 November 2022.

10. 'OnlyFans Is One of the 2021 TIME 100 Most Influential Companies', *Time*, 26 April 2021.

11. 'OnlyFans Porn Ban a "Kick in the Teeth" for Creators', *BBC Online News*, 21 August 2021.

12. Ibid.

13. Kari Paul, 'OnlyFans Ban on Sexually Explicit Content Will Endanger Lives, Say US Sex Workers', *The Guardian*, 20 August 2021.

14. 'OnlyFans Founder Blames Banks for Ban on Porn', *Financial Times*, 24 August 2021.

15. @OnlyFans (OnlyFans), twitter.com/OnlyFans/status/1430499277302816773, 25 August 2021.

16. 'Ask First at Antioch', *The New York Times*, 11 October 1993.

17. 'The History Behind Sexual Consent Policies', *NPR News*, 5 October 2014, www.kunc.org/2014-10-05/the-history-behind-sexual-consent-policies.

18. Alan E. Guskin, '. . . To the Rules of Antioch', *The Washington Post*, 10 November 1993.

19. Jeannie Suk Gersen, 'The Politics of Bad Sex', *The New Yorker*, 30 March 2021.

20. See antiochcollege.edu/campus-life/sexual-offense-prevention-policy-title-ix/.

21. Jeannie Suk Gersen and Jacob Gersen, 'The Sex Bureaucracy', *California Law Review*, 104.4 (2016), pp. 881–948.

22. Nick Hillman, 'Sex and Relationships Among Students: Summary Report', 21 April 2021, www.hepi.ac.uk/2021/04/29/most-students-think-passing-a-sexual-consent-test-should-be-compulsory-before-starting-higher-education/.

23. William Turvill and Stephen McGinty, 'ITV Tells Staff to Declare Friendships or Face Sack After Schofield Scandal', *The Sunday Times*, 22 October 2022.

24. Katherine Angel, *Tomorrow Sex Will Be Good Again: Women and Desire in the Age of Consent* (New York: Verso, 2021), p. 99.

25. Samantha Harris and Michael Thad Allen, 'Bad Vibrations: The Lies Universities Tell Their Students About Sex', *Quillette*, 17 July 2020, quillette.com/2020/06/17/bad-vibrations-the-lies-universities-tell-their-students-about-sex/.

26. Ibid.

27. 'Sexual health', Wellness and Health Advocacy, UW-La Crosse, https://www.uwlax.edu/wellness/sexual-health/.

28. Nicola Lacey, Celia Wells and Oliver Quick, *Reconstructing Criminal Law: Text and Materials* (Cambridge: Cambridge University Press, 2003), p. 488.

29. bell hooks, *Feminist Theory from Margin to Center*, in Hannah Dawson (ed.), *The Penguin Book of Feminist Writing* (London: Penguin, 2021), p. 452.

CHAPTER 24

1. 'You Should Be Freaking Out About Privacy', *The New York Times*, 20 December 2019; 'Be Paranoid About Privacy', *The New York Times*, 24 December 2019; 'You Are Now Remotely Controlled', *The New York Times*, 24 January 2020.

2. Conor Skelding, 'Canada Secretly Tracked 33 Million Phones During Covid-19 Lockdown', *New York Post*, 25 December 2021; David Lyon, *Pandemic Surveillance* (Cambridge: Polity, 2022).

3. Ellen Nakashima and Reed Albergotti, 'The FBI Wanted to Unlock the San Bernardino Shooter's iPhone. It turned to a little-known Australian firm', *The Washington Post*, 14 April 2021.

4. Jennifer Senior, 'You Are Not Alone When You Are on Google', *The New York Times*, 17 May 2019.

5. Eric Nagourney, 'Cameras Came to the Newsroom. What if They Catch Us Printing Springsteen Tickets?' *The New York Times*, 2 June 2019.

6. James Bennet, 'Do You Know What You've Given Up?', *The New York Times*, 10 April 2019.

7. Lauren Jackson, 'Shoshana Zuboff Explains Why You Should Care About Privacy', *The New York Times*, 21 May 2021.

8. Carissa Véliz, *Privacy Is Power: Why and How You Should Take Back Control of Your Data* (London: Bantam Press, 2020), p. 1.

9. Derek Thompson, 'Google's CEO: "The Laws Are Written by Lobbyists"', *The Atlantic*, 1 October 2010.

10. Carol Cadwalladr, 'I Made Steven Bannon's Psychological Warfare

Tool: Meet the Data Whistleblower', *The Guardian*, 18 March 2018.

11. Carole Cadwalladr, 'The Great British Brexit Robbery: How Our Democracy Was Hijacked', *The Observer*, 7 May 2017.

12. 'Letter from the Information Commissioner to Julian Knight MP', Information Commissioner's Office, 2 October 2020, https://ico.org.uk/media/action-weve-taken/2618383/20201002_ico-o-ed-l-rtl-0181_to-julian-knight-mp.pdf. Izabella Kaminska, 'ICO's Final Report into Cambridge Analytica Invites Regulatory Questions', *Financial Times*, 8 October 2020.

13. Yuval Noah Harari, 'The World After Coronavirus', *Financial Times,* 20 March 2020.

CHAPTER 25

1. Jim Waterson, 'Boris Johnson: Police Called to Loud Altercation at Potential PM's Home', *The Guardian*, 21 June 2019.

2. Henry Zeffman, George Gryllis, Geraldine Scott and Matt Dathan, 'WhatsApp Chats Vanish – and Take Scrutiny With Them', *The Times*, 3 June 2023.

3. Ibid.

4. Tony Blair, '"My Commitment" – Extracts from a Speech by Tony Blair on 25 March 1996 Before He Became Prime Minister', *The Guardian*, 22 June 1999.

5. Tony Blair, *A Journey* (London: Hutchinson, 2010), pp. 1578–9.

6. Peter Walker, 'Rishi Sunak Tells Covid Inquiry He Was Not Told to Save Whatsapp Messages', *The Guardian*, 11 December 2023.

7. 'UK Covid Inquiry: Nicola Sturgeon's Covid WhatsApp Messages "All Deleted"', *BBC News Online*, 19 January 2023.

8. Isabel Oakeshott, 'I Had to Release Matt Hancock's Covid WhatsApp Messages to Avoid a Whitewash', *The Telegraph*, 28 February 2023.

9. Stuart Heritage, 'The WhatsApp Messages that Should Have Been Edited', *The Times*, 23 May 2023.

10. Tom Gordon, 'MSPS Back Criminalising Hate Speech at the Dinner Table', *The Herald*, 9 February 2021; Justice Committee,

Tuesday 27 October 2020, Session 5, Scottish Parliament,
www.parliament.scot/api/sitecore/CustomMedia/
OfficialReport?meetingId=12903.

11. Carly Page, 'An Encryption Exodus Looms over UK's Online
    Safety Bill', *Techcrunch*, 27 June 2023.

12. Siba Jackson, 'Ex-cop Found Guilty of Sending "Grossly Offensive"
    Racist Parrot Message', *Metro*, 6 November 2023.

13. Jess Warren, 'Ex-Met Officer Guilty of Sending Racist Message',
    BBC News Online, 6 November 2023.

14. CPS News, 'Ex-Metropolitan Police Officers Sentenced After
    Sending Racist Messages', 7 December 2023.

15. Ed West, 'Why Britain Needs a First Amendment', *Wrong Side of
    History*, Substack, 15 June 2022.

16. Orlando Figes, *The Whisperers: Private Life in Stalin's Russia*
    (London: Allen Lane, 2007), p. 129.

17. Ibid., p. xxxi.

Select Bibliography

Allen, Anita L., *Unpopular Privacy: What Must We Hide?* (New York: Oxford University Press, 2011)

Anderson, Elizabeth, *Private Government: Why Employers Rule Our Lives (And Why We Don't Talk About It)* (Princeton, NJ: Princeton University Press, 2017)

Angel, Katherine, *Tomorrow Sex Will Be Good Again: Women and Desire in the Age of Consent* (London: Verso, 2021)

Arendt, Hannah, *The Human Condition* (Chicago: University of Chicago Press, 1958)

Aries, Philippe, and Georges Duby (eds), *A History of Private Life*, 5 vols (Cambridge, MA: Belknap Press, 1987–94)

Bejan, Teresa M., *Mere Civility: Disagreement and the Limits of Toleration* (Cambridge, MA: Harvard University Press, 2017)

Berger, Brigitte, and Peter Berger, *The War Over the Family: Capturing the Middle Ground* (New York: Doubleday, 1984)

Boling, Patricia, *Privacy and the Politics of Intimate Life* (New York: Cornell University Press, 1996)

Boyd, Dana, *It's Complicated: The Social Lives of Networked Teens* (New Haven, CT: Yale University Press, 2014)

Braddick, Michael, *God's Fury, England's Fire: A New History of the English Civil Wars* (London: Penguin, 2008)

Chase, Karen, and Michael Levenson, *The Spectacle of Intimacy: A Public Life for the Victorian Family* (Princeton, NJ: Princeton University Press, 2020)

Cohen, Deborah, *Family Secrets: The Things We Used to Hide* (London: Penguin, 2014)

Cohen, Josh, *The Private Life: Why We Remain in the Dark* (London: Granta, 2014)

Coontz, Stephanie, *The Social Origins of Private Life: A History of American Families 1600–1900* (London: Verso, 1988)

Cummings, Brian, *Mortal Thoughts: Religion, Secularity and Identity in Shakespeare and Early Modern Culture* (Oxford: Oxford University Press, 2013)

Dabhoiwala, Faramerz, *The Origins of Sex: A History of the First Sexual Revolution* (London: Allen Lane, 2012)

DeBrabander, Firmin, *Life After Privacy: Reclaiming Democracy in a Surveillance Society* (Cambridge: Cambridge University Press, 2020)

Elshtain, Jean Bethke, *Public Man, Private Woman: Women in Social and Political Thought* (Princeton, NJ: Princeton University Press, 1993)

Flaherty, David, *Privacy in Colonial England* (Charlottesville: University of Virginia Press, 1972)

Foucault, Michel, *The History of Sexuality: An Introduction*, vol. 1, trans. Robert Jurley (Harmondsworth: Penguin Books, 1990 [1978])

Friedman, Lawrence M., *Guarding Life's Dark Secrets: Legal and Social Controls Over Reputation, Propriety, and Privacy* (Stanford, CA: Stanford University Press, 2007)

Furedi, Frank, *Therapy Culture: Cultivating Vulnerability in an Uncertain Age* (London and New York: Routledge, 2004)

Gajda, Amy, *Seek and Hide: The Tangled History of the Right to Privacy* (New York: Viking, 2022)

Gandy, Oscar H. Jr, *The Panoptic Sort: A Political Economy of Personal Information* (New York: Oxford University Press, 1993)

Geuss, Raymond, *Public Goods, Private Goods* (Princeton, NJ: Princeton University Press, 2009)

Giddens, Antony, *The Transformation of Intimacy: Sexuality, Love and Eroticism in Modern Societies* (Cambridge: Polity, 2008 [1993])

Goffman, Erving, *The Presentation of Self in Everyday Life* (London: Penguin, 1969 [1959])

Gurstein, Rochelle, *The Appeal of Reticence: America's Cultural and Legal Struggles Over Free Speech, Obscenity, Sexual Liberation and Modern Art* (New York: Hill and Wang, 1996)

Habermas, Jürgen, *The Transformation of the Public Sphere* (Cambridge, MA: MIT Press, 1989)

Han, Byung-Chul, *The Disappearance of Rituals: A Topology of the Present* (Cambridge: Polity, 2020)

Haahr Henriksen, Anni, 'The Private Mind in Elizabethan England: Representations of the Mind in Literary, Political, Religious, and Legal Discourse' (PhD diss., University of Copenhagen, Centre for Privacy Studies, 2022)

Hochman, Brian, *The Listeners: A History of Wiretapping in the United States* (Cambridge, MA: Harvard University Press, 2022)

Hochschild, Arlie Russell, *The Outsourced Self: What Happens When We Pay Others to Live Our Lives for Us* (New York: Metropolitan Books, 2012)

Huebert, Ronald, *Privacy in the Age of Shakespeare* (Toronto: University of Toronto Press, 2016)

Igo, Sarah, *The Averaged American: Surveys, Citizens, and the Making of a Mass Public* (Cambridge, MA: Harvard University Press, 2008)

Igo, Sarah, *The Known Citizen: A History of Privacy in Modern America* (Cambridge, MA: Harvard University Press, 2018)

Illouz, Eva, *Cold Intimacies: The Making of Emotional Capitalism* (Cambridge: Polity, 2007)

Innes, Julie C., *Privacy, Intimacy, and Isolation* (Oxford: Oxford University Press, 1992)

Kennedy, Angus, and James Panton (eds), *From Self to Selfie: A Critique of Contemporary Forms of Individualism* (London: Bloomsbury Academic, 2019)

Kipnis, Laura, *Unwanted Advances: Sexual Paranoia Comes to Campus* (New York: Verso, 2018)

Kumar, Krishan, and Jeff Weintraub (eds), *Public and Private in Thought and Practice: Perspectives on a Grand Dichotomy* (Chicago: University of Chicago Press, 1997)

Lane, Frederick S., *American Privacy: The 400-Year History of Our Most Contested Right* (Boston: Beacon Press, 2009)

Lasch, Christopher, *The Culture of Narcissism: American Life in an Age of Diminishing Expectations* (New York: W. W. Norton and Company, 1979)

Lasch, Christopher, *Haven in a Heartless World: The Family Besieged* (New York: Basic Books, 1997)

Lasch, Christopher, *The Minimal Self: Psychic Survival in Troubled Times* (New York: Picador, 1984)

Lasch-Quinn, Elizabeth, *Ars Vitae: The Fate of Inwardness and the Return of the Ancient Arts of Living* (Notre Dame, IN: University of Notre Dame Press, 2020)

Ljungberg, Johannes, and Natasha Klein Käfer (eds), *Tracing Private Conversations in Early Modern Europe: Talking in Everyday Life* (London: Palgrave Macmillan, 2024)

Lyon, David, *Surveillance Society: Monitoring Everyday Life* (Oxford: Oxford University Press, 2001)

MacKinnon, Catharine A., *Toward a Feminist Theory of the State* (Cambridge, MA: Harvard University Press, 1989)

Maier, Charles S., *Changing Boundaries of the Political: Essays on the Evolving Balance Between the State and Society, Public and Private, in Europe* (Cambridge: Cambridge University Press, 2012)

McKeon, Michael, *The Secret History of Domesticity* (Baltimore: Johns Hopkins Press, 2005)

Melton, James Van Horn, *The Rise of the Public in Enlightenment Europe* (Cambridge: Cambridge University Press, 2001)

Moore, Barrington Jr, *Privacy: Studies in Social and Cultural History* (Armonk, NY: M. E. Sharpe, Inc., 1984)

Nelson, Deborah, *Pursuing Privacy in Cold War America* (New York: Columbia University Press, 2002)

Nippert-Eng, Christena, *Islands of Privacy* (Chicago: University of Chicago Press, 2010)

O'Mara, Margaret, *The Code: Silicon Valley and the Remaking of America* (New York: Penguin, 2019)

Orlin, Lena Cowen, *Locating Privacy in Tudor London* (Oxford: Oxford University Press, 2007)

Panton, James, 'Politics, Subjectivity and the Public/Private Distinction: The Problematisation of the Public/Private Relationship in Political Thought After World War II' (PhD diss., New College, University of Oxford, 2010)

Pateman, Carole, 'Feminist Critiques of the Public/Private Dichotomy', in *Public and Private in Social Life*, Stanley I. Benn and Gerald F. Gaus (eds) (Croom Helm and St Martin's Press, 1983), pp. 281–307

Pratt, Walter F., *Privacy in Britain* (Lewisburg, PA: Bucknell University Press, Associated Universities Press, 1979)

Pressly, Lowry, *The Right to Oblivion: Privacy and the Good Life* (Cambridge, MA Harvard University Press, 2024)

Putnam, Robert D., *Bowling Alone: The Collapse and Revival of American Community* (New York: Simon & Schuster, 2001)

Richards, Neil, *Why Privacy Matters* (Oxford: Oxford University Press, 2022)

Richardson, Megan, *The Right to Privacy: Origins and Influence of a Nineteenth-Century Idea* (Cambridge: Cambridge University Press, 2017)

Rieff, Philip, *The Triumph of the Therapeutic: Uses of Faith After Freud* (New York: Harper and Row, 1966)

Riesman, David, Nathan Glazer and Reuel Denney, *The Lonely Crowd: A Study of the Changing American Character* (New Haven, CT: Yale University Press, 2001 [1961])

Rosen, Jeffrey, *The Naked Crowd: Reclaiming Security and Freedom in an Anxious Age* (New York: Random House, 2004)

Rosen, Jeffrey, *The Unwanted Gaze: The Destruction of Privacy in America* (New York: Vintage, 2001)

Schudson, Michael, *The Rise of the Right to Know: Politics and the Culture of Transparency 1945–1975* (Cambridge, MA: Belknap Press, 2016)

Seigel, Jerrold, *The Idea of the Self: Thought and Experience in Western Europe Since the Seventeenth Century* (Cambridge: Cambridge University Press, 2005)

Self, Robert O., *All in the Family: The Realignment of American Democracy Since the 1960s* (New York: Hill and Wang, 2012)

Sennett, Richard, *The Fall of Public Man* (New York: Alfred A. Knopf, 1977)

Shadbolt, Nigel, and Roger Hampson, *As if Human: Ethics and Artificial Intelligence* (New Haven, CT: Yale University Press, 2024)

Smith, Janna Malamud, *Private Matters: In Defence of the Personal Life* (London: Addison-Wesley, 1997)

Sofsky, Wolfgang, *Privacy: A Manifesto* (Princeton, NJ: Princeton University Press, 2008)

Spacks, Patricia Meyer, *Privacy: Concealing the Eighteenth-Century Self* (Chicago: University of Chicago Press, 2003)

Suk, Jeannie, *At Home in the Law: How the Domestic Violence Revolution is Transforming Privacy* (New Haven, CT: Yale University Press, 2009)

Taylor, Charles, *The Sources of the Self: The Making of Modern Identity* (Cambridge, MA: Harvard University Press, 1989)

Thomas, Keith, 'Cases of Conscience in Seventeenth-Century England', in John Morrill, Paul Slack and Daniel Woolf (eds), *Public Duty and Private Conscience in Seventeenth-Century England: Essays Presented to G. E. Aylmer* (Oxford: Clarendon Press, 1993), pp. 29–56

Thomas, Keith, *In Search of Civility: Common Curiosity and the Politics of the Public Sphere* (New Haven, CT: Yale University Press, 2018)

Trilling, Lionel, *Sincerity and Authenticity* (Cambridge, MA: Harvard University Press, 1971)

Turner, Fred, *From Counterculture to Cyberculture: Stewart Brand, the Whole Earth Network, and the Rise of Digital Utopianism* (Chicago: University of Chicago Press, 2008)

Veliz, Carissa, *Privacy is Power: Why and How You Should Take Back Control of Your Data* (London: Penguin, Bantam Press, 2020)

Vincent, David, *The Culture of Secrecy: Britain 1832–1998* (Oxford: Oxford University Press, 1998)

Vincent, David, *I Hope I Don't Intrude: Privacy and Its Dilemmas in Nineteenth-Century Britain* (Oxford: Oxford University Press, 2015)

Vincent, David, *Privacy: A Short History* (Cambridge: Polity, 2016)

Westin, Alan, *Privacy and Freedom* (New York: Simon & Schuster, 1967)

Westin, Alan, 'Privacy in Western History: From the Age of Pericles to the American Republic' (PhD diss., Harvard University, Harvard University Thesis Collection, 1967)

Ziegler, Mary, *Beyond Abortion: Roe. v. Wade and the Battle for Privacy* (Cambridge, MA: Harvard University Press, 2018)

Zuboff, Shoshana, *The Age of Surveillance Capitalism: The Fight for a Human Future at the New Frontier of Power* (London: Profile Books, 2019)

Index

Page numbers in **bold** refer to figures.